Fodor's 95 The Carolinas & the Georgia Coast

PRAISE FOR FODOR'S GUIDES

"Fodor's guides . . . are an admirable blend of the cultural and the practical."

—The Washington Post

"Researched by people chosen because they live or have lived in the country, well-written, and with good historical sections . . . Obligatory reading for millions of tourists."

—The Independent, *London*

"Usable, sophisticated restaurant coverage, with an emphasis on good value."

—*Andy Birsh,* Gourmet *restaurant columnist, quoted by Gannett News Service*

"Packed with dependable information."

—Atlanta Journal Constitution

"Fodor's always delivers high quality . . . thoughtfully presented . . . thorough."

—Houston Post

"Valuable because of their comprehensiveness."

—Minneapolis Star-Tribune

Portions of this book appear in Fodor's *The South '95*

Fodor's Travel Publications, Inc.
New York • Toronto • London • Sydney • Auckland

 Published in the United States by Fodor's Travel Publications, Inc., a subsidiary of Random House, Inc., New York, and simultaneously in Canada by Random House of Canada Limited, Toronto. Distributed by Random House, Inc., New York.

ISBN 0-679-02706-8

Fodor's The Carolinas & the Georgia Coast

Editor: Jillian L. Magalaner
Contributors: Steven Amsterdam, Andrew Collins, Suzanne DeGalan, Echo Garrett, Kevin Garrett, Susan Ladd, Bevin McLaughlin, Linda K. Schmidt, Mary Ellen Schultz, Carol L. Timblin, Nancy van Itallie
Creative Director: Fabrizio La Rocca
Cartographer: David Lindroth
Illustrator: Karl Tanner
Cover Photograph: Erik Horan/Nawrocki Stock Photo

Design: Vignelli Associates

Special Sales

Fodor's Travel Publications are available at special discounts for bulk purchases for sales promotions or premiums. Special editions, including personalized covers, excerpts of existing guides, and corporate imprints, can be created in large quantities for special needs. For more information, contact your local bookseller or write to Special Markets, Fodor's Travel Publications, 201 East 50th Street, New York, NY 10022. Inquiries from Canada should be directed to your local Canadian bookseller or sent to Random House of Canada, Ltd., Marketing Department, 1265 Aerowood Drive, Mississauga, Ontario L4W 1B9. Inquiries from the United Kingdom should be sent to Fodor's Travel Publications, 20 Vauxhall Bridge Road, London, England SW1V 2SA.

MANUFACTURED IN THE UNITED STATES OF AMERICA
10 9 8 7 6 5 4 3 2 1

Contents

Maps

Foreword

While every care has been taken to ensure the accuracy of the information in this guide, the passage of time will always bring change and, consequently, the publisher cannot accept responsibility for errors that may occur.

All prices and opening times quoted here are based on information supplied to us at press time. Hours and admission fees may change, however, and the prudent traveler will avoid inconvenience by calling ahead.

Fodor's wants to hear about your travel experiences, both pleasant and unpleasant. When a hotel or restaurant fails to live up to its billing, let us know and we will investigate the complaint and revise our entries where the facts warrant it.

Fodor's wishes to express our gratitude to the following contributors for their assistance in the preparation of this guide: Dorri Harty of the Dare County Tourist Bureau (NC), Sally Hekkers and the Chattanooga Chamber of Commerce, Bruce Morgan of the Louisiana Office of Tourism, Gene Pindar and the Tennessee Aquarium, Caryn Shoffner and Debbie Geiger of Geiger and Associates, and Ami Simpson of the Alabama Bureau of Tourism and Travel.

Send your letters to the editors of Fodor's Travel Publications, 201 E. 50th Street, New York, NY 10022.

Highlights'95 and Fodor's Choice

Highlights '95

Georgia Anticipation of the **1996 Olympic Games** has inspired much new construction in the host city of Atlanta. A new **85,000-seat stadium** is being built for the games (after the Olympics it will be used for Atlanta Braves games). The **Velodrome,** an indoor bicycle track, is under construction at Stone Mountain Park, and the **Olympic Village,** which will be home to athletes and their families during the games, is being constructed on the Georgia Tech campus. Opened in fall 1992, the **Georgia Dome**—the home of the NFL's Atlanta Falcons—will be the site of several Olympic events.

Also in Atlanta, the 30,000-square-foot **Atlanta History Center** opened in October 1993. The center has exhibits on Atlanta's history from its earliest Indian settlements to the present, including provocative displays juxtaposing *Gone with the Wind* romanticism with the grim reality of Ku Klux Klan racism.

North Carolina The biggest news in North Carolina is the acquisition of another professional sports team: The **Carolina Panthers** NFL football team will take to the field in Clemson, South Carolina, in 1995, until their new stadium in Charlotte is completed, most likely in 1996. Once the team is in their new stadium, the city expects sellout crowds for every game. Panther mania has already gripped the state, perhaps even more intensely than Hornet fever. Since the Charlotte Hornets built their hive in Charlotte, the team has set NBA attendance—and merchandise sales—records.

NationsBank Corporate Center, a 60-story Pelli-design skyscraper that includes the **North Carolina Blumenthal Center for the Performing Arts** and **Founders Hall,** a shopping-restaurant complex, opened in uptown Charlotte in late 1992. The bank's lobby, the tallest in the Southeast, has three large frescoes by Ben Long, the same artist who painted the Blue Ridge frescoes in Ashe County. Also Uptown on Stonewall Street are the **Visitor Information Center** and the **Mecklenburg County Aquatic Center.**

South Carolina By spring 1995 **Kiawah Island Resort** will have a brand new look. If all goes according to schedule, by this time the resort's 150 inn rooms and 300 villas will have been overhauled, and a state-of-the-art health and fitness spa will have been added. Already well-known for its great golfing and tennis and its children's programs, Kiawah now also has an excellent nature program—with activities ranging from naturalist-led walks and canoe trips, to ecology seminars—making good use of the island's undeveloped regions, which include wildlife marshes. Kiawah stands to become one of the East Coast's most luxurious outdoors-oriented resorts.

South Carolina's tourist crop has traditionally centered on the coastal areas of Myrtle Beach, Georgetown, Charleston, Beaufort, and Hilton Head, but the inland communities of **Aiken and Camden** have recently made impressive strides toward drawing visitors to the Heartland. Aiken has been promoting its prestigious thoroughbred horse-racing past and its lovely setting of wooded parkland, historic mansions, and tony shopping. Camden, a center of Revolutionary War history and thoroughbred horse-racing, added a charming B&B (the **Greenleaf Inn**) and two outstanding restaurants (**1890 McLean's House** and the **Mill Pond Restaurant**) in 1994. Both of these genteel towns offer excellent two- to five-day getaways for much less than you'd pay for comparable vacations along the coast.

Myrtle Beach continues in its quest to become the next Branson, Missouri, with rapid expansion in the country music and amusements scenes. The **Gatlin brothers** chose Myrtle Beach as the site for their $7.5 million, 2,000-seat country music theater, which opened in July 1994 as part of the 200-acre **Waccamaw Harbour** complex. The complex will add 14 theaters, 12 restaurants, four hotels, and more than 200,000 square feet of shops over the next seven years. Also in summer 1994, Waccamaw Harbour saw the opening of the 21,000-square-foot **Magic On Ice Theatre,** where live ice-skating shows take place year-round. Another long-term project is in the works for Myrtle Beach: the $250 million **Broadway at the Beach** will be built on a 350-acre tract along the U.S. 17 Bypass where it hits 21st Street North. This family-oriented park will include 12 theaters, a 14-acre lake, and scores of shops and restaurants.

Fodor's Choice

No two people will agree on what makes a perfect vacation, but it's fun and helpful to know what others think. We hope you'll have a chance to experience some of Fodor's Choices yourself while visiting the Carolinas and the Georgia Coast. For detailed information about each entry, refer to the appropriate chapters within this guidebook.

Georgia

Special Moments Observing the eternal flame burning at Martin Luther King, Jr.'s tomb in front of the King Center

View from the lounge atop the Westin Peachtree Plaza Hotel, Atlanta

Sights, scents, and sounds of Harry's Farmer's Market, several locations, suburban Atlanta

St. Patrick's Day in Savannah

Dining Dining Room in the Ritz-Carlton Buckhead, Atlanta, *$$$$*

Elizabeth on 37th, Savannah, *$$$*

Buckhead Diner, Atlanta, *$$–$$$*

Indigo Coastal Grill, Atlanta, *$$–$$$*

Mrs. Wilkes Boarding House, Savannah, *$*

Lodging Cloister Hotel, Sea Island, *$$$$*

Ritz-Carlton Atlanta, *$$$$*

Ritz-Carlton, Buckhead, *$$$$*

The Mulberry, Savannah, *$$$–$$$$*

Eliza Thompson House, Savannah, *$$$*

Museums High Museum of Art, Atlanta

The World of Coca-Cola Pavilion, Underground Atlanta

Nightlife Early-morning crowds partying in Buckhead, Atlanta

Live jazz at Dante's Down the Hatch, Underground Atlanta

North Carolina

Special Moments Standing under the Gothic arches of Duke Chapel, at Duke University

Shooting the rapids on the Nantahala River

Observing 19th-century living at Old Salem

Dining Lamplighter, Charlotte, *$$$$*

Longhorn Steaks Restaurant and Saloon, Charlotte, *$$–$$$*

Grady's American Grill, Charlotte, *$–$$*

Lodging Fearrington House, Chapel Hill, *$$$$*

The Blooming Garden Inn, Durham, *$$$*

The Homeplace, Charlotte, *$$*

Museums Discovery Place, Charlotte

Mint Museum of Art, Charlotte

North Carolina Museum of Art, Raleigh

Museum of Early Southern Decorative Arts (MESDA), Winston-Salem

South Carolina

Special Moments Riding a mule-drawn farm wagon at the Plantation Stableyards in Middleton Place

Collecting shells and sand dollars on the beach at Kiawah Island

Boat tour among spring blooms reflecting in the black waters at Cypress Gardens

Relaxing in a rocking chair overlooking luxury yachts in the Harbour Town marina, Sea Pines on Hilton Head

Dining Louis's Charleston Grill, Charleston, *$$$*

82 Queen, Charleston, *$$*

Sea Captain's House, Myrtle Beach, *$$*

Magnolias–Uptown/Down South, Charleston, *$*

Lodging John Rutledge House Inn, Charleston, *$$$$*

Radisson Resort Hotel at Kingston Plantation, Myrtle Beach, *$$$$*

Westin Resort, Hilton Head Island, *$$$$*

Omni Hotel at Charleston Place, Charleston, *$$$*

Museums Charleston Museum, Charleston

Gibbes Museum of Art, Charleston

Patriots Point, East of the Cooper River, Charleston

Brookgreen Gardens, Murrells Inlet

Rice Museum, Georgetown

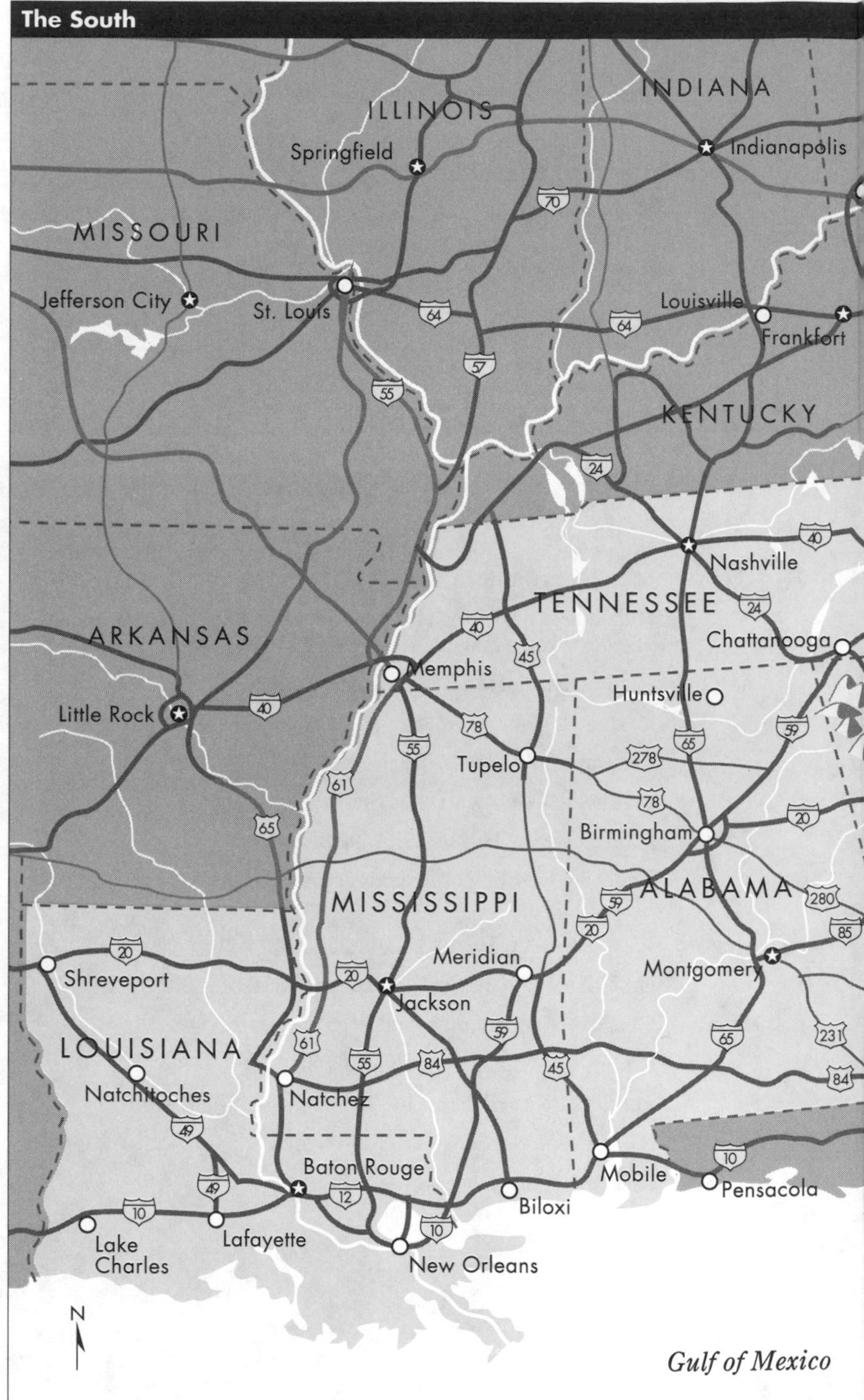
The South
ILLINOIS
INDIANA
Springfield
Indianapolis
MISSOURI
Jefferson City
St. Louis
Louisville
Frankfort
KENTUCKY
Nashville
TENNESSEE
Chattanooga
ARKANSAS
Memphis
Huntsville
Little Rock
Tupelo
Birmingham
ALABAMA
MISSISSIPPI
Shreveport
Meridian
Montgomery
Jackson
LOUISIANA
Natchitoches
Natchez
Baton Rouge
Mobile
Pensacola
Biloxi
Lake Charles
Lafayette
New Orleans
N
Gulf of Mexico

OHIO
Columbus
Cincinnati
WEST VIRGINIA
Charleston
Lexington
APPALACHIAN MTS.
Baltimore
Dover
MD.
DEL.
Washington, DC
Annapolis
Charlottesville
Richmond
VIRGINIA
Norfolk
Lynchburg
Petersburg
Virginia Beach
Roanoke
Edenton
Nags Head
Greensboro
Raleigh
Winston-Salem
Knoxville
NORTH CAROLINA
New Bern
Asheville
Charlotte
Greenville
Wilmington
Columbia
Myrtle Beach
SOUTH CAROLINA
Atlanta
Augusta
Charleston
Macon
Beaufort
GEORGIA
Columbus
Savannah
Albany
ATLANTIC OCEAN
Brunswick
Jacksonville
Tallahassee
FLORIDA
Orlando
Tampa
0
100 miles
0
100 km
70
64
75
81
85
40
26
77
20
95
17
221
16
301
82
84
10

The United States

ONTARIO
CANADA
QUÉBEC
NEW BRUNSWICK
Fredericton
Québec
MAINE
Montréal
Augusta
Ottawa
Montpelier
VT.
Concord
N.H.
Boston
MASS.
R.I.
Providence
Lake Superior
MINNESOTA
Duluth
WISCONSIN
MICHIGAN
Lake Huron
Lake Michigan
St. Paul
Minneapolis
Green Bay
Toronto
Lake Ontario
Albany
Hartford
Buffalo
NEW YORK
Hudson R.
CONN.
Milwaukee
Lansing
Madison
Lake Erie
New York
Detroit
Cleveland
N.J.
PENNSYLVANIA
Trenton
Harrisburg
Philadelphia
IOWA
Chicago
Pittsburgh
OHIO
MD
Dover
DEL.
Des Moines
Omaha
INDIANA
Baltimore
Annapolis
ILLINOIS
Columbus
WEST VIRGINIA
Washington, D.C.
Springfield
Indianapolis
Charleston
Richmond
Mississippi R.
Topeka
Cincinnati
Norfolk
Kansas City
Jefferson City
St. Louis
Louisville
Frankfort
VIRGINIA
MISSOURI
Ohio R.
KENTUCKY
Raleigh
Nashville
NORTH CAROLINA
TENNESSEE
Tulsa
ARKANSAS
Memphis
Columbia
SOUTH CAROLINA
Little Rock
Tennessee R.
Savannah R.
Atlanta
Birmingham
GEORGIA
ATLANTIC OCEAN
MISSISSIPPI
Savannah
Montgomery
Jackson
ALABAMA
Jacksonville
Mobile
Tallahassee
Baton Rouge
FLORIDA
New Orleans
Orlando
Houston
LOUISIANA
Bahama Islands
Miami
Nassau
Gulf of Mexico
N
0
200 miles
0
300 km

World Time Zones

+11 +12 - -11 -10 -9 -8 -7 -6 -5 -4 -3 -2

Numbers below vertical bands relate each zone to Greenwich Mean Time (0 hrs.). Local times frequently differ from these general indications, as indicated by light-face numbers on map.

Algiers, **29**
Anchorage, **3**
Athens, **41**
Auckland, **1**
Baghdad, **46**
Bangkok, **50**
Beijing, **54**
Berlin, **34**
Bogotá, **19**
Budapest, **37**
Buenos Aires, **24**
Caracas, **22**
Chicago, **9**
Copenhagen, **33**
Dallas, **10**
Delhi, **48**
Denver, **8**
Djakarta, **53**
Dublin, **26**
Edmonton, **7**
Hong Kong, **56**
Honolulu, **2**
Istanbul, **40**
Jerusalem, **42**
Johannesburg, **44**
Lima, **20**
Lisbon, **28**
London (Greenwich), **27**
Los Angeles, **6**
Madrid, **38**
Manila, **57**

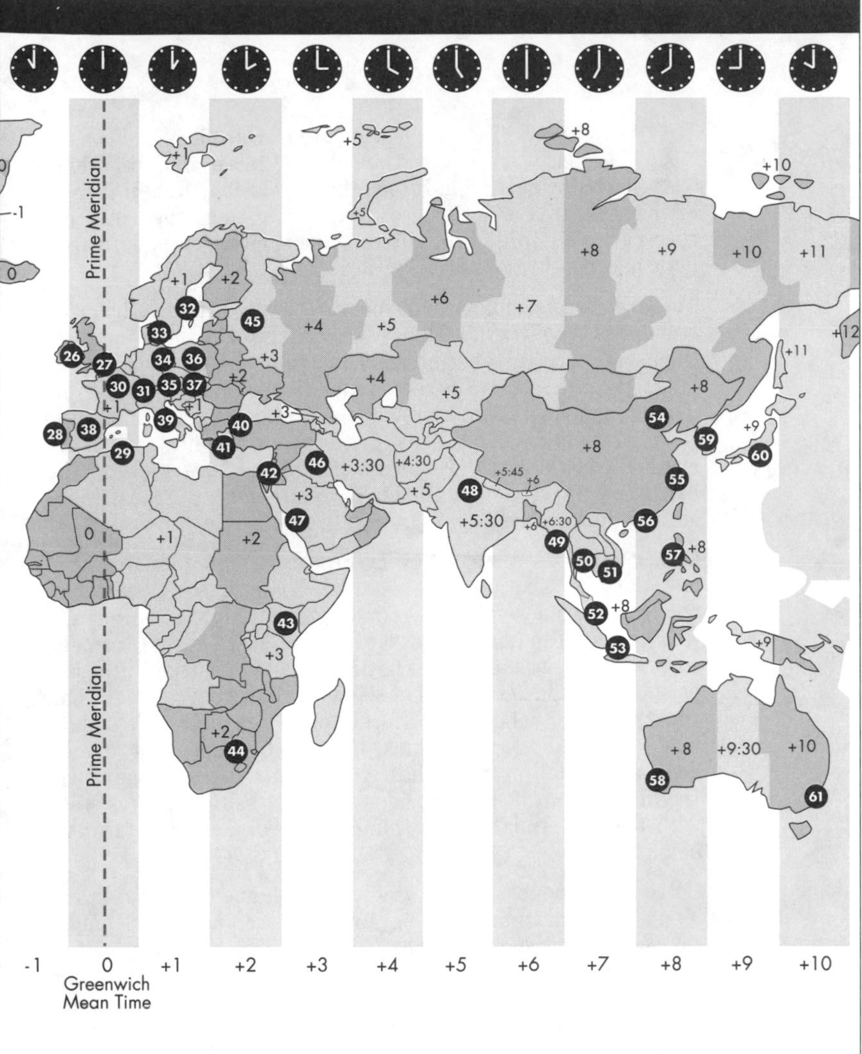

Mecca, **47**
Mexico City, **12**
Miami, **18**
Montréal, **15**
Moscow, **45**
Nairobi, **43**
New Orleans, **11**
New York City, **16**
Ottawa, **14**
Paris, **30**
Perth, **58**
Reykjavík, **25**
Rio de Janeiro, **23**
Rome, **39**
Saigon (Ho Chi Minh City), **51**
San Francisco, **5**
Santiago, **21**
Seoul, **59**
Shanghai, **55**
Singapore, **52**
Stockholm, **32**
Sydney, **61**
Tokyo, **60**
Toronto, **13**
Vancouver, **4**
Vienna, **35**
Warsaw, **36**
Washington, D.C., **17**
Yangon, **49**
Zürich, **31**

Introduction

Throw away all the clichés about the Carolinas and coastal Georgia. Very few of them fit anymore and the others probably never did. It took the world a long time to discover that this area is not tobacco road but, rather, energetic, nature-rich, and quietly dignified. It's a thriving area with very little bustle—there is drive without push.

This area has never been "dirt-poor." Its agriculture is, by many standards, "soil-rich." Things grow here, almost in spite of themselves. Everywhere but on the sandy strip of coastal islands, trees dominate the region's landscape. Pines are the overwhelming favorites of nature here, growing solid and thick over the mountaintops and tall and graceful in the sandy soils of the eastern coastal plain. They camouflage the bare limbs of the hardwoods in winter and add vivid green contrast to the flame of autumn just before Thanksgiving.

Closer to sea level, almost everything can—and does—grow in one part or another of the area. Even in tidy suburban backyards, honeysuckle can scent a summer night so powerfully that one is often tempted to "let it grow" just because it smells so nice. (Few succumb to this notion twice—like its anthitheses, poison ivy, kudzu, and Spanish moss, it spreads faster than you'd believe.) Jonquils and forsythia begin their yellow show long before the vernal equinox, followed by azaleas and camellias, and finally, magnolias with their lemon fragrance. Daylilies sprout along roadsides, and English ivy climbs trees with alacrity. And these are things that grow without a farmer's help!

Cotton is no longer agricultural king here, and tobacco is losing its place as crown prince. They are being replaced by peanuts, soybeans, cucumbers, grapes, Christmas trees, and peaches. (You have never *really* tasted a peach until you have had one grown in the surrounding Sandhills orchards and bought from a roadside stand.) More and more cornfields are appearing across the Piedmont, as are herds of dairy cows, feeding on the lush grassy fields. Pickle production is up, along with that of peanut butter and a new product, wine.

There are four seasons here—spring is wet and fall is dry, but they are just about the loveliest spring and fall to be found in the continental United States. The hardwood trees bud in March, and the profusion of flowers, both wild and cultivated, is breathtaking. Everyone comes outdoors to look, and feel, and to wake up. Golfers, tennis players, gardeners, and sunbathers appear with renewed energy. The rains are warm and usually brief. Fall is even prettier, with foliage that rivals the gold of the sun. Outdoor activity continues until at least the end of November, when the leaves finally fall.

That leaves summer and winter—surely too hot and too cold to enjoy? Definitely not. Air conditioning is a fact of life in the humid summers, when the sun bakes the air until thunderheads pile up. But the beaches, the myriad lakes, and the local swimming pools beckon even the nonswimmers, and mountains—a cool haven—are less than a day's drive from anywhere. In winter the mountains are often snowy while the rest of the area is just chilly. Skiers scurry to the slopes, but those who remain in the low country probably can't remember where they put boots after last year's one day of snow. If and when that snowfall comes to the low country (as it usually does a couple of times each year) everything comes to a halt—schools close and meetings are cancelled, and local disc jockeys recount their harrowing journey into the station through a couple of inches of serious snow. (Low-country people do not handle driving in the snow at all well, and local governments have no snow removal equipment. If it snows, be content to stay where you are.) It's almost a holiday when winter weather comes to the southeast. Adults and children alike find the slightest rise in land countour an excuse to go sledding "before it's gone tomorrow." A sprinkle of snow along the coast draws crowds.

Not too long ago the geography books described this area as "agriculture." We've told you what grows here, but what is more important now is what is *made* here—fabrics and pharmaceuticals, bath towels and beer, furniture and films, chemicals, electronic components, lumber, tobacco products, and nuclear power. Most of the current boom is, of course, concentrated in the metropolitan centers. Atlanta and surrounding cities will host the 1996 summer Olympics, and Charlotte is fast becoming one of America's preeminent banking empires. However, commercial success is emerging rapidly in rural areas, too. Tourism is a major industry all over and is widely supported. Officials in charge of such things have already awakened to the need for long-range planning to maintain the quality of the environment. Visitors are welcomed warmly, and there are plenty of accommodations available, but development is being programmed to avoid destruction of natural resources and precious beaches. Even in the dense-built Grand Strand at Myrtle Beach in South Carolina one doesn't have to step over recumbent bodies to reach the water. And on most of the beaches, even at the height of the summer season, a lonesome dawn stroll is still possible.

Winston Churchill once said that "change is not necessarily progress." It is *here*, with one exception—the people. If there should come a change in the courteous, friendly, and helpful attitudes of these charming inhabitants of North and South Carolina and the Georgia Coast, it will be a shame. The men are courtly—not antifeminist, but apt to address a woman as "young lady" regardless of her age.

And the women, although generally not antifeminist, are nonetheless, soft-spoken. The children learn "ma'am" and "sir" when they're toddlers, and all of this politeness is contagious. Service people (the plumber, the shoe clerk, the auto mechanic) go far out of their way to accommodate, and they know you'll understand if things move just a *mite* slower here than in some other places. There are smiling faces everywhere, and "Hey, how are you?" sounds genuine. The pace is steady but relaxed; the ambience is open and friendly; the geniality is authentic. Once you've been here, you'll be quick to respond to "y'all come bac, y'heah."

1 Essential Information

Before You Go

Tourist Information

Contact the **Georgia Department of Industry, Trade and Tourism** (Box 1776, Atlanta, GA 30301, tel. 404/656–3590 or 800/847–4842, fax 404/651–9063), the **North Carolina Division of Travel and Tourism** (430 N. Salisbury St., Raleigh, NC 27611, tel. 919/733–4171 or 800/847–4862, fax 919/733–8582), and the **South Carolina Division of Tourism** (1205 Pendleton St., Box 71 Columbia, SC 29202, tel. 803/734–0122, fax 803/734–0133).

Tours and Packages

Should you buy your travel arrangements to the South packaged or do it yourself? There are advantages either way. Buying packaged arrangements saves you money, particularly if you can find a program that includes exactly the features you want. You also get a pretty good idea of what your trip will cost from the outset. Generally, you have two options: independent packages and fully escorted tours. Escorted tours are most often via motorcoach, with a tour director in charge. They're ideal if you don't mind having limited free time and traveling with strangers. Your baggage is handled, your time rigorously scheduled, and most meals planned. Such tours are therefore the most hassle-free way to see a destination, as well as generally the least expensive. Independent packages allow plenty of flexibility. They generally include airline travel and hotels, with certain options available, such as sightseeing, car rental, and excursions. Such packages are usually more expensive than escorted tours, but your time is your own.

While you can book directly through tour operators, you will pay no more to go through a travel agent, who will be able to tell you about tours and packages from a number of operators. Whatever program you ultimately choose, be sure to find out exactly what is included: taxes, tips, transfers, meals, baggage handling, ground transportation, entertainment, excursions, sports or recreation (and rental equipment if necessary). Ask about the level of hotel used, its location, the size of its rooms, the kind of beds, and its amenities, such as pool, room service, or programs for children, if they're important to you. Find out the operator's cancellation penalties. Nearly everyone charges them, and the only way to avoid them is to buy trip-cancellation insurance. Also ask about the single supplement, a surcharge assessed to solo travelers. Some operators do not make you pay it if you agree to be matched up with a roommate of the same sex, even if one is not found by departure time. Remember that a program that has features you won't use may not be the most cost-wise choice.

Fully Escorted Tours

Escorted tours are usually sold in three categories: deluxe, first-class, and tourist or budget class. The most important differences are the price, of course, and the level of accommodations. Some operators specialize in one category, while others offer a range.

Top operators include **Maupintour** (Box 807, Lawrence, KS 66044, tel. 913/843–1211 or 800/255–4266) and **Tauck Tours** (11 Wilton Rd., Westport, CT 06881, tel. 203/226–6911 or 800/468–2825) in the deluxe category; **Bixler Tours** (Box 37 Hiram, OH 44234, tel. 216/569–3222 or 800/325–5087), **Brendan Tours** (15137 Califa St., Van Nuys, CA 91411, tel. 818/785–9696 or 800/421–8446), **Caravan** (401 N. Michigan Ave., Chicago, IL 60611, tel. 800/227–2862), **Collette**

Tours (162 Middle St., Pawtucket, RI 02860, tel. 401/728–3805 or 800/832–4656), **Domenico Tours** (751 Broadway, Bayonne, NJ 07002, tel. 201/823–8687 or 800/554–8687), **Gadabout Tours** (700 E. Tahquitz Way, Palm Springs, CA 92262, tel. 619/325–5556 or 800/952–5068), **Globus** (5301 S. Federal Circle, Littleton, CO 80123, tel. 303/797–2800 or 800/221–0090), **Go America Tours** (733 Third Ave., 7th floor, New York, NY 10017, tel. 212/370–5080), **Landmark Tour and Travel** (4363 First Ave., N. Birmingham, AL 35222, tel. 205/592–2001 or 800/338–4714), **Mayflower Tours** (1225 Warren Ave., Downers Grove, IL 60515, tel. 708/960–3430 or 800/323–7604), **Parker Tours** (218-14 Northern Blvd., Bayside, NY 11361, tel. 718/428–7800 or 800/833–9600), and **Trieloff Tours** (24301 El Toro Rd., Suite 140, Laguna Hills, CA 92653, tel. 800/248–6877; 800/432–7125 in CA) in the first-class category; and Globus's sister company, **Cosmos Tourama,** in the budget category.

Independent Packages Independent packages are offered by airlines, tour operators who may also do escorted programs, and any number of other companies from large, established firms to small, new entrepreneurs.

Most of the airlines that fly to southern destinations offer independent tour packages. Contact **American Airlines' Fly AAway Vacations** (tel. 800/321–2121), **Continental Airlines' Grand Destinations** (tel. 800/634–5555), **Delta Dream Vacations** (tel. 800/872–7786), **TWA Getaway Vacations** (tel. 800/438–2929), **United Airlines' Vacation Planning Center** (tel. 800/328–6877), and **USAir Vacations** (tel. 800/428–4322). **SuperCities** (139 Main St., Cambridge, MA 02142, tel. 617/621–9988 or 800/333–1234) also offers a variety of packages.

Their programs come in a wide range of prices based on levels of luxury and options—in addition to hotel and airfare, sightseeing, car rental, transfers, admission to local attractions, and other extras. Note that when pricing different packages, it sometimes pays to purchase the same arrangements separately, as when a rock-bottom promotional airfare is being offered, for example. Again, base your choice on what's available at your budget for the destinations you want to visit.

Special-Interest Travel Special-interest programs may be fully escorted or independent. Some require a certain amount of expertise, but most are for the average traveler with an interest and are usually hosted by experts in the subject matter. The price range is wide, but the cost is usually higher—sometimes a lot higher—than for ordinary escorted tours and packages, because of the expert guiding and special activities.

Bicycling Look into **Appalachian Valley Bicycle Touring** (31 E. Fort Ave., Box 27079, Baltimore, MD 21230, tel. 410/837–8068), **Backroads** (1516 5th St., Suite L101, Berkeley, CA 94710, tel. 510/527–1555 or 800/462–2848), **Classic Adventures** (Box 153-P, Hamlin, NY 14464, tel. 716/964–8488 or 800/777–8090), and **Nantahala Outdoor Center** (13077 Hwy. 19W, Bryson City, NC 28713, tel. 704/488–2175, ext. 333).

Crafts School Some of the nation's top crafts centers draw serious amateurs and professionals alike to weekend and week-long courses. Best bests include the **Penland School of Crafts** (Penland School Rd., Penland, NC 28765, tel. 704/765–2359) and **John C. Campbell Folk School** (Rte. 1, Box 14A, Brasstown, NC 28902, tel. 704/837–2775).

Cultural and History Tours The nonprofit **Pepper Bird Foundation** (Box 69081, Hampton, VA 23669, tel. 804/723–1106) runs group tours exploring the African, Hispanic, Native American, and Asian cultures as they have developed in the South. The **Beach Institute** (502 E. Harris St., Savannah, GA 31401, tel. 912/234–8000) offers Black heritage tours of Savannah.

Outdoor Trips Contact **Nantahala Outdoor Center** (13077 Hwy. 19W, Bryson City, NC 28713, tel. 704/488–2175, ext. 333) for everything from rafting and backpacking to biking. There are **Sierra Club Base Camps** in the Smokies (730 Polk St., San Francisco, CA 94109, tel. 415/776–2211). **Outward Bound** (Rte. 9D, R2 Box 280, Garrison, NY 10524, tel. 914/424–4000 or 800/243–8520) runs wilderness skills programs with personal growth as an objective. **TrekAmerica** (Box 470, Blairstown, NJ 07825, tel. 908/362–9198 or 800/221–0596) includes hiking, camping, and hotels on its *Dixieland* tours. **Earthwatch** (680 Mount Auburn St., Watertown, MA 02272, tel. 617/926–8000) recruits volunteers to serve as short-term assistants to scientists on research expeditions.

Tips for British Travelers

Visitor Information Write or fax the **United States Travel and Tourism Administration** (Box 1EN, London WIA 1EN, tel. 0171/495–4466, fax 0171/409–0566) for a free USA pack.

Passports and Visas British subjects need a valid 10-year passport. A visa is not necessary unless (1) you are planning to stay more than 90 days; (2) your trip is for purposes other than vacation; (3) you have at some time been refused a visa, or refused admission to, the United States, or have been required to leave by the U.S. Immigration and Naturalization Service; or (4) you do not have a return or onward ticket. You will need to fill out the Visa Waiver Form 1–94W, supplied by the airline.

To apply for a visa or for more information, call the U.S. Embassy's Visa Information Line (tel. 0891/200–290); calls cost 48p per minute or 36p per minute cheap rate). If you require a visa, call 0891/234–224 to schedule an interview.

Customs British visitors aged 21 or over may import the following into the United States: 200 cigarettes or 50 cigars or 2 kilograms of tobacco; one U.S. liter of alcohol; gifts to the value of $100. Restricted items include meat products, seeds, plants, and fruits. Never carry illegal drugs.

Insurance The **Association of British Insurers,** a trade association representing 450 insurance companies, advises extra medical coverage for visitors to the United States.

For advice by phone or a free booklet, "Holiday Insurance," that sets out what to expect from a holiday-insurance policy and gives price guidelines, contact the Association of British Insurers (51 Gresham St., London EC2V 7HQ, tel. 0171/600–3333; 30 Gordon St., Glasgow G1 3PU, tel. 0141/226–3905; Scottish Provincial Bldg., Donegall Sq. W, Belfast BT1 6JE, tel. 01232/249176; call for other locations).

Tour Operators Tour operators offering packages to the Southern states include **Jetsave** (Sussex House, London Rd., East Grinstead, West Sussex RH19 1LD, tel. 0342/312033); **Key to America** (15 Feltham Rd., Ashford Middlesex, TW15 1DQ, tel. 0784/248777); **Premier Holidays** (Premier Travel Center, Westbrook, Milton Rd., Cambridge CB4 1YQ, tel. 0223/355977); and **Trailfinders** (194 Kensington High St., London W8 7RG, tel. 0171/937–5400; 58 Deansgate, Manchester M3 2FF, tel. 061/839–6969).

Airlines Major airlines fly to most Southern cities, including **American Airlines** (tel. 0345/789789), **British Airways** (tel. 081/897–4000), **Continental Airlines** (tel. 0293/776464), **Delta Airlines** (tel. 0800/414767), and **TWA** (tel. 071/439–0707).

When to Go

Spring is probably the most attractive season in this part of the United States. Cherry blossoms are followed throughout the region by azaleas, dogwood, and camellias from April into May, and by apple blossoms in May. Folk, craft, art, and music festivals tend to take place in summer, as do sports events. State and local fairs are held mainly in August and September, though there are a few in early July and into October.

Climate In winter, temperatures generally average in the low 40s inland, in the 60s by the shore. Summer temperatures, modified by mountains in some areas, by water in others, range from the high 70s to the mid-80s, now and then the low 90s.

The following are average daily maximum and minimum temperatures for key cities.

Atlanta, Georgia

Jan.	52F	11C	**May**	79F	26C	**Sept.**	83F	28C
	36	2		61	16		65	18
Feb.	54F	12C	**June**	86F	30C	**Oct.**	72F	22C
	38	3		67	19		54	12
Mar.	63F	17C	**July**	88F	31C	**Nov.**	61F	16C
	43	6		70	21		43	6
Apr.	72F	22C	**Aug.**	86F	30C	**Dec.**	52F	11C
	52	11		70	21		38	3

Raleigh, North Carolina

Jan.	50F	10C	**May**	78F	26C	**Sept.**	81F	27C
	29	- 2		55	13		60	16
Feb.	52F	11C	**June**	85F	29C	**Oct.**	71F	22C
	30	- 1		62	17		47	8
Mar.	61F	16C	**July**	88F	31C	**Nov.**	61F	16C
	37	3		67	19		38	3
Apr.	72F	22C	**Aug.**	87F	31C	**Dec.**	52F	11C
	46	8		66	18		52	11

Charleston, South Carolina

Jan.	59F	15C	**May**	81F	27C	**Sept.**	84F	29C
	41	6		64	18		69	21
Feb.	60F	16C	**June**	86F	30C	**Oct.**	76F	24C
	43	7		71	22		59	15
Mar.	66F	19C	**July**	88F	31C	**Nov.**	67F	19C
	49	9		74	23		49	9
Apr.	73F	23C	**Aug.**	88F	31C	**Dec.**	59F	11C
	56	13		73	23		42	6

Information Sources For current weather conditions and forecasts for cities in the United States and abroad, plus the local time and helpful travel tips, call the **Weather Channel Connection** (tel. 900/932–8437; 95¢ per minute) from a touch-tone phone.

Festivals and Seasonal Events

January In South Carolina, Orangeburg invites the country's finest coon dogs to compete in the **Grand American Coon Hunt.** The **Savannah Marathon** and **Half Marathon** in Savannah, Georgia; and the **Charlotte Observer Marathon** and **Runner's Expo** in Charlotte, North Carolina, attract the region's runners. **Martin Luther King, Jr., Week** is celebrated in Atlanta.

February **Black History Month** is observed throughout the South. In North Carolina, Asheville welcomes visitors to its annual **Winterfest Arts and Crafts Show,** and Wilmington stages the **North Carolina Jazz Festival.**

March The Old South comes alive: **Antebellum mansion and garden tours** are given in Charleston and Beaufort, South Carolina. A Revolutionary War battle is reenacted on the **Anniversary of the Battle of Guilford Courthouse** in Greensboro, North Carolina. Spring is celebrated with a **Cherry Blossom Festival** in Macon, Georgia, and **Springfest** on Hilton Head Island, South Carolina.

April Spring festivals abound, including **Dogwood Festivals** in Atlanta, and Fayetteville, North Carolina. Also consider the **Okefenokee Spring Fling** in Waycross, Georgia. In Wilkesboro, North Carolina, the **Merle Watson Memorial Festival** features Doc Watson's renowned bluegrass picking.

May Festivals take to the air this month with the annual **Hang Gliding Spectacular** in Nags Head, North Carolina. **Spoleto Festival USA** in Charleston, South Carolina, is one of the world's biggest arts festivals; **Piccolo Spoleto,** running concurrently, showcases local and regional talent. In South Carolina, Beaufort's **Gullah Festival** highlights the fine arts, customs, language, and dress of Lowcountry blacks.

June Summer gets underway at the **Sun Fun Festival** on Myrtle Beach's Grand Strand on the South Carolina coast.

July **Independence Day** celebrations are annual traditions around the South, including in Atlanta, Savannah, and Columbus, Georgia; and in Greenville, South Carolina, which hosts **Freedom Weekend Aloft,** the second-largest balloon rally in the country. In North Carolina, clog and figure dancing are part of the **Shindig-on-the-Green** in Asheville, and the annual **Highland Games & Gathering of the Scottish Clans** is held on Grandfather Mountain near Linville.

August Happenings include North Carolina's **Apple Festival** in Hendersonville. August music festivals include a **Beach Music Festival** in Jekyll Island, Georgia, and the annual **Mountain Dance and Folk Festival** in Asheville, North Carolina.

September In Georgia, Atlanta's **Fine Arts and Crafts Festival** is held in Piedmont Park, and the **Hot Air Balloon Festival** floats over Helen. The annual **Woolly Worm Festival** takes place in Banner Elk, North Carolina.

October The **National Pecan Festival** is held in Albany, Georgia. A barbecue and parade of pigs guarantee fun at the **Lexington Barbecue Festival** in North Carolina. **Oktoberfest** is celebrated in Savannah, Georgia, and in Myrtle Beach and Walhalla, South Carolina. The "Ghost Capital of the World"—Georgetown, South Carolina—stages a **Ghost Tour.**

November Christmas preparations include **Mistletoe Markets** in Albany, Georgia. The **Catfish Festival** takes place in Society Hill, South Carolina, and the **Chitlin' Strut** in Salley, South Carolina.

December Christmas is celebrated all over the South, with events in almost every city. Highlights include **Old Salem Christmas,** which recreates a Moravian Christmas in Winston-Salem, North Carolina. New Year's events include the **Peach Bowl,** played in Atlanta, and the **First Night Charlotte** festival, held on the Town Square in Charlotte, North Carolina.

The Olympic Games The Olympic Games will be held in Atlanta, Georgia, July 19–August 4, 1996. Tickets for Olympic events will go on sale in spring 1995. They will range in price from $6 to $250, but about 95% of them will sell for less than $75. Details on how to buy tickets had not been released at press time; for more information, contact the **Atlanta Committee for the Olympic Games** (ACOG, Box 1996, Atlanta, GA 30301, tel. 404/224-1996, fax 404/224-1993).

What to Pack

Clothing Much of the South has hot, humid summers and sunny, mild winters. For colder months, pack a lightweight coat, slacks, and sweaters; you'll need heavier clothing in the more northern states, where cold, damp weather prevails and snow is not unusual. Keeping summer's humidity in mind, pack absorbent natural fabrics that breathe; bring an umbrella, but leave the plastic raincoat at home. You'll want a jacket or sweater for summer evenings and for too-cool air-conditioning. And don't forget insect repellent.

Miscellaneous Bring an extra pair of eyeglasses or contact lenses in your carry-on luggage. If you have a health problem that requires a prescription drug, pack enough to last the duration of the trip. Don't pack them in luggage that you plan to check, in case your bags go astray. Pack a list of the offices that supply refunds for lost or stolen traveler's checks.

Luggage

Regulations Free airline baggage allowances depend on the airline, the route, and the class of your ticket; ask in advance. In general, on domestic flights you are entitled to check two bags—neither exceeding 62 inches, or 158 centimeters (length + width + height), or weighing more than 70 pounds (32 kilograms). A third piece may be brought aboard; its total dimensions are generally limited to less than 45 inches (114 centimeters), so it will fit easily under the seat in front of you or in the overhead compartment. In the U.S. the Federal Aviation Administration gives airlines broad latitude to limit carry-on allowances and tailor them to different aircraft and operational conditions. Charges for excess, oversize, or overweight pieces vary.

Safeguarding Your Luggage Before leaving home, itemize your bags' contents and their worth, in case they go astray. To minimize that risk, tag them inside and out with your name, address, and phone number. (If you use your home address, cover it so that potential thieves can't see it.) Put a copy of your itinerary inside each bag, so that you can easily be tracked. At check-in, make sure that the tag attached by baggage handlers bears the correct three-letter code for your destination. If your bags do not arrive with you, or if you detect damage, immediately file a written report with the airline before you leave the airport.

Insurance In the event of loss, damage, or theft on domestic flights, airlines' liability is $1,250 per passenger, excluding the valuable items such as jewelry, cameras, and more that are listed in the fine print on your ticket. Excess-valuation insurance can be bought directly from the airline at check-in. Your homeowner's policy may fill the gap; or firms such as **The Travelers Companies** (1 Tower Sq., Hartford, CT 06183, tel. 203/277–0111 or 800/243–3174) and **Wallach & Company, Inc.** (107 W. Federal St., Box 480, Middleburg, VA 22117, tel. 703/687–3166 or 800/237–6615) sell baggage insurance.

Traveler's Checks

Traveler's checks are preferable in metropolitan centers, although you'll need cash in rural areas and small towns. The most widely recognized are **American Express, Citicorp, Diners Club, Thomas Cook,** and **Visa,** which are sold by major commercial banks. Both American Express and Thomas Cook issue checks that can be counter-signed and used by you or your traveling companion. Typically the issuing company or the bank at which you make your purchase charges 1% to 3% of the checks' face value as a fee. Some foreign banks charge as much as 20% of the face value as the fee for cashing travelers' checks in a foreign currency. Buy a few checks in small denominations to cash toward the end of your trip, so you won't be left with excess foreign currency. Record the numbers of checks as you spend them, and keep this list separate from the checks.

Getting Money from Home

Cash Machines Many automated-teller machines (ATMs) are tied to international networks such as **Cirrus** and **Plus.** You can use your bank card at ATMs to withdraw money from an account and get cash advances on a credit-card account if your card has been programmed with a personal identification number, or PIN. Check in advance on limits on withdrawals and cash advances within specified periods. On cash advances you are charged interest from the day you receive the money from ATMs as well as from tellers. Transaction fees for ATM withdrawls outside your home turf may be higher than for withdrawals at home.

For specific Cirrus locations in the United States and Canada, call 800/424–7787. For U.S. Plus locations, call 800/843–7587 and press the area code and first three digits of the number you're calling from (or of the calling area where you want an ATM).

Wiring Money You don't have to be a cardholder to send or receive a **MoneyGram from American Express** for up to $10,000. Go to a MoneyGram agent in retail and convenience stores and American Express travel offices, pay up to $1,000 with a credit card and anything over that in cash. You are allowed a free long-distance call to give the transaction code to your intended recipient, who needs only to present identification and the reference number to the nearest MoneyGram agent to pick up the cash. MoneyGram agents are in more than 70 countries (call 800/926–9400 for locations). Fees range from 3% to 10%, depending on the amount and how you pay.

You can also use **Western Union.** To wire money, take either cash or a cashier's check to the nearest agent or call and use Mastercard or Visa. Money sent from the United States or Canada will be available for pickup at agent locations in 100 countries within minutes. Once the money is in the system it can be picked up at *any* one of 25,000 locations (call 800/325–6000 for the one nearest you; 800/321–2923 in Canada). Fees range from 4% to 10%, depending on the amount you send.

Traveling with Cameras, Camcorders, and Laptops

Film and Cameras If your camera is new or if you haven't used it for a while, shoot and develop a few test rolls of film before you leave. Store film in a cool, dry place—never in the car's glove compartment or on the shelf under the rear window.

Airport security X-rays generally aren't harmful to film with ISO below 400. To protect your film, carry it with you in a clear plastic bag and ask for a hand inspection. Such requests are honored at U.S. airports. Don't depend on a lead-lined bag to protect film in checked luggage—the airline may increase the radiation to see what's inside. Call the Kodak Information Center (tel. 800/242–2424) for details.

Camcorders and Videotape Before your trip, put camcorders through their paces, invest in a skylight filter to protect the lens, and check all the batteries.

Videotape is not damaged by X-rays, but it may be harmed by the magnetic field of a walk-through metal detector, so ask for a hand-check. Airport security personnel may ask you to turn on the camcorder to prove that it's what it appears to be, so make sure the battery is charged.

Laptops Security X-rays do not harm hard-disk or floppy-disk storage, but you may request a hand-check, at which point you may be asked to turn on the computer to prove that it is what it appears to be. (Check your battery before departure.) Most airlines allow you to use your laptop aloft except during takeoff and landing (so as not to interfere with navigation equipment). Before departure, find out about repair facilities at your destination.

Car Rentals

All major car-rental companies are represented in the South, including **Alamo** (tel. 800/327–9633); **Avis** (tel. 800/331–1212, 800/879–2847 in Canada); **Budget** (tel. 800/527–0700); **Hertz** (tel. 800/654–3131, 800/263-0600 in Canada); and **National** (tel. 800/227–7368). **Agency** (tel. 800/321–1972) and **Enterprise** (tel. 800/325–8007) offer some of the region's lowest rates, though they do not have offices in all cities. In cities, unlimited-mileage rates range from $35 per day for an economy car to $60 for a large car; weekly unlimited-mileage rates range from $150 to $230. This does not include sales tax, which varies from state to state.

Extra Charges Picking up the car in one city and leaving it in another may entail substantial drop-off charges or one-way service fees. The cost of a collision or loss-damage waiver (*see below*) can be high, also. Some rental agencies will charge you extra if you return the car *before* the time specified on your contract. Ask before making unscheduled drop-offs. Be sure the rental agent agrees *in writing* to any changes in drop-off location or other items of your rental contract. Fill the tank when you turn in the vehicle to avoid being charged for refueling at what you'll swear is the most expensive pump in town.

Be careful when renting a car for a multistate Southern trip: Many rental companies tack in-state driving restrictions onto their unlimited-mileage specials.

Cutting Costs Major international companies have programs that discount their standard rates by 15%–30% if you make the reservation before departure (anywhere from 24 hours to 14 days), rent for a minimum number of days (typically three or four), and prepay the rental.

More economical rentals may come as part of fly/drive or other packages, even bare-bones deals that only combine the rental and an airline ticket (*see* Tours and Packages, *above*).

Insurance and Collision Damage Waiver Until recently, standard rental contracts included liability coverage (for damage to public property, injury to pedestrians, and so on) and coverage for the car against fire, theft, and collision damage with a deductible. Due to law changes in some states and rising liability costs, several car rental agencies have reduced the type of coverage they offer. Before you rent a car, find out exactly what coverage, if any, is provided by your personal auto insurer. Don't assume that you are covered. If you do want insurance from the rental company, secondary coverage may be the only type offered. You may already have secondary coverage if you charge the rental to a credit card. Only Diner's Club (tel. 800/234–6377) provides primary coverage in the U.S. and worldwide.

In general if you have an accident, you are responsible for the automobile. Car rental companies may offer a collision damage waiver (CDW), which ranges in cost from $4 to $14 a day. You should decline the CDW only if you are certain you are covered through your personal insurer or credit card company. In many states, laws mandate that renters be told what the CDW costs, that it's optional, and that their own auto insurance may provide the same protection.

Traveling with Children

Publications *Local Guides* Publications filled with events listings, resources, and advice for parents include ***Atlanta Parent*** (4330 Georgetown Sq., Ste. 506, Atlanta, GA 30338, tel. 404/454–7599), which regularly features a "Family Calendar" of events that's especially for visiting families. It's available free at area libraries, supermarkets, and museums, or by mail for a small fee.

Newsletter ***Family Travel Times,*** published 10 times a year by **Travel With Your Children** (TWYCH, 45 W. 18th St., New York, NY 10011, tel. 212/206–0688; annual subscription $55), covers destinations, types of vacations, and modes of travel. TWYCH also publishes *Cruising with Children* ($22) and *Skiing with Children* ($29).

Books *Great Vacations with Your Kids,* by Dorothy Jordon and Marjorie Cohen ($13; Penguin USA, 120 Woodbine St., Bergenfield, NJ 07621, tel. 800/253–6476), and *Traveling with Children—And Enjoying It,* by Arlene K. Butler ($11.95 plus $3 shipping per book; Globe Pequot Press, Box 833, 6 Business Park Rd., Old Saybrook, CT 06475, tel. 800/243–0495, or 800/962–0973 in CT) help plan your trip with children, from toddlers to teens. From the same publisher are *Recommended Family Resorts in the United States, Canada, and the Caribbean,* by Jane Wilford with Janet Tice ($12.95), and *Recommended Family Inns of America* ($12.95).

Tour Operators **Rascals in Paradise** (650 5th St., Suite 505, San Francisco, CA 94107, tel. 415/978–9800, or 800/872–7225) specializes in adventurous, exotic, and fun-filled vacations for families to carefully screened resorts and hotels around the world.

Getting There *Air Fares* On domestic flights, children under 2 not occupying a seat travel free, and older children currently travel on the "lowest applicable" adult fare.

Baggage The adult baggage allowance applies for children paying half or more of the adult fare. Check with the airline for particulars.

Safety Seats The FAA recommends the use of safety seats aloft and details approved models in the free leaflet **"Child/Infant Safety Seats Recommended for Use in Aircraft"** (available from the Federal Aviation Administration, APA-200, 800 Independence Ave. SW, Washington, DC 20591, tel. 202/267–3479; Information Hotline, tel. 800/322-7873). Airline policy varies. U.S. carriers allow FAA-approved models bearing a sticker declaring their FAA approval. Because these seats are strapped into regular passenger seats, airlines may require that a ticket be bought for an infant who would otherwise ride free.

Facilities Aloft Some airlines provide other services for children, such as children's meals and freestanding bassinets (only to those with seats at the bulkhead, where there's enough legroom). Make your request when reserving. Bi-annually the February issue of *Family Travel Times* details children's services on three dozen airlines ($12; *see above*). "Kids and Teens in Flight," free from the U.S. Department of Transportation's Office of Consumer Affairs (R-25, Washington, D.C. 20590, tel. 202/366–2220) offers tips for children flying alone.

Lodging **Guest Quarters Suite Hotels** (tel. 800/424–2900) offer the luxury of two-room suites with kitchen facilities, plus children's menus in the restaurants. Many hotels in this chain also allow children under 17 to stay free in their parents' suite. Many **Days Inns** (tel. 800/325–2525) allow children under 18 to stay free and some have housekeeping units or provide free meals to very young children.

Hints for Travelers with Disabilities

Organizations Several organizations provide travel information for people with disabilities, usually for a membership fee, and some publish newsletters and bulletins. Among them are the **Information Center for Individuals with Disabilities** (Fort Point Pl., 27–43 Wormwood St., Boston, MA 02210, tel. 617/727–5540 or 800/462–5015 in MA between 11 AM and 4 PM, or leave message; TTY 617/345–9743); **Mobility International USA** (Box 10767, Eugene, OR 97440, tel. and TTY 503/343–1284; fax 503/343–6812), the U.S. branch of an international organization based in Britain (*see below*) that has affiliates in 30 countries; **MossRehab Hospital Travel Information Service** (tel. 215/456–9603, TTY 215/456–9602); the **Travel Industry and Disabled Exchange** (TIDE, 5435 Donna Ave., Tarzana, CA 91356, tel. 818/344–3640, fax 818/344–0078); and **Travelin' Talk** (Box 3534, Clarksville, TN 37043, tel. 615/552–6670, fax 615/552–1182).

In the United Kingdom Important information sources include the **Royal Association for Disability and Rehabilitation** (RADAR, 12 City Forum, 250 City Rd., London EC1V 8AF, tel. 0171/250–3222), which publishes travel information for people with disabilities in Britain, and **Mobility International** (228 Borough High St., London SE1 1JX, tel. 0171/403–5688), an international clearinghouse of travel information for people with disabilities.

Travel Agencies and Tour Operators **Flying Wheels Travel** (143 W. Bridge St., Box 382, Owatonna, MN 55060, tel. 507/451–5005 or 800/535–6790) is a travel agency specializing in domestic and worldwide cruises, tours, and independent travel itineraries for people with mobility problems. Adventurers should contact **Wilderness Inquiry** (1313 Fifth St. S.E., Minneapolis, MN 55414, tel. and TTY 612/379–3858 or 800/728–0719), which orchestrates action-packed trips like white-water rafting, sea kayaking, and dog sledding for people with disabilities. Tours are designed to bring together people who have disabilities with those who don't.

Publications Several free publications are available from the U.S. Consumer Information Center (Pueblo, CO 81009): "New Horizons for the Air Traveler with a Disability" (include Dept. 608Y in the address), a U.S. Department of Transportation booklet describing changes resulting from the 1986 Air Carrier Access Act and from the 1990 Americans with Disabilities Act, and the Airport Operators Council's *Access Travel: Airports* (Dept. 5804), which describes facilities and services for people with disabilities at more than 500 airports worldwide.

Fodor's publishes *Great American Vacations for Travelers with Disabilities* (available in bookstores, or call 800/533–6478) detailing services and accessible attractions, restaurants, and hotels in the South and other U.S. destinations. The 500-page *Travelin' Talk Directory* (*see* Organizations, *above*; $35 check or money order with a money-back guarantee) lists names and addresses of people and organizations offering help for travelers with disabilities. Twin Peaks Press (Box 129, Vancouver, WA 98666, tel. 206/694–2462 or 800/637–2256) publishes the *Directory of Travel Agencies for the Disabled* ($19.95, plus $2 for shipping), listing more than 370 agencies worldwide. The Sierra Club publishes *Easy Access to National Parks* ($16 plus $3 shipping; 730 Polk St., San Francisco, CA 94109, tel. 415/776–2211).

Hints for Older Travelers

Organizations The **American Association of Retired Persons** (AARP, 601 E St. NW, Washington, DC 20049, tel. 202/434–2277) provides independent travelers who are members of the AARP (open to those age 50 or older; $8 per person or couple annually) with the Purchase Privilege Program, which offers discounts on lodging, car rentals, and sightseeing, and the AARP Motoring Plan, provided by Amoco, which furnishes domestic trip-routing information and emergency road-service aid for an annual fee of $39.95 per person or couple ($59.95 for a premium version). AARP also arranges group tours, cruises, and apartment living through AARP Travel Experience from American Express (400 Pinnacle Way, Suite 450, Norcross, GA 30071, tel. 800/927–0111 or 800/745–4567).

Two other organizations offer discounts on lodgings, car rentals, and other travel products, along with such nontravel perks as magazines and newsletters: the **National Council of Senior Citizens** (1331 F St. NW, Washington, DC 20004, tel. 202/347–8800; membership $12 annually) and **Mature Outlook** (6001 N. Clark St., Chicago, IL 60660, tel. 800/336–6330; $9.95 annually).

Note: Mention your senior-citizen identification card when booking hotel reservations for reduced rates, not when checking out. At restaurants, show your card before you're seated; discounts may be limited to certain menus, days, or hours. If you are renting a car, ask about promotional rates that might improve on your senior-citizen discount.

Educational Travel The nonprofit **Elderhostel** (75 Federal St., 3rd floor, Boston, MA 02110, tel. 617/426–7788) has offered inexpensive study programs for people 60 and older since 1975. Held at more than 1,800 educational and cultural institutions, courses cover everything from marine science to Greek myths and cowboy poetry. Participants generally attend lectures in the morning and spend the afternoon sightseeing or on field trips; they live in dormitory-type lodgings. Fees for programs in the United States and Canada, which usually last one week, run about $300, not including transportation.

Tour Operators The following tour operators specialize in older travelers. **Saga International Holidays** (222 Berkeley St., Boston, MA 02116, tel. 800/343–0273) caters to those over age 60 who like to travel in groups; **SeniorTours** (508 Irvington Road, Drexel Hill, PA 19026, tel. 215/626–1977 or 800/227–1100) arranges motorcoach tours throughout the U.S. and Nova Scotia, as well as Caribbean cruises.

Publications *The 50+ Traveler's Guidebook: Where to Go, Where to Stay, What to Do* by Anita Williams and Merrimac Dillon ($12.95, St. Martin's Press, 175 Fifth Ave., New York, NY 10010) is available in bookstores and offers many useful tips. "The Mature Traveler" (Box 50820, Reno, NV 89513, tel. 702/786–7419; $29.95), a monthly newsletter, contains many travel deals.

Hints for Gay and Lesbian Travelers

Organizations The **International Gay Travel Association** (Box 4974, Key West, FL 33041, tel. 800/448–8550), which has 700 members, will provide you with names of travel agents and tour operators who specialize in gay travel. The **Gay & Lesbian Visitors Center of New York Inc.** (135 West 20th St., 3rd floor, New York, NY 10011, tel. 212/463–9030 or 800/395–2315; $100 annually) mails a monthly newsletter, valuable coupons, and more to its members.

Tour Operators and Travel Agencies The dominant travel agency in the market is **Above and Beyond** (3568 Sacramento St., San Francisco, CA 94118, tel. 415/922–2683 or 800/397–2681). Tour operator **Olympus Vacations** (8424 Santa Monica Blvd.. #721, West Hollywood, CA 90069, tel. 310/657–2220) offers all-gay-and-lesbian resort holidays. **Skylink Women's Travel** (746 Ashland Ave., Santa Monica, CA 90405, tel. 310/452–0506 or 800/225-5759) handles individual travel for lesbians all over the world and conducts two international and five domestic group trips annually.

Publications The premiere international travel magazine for gays and lesbians is *Our World* (1104 North Nova Rd., Suite 251, Daytona Beach, FL 32117, tel. 904/441–5367; $35 for 10 issues). *Out & About* (tel. 203/789–8518 or 800/929–2268; $49 for 10 issues, full refund if you aren't satisfied) is a 16-page monthly newsletter with extensive information on resorts, hotels, and airlines that are gay-friendly.

Home Exchange

You can find a house, apartment, or other vacation property to exchange for your own by becoming a member of a home-exchange organization, which then sends you its annual directories listing available exchanges and includes your own listing in at least one of them. Arrangements for the actual exchange are made by the two parties to it, not by the organization. For more information contact the **International Home Exchange Association** (IHEA, 41 Sutter St., Suite 1090, San Francisco, CA 94104, tel. 415/673–0347 or 800/788–2489). Principal clearinghouses include **Intervac International** (Box 590504, San Francisco, CA 94159, tel. 415/435–3497), with three annual directories; membership is $62, or $72 if you want to receive the directories but remain unlisted. **Loan-a-Home** (2 Park La., Apt. 6E, Mount Vernon, NY 10552, tel. 914/664–7640) specializes in long-term exchanges; there is no charge to list your home, but the directories cost $35 or $45 depending on the number you receive.

Apartment and Villa Rentals

If you want a home base that's roomy enough for a family and comes with cooking facilities, a furnished rental may be the solution. It's generally cost-wise, too, although not always—some rentals are luxury properties (economical only when your party is large). Home-exchange directories do list rentals—often second homes owned by prospective house swappers—and some services search for a house or apartment for you (even a castle if that's your fancy) and handle the paperwork. Some send an illustrated catalogue and others send photographs of specific properties, sometimes at a charge; up-front registration fees may apply.

Among the companies are **Interhome Inc.** (124 Little Falls Rd., Fairfield, NJ 07004, tel. 201/882-6864); **The Invented City** (*see* IHEA, *above*); and **Vacation Home Rentals Worldwide** (235 Kensington Ave., Norwood, NJ 07648, tel. 201/767-9393 or 800/633-3284). **Hideaways International** (767 Islington St., Box 4433, Portsmouth, NH 03802, tel. 603/430-4433 or 800/843-4433) functions as a travel club, and offers rentals in the South. Membership ($99 yearly per person or family at the same address) includes two annual guides plus quarterly newsletters; rentals are arranged directly between members, not by the club staff.

See ***The Condo Lux Vacationer's Guide to Condominium Rentals in the Southeast,*** by Jill Little ($9.95; Vintage Books/Random House, New York).

Credit Cards

The following credit card abbreviations are used: AE, American Express; D, Discover; DC, Diners Club; MC, MasterCard; V, Visa.

Further Reading

For background on Southern writers, take along Paul Buiding's *A Separate Country: A Literary Journey Through the American South.* Chet Fuller's *I Hear Them Calling My Name* is a narrative of a journalist traveling through the South. The *Encyclopedia of Southern Culture,* edited by Reagan Wilson and William Ferris, with a foreword by Alex Haley, offers an extraordinary portrait of the South. Two volumes edited by Ben Forkner and Patrick Samway—*Modern Southern Reader* and *A New Reader of the Old South*—portray the South through stories, plays, poetry, essays, diaries, interviews, and songs.

Eugenia Price's novels *Savannah* and *The Beloved Invader* provide a keen sense of place in a historical-romance frame. Also look for *Cold Sassy Tree,* by Olive Ann Burns. *Midnight in the Garden of Good and Evil* is John Berendt's nonfiction account of a murder in Savannah.

2 Georgia

Updated by Echo and Kevin Garrett

Georgia, like a cleverly made patchwork quilt, is a state full of surprises. First, consider its wildly varied landscapes: from the Appalachian mountains in the north to the pristine white beaches of the Atlantic; to the pine barrens dotted with azaleas and the black, gator-infested swamps that make up the state's southern portion. Next, observe its towns, each with its own brand of southern charm: from Dahlonega, site of the nation's first gold rush in 1828; to Alpine Helen, a re-creation of a Bavarian village in the Blue Ridge Mountains; to graceful Savannah, so beautiful that General Sherman spared the city during the Union Army's destructive march to the sea; to Macon, full of flowering Japanese cherry trees and the ghosts of the antebellum South.

Atlanta, a world apart from all of these, catapulted into the international spotlight when it was named the host city for the 1996 Olympic Games. The undisputed boomtown of the southeast, Atlanta is a vibrant city with a gleaming skyline, largely designed by local architect John Portman. Yet despite the progress, Atlanta has retained its reputation as a city of trees; a bird's eye view of the city from one of those skyscrapers will tell you why.

A five-hour car ride away lies another world. Georgia's 100-mile coast runs from the mouth of the Savannah River south to the mouth of the St. Mary's. Colonial Savannah lures visitors to its 21 cobblestone squares, giant parterre gardens, waterfront gift shops, jazz bars, and parks draped in Spanish moss.

The seaside resort communities blend southern elegance with a casual sensibility. St. Simons Island, about 70 miles south, attracts a laid-back crowd of anglers, beach-goers, golfers, and tennis players. On nearby Jekyll Island,the lavish lifestyle of America's early 19th-century rich and famous is still evident in their stately Victorian "cottages." Cumberland Island's protected forests and miles of sandy coastline and the dark waters of Okefenokee Swamp are favorite haunts of nature lovers.

Other historical riches include thousand-year-old Native-American homesites and burial mounds, antebellum mansions, war heroes' memorials, and intriguing monuments built by eccentric folk artists and obsessive gardeners. Georgia's large number of parks offer superb facilities for white-water rafting, canoeing, fishing, golf, and tennis, plus nature trails through mountain forests delicately laced with wild rhododendron, dogwoods, and azaleas.

Atlanta

"Her patron saint is Scarlett O'Hara," the writer James Street once said of Atlanta, "and the town is just like her—shrewd, proud and full of gumption—her Confederate slip showing under a Yankee mink coat."

The Yankee influence in metropolitan Atlanta is indeed undeniable, and the city has never been part of the moonlight and magnolias romance common to many antebellum cities. But make no mistake: Atlanta is in the heart of the Old South: *The Atlanta Journal & Atlanta Constitution's* Sunday section of regional news is still called "Dixie Living," and a top tourist attraction remains the Cyclorama, depicting the Battle of Atlanta in the "War Between the States."

From its founding in 1837, Atlanta–then called Terminus–was a vital freight center. Today it's called the "Crossroads of the South": Three interstates converge near downtown, and Hartsfield Atlanta

International Airport is one of the nation's busiest. Atlanta has emerged as a banking center, and the city acts as world headquarters for several Fortune 500 companies, including CNN, Coca-Cola, Delta Air Lines, Georgia-Pacific, Holiday Inn Worldwide, Home Depot, Scientific-Atlanta, and United Parcel Service.

Part of the city's vibrancy comes from its international community. Direct flights to Europe, South America, and Asia have helped to lure some of the 1,200 international businesses that operate here, and 48 countries have representation in the city through consular and trade offices and foreign chambers of commerce.

For more than three decades, Atlanta has been linked to the civil rights movement. Among the many accomplishments of Atlanta's African-American community is the Nobel Peace Prize that Martin Luther King, Jr., won in 1964. Dr. King's widow, Coretta Scott King, continues to operate the King Center, which she founded after her husband's assassination in 1968, and their four children maintain a high profile in the community. In 1972, Andrew Young was elected the first black congressman from the South since Reconstruction. After serving as Ambassador to the United Nations during President Jimmy Carter's administration, Young was elected mayor of Atlanta. Today, he serves on the city's Olympic committee.

The coming Olympics have been the talk of the town ever since Atlanta was picked to join the 20 international cities that have hosted the summer games since 1896 in Athens, Greece. Athletes from 200 countries will descend on Atlanta, accompanied by an estimated 2 million other visitors.

Arriving and Departing

By Plane Hartsfield Atlanta International Airport, off I–85 and I–285, 13 miles south of downtown, is the nation's fourth busiest. Airlines serving it include **Air Jamaica, ALM Antillean, America West, American, British Airways, Cayman Airways, Continental, Delta, Japan Airlines, Kiwi International, KLM, Lufthansa German, Markair, Midwest Express, Northwest, Private Jet, Swissair, TWA, United, USAir** and **ValuJet.**

Between the Airport and Center City **Atlanta Airport shuttle vans** (tel. 404/766–5312) operate every half hour between 7 AM and 11 PM. The downtown trip ($8 one-way) takes about 20 minutes and stops at major hotels. Vans also go to Emory University and Lenox Square ($12 one-way).

If your luggage is light, you can take **MARTA**'s (Metropolitan Atlanta Rapid Transit Authority, tel. 404/848–4711) high-speed trains between the airport and downtown and other locations. Trains operate 4:30 AM–1:16 AM (weekdays) and 5:30 AM–1:30 AM (weekends). The trip downtown takes about 15 minutes, and the fare is $1.25.

Taxi fare between the airport and downtown hotels is fixed at $15 for one person; $8 each for two people; $6 each for three people. Taxi drivers sometimes appear as befuddled by Atlanta's notoriously confusing street names as visitors are. The problem gets worse when big events are in town, because out-of-town operators from smaller Southern cities come into Atlanta to pick up business. These drivers are even less familiar with the roads, so come armed with directions if your destination is something other than a major hotel or other well-known site.

By Train **Amtrak's** *Crescent* (tel. 404/881–3060 or 800/872–7245) operates daily to New Orleans; Washington, DC; and New York from Atlanta's

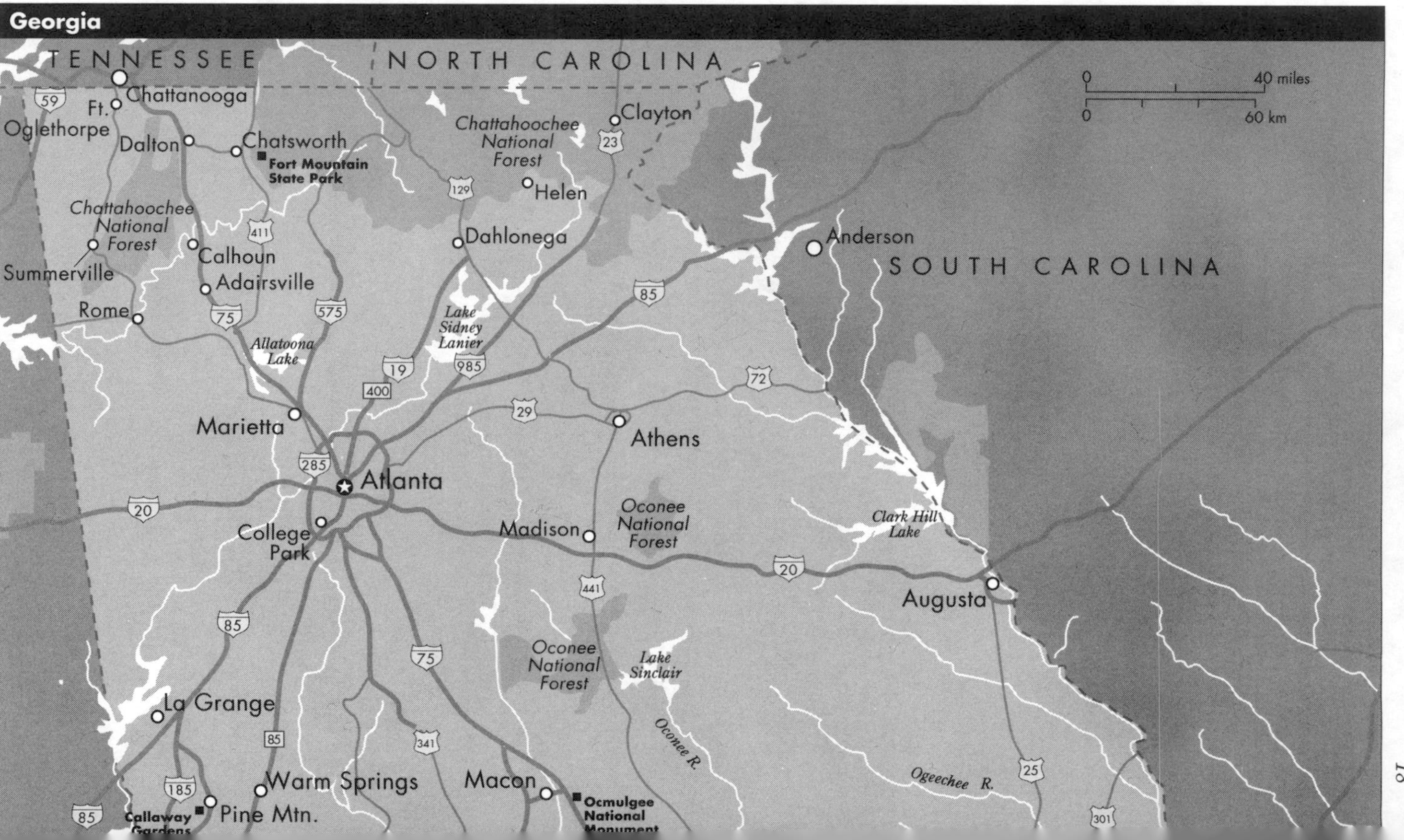
Georgia
TENNESSEE
NORTH CAROLINA
SOUTH CAROLINA
0 40 miles
0 60 km
Chattanooga
Ft. Oglethorpe
Dalton
Chatsworth
Fort Mountain State Park
Chattahoochee National Forest
Summerville
Rome
Calhoun
Adairsville
Allatoona Lake
Marietta
Atlanta
College Park
La Grange
Pine Mtn.
Callaway Gardens
Warm Springs
Macon
Ocmulgee National Monument
Oconee National Forest
Lake Sinclair
Oconee R.
Madison
Athens
Dahlonega
Lake Sidney Lanier
Helen
Clayton
Anderson
Clark Hill Lake
Augusta
Ogeechee R.
59
411
75
575
285
400
19
985
129
23
29
85
72
20
441
341
185
25
301

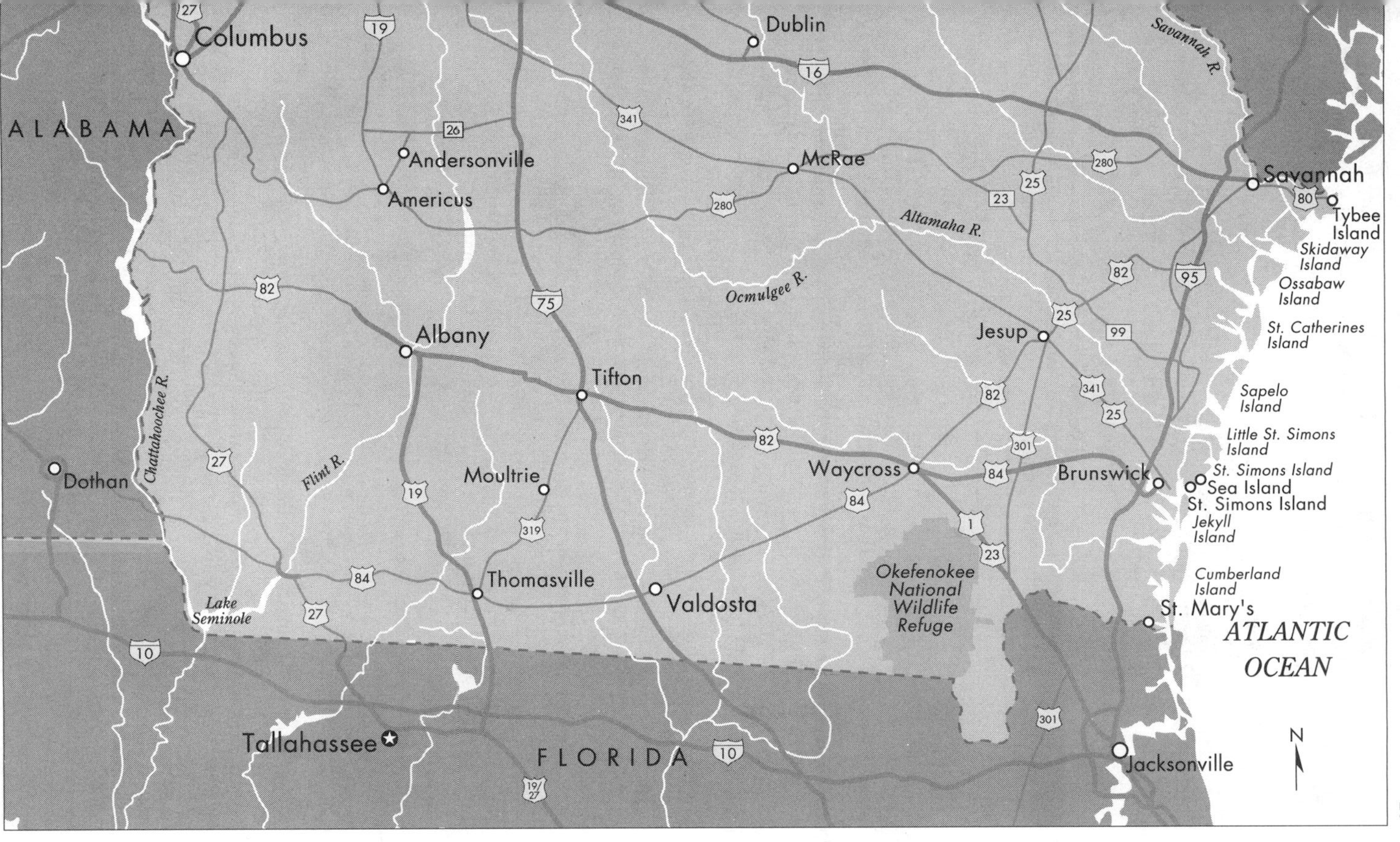

Columbus
Dublin
Savannah R.
ALABAMA
Andersonville
McRae
Savannah
Americus
Tybee Island
Altamaha R.
Skidaway Island
Ossabaw Island
Ocmulgee R.
Albany
Jesup
St. Catherines Island
Tifton
Sapelo Island
Chattahoochee R.
Little St. Simons Island
Waycross
St. Simons Island
Dothan
Flint R.
Moultrie
Brunswick
Sea Island
St. Simons Island
Jekyll Island
Okefenokee National Wildlife Refuge
Thomasville
Cumberland Island
Valdosta
Lake Seminole
St. Mary's
ATLANTIC OCEAN
Tallahassee
FLORIDA
Jacksonville
N
27
19
16
341
26
280
25
23
80
280
82
95
82
75
25
99
341
82
25
301
82
27
84
19
84
319
1
23
84
27
10
301
10
19/27

Brookwood Station (1688 Peachtree St.). Its *Gulf Breeze* travels from Atlanta to Birmingham and Mobile, Alabama.

By Bus **Greyhound Bus Lines** (81 International Blvd., tel. 404/522–6300 or 800/231–2222) also provides transport to downtown Atlanta.

By Car Some refer to Atlanta as the Los Angeles of the South, because travel by car is virtually the only way to get to most parts of the city. Although the congestion isn't comparable to L.A.'s yet, Atlantans have grown accustomed to frequent delays at rush hour. Perhaps in a desperate attempt to get somewhere, Atlantans are known for high-speed driving and reckless cutting across lanes of traffic. Visiting drivers should be vigilant.

The city is encircled by I–285. Three interstates—I–85, running northeast–southwest from Virginia to Alabama; I–75, north–south from Michigan to Florida; and I–20, east–west from South Carolina to Alabama—also criss-cross Atlanta.

Getting Around

By Bus **The Metropolitan Atlanta Rapid Transit Authority (MARTA)** (tel. 404/848–4711) operates a bus system with 150 routes covering 1,500 miles. The fare is $1.25, and exact change is required. In much of the city, service is so infrequent that it's barely an option, and many areas are not served at all. (An additional 1,923 buses–some loaned from as far away as New Jersey–will be used during the Olympics.)

By Subway MARTA's clean rapid-rail subway trains have somewhat limited routes but do link downtown with many major landmarks. The rail system's two lines connect at the **Five Points Station** downtown, where information on public transportation is available at the **Ride Store** (weekdays 7 AM–7 PM and Sat. 8:30 AM–5 PM). Trains run 5 AM–1 AM, and parking (free) can be found around most suburban stations. Tokens, which can be bought from machines with exact change, cost $1.25. Transfers, valid on buses or trains, are free.

By Taxi Taxi fares start at $1.50 and go up $1.20 each mile or 40 seconds of waiting time. Each additional person is charged another $1. Within the Downtown Convention Zone a flat rate of $3 for one person or $2 each for more than one will be charged for any destination. **Executive Limousine** (tel. 404/223-2000), **North Atlanta Cab** (tel. 404/451–4524), and **Yellow Cabs** (tel.404/521–0200) offer 24-hour service.

Guided Tours

Orientation **Gray Line of Atlanta** (tel. 404/767–0594, 3½-hour tour $15 per person, full-day tour $25 per person) gives tours of Downtown, Midtown, and Buckhead, plus a day-long tour that includes Stone Mountain and the King Center. **Historic Air Tours** (1954 Airport Rd. Suite 66, 30341, tel. 404/457–5217; 4 tours; $60-$85 per person per tour) takes visitors high above the city in a private airplane.

Walking Tours **The Atlanta Preservation Center** (The DeSoto, 156 7th St. NE, Suite 3, tel. 404/876–2041 or 876–2040) offers 10 walking tours of historic areas and neighborhoods ($5 adults, $4 senior citizens, $3 students; children under 19 free). Especially noteworthy are tours of Sweet Auburn, the neighborhood associated with Martin Luther King, Jr. and other leaders in Atlanta's African-American community; Druid Hills, the verdant, genteel neighborhood where "Driving Miss Daisy" was filmed; and the Fox Theatre, the elaborate, Moorish 1920s picture palace.

Important Addresses and Numbers

Tourist Information To plan your trip write to the **Department of Tourism** (233 Peachtree St. NE, Suite 2000, Atlanta 30303). For information on the 1996 Olympic Games (July 19–Aug. 4), contact the **Atlanta Committee for the Olympic Games** (Box 1996, Atlanta 30301-1996, tel. 404/224–1996.) Once in Atlanta, the **Convention and Visitors Bureau (ACOG)** (tel. 404/222–6688) has four visitor information centers stocked with maps and brochures: **Peachtree Center Mall** (233 Peachtree St. NE), **Underground Atlanta** (65 Upper Alabama St.), World Congress Center (285 International Blvd.), and **Lenox Square Mall** (3393 Peachtree Rd. NE). The ACOG also runs The Olympic Experience, a public information gallery/gift shop at Underground Atlanta.

Olympic Countdown

The Atlanta Committee for the Olympic Games (ACOG) is in the process of spending $500 million to ready Atlanta for the event. A new stadium—where the Atlanta Braves will eventually play—will seat 85,000. The Velodrome, an indoor bicycle race track; is under construction at Stone Mountain Park. The Olympic Village, where athletes and their families will stay, will be on the Georgia Tech campus in the heart of the city. At press time, about 11 million tickets were scheduled to go on sale in spring 1995. Tickets to the most sought-after events will be distributed through a lottery system; other tickets will be sold on a first-come, first-served basis, first by mail-order and then by phone-order. To get on a mailing list for ticket information, contact ACOG (tel. 404/224–1996).

Emergencies Dial 911 for assistance. Both **Grady Memorial Hospital** (80 Butler St. SE, tel. 404/616–4307) and **Georgia Baptist Medical Center** (300 Boulevard NE, tel. 404/653–4000) have 24-hour emergency rooms.

Pharmacy **Big B Drug** (1061 Ponce de Leon Ave. NE, tel. 404/876–0381) is open 24 hours, seven days a week.

Exploring Atlanta

Orientation In the past decade, Atlanta has experienced unprecedented growth. A good measure of that is its ever-changing skyline. More than a dozen architecturally dazzling skyscrapers have continually reshaped the city's profile since the late 1970s. Architect John Portman, who graduated from Atlanta's Georgia Tech in 1950, has designed numerous projects, including Peachtree Center, notable as a city within the city. Residents, however, are less likely to measure the city's growth by skyscrapers than by increasing traffic jams and the ever-burgeoning subdivisions that have pushed the city's limits further and further into surrounding rural areas. Most of metro Atlanta is within Fulton and DeKalb counties, but the southern part of the city is in Clayton County. Cobb and Gwinnett counties are experiencing much of Atlanta's population increase.

Although downtown offers interesting architecture and some excellent restaurants, nighttime and weekends find it practically empty; for locals, a night on the town usually means a visit to the Buckhead, Virginia-Highland, or Little Five Points neighborhoods. Residents love the area's recreational opportunities—from "shooting the 'hooch" (local talk for riding the rapids of the Chattahoochee River) to water skiing at Lake Lanier. Atlanta is a young city. At last count, the median age was 28. This youthful face helps account for much of the energy here and has helped Atlanta gain a reputation for nightlife, especially live music.

One of residents' main complaints is traffic—and it may become yours when you visit. With attractions scattered and public transportation limited, it's difficult to get somewhere without your own wheels. Rush-hour traffic runs from around 7 AM (sometimes earlier) to 9 AM and from 4:30 PM to about 7 PM. If you can, avoid interstates and such main streets as Piedmont Road, Peachtree Road, and Ponce de Leon Avenue during these hours. In particular, steer clear of I–285, which encircles the city and is dubbed "the perimeter." It's the unavoidable route for many a commuter and is notorious for traffic snarls and delays.

Atlanta's lack of a grid system and its confluence of streets into five-point intersections make for confusion. The streets were originally cow paths and Indian trails, which were paved, renamed, and given lights. The city's many hills and the meandering Chattahoochee River also throw a kink into any attempts at street planning. The city is shaped like a cursive capital *I*. At the bottom is the downtown area, and at the top is the Lenox Square-Phipps Plaza area. Along the shank of the *I* runs the famed Peachtree Street, the city's main thoroughfare, which changes its name without notice to Peachtree Road, then Peachtree Industrial Boulevard—Atlanta has a dozen arteries with "Peachtree" in their names. And there are several roads with "Roswell" in their names as well, a source of frustration to tourists and locals alike. Before setting out anywhere, get the complete street address of your destination.

Numbers in the margin correspond to points of interest on the Downtown Atlanta and Atlanta Vicinity maps.

Downtown The Martin Luther King, Jr., National Historic District occupies several blocks on Auburn Avenue, a couple of blocks north on Boulevard Drive. In the black business community of Sweet Auburn, the neighborhood was the birthplace of Martin Luther King, Jr., the undisputed leader of the civil rights movement, in 1929. After his assassination in 1968, King's widow, Coretta Scott King, estab-
1 lished the **King Center.** It contains a museum with King's Nobel Peace Prize, Bible, and typewriter, as well as photos chronicling the Civil Rights Movement, a library, and a souvenir gift shop, and it frequently sponsors educational programs. Tours of Sweet Auburn commence from here. In front of the King Center is King's white marble tomb, where an eternal flame burns and the inscription reads, "Free at last!" *449 Auburn Ave. NE, tel. 404/524–1956. Admission free. Open daily 9–5:30.*

2 Next door is **Ebenezer Baptist Church** (407 Auburn Ave. N.E., tel. 404/688–7263), a Gothic-Revival style building completed in 1922, which became known as the spiritual center for the movement after Dr. King won the Nobel Peace Prize in 1964. Members of the King family have preached at the church for three generations; Dr. King's funeral was here.

3 **Dr. King's birthplace** (501 Auburn Ave.), a Queen Anne-style bungalow, is managed by the National Park Service and is open to the public daily.

Auburn Avenue is still the heart of the black community's entrepre-
4 neurial district. The landmark **Atlanta Life Insurance Company,** founded by Alonzo Herndon, was located in modest quarters at 148 Auburn Avenue until the modern complex at No. 100 was opened in 1980.

5 At 145 Auburn Avenue is the **Atlanta Daily World** building, home of
one of the nation's oldest black newspapers. The church with the
"Jesus Saves" sign on its steeple is the Big Bethel African Methodist
6 Episcopal Church. Nearby is the **Royal Peacock Club,** (186 Auburn
Ave. N.E., tel. 404/880–0745) where the king and queen of soul—
James Brown and Aretha Franklin—frequently held court in the
Sixties. Now it's the home of reggae on the weekends.

For a history of Sweet Auburn, view the permanent exhibit at the
7 **African American Panoramic Experience;** there are also changing
exhibits on African-American culture. *135 Auburn Ave., tel. 404/
521–2654. Admission: $2 adults, $1 children. Open Sept.–May,
Tues.–Sat. 10–5; June–Aug., Tues.–Sat. 10–5, Sun. 1–5.*

8 On Edgewood Avenue is the **Municipal Market** (209 Edgewood Ave.,
open 8 AM –5:45 PM, except on Sun.), a thriving food market where you
can buy every part of the pig but the oink–as well as vegetables, fish,
and meat. At 125 Edgewood Avenue is the site of the first bottling
9 plant for the Coca-Cola Company—today occupied by the **Baptist Student Center** for the adjoining campus of **Georgia State University.**
Take a shortcut through the urban GSU campus toward the glitter-
10 ing gold dome of the **Georgia State Capitol building** (206 Washington
St.), a Renaissance-style building dedicated on July 4, 1889. State
historical markers on the grounds reveal that Atlanta has been virtually rebuilt since General Sherman's urban renewal program destroyed 90% of the city in 1864. The capitol's dome was gilded in 1958
with gold leaf mined from Dahlonega, a small town in north Georgia.
In addition to housing politicos, it also contains a Georgia history
museum, which is open to the public. *Georgia State Capitol, tel. 404/
656–2844. Free guided tours weekdays at 10, 11, 1, and 2.*

11 Behind the capitol is the **Fulton County Stadium,** home of the city's
beloved Atlanta Braves. By the time you read this, however, the
Braves will have a new stadium—initially called Olympic Stadium,
then christened Braves stadium—across the street. Across the
12 street from the capitol is Atlanta's **City Hall** (68 Mitchell St.). When
this 14-story, neo-Gothic structure with lavish marble interior was
built in 1926, wags dubbed it "The Painted Lady of Mitchell Street."

13 The **Five Points MARTA** station (corner of Peachtree and Alabama streets, downtown) services Underground Atlanta and nearby Woodruff Park, Georgia State University, city and county government offices, and CNN Center. Stand on the corner of Peachtree and Alabama streets, outside the station, and notice the old-fashioned gas street light, with its historic marker proclaiming it as the **Eternal Flame of the Confederacy.**

Up Central Avenue to Upper Alabama Street lies an entrance to
14 **Underground Atlanta** (tel. 404/523–2311). This six-block entertainment and shopping district was created from of the web of underground brick streets, ornamental building facades, and tunnels that
fell into disuse in 1929, when the city built viaducts over the train
tracks. Merchants moved their storefronts to the new viaduct level,
leaving the original street level for storage.

When Underground was developed five years ago by Rouse Company, the creators of Baltimore's highly successful Harborplace, it was expected to draw scores of residents and visitors back to the downtown area. The result has been disappointing, with conventioneers and tourists a stronger presence than locals, who opt for Midtown, Buckhead, and Virginia-Highland night spots instead. Still, Underground's atmosphere is lively enough—if a bit contrived—on weekend nights. The complex accommodates some 100 specialty

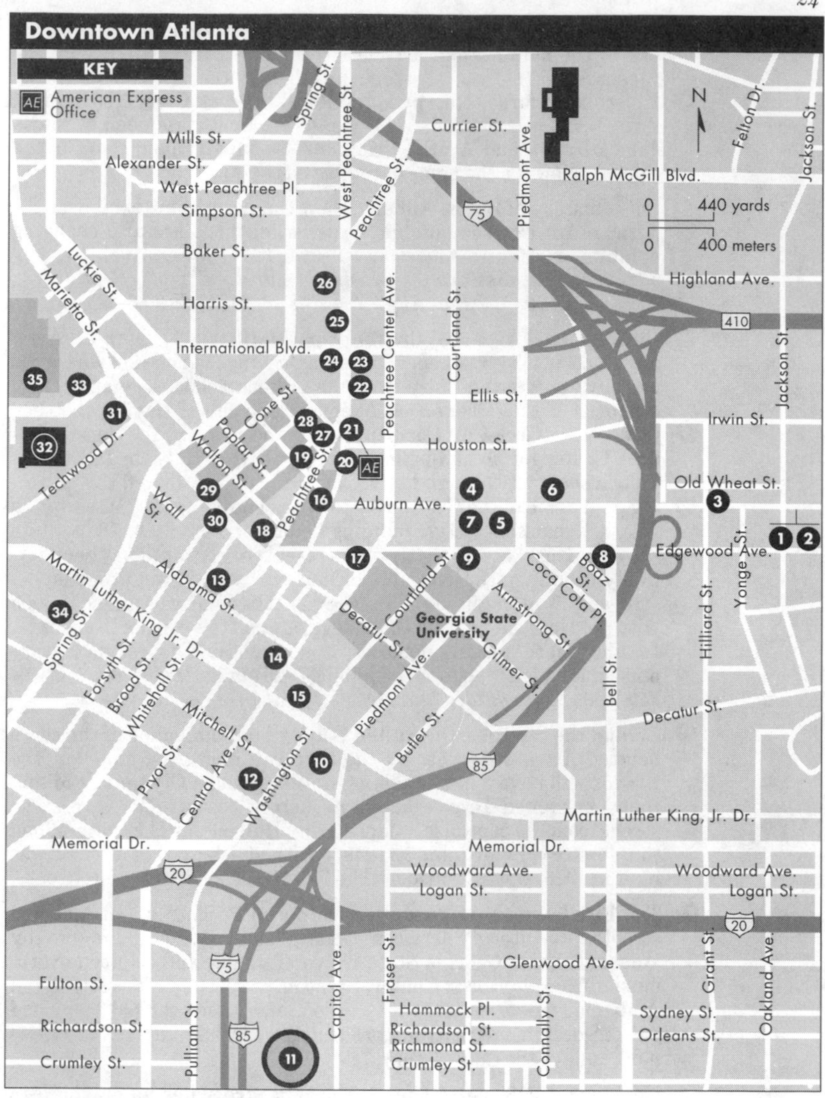

African American Panoramic Experience, **7**
Atlanta Daily World, **5**
Atlanta-Fulton County Public Library, **28**
Woodruff Park, **16**
Atlanta History Center, **46**
Atlanta Life Insurance Company, **4**
Bank South Building, **29**
Baptist Student Center, **9**
The Candler Building, **20**
Capital City Club, **26**
City Hall, **12**
CNN Center, **31**
Dr. King's birthplace, **3**
Ebenezer Baptist Church, **2**
Fay Gold Gallery, **44**
Fernbank Museum of Natural History, **51**
Fernbank Science Center, **52**
Five Points MARTA, **13**
The Flatiron Building, **19**
Fox Theatre, **37**
Fulton County Stadium, **11**
Georgia Dome, **35**
Georgia Governor's Mansion, **45**

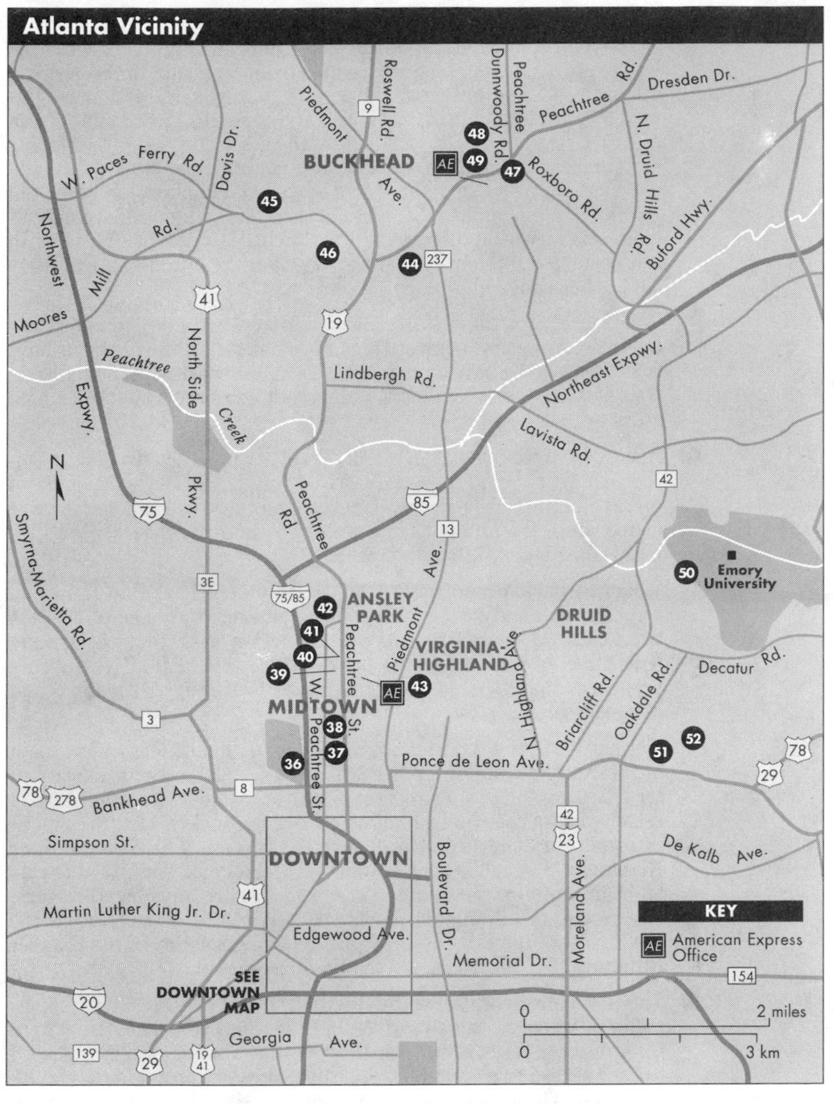

Georgia-Pacific Building, **21**

Georgia State Capitol Building, **10**

High Museum of Art, **41**

The Hurt Building, **17**

King Center, **1**

Lenox Square, **47**

Margaret Mitchell Park, **27**

Michael C. Carlos Museum, **50**

Municipal Market, **8**

Nation's Bank Tower, **36**

Omni, **32**

One Atlantic Center/ IBM Tower, **39**

One Ninety One Peachtree Tower, **23**

Peachtree Center, **25**

Phipps Plaza, **48**

Piedmont Park, **43**

Rhodes Memorial Hall, **42**

Richard B. Russell Federal Building, **34**

Ritz-Carlton Buckhead, **49**

Ritz-Carlton Hotel, **22**

Road to Tara Museum, **38**

Royal Peacock Club, **6**

Statue of Henry Grady, **30**

Underground Atlanta, **14**

Westin-Peachtree Plaza Hotel, **24**

The William Oliver Building, **18**

Woodruff Arts Center, **40**

Woodruff Park, **16**

World Congress Center, **33**

The World of Coca-Cola, **15**

retailers—many specializing in African-American goods—as well as 20 food-court vendors and 22 restaurants and nightclubs on three levels. Merchants selling their wares from carts add to the carnival atmosphere. The entertainment strip, Kenny's Alley—once occupied by saloons and livery stables—styles itself as Atlanta's version of New Orleans's Bourbon Street, with bars and night spots offering comedy acts, a variety of music (rock, country, pop, folk, jazz), and dancing. **Dante's Down the Hatch** stars live alligators, fondue, and jazz and is a favorite of locals and tourists alike. Underground's main entrance is highlighted by the Peachtree Fountains Plaza, with its distinctive 138-foot light tower. Two parking garages are on Martin Luther King, Jr. (locally, MLK) Drive.

Look closely for the historic markers that dot Underground Atlanta. One of the city's oldest remaining buildings, the Georgia Railroad Freight Depot, built in 1809 as three stories, remains here. Once it was the city's tallest building, but a fire reduced it to a single story in 1935.

15 Across from Kenny's Alley is **The World of Coca-Cola** (55 Martin Luther King, Jr. Dr., tel. 404/676–5151), where you can sip samples of more than 100 Coke products from around the world and marvel over memorabilia from more than a century's worth of corporate archives in this four-story, $10 million facility.

16 **Woodruff Park** (corner of Peachtree Street and Park Place), named after the city's great philanthropist, Robert W. Woodruff, the late Coca-Cola magnate, presents a cross section of Atlanta life. During lunchtime on weekdays, the park is filled with executives, street preachers, politicians, Georgia State University students, and homeless people.

Not much of old Atlanta still exists downtown, although a few turn-
of-the-century buildings remain. These elaborately decorated
structures stand in sharp contrast to the postmodern skyscrapers of
17 recent years. **The Hurt Building** (45 Edgewood Ave.) features intri-
18 cate grillwork and an elaborate marble staircase. **The William Oliver
Building** (32 Peachtree St.) is an Art Deco gem. Walk through its
lobby and admire the ceiling mural, brass grills, and elevator doors.
19 **The Flatiron Building** (84 Peachtree St.) dates from 1897 and is the
20 city's oldest high rise. The magnificent mosaic lobby of the **Candler
Building** (127 Peachtree St.) shouldn't be missed.

21 The towering **Georgia-Pacific Building** (133 Peachtree St.) occupies hallowed ground, the site of the old Loew's Grand Theatre, where *Gone with the Wind* premiered in 1939. One of the architectural oddities of this red-marble high rise is that from certain angles the building appears to be two-dimensional, or flat against the sky. The **High Museum of Art Folk Art and Photography Galleries** is inside the building. *30 John Wesley Dobbs Ave., tel. 404/577–6940. Admission free. Open Mon.–Sat. 10–5.*

22 On the adjacent corner is the downtown **Ritz-Carlton Hotel** (181
Peachtree St.), elegant with the company's trademark 18th- and
19th-century English antiques. The Ritz-Carlton's new neighbor is
23 the **One Ninety One Peachtree Tower,** designed by Philip Johnson.

Next to **Macy's** department store (180 Peachtree St.), is the 73-story
24 **Westin–Peachtree Plaza Hotel** (210 Peachtree St.) Designed by Atlanta architect John Portman, the round tower with its trademark
exterior elevator features a postmodern interior and the Sundial, a
revolving bar/restaurant offering the best panoramic view of the
city.

25 In the next block, on both sides of the street, is **Peachtree Center,** also designed by John Portman. This complex, with its connecting skywalks, includes the massive **Atlanta Market Center,** housing the **Merchandise Mart, Apparel Mart, Gift Mart and Inforum** (where ACOG is headquartered); the twin office towers of Peachtree Center, with an underground arcade and plaza; and the **Hyatt Regency Hotel.** Portman created a blueprint for American hotels when he designed this Hyatt—with its bunkerlike exterior, low entrance, soaring atrium and blue-domed Polaris Lounge—in 1967.

Within Peachtree Center, the **Atlanta International Museum of Art and Design** exhibits crafts from around the globe. *285 Peachtree Center Ave., tel. 404/688–2467. Admission free. Open Tues.–Sat. 11–5, Sun. noon–5.*

Dwarfed by the skyscrapers around it, the modestly sized Italian
26 Renaissance-style **Capital City Club** (7 Harris St.), built in 1911,
continues to attract the city's power brokers.

27 Across from the Georgia-Pacific building is **Margaret Mitchell Park,**
with its cascading waterfall and columned sculpture. Within sight of
the park named for Atlanta's most famous author is the
28 **Atlanta-Fulton County Public Library** (126 Carnegie Way), which
houses a large collection of *Gone with the Wind* memorabilia.

Head down Forsyth Street five blocks, to Marietta Street. Notice
the renovated **Healy Building** (57 Forsyth St.), an early skyscraper
29 with Tudor decoration. The **Bank South Building** (55 Marietta St.
NW) was Atlanta's tallest building from 1955 until 1964 and was constructed on the former site of City Hall.

30 At the corner of Marietta and Forsyth streets is a bronze **statue of Henry Grady,** the post–Civil War editor of *The Atlanta Constitution* and early champion of the so-called "New South." Farther down Marietta Street are the offices of the **Atlanta Journal & Atlanta Constitution.** Next door is the **Federal Reserve Bank.** Tours of its monetary museum can be arranged. *104 Marietta St., tel. 404/521–8747. Admission free. Open weekdays 9–4.*

Two blocks away, at the corner of Marietta Street and Techwood
31 Drive, is **CNN Center** (1 CNN Center, 100 International Blvd.), the
home of Ted Turner's Cable News Network. The 45-minute CNN
studio tour begins with a ride up the world's longest escalator to an
eighth-floor exhibit on Turner's global broadcasting empire. This
center will serve as the command post to thousands of international
journalists during the Olympics. *Tours: tel. 404/827–2300 or 404/
827–2400 for reservations, which are strongly recommended. $6
adults, $3.50 children under 19. Not recommended for children un-
der 6. Open daily 9–5:30 except major holidays. MC, V.*

32 Behind the CNN Center is the **Omni** (100 Techwood Dr.), home to
the Atlanta Hawks basketball team and site of special events, from
rock concerts to the 1988 Democratic National Convention. The
Hawks plan to build a new arena in the north suburbs by 1996, leav-
33 ing the Omni's future in doubt. The **World Congress Center** (285 International Blvd.), where Jimmy Carter held his rally the night he
was elected president, is also nearby. A short distance away is the
34 **Richard B. Russell Federal Building** (Spring Street between Mitchell Street and Martin Luther King, Jr. Drive), where former President Carter has an office. The lobby features magnificent tile
mosaics.

35 The 70,500-seat **Georgia Dome** (1 Georgia Dome Dr.), with a white, plum, and turquoise facade, is the site of Atlanta Falcons football

games, major rock concerts, and conventions and trade shows. A design team of local architects crowned the 1-million-square-foot facility with the world's largest cable-supported oval, giving the roof a circus-tent top.

Midtown Just north of downtown lies this thriving area, a former hippie hangout in the late Sixties and Seventies and now dominated by 1920s bungalows and mansions converted into multiunit apartments. Gentrification and gleaming new office towers have filled once-drab streets with trendy eateries and bars. Much of Atlanta's cultural scene happens in Midtown, and some of the city's most impressive new buildings have sprung up here, giving the area a skyline to rival that of downtown. Our tour takes you north along Peachtree Street and then east to Piedmont Park.

36 Built in 1992, **Nation'sBank** tower (600 W. Peachtree St.), its graceful birdcage roof easily visible from the interstate, is the South's tallest building at 1,023 ft. It's also one of Atlanta's most beautiful.

37 The not-to-be-missed **Fox Theatre** is one of only a handful of classic movie palaces in the nation saved from the wrecker's ball. It was built in 1929 in a fabulous Moorish-Egyptian style; the interior's crowning glory is its "sky" —complete with clouds and stars above Alhambra-like minarets. The Fox is still a prime venue for Broadway shows, rock concerts, dance performances, and film festivals. *660 Peachtree St., tel. 404/881–2100. Tours given Mon. and Thurs. at 10 AM, Sat. at 10 AM and 11:30 AM (cost: $5 adults, $4 senior citizens, $3 students).*

Time Out A few blocks from the Fox, in an old drugstore with the original tile floors and pressed tin ceilings, is a branch of **Mick's** (557 Peachtree St. at Linden St., tel. 404/875–6425), a popular Atlanta chain featuring old fashioned American food.

---

38 Across the street from the Fox is the **Road to Tara Museum** (The Georgian Terrace, 659 Peachtree St., tel. 404/897–1939; Mon.–Sat. 10–6; Sun. 1–6). This museum, named for the original title of *Gone with the Wind*, houses an impressive collection of *Gone with the Wind* memorabilia from around the world. Especially peachy are David O. Selznick's Screening Room, where clips on the making of the film classic are shown, and the new costume gallery.

At Peachtree and 10th streets is one piece of Atlanta history that has yet to find a savior: the dilapidated apartment house where Margaret Mitchell penned "Gone with the Wind" has practically lived up to her famous book's title. Mitchell derisively referred to the place as **"The Dump,"** and, indeed, Tara it ain't.

39 Down 14th Street is **One Atlantic Center** (1201 W. Peachtree St. NE), also known as the **IBM Tower.** Visible from many parts of the city, this pyramid-topped high rise with a Gothic motif, built in 1987, was designed by Philip Johnson.

40 The **Woodruff Arts Center** (1280 Peachtree St.) is home to the world-renowned **Atlanta Symphony Orchestra (ASO),** and the **Alliance Theatre.** The Alliance has a primary stage, where mainstream works are produced for general audiences, and a downstairs studio that offers innovative productions.

41 Next door is the bold white porcelain paneled **High Museum of Art,** a building that many call far superior to the collection within. This high-tech showplace built in 1983 is the award-winning design of premier architect Richard Meier. In 1991, the American Institute of

Architects listed the sleek museum among the 10 best works of American architecture of the 1980s. Best bets among the museum's permanent collection are its American decorative arts collection and its African folk art collection. Also check out temporary exhibits while you are here. *1280 Peachtree St., tel. 404/892–9284 or 404/892–HIGH for recorded information. Admission: $5 adults, $3 students and senior citizens, $1 children 6–17; free Thurs. after 1. Special exhibits often have an additional charge. Open Tues.–Thurs. 10–5, Fri. 10–9, Sat. 10–5, Sun. noon–5.*

42 North on Peachtree Street, **Rhodes Memorial Hall,** headquarters of the **Georgia Trust for Historic Preservation,** is one of the finest works of Willis F. Denny II. Built of Stone Mountain granite in 1904 for the wealthy founder of a local furniture chain, the hall now shelters a permanent exhibit on Atlanta architecture of bygone eras. *1516 Peachtree St., tel. 404/881–9980. Admission: $2. Open weekdays 11–4.*

43 A few blocks off Peachtree Street is beautiful **Piedmont Park,** the city's outdoor recreation center and the site of most *plein air* festivals and events in Atlanta's calendar (a source of rancor for those who say the park is damaged by the numerous mega-events scheduled there each year). Tennis courts, a swimming pool, and paths for walking, jogging, and rollerblading are part of the attraction, but many retreat to the park's great lawn for picnics with a smashing view of the Midtown skyline. Each April the park hosts the popular Dogwood Festival, emphasizing ecology. **The Atlanta Botanical Garden** (tel. 404/876–5858), occupying 60 acres inside the park, has 15 acres of formal gardens; a 15-acre hardwood forest with walking trails; a serene Japanese garden; and the Fuqua Conservatory, featuring unusual and threatened flora from tropical and desert climates. A whimsical dragon topiary guards the entrance. *Tel. 404/876–5858. Admission: $4.50 adults, $2.25 children 6–12 and senior citizens; free Thurs. 1–6. Open Tues.–Sun. 9–6.*

Buckhead Take to the road for the remainder of the tours; Atlanta's sprawl doesn't lend itself to walking. Drive north on Peachtree Road past Peachtree Hills and Garden Hills to **Buckhead,** the heart of affluent and trendy Atlanta. Many of Atlanta's see-and-be-seen restaurants, chic shops, and hip art galleries are concentrated in this neighborhood. Finding a parking spot on the weekends can be a real headache, and waits of two hours or more are common in the hottest restaurants.

44 Start a tour of the art district at the **Fay Gold Gallery** (247 Buckhead Ave., tel. 404/233–3843; open weekdays 9:20 AM–5:30 PM; Sat. 10 AM–6 PM), a favorite of Atlanta transplant Elton John, and pick up a guidebook for other gallery locations. Fine photography is sold at the **Jackson Fine Art Gallery** (3115 E. Shadownlawn, tel. 404/233–3739).

Time Out **Café Tutu Tango** (220 Pharr Rd. NE, tel. 404/841–6222), a small space with local art—and artists—in every nook and cranny, serves tasty tapas throughout the day. At night, the crush of Buckhead's beautiful people often means two-hour waits for tables.

---

45 The **Georgia Governor's Mansion** is a short drive away on West Paces Ferry Road. Built in the late 1970s in Greek Revival style, the house features Federal-period antiques in its public rooms. *391 W. Paces Ferry Rd., tel. 404/261–1776. Open for free guided tours Tues.–Thurs. 10–11:30 AM.*

46 Continue left on West Paces Ferry Road to the **Atlanta History Center,** opened in 1993. Its 28-foot-high atrium highlights materials native to Georgia and has a floor of heart pine and polished Stone Mountain granite. Displays are provocative, juxtaposing "Gone with the Wind" romanticism with the grim reality of Ku Klux Klan racism. Also on the 32-acre site, but not new to it, are the elegant **Swan House,** a Palladian mansion designed by architect Philip Trammell Shutze in 1926; the **Tullie Smith Plantation,** a two-story plantation house built in 1845; and **McElreath Hall,** an exhibition space for artifacts from Atlanta's history. *130 W. Paces Ferry Rd. NW, tel. 404/814–4000. Admission: $6 adults, $4.50 senior citizens and students, $3 children 6–17, under 6 free. Open Mon.–Sat. 9–5:30, Sun. noon–5:30.*

Follow the green-and-white "Scenic Drive" signs along Tuxedo, Valley, and Habersham roads to get a look at the lawns, gardens, and mansions of Atlanta's well-to-do. Greek Revival, Spanish, Italianate, English Tudor, and French château and mansions vie for viewers' attention.

At the intersection of Peachtree Street and Lenox Road are
47 Atlanta's two premier shopping malls: **Lenox Square,** centered
around a four-story open atrium, and the newly refurbished and en-
48 larged **Phipps Plaza.** At the latter, shoppers dressed to the nines
take such amenities as valet parking and concierge service in stride. Break up boutique visits with a stop at **Il Centro,** the center's chic coffee bar, or one of several restaurants here.

49 Across the street lies the **Ritz-Carlton Buckhead,** next door to the luxury hotel chain's headquarters. Considered one of the finest hotels in the country, it contains one of the South's most valuable private art collection, primarily 18th- and 19th-century American and European painting, sculpture, and porcelain. It's also home to Atlanta's only five-star restaurant, **The Dining Room** (*see* Dining, *below*).

Virginia-Highland and the Emory Area

Restaurants, bars, and art galleries are the backbone of the eclectic Virginia-Highland/Morningside neighborhood, northeast of Midtown. Emory University, site of the Centers for Disease Control and one of the city's cultural and academic hubs, lies east of here. A number of museums and other attractions are scattered throughout the area.

50 The postmodern **Michael C. Carlos Museum**'s interior was designed by architect Michael Graves. Exhibits range from an Egyptian mummy to contemporary art. *Emory University, Kilgo St., tel. 404/727–4282. Suggested donation: $3. Open Mon.–Sat. 10–4:30, Fri. 10–9, Sun. noon–5.*

Drive east on North Decatur Avenue, turn right on Clifton Road,
51 and continue for 1 mile. **Fernbank Museum of Natural History,**
opened in October 1992, maintains the largest natural history collection south of the Smithsonian. A permanent exhibit, "A Walk Through Time in Georgia," takes the visitor through 15 galleries to explore the beauty of the state. The museum's IMAX theater shows films on a six-story screen. *767 Clifton Rd. NE, tel. 404/378–0127 or directions hot line 404/370–0850. Admission: $5.50 adults, $4.50 students and senior citizens, under 2 free. Open Mon.–Sat. 9–6; Sun. noon–6.*

Head left on Ponce de Leon Avenue and left again on Altwood Road. A right onto Heaton Park Drive takes you to the large planetarium
52 at the **Fernbank Science Center,** the only one in the nation owned by

a public school system. This small museum focuses on geology, space exploration, and ecology; older children will likely find its displays outdated. *156 Heaton Park Dr. NE, tel. 404/378–4311. Museum admission free (planetarium shows: $2 adults, $1 students). Open Tues.–Fri. 8:30–10, Mon. 8:30–5, Sat. 10–5, and Sun. 1–5.*

Although you can walk much of the Virginia-Highland area, as many points of interest lie along or off of a single street (N. Highland Avenue), you'll often find clusters of shops, restaurants, and galleries separated by longish stretches of residential area. A car may still be your best bet, although parking can be scarce. Virginia-Highland's galleries are abundant; art is usually contemporary and often reasonably priced. The **Modern Primitive Gallery** (1402 N. Highland Ave., tel. 404/892–0556) features the folk art of Howard Finster, a local legend in the arts scene. Hipsters enjoy **20th Century Antiques** (1044 N. Highland Ave., tel. 404/892–2065).

When you tire of gallery-hopping, some of the city's best restaurants and bars are here (*see* Dining, *below*).

Atlanta for Free

Alonzo F. Herndon Home. Former slave and founder of the Atlanta Life Insurance Co., the nation's second-largest black-owned insurance company, Alonzo Herndon built this 15-room mansion in 1910. A museum contains furnishings, artwork, and memorabilia. *587 University Pl., tel. 404/581–9813. Open Tues.–Sat. 10–4.*

Georgia Governor's Mansion (*see* Exploring, *above*).

Michael C. Carlos Museum (*see* Virginia-Highlands and the Emory Area, *above*.

What to See and Do with Children

The "Weekend" tabloid section of Saturday's *Atlanta Journal & Atlanta Constitution* has a listing called "Kids," which highlights special happenings around the city for youngsters.

American Adventures/White Water Atlanta. The former has recently opened a $1 million tree house and features 15 indoor and outdoor rides, miniature golf, a race-car track, and Imagination Station. The latter features more than 40 water attractions, including the largest kid's water playground in the country. *North Cobb Parkway, Marietta, tel. 404/424–9283. Admission to grounds free. Open Memorial Day–Labor Day, Mon.–Thurs. 11–7, weekends 10–9; rest of the year hours vary—call ahead.*

Center for Puppetry Arts Museum. The large display of puppets from all over the world is designed to teach visitors about the craft. Children who attend a workshop on puppetmaking take home their creation. Performances here leave youngsters spellbound. *1404 Spring St. at 18th St., tel. 404/873–3391. Admission: $3 adults, $2 children 13 and under. Recommended for age 4 and up. Open Mon.–Sat. 9–4.*

Chattahoochee Nature Center. Residents delight in the nature trails and boardwalk winding through 100 acres of woodlands and wetlands. *9135 Willeo Rd., Roswell, tel. 404/992–2055. Admission: $2 adults, $1 children and senior citizens. Open daily 9–5.*

SciTrek. The Science and Technology Museum of Atlanta, opened in 1988, covers 96,000 square feet of space and has about 100 hands-on exhibits in four halls: Simple Machines; Light, Color, and Perception; Electricity and Magnetism; and Kidspace, for children ages two to seven. *395 Piedmont Ave. NE, tel. 404/522–5500. Admission: $6 adults, $4 children 3–17, under 3 free. Open daily 10–5.*

Six Flags Over Georgia. This is Atlanta's major theme park, with more than 100 rides, many of them heart-stopping roller coasters and water rides (the latter best saved for last to prevent being damp all day). An especially popular spectacle is the Batman Stunt Show. The park also features well-staged musical revues, diving shows, performing tropical birds and dolphins, and concerts by top-name artists. *I–20W at Six Flags Dr., tel. 404/948–9290. Admission: (all-inclusive 1-day pass) $25 adults, $11 ages 55 and older, $18 children 3–9, under 3 free; $5 parking fee. Opens 10 AM daily in summer, with weekend-only operations Mar.–May and Sept.–Oct. Closed Nov.–Feb.; closing times vary. Take MARTA's West Line to Hightower Station and then Six Flags bus (No. 201).*

Stone Mountain Park is the largest granite outcropping on earth. The Confederate Memorial on the north face of the 825-foot-high, 5-mile-around monolith is the world's largest sculpture. The 3,200-acre park has a skylift–scheduled for expansion in time for the Olympics–to the mountaintop, a steam locomotive ride around the mountain's base, an antebellum plantation, an ice-skating rink, golf course, swimming beach, campground, paddlewheel steamboat, and Civil War museum. Summer nights are capped with a laser light show. *U.S. 78, Stone Mountain Freeway, tel. 404/498–5600. Admission: $5 per car, additional fees for attractions. Open daily 6 AM–midnight.*

Zoo Atlanta has nearly 1,000 animals inhabiting its redeveloped property. An ongoing $35-million renovation program has already produced the Birds of Prey Amphitheater, the Ford African Rain Forest, Flamingo Lagoon, and the Sumatran Tiger Exhibit. Recent big news at the zoo is the much-heralded birth of a baby gorilla after a decade of trying. The baby's name is Kudzu, after the vine introduced from Japan that has now taken over much of the South's native vegetation. *Grant Park, 800 Cherokee Ave., tel. 404/624–5600. Admission: $7.50 adults and children 12 and older, $5 children 3–11, under 3 free. Open daily 10–4:30 except major holidays.*

Off the Beaten Track

Just 30 minutes north of Atlanta, Chateau Elán (7000 Old Winder Highway, I-85 to exit 48, Braselton, tel. 404/932–0900 or 800/233–9463, fax 404/271–6005), a 16th-century–style French chateau and Georgia's premiere winery, sits on 2,400 rolling acres. Winery tours and tastings are free; European luxury blends with southern hospitality at the 146-room inn and newly opened spa. Two golf courses, fishing, tennis, and equestrian centers round out the offerings.

Carter Presidential Center. The museum and archives focus on Jimmy Carter's political career. The center, located on the site where General Sherman orchestrated the Battle of Atlanta, sponsors foreign affairs conferences and projects on such issues as world food supply. Its Japanese garden is a serene spot to unwind. *1 Copenhill Ave. NE, tel. 404/420–5100. Admission: $2.50 adults, $1.50 senior citizens, under 15 free. Open Mon.–Sat. 9–4:45, Sun. noon–4:45 except major holidays. Cafeteria open Mon.–Sat. 11–4, Sun. noon–4:30.*

Shopping

Atlanta is second only to Chicago in space devoted to shopping areas, and its department stores, specialty shops, and flea markets draw shoppers from across the Southeast. Most stores are open Monday–Saturday 10–9:30, Sunday noon–6. Many downtown stores close Sunday. Sales tax is 6% in the city of Atlanta and Fulton County; rates vary in the suburbs.

Unlike many urban centers, downtown stores—although not abundant—do a steady business. Stores here are anchored on the north by **Macy's** (180 Peachtree St., tel. 404/221–7221). Smaller stores include **Brooks Brothers** (235 Peachtree St., tel. 404/577–4040), on the ground floor of Peachtree Center's Gaslight Tower, **The Limited** (209 Peachtree St., tel. 404/523–1728), and 80 retail shops and 40 cart vendors inside Underground Atlanta.

At the intersection of Peachtree and Lenox roads, 8 miles north of downtown, is Atlanta's high-fashion shopping district (*see* Buckhead, *above*). **Lenox Square Mall** has branches of **Neiman Marcus, Macy's, Rich's,** and 200 other specialty stores and restaurants. Practically across the street from Lenox and neck and neck with the former in the race for customers, **Phipps Plaza** houses branches of **Saks Fifth Avenue, Lord & Taylor, Parisians, Gucci,** and **Tiffany & Co.** Phipps recently announced it will add a branch of Bloomingdale's in time for the Olympics, while Lenox says it will add about 60 stores.

Cumberland Mall (Cobb Parkway at I-285 & I-75, tel. 404/435–2206) and the more upscale Galleria Specialty Mall (One Galleria Parkway, tel. 404/955–9100), offer prime shopping for residents of Atlanta's northwestern suburbs. The newest entry on the mall scene, the vast North Point Mall (1000 North Point Circle, Alpharetta, tel. 404/740–8636), has five department stores. About 15 minutes north of Lenox is Perimeter Mall (4400 Ashford-Dunwoody, tel. 404/394–4270), known for upscale family shopping, with shops such as the High Museum of Art's gift shop, Gap Kids, and The Nature Company. Also child-friendly are Town Center (400 Barrett Parkway, Kennesaw, tel. 404/424–9486) and Gwinnett Place Mall (2100 Pleasant Hill Rd., Duluth, tel. 404/476–5160), both with on-site child-care facilities.

Outlets Atlanta and surrounding towns are a bargain-hunter's delight. Macy's Close-Out at Avondale Mall (3588 Memorial Dr., Decatur, tel. 404/286–0829) and Rich's Finale at Greenbriar Mall (2841 Greenbriar Parkway S.W., tel. 404/346–2615) are two of the many discounters here. Ballard's Backroom Catalog Clearance Center (1670 Defoor Ave., tel. 404/352–2776) carries the uniquely designed rugs, lamps, tables, and pillows usually available only through Ballard Design's stylish catalogs.

Outlets at **Chattahoochee Avenue** (Exit 105 off I–75) include designer stops such as Joan Vass. The Dalton Factory Stores (80 miles north of Atlanta; exit 136 off I-75, tel. 706/278–0399) offer Jones of New York, West Point Pepperell, and more. Outlets Ltd. Mall (two locations: 3750 Venture Dr., Duluth, tel. 404/476–8552; 750 George Busbee Parkway, Kennesaw, tel. 404/424–9500) yields good buys in men's, women's, and children's clothing, as well as numerous specialty items. The Outlet Square of Atlanta (4166 Buford Highway N.E., tel. 404/633–2566) is anchored by the Burlington Coat Factory and Marshall's.

Specialty Shops

Antiques

Buckhead is home to several antique areas. Expect rare goods and high prices in many stores. More than 25 shops line the cobblestone courtyard of Buckhead's **2300 Peachtree Road** complex. The **Miami Circle** district, off Piedmont Road, is another enclave for antique and decorative arts lovers. **The Stalls** (116 Bennett St., tel. 404/352-4430), is an upscale flea market.

"Junking" addicts find nirvana in Little Five Points, around the intersection of Moreland and Euclid avenues. The neighborhood is characterized by vintage clothing stores, used record and book shops, and some stores that defy description.

Other fertile ground for serious antique shoppers includes several stores on Peachtree Industrial Boulevard, near the MARTA station; and historic Roswell, about a 30-minute drive north of downtown.

Books

Atlanta's largest selection of books and newspapers is at **Oxford Books at Buckhead** (360 Pharr Rd., tel. 404/262-3333), a local institution where frequent book signings are prominently noted on the store's marquee. Oxford's narrow balcony is a coffee shop, and the store also contains a full-service art gallery that emphasizes local artists' works.

Food

DeKalb Farmers Market (3000 E. Ponce de Leon Ave., Decatur, tel. 404/377-6400) has 106,000 square feet of exotic fruits, cheeses, seafood, sausages, breads, and delicacies from around the world. Gourmands stock up at **Harry's Farmers Markets** (1180 Upper Hembree Rd., Alpharetta, tel. 404/664-6300; plus three other locations) north of the city, with their dazzling array of prepared foods as well as produce, meats, seafood, and wines.

Participant Sports

In a city where outdoor recreation is possible almost year-round, sports play a major role. At almost any time of the year, in parks, private clubs, and neighborhoods throughout the city, you'll find Atlantans pursuing everything from tennis to soccer to rollerblading. *Atlanta Sports & Fitness Magazine* (tel. 404/842-0359), available at many grocery stores and health clubs, is a good link to Atlanta's athletic community.

Bicycling

Piedmont Park (Piedmont Ave. between 10th and 14th Sts.) is closed to traffic and popular for rollerblading. **Skate Escape** (across from the park at 1086 Piedmont Ave., tel. 404/892-1292) has rental bikes and skates. The **Southern Bicycle League** (tel. 404/594-8350) has regularly scheduled tours. Contact The Bicycle Club of Atlanta (tel. 404/483-2557) for more information.

Golf

Golf is enormously popular here, as the many courses will attest. The public courses most convenient to downtown are **Stone Mountain Park** (U.S. 78, 16 mi east of downtown, tel. 404/498-4715), N. Fulton Golf Course (216 W. Wieuca Rd., tel. 404/255-0723), and **Sugar Creek** (2706 Bouldercrest Rd., tel. 404/241-7671). Other good choices are Southerness Golf Club (4871 Flat Bridge Rd., Stockbridge, tel. 404/808-6000; 25 minutes east of Atlanta) and Eagle Watch Golf Club (3055 Eagle Watch Dr., Woodstock, tel. 404/591-1000; 35 minutes north of Atlanta.) Golf Atlanta! (tel. 404/255-7559) provides centralized tee-time reservations for several courses.

Health Clubs

SportsLife (1775 Water Pl., tel. 404/952-3200) and the **YMCA** (tel. 404/588-9622; 15 locations) are both open to the public. Hotels with health clubs include the **Ritz-Carlton Buckhead, Westin Peachtree**

Plaza, Hotel Nikko, the **Swissotel,** and the **Atlanta Marriott Marquis** (*see* Lodging, *below*).

Jogging This is one of the city's most popular sports. The **Peachtree Road Race 10K,** held annually on July 4, has become so competitive that there are no longer enough slots for those wanting to sign up. Atlanta's hills provide joggers with plenty of challenges. On the plus side, most streets are heavily shaded, offering some respite from the miserable summer humidity. Traffic-free **Piedmont Park** is ideal for running, as is the **Chattahoochee National Recreation Area.** Contact the **Atlanta Track Club** (3097 Shadowlawn Ave., tel. 404/231–9064) or Chattahoochee Road Runners (Box 724745, 31139, tel. 404/916–2790) for other suggestions.

Rafting and Rowing The **Chattahoochee River** is a favorite among rafters and rowers alike. The Atlanta Rowing Club (tel. 404/993–1879) provides information.

Swimming Climate-controlled facilities are housed in the **Martin Luther King Jr. Natatorium** (70 Boulevard, tel. 404/688–3791). **White Water Park** (250 North Cobb Pkwy. U.S. 41, Marietta, tel. 404/424–9283) has a huge wave pool, several water slides, picnic areas, lockers, and showers.

Tennis **Bitsy Grant Tennis Center** (2125 Northside Dr., tel. 404/351–2774; open weekdays 9–7, weekends 9–5),with 13 clay courts and 10 hard courts, is the area's best public facility. **Piedmont Park** (tel. 404/872–1507) has 12 hard courts with night lights available, but no locker facilities (open weekdays noon–9, weekends 9–5).

Water Skiing Lake Lanier and Callaway Gardens both offer superior water skiing, although the former can be extremely crowded on weekends. Contact The Atlanta Water Ski Club (tel. 404/425–7166).

Spectator Sports

As much as they play sports, Atlantans love to watch them. Sports fever grew in 1991 and 1992, when the Atlanta Braves won back-to-back National League titles. The Braves play home games at **Atlanta–Fulton County Stadium** (521 Capitol Ave., tel. 404/577–9100). The National Basketball Association's Atlanta Hawks play home games at the **Omni Coliseum** (100 Techwood Dr., tel. 404/827-DUNK). The National Football League's Atlanta Falcons play home games at the **Georgia Dome** (285 International Blvd., tel. 404/223–8000). One of the newest entrants to the International Hockey League is the Atlanta Knights. The team plays at the Omni (tel. 404/525–5800.)

Dining

Atlanta offers a range of eating options worthy of its image as a dynamic international city. From a million-dollar diner to a humble meat-and-three, one can find almost anything in the capital of the New South: prestigious kitchens run by world-class chefs, a multitude of ethnic restaurants—Thai in particular—and more fried-chicken outlets than anywhere else in the country.

As is probably inevitable in a city where enthusiasm and growth has outstripped experience, however, some of the so-called hottest or trendiest Atlanta restaurants can be something of a letdown. Experimentation with such cuisines as Pacific Rim and fusion cooking can produce overwrought combinations and bizarre flavors. Service, too, has a long way to go at many popular establishments. Visitors would do well to approach each meal here with cautious optimism. One nice surprise: Prices here are still much lower—even at most upscale restaurants—than in most major American cities.

The local taste for things sweet and fried holds true for restaurants serving traditional Southern food. Try to catch the flavor of the South at breakfast and lunch in modest establishments. Reserve your evenings for more ambitious culinary exploration.

The most highly recommended restaurants in each price category are indicated by a star ★.

Category	Cost*
$$$$	over $45
$$$	$35–$45
$$	$25–$35
$	under $15

**per person without tax (6%), service, or drinks*

Downtown
$$$$
★ **City Grill.** This posh but breezy restaurant has made the most of its grand location in the elegantly renovated historic Hurt building. The bustle of success greets you at the door, while bucolic murals and stunning high ceilings create a feeling of glamour. The primarily modern French menu has a few weaknesses, but you can't go wrong with the free-range chicken, the lamb, or any of the delicious vegetable specialties. Local heavyweights like to lunch here. *50 Hurt Plaza, tel. 404/524–2489. Valet parking. Reservations recommended, weeks ahead for weekend dining. Jacket required. AE, D, DC, MC, V. No lunch weekends.*

$$$ **Morton's of Chicago.** Signature porterhouse and prime dry-age steaks are served in a clubby, sophisticated setting of gleaming hardwood floors and comfortable banquettes. The dinner menu offers fish and chicken entrées for those with lighter appetites. *245 Peachtree Center Ave., tel. 404/577–4366. Reservations accepted. Jacket and tie requested. AE, DC, MC, V.*

Ocean Club. The stunning mosaic oyster bar and brilliant turquoise interior set an upbeat mood at this seafood restaurant in Peachtree Center. Good choices include fried shrimp with jalapeño tartar sauce, grilled grouper with black bean sauce, and a teriyaki tuna sandwich. Service is snappy. *Peachtree Center, 231 Peachtree St., tel. 404/688–9330. No reservations at lunch. Dress: casual. AE, MC, V.*

Savannah Fish Company. Have a drink in the revolving lounge at the top of the hotel, but come to the ground floor for a smashingly good and simple meal of fresh fish, grilled or sautéed without ado. Ignore overpriced appetizers and enjoy the house's saffron- and fennel-flavored fish stew. Pass up generic cakes for the simple Savannah Hot Puffs, fried dough sprinkled with sugar and cinnamon and served with three sauces. The pared-down decor speaks Asian simplicity. *Westin Peachtree Plaza, 210 Peachtree St. at International Blvd., tel. 404/589–7456. No reservations at dinner. Jacket advised at dinner. AE, D, DC, MC, V.*

$$ **Dailey's.** The downstairs dining room of this enormous converted warehouse is casual fun. Upstairs there's spectacular decor (merry-go-round horses and huge shop lamps) and more serious dining: au poivre swordfish, Georgia peach rack of lamb, crisp duck, generous salad, and fried rolls. Revved-up versions of pastry classics are pa-

raded before the adoring eyes of the crowd. *17 International Blvd., tel. 404/681–3303. No reservations; expect a wait. Dress: casual. AE, D, DC, MC, V. Entertainment nightly in downstairs lounge. No lunch Sunday.*

$ **Burton's Grill.** The Deacon who presided over this soul-food standby is gone, but his affable son stands in, presiding over the best fried chicken in town. Opposite the Inman Park MARTA station, this modest eatery serves up standard down-home collards, hoe cakes, mashed potatoes and gravy, and peach cobbler. No alcohol is served. *1029 Edgewood Ave. N.E., 404/658–9452. No reservations. No credit cards.*

★ **Delectables.** One of downtown's best-kept secrets; don't let the location (inside the Central Public Library) or the format (cafeteria) deter you. This is a sophisticated little operation serving ravishing salads, wholesome soups, yummy cookies, and freshly baked cakes. Sandwiches are fair. Enjoy your meal immersed in classical music and sunshine on the patio. *Public Library, corner of Margaret Mitchell Sq. and Carnegie Way (enter through Carnegie Way), tel. 404/681–2909. Dress: casual. AE, V, MC. Lunch only; closed weekends.*

Harold's Barbecue. Legislators, political groupies, and small fry from the capitol sit side by side, wolfing down delicious sliced pork sandwiches, huge platters of freshly sliced meat, and overflowing bowls of Brunswick stew. Don't miss the crackling bread. The knotty pine, tacky art, and management haven't changed in 25 years. It's a short distance from downtown, but worth the ride. *171 McDonough Blvd., tel. 404/627–9268. No reservations. Dress: casual. No credit cards. Closed Sun.*

Thelma's Kitchen. Honest-to-goodness soul food is served in a squat cinder block building located in the proposed Olympic Park district downtown. Ambience here means a cafeteria counter and cramped dining room, but that's not why folks come to this cheerful, family-run eatery. Go early at lunchtime to beat the crowds lining up for tasty fried chicken, okra cakes, black eyed peas, twice-cooked potatoes, and some of the best flavored greens around. Save room for the sweet potato pie. *190 Luckie St. N.W., tel. 404/688–5855. No reservations. Dress: casual. No credit cards. No dinner; closed weekends.*

The Varsity. Part of Atlanta's collective past, this sprawling diner near the Georgia Tech campus attracts people from all walks of life. It offers famous chili dogs, glorified hamburgers, and gigantic orders of fresh and delicious—but greasy—onion rings. Line up behind the locals and pay close attention to the lingo: "One naked dog, walking and a bag o' rags," will get you a plain hot dog and some french fries. Connoisseurs drink orange frosties. Folks in a hurry get curb service. *61 North Ave., tel. 404/881–1706. No reservations. Dress: casual. No credit cards. Open late.*

Midtown

$$$$ **Ciboulette.** French-bistro food and atmosphere from Jean Banchet and Tom Coohill have Atlantans lining up for hot smoked salmon with wild mushrooms and ginger, Amish capon "grand mere," cassoulet Toulousain, and wild mushroom sauces. The dining room is a bit French-fussy in decor, but the counter seats, with their kitchen view, provide a true bistro ambience. *1529 Piedmont Ave.N.E. tel. 404/874–7600. Reservations accepted Mon.–Thurs. Jacket advised. AE, DC, MC, V. No lunch; closed Sun.*

$$–$$$ **Chef's Grill.** This casual San Francisco–style bistro located inside the Woodruff Arts Center is a popular pre- and posttheater dining spot. The menu changes with the seasons, but grilled fish, gourmet

Dining
Burton's Grill, **22**
Chef's Grill, **2**
Ciboulette, **4**
City Grill, **20**
Dailey's, **15**
Delectables, **17**
Harold's Barbecue, **21**
Indigo Coastal Grill, **6**
Morton's of Chicago, **8**
Ocean Club, **13**
Partners Morningside Cafe, **7**
Savannah Fish Company, **14**
Thelma's Kitchen, **10**
The Varsity, **5**

Lodging
Ansley Inn, **3**
Atlanta Marriott Marquis, **9**
Barclay Hotel, **11**
Colony Square Hotel, **1**
Hyatt Regency, **18**
Omni Hotel at CNN Center, **16**
The Ritz-Carlton Atlanta, **19**
Westin Peachtree Plaza, **12**

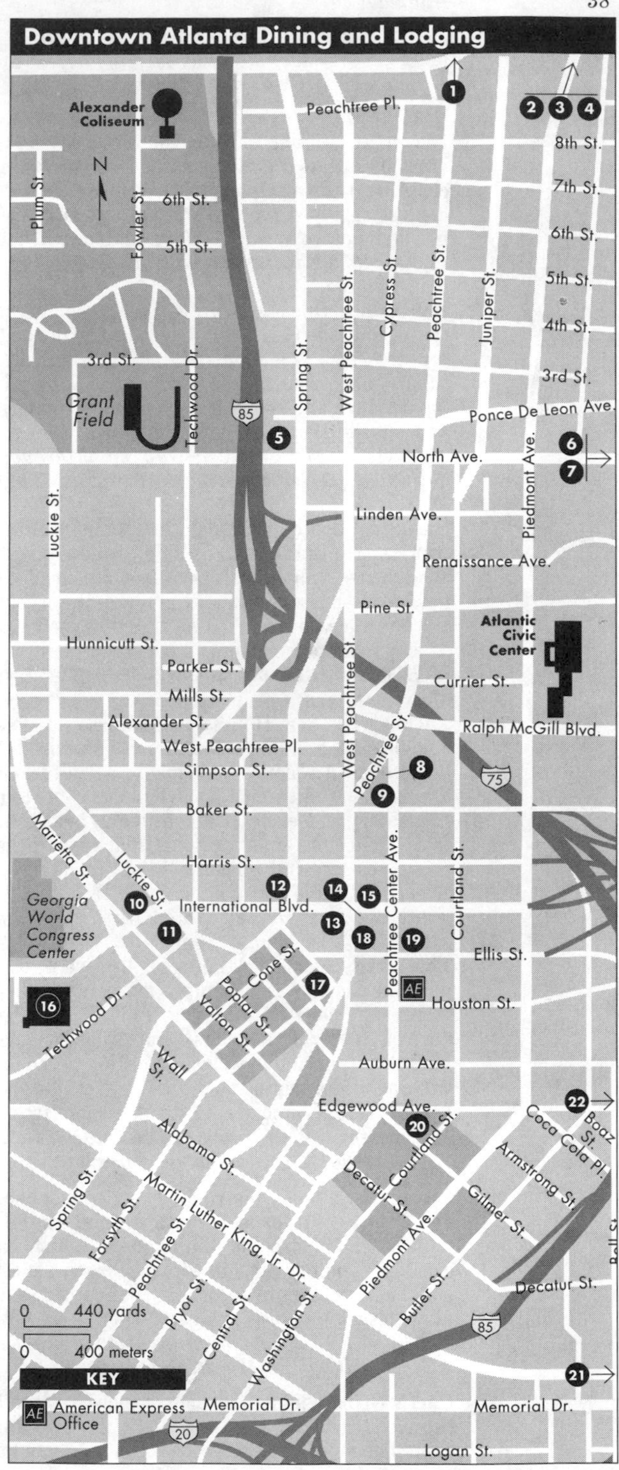

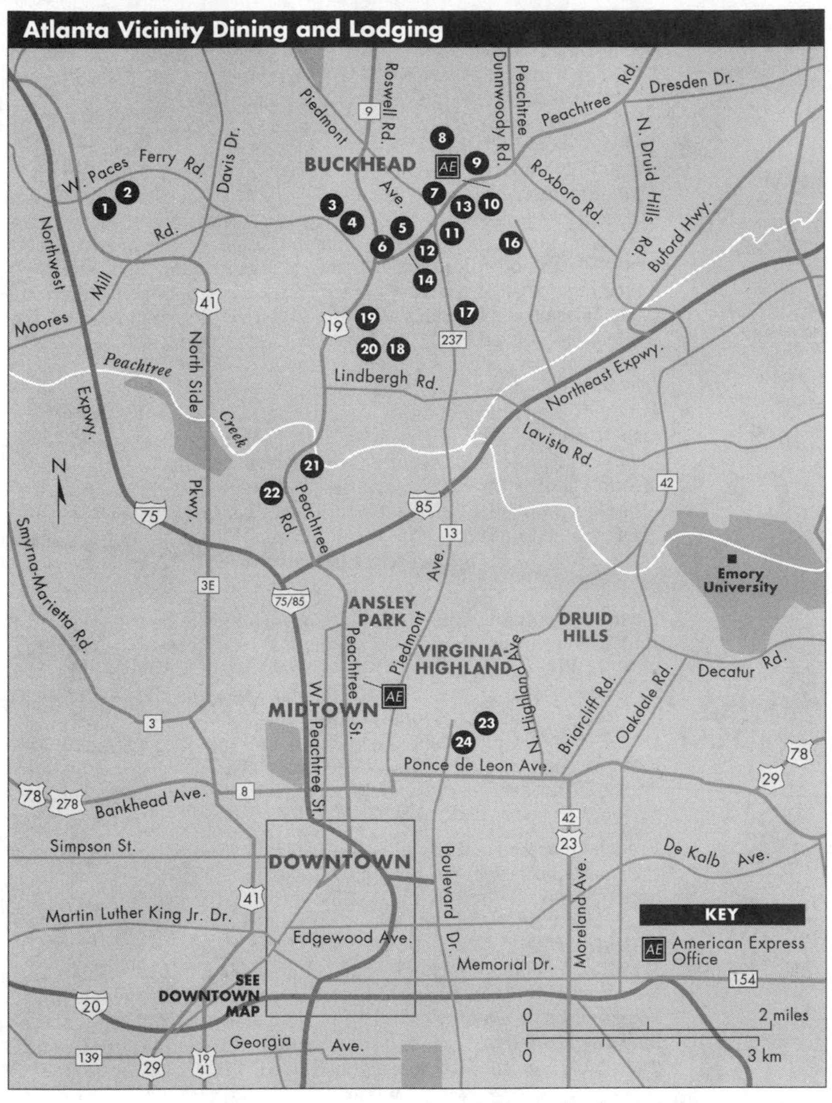

Dining

Abruzzi Ristorante, **15**
Annie's Thai Castle, **5**
Atlanta Fish Market, **19**
Azalea, **12**
Basil's Mediterranean Cafe, **20**
Bone's, **11**
Buckhead Diner, **17**
Chops, **4**
Dining Room, in the Ritz-Carlton Buckhead, **9**
French Quarter Food Shop, **25**
Kudzo Cafe, **14**
La Grotta, **6**
Luna Si, **21**
OK Café, **1**
103 West, **3**
Pano's and Paul's, **2**
Pricci, **18**
Rocky's Brick Oven Pizzeria, **22**
Surin of Thailand, **23**
Tortillas, **24**

Lodging

Embassy Suites, **13**
Hotel Nikko, **7**
JW Marriott, **16**
Ritz-Carlon, Buckhead, **9**
Swissotel, **10**
Windham Garden Hotel, **8**

pizzas, and creative appetizers are constant. Grilled eggplant, warm Georgia goat cheese, and crab cakes are among the specialties. The wine list is excellent. *1280 Peachtree St., tel. 404/881–0652. Reservations advised. Dress: casual. AE, MC, V. Closed Sun.–Mon. dinner and weekend lunch.*

★ **Indigo Coastal Grill.** Trendy coastal cuisine packs them in at this lively Virginia-Highland eatery run by Chef/Owner Alix Kenagy, a former fashion editor with an eye for catchy details. Cuisine is more fun than fabulous, with some dishes suffering from overwrought flavors and mediocre preparation. Popular here are conch fritters, heavy-cream biscuits, lobster corn chowder, and fish and fresh herbs in a twist of parchment. Don't miss the refreshing Key lime pie or the sautéed bananas with rum and lime. Sunday breakfast and brunch are served. *1397 N. Highland Ave., tel. 404/876–0676. No reservations; expect a wait. Dress: casual. AE, MC, V. No sit-down lunch, but take-out service available.*

★ **Partners Morningside Cafe.** This upbeat, noisy, and colorful spot also owned by Kenagy is next door to Indigo Coastal Grill (*see above*). Cuisine blends several influences, particularly Mediterranean and Pacific Rim. Ravioli stuffing and sauce changes daily; there's also Cajun mixed grill, Vietnamese chicken cakes, and nostalgic, old-fashioned desserts. An appealing small wine list is full of good values. *1399 N. Highland Ave., tel. 404/876–0104. No reservations; expect a wait. Dress: casual. AE, MC, V. No lunch.*

$$ **Surin of Thailand.** Considered by some to be the best Thai restaurant in town, this dining spot opened in 1991 in a renovated drugstore in Virginia-Highland. Big windows let in plenty of light, and the owners' own photographs of Thailand hang on the yellow walls. Try the French basil rolls stuffed with shrimp, cucumber, and pork—one of Chef Surin Techarukpong's best dishes—but save room for the delicately flavored, homemade coconut or mango ice cream for dessert. *810 Highland Ave., tel. 404/892–7789. No reservations. Dress: casual. AE, D, MC, V.*

$ **French Quarter Food Shop.** Sandwiched between two bars, this ultra-casual eatery has a pleasant sidewalk café. Sit down to some crawfish etouffée or a shrimp po'boy; takeout is also available. *923 Peachtree Rd. NE, tel. 404/875–2489. No reservations. Dress: informal. AE, D, MC, V. Closed Sun.*

Tortillas. The neighborhood is no great shakes, but this funky Tex-Mex joint rates raves from the business crowd it attracts at lunch. Weekends and evenings find it packed with 20-somethings. The burritos stuffed with pork or shrimp and extras like green salsa, guacamole, and potatoes are well-spiced. *774 Ponce de Leon Ave. N.E., tel. 404/892–3493. No reservations. Dress: casual. No credit cards.*

Buckhead
$$$$ **Bone's.** In this brash, New York–style steakhouse, sports celebs and fast-track businesspeople rub egos and compare lifestyles over excellent prime beef, chops, Maine lobster, and potatoes baked in a crust of salt. Most patrons wear jackets, but if your idea of fun is spending big bucks in a sport shirt, they won't turn you down. Private dining rooms are available, and the deluxe model even has a shoeshine booth. *3130 Piedmont Rd., tel. 404/237–2663. Reservations advised. Jacket and tie advised. AE, DC, MC, V. No lunch weekends.*

★ **Chops.** This clubby steakhouse is a favorite of the city's power brokers. The interior's sleek Mission-style setting features a redwood bar and a carved glass screen. You're served generous portions of grain-fed Midwestern beef cooked on an indoor grill, and a wide variety of seafood. *70 W. Paces Ferry Rd., tel. 404/262–2675. Reservations advised. Jacket and tie advised. AE, D, DC, MC, V. No lunch weekends.*

★ **Dining Room, in the Ritz-Carlton Buckhead.** This is the best restaurant in town and among the country's 10 greatest. Under Chef Guenter Seeger, haute cuisine is not flashy or ostentatious. Strictly limiting himself to the freshest regional products, Seeger doesn't like calling attention to the culinary process. The menu, handwritten every day, is likely to involve local sun-dried sweet potatoes (in ravioli), Vidalia onions (with lobster and lobster coral sauce), or persimmons (in a mousse with muscadine sorbet and Georgia golden raspberries). Don't ask for your food to be well-done. Surrender to this imperious genius and the exquisite, discreet service. *3434 Peachtree Rd., tel. 404/237–2700. Reservations required, several days ahead for weekend dining. Jacket and tie requested. AE, D, DC, MC, V. Dinner only. Closed Sun.*

★ **La Grotta.** Despite its odd location in the basement of an apartment building, this is one of the best-managed dining rooms in town. Magnetic, dynamic Sergio Favalli is a superb host, and waiters are on their toes. The kitchen experiments cautiously with new concepts and trendy ingredients, but old Northern Italian favorites remain at the core of the menu. Don't miss the cold grilled wild mushrooms, the baby quails over polenta, or the tiramisu. Veal and fresh pasta are outstanding. There's an excellent wine list. *2637 Peachtree Rd., tel. 404/231–1368. Reservations required well in advance. Jacket and tie advised. AE, D, DC, MC, V. Dinner only. Closed Sun.*

★ **103 West.** An ornate facade and porte cochere add to the proud image of Atlanta's poshest, most palatial restaurant. Antique tapestries, watered silks, and glorious details fill the dining rooms. The kitchen matches this lavish classicism. Here's the place to indulge in crab cakes with beurre blanc, sweet basil and red pepper rouille; or fresh veal sweetbreads with madeira sauce and fresh grapes on a bed of wilted spinach. Glamour dishes include smoked mountain trout with lump crabmeat, venison with wild mushrooms and mustard fruit, and an amazing "Grand Dessert" sampler. *103 W. Paces Ferry Rd., tel. 404/233–5993. Reservations required. Jacket required. AE, D, DC, MC, V. Dinner only. Closed Sun.*

$$$ **Abruzzi Ristorante.** "Understated elegance" is the buzz phrase for
★ this modern yet traditional restaurant frequented by the city's old guard. If you're not taken with one of the myriad menu-offerings, have managing partner Nico Petrucci suggest a specialty. Excellent dishes include salmon carpaccio, green-and-white gnocchi in pesto, sautéed sweetbreads, veal chop, baked fish with rosemary, and ricotta cheesecake. *2355 Peachtree Rd., tel. 404/261–8186. Reservations advised. Jacket advised at dinner. AE, DC, MC, V. Closed Sat. lunch and Sun.*

Pano's and Paul's. An Atlanta classic that's known for stylish pampering. Pano Karatassos and Paul Albrecht hit gold with their single-minded devotion to their customers' needs, from whims to dietary restriction. Many new ideas percolate through the kitchen; state-of-the-art dishes are introduced as specials and eventually included in the menu. Look for lemon-roasted, farm-raised chicken with a crisp, celery-potato cake, sautéed gulf red snapper fillet, and jumbo cold lobster tail fried in a light batter and served with Chinese honey mustard. *1232 W. Paces Ferry Rd., tel. 404/261–3662. Reservations required (days, sometimes weeks ahead for a prime slot). Jacket required. AE, D, DC, MC, V. No lunch. Closed Sun.*

$$ **Luna Si.** The emphasis is on fun at this New York loft–style restaurant where Latin music blares, and customers are encouraged to

write on the walls. The menu, which changes weekly, is dominated by seafood—seared Atlantic salmon with a ginger crust is a favorite. The chef eschews cream and butter in the preparations. *1931 Peachtree Rd. NE, tel. 404/355-5993. Reservations accepted for large parties. Dress: casual. AE, D, MC, V. Closed Mon., and Sun. lunch.*

$$–$$$ **Annie's Thai Castle.** A family-run delight transplanted from a suburban location into the heart of Buckhead, this small restaurant is lovingly decorated with objets d'art from Annie's native Thailand. The soup is perfectly flavored with spices and lemon grass, and the seafood salad dazzles. Nam sod, chicken satay, and spicy catfish are excellent choices. *3195 Roswell Rd. N.E., tel. 404/264-9546. Reservations advised on weekends. Dress: casual. AE, MC, V.*

Atlanta Fish Market. An overwhelming selection of fresh seafood is served in this cavernous space, reminiscent of an old train station. Swordfish with roasted cashew and cracked-pepper crust, served with white-corn cheese grits, exemplifies the creatively prepared cuisine on the ever-changing menu. The noise level is high. *265 Pharr Rd., tel. 404/262-3165. Reservations advised. AE, D, DC, MC, V. Closed Sun. lunch.*

★ **Buckhead Diner.** This million-dollar fantasy by the owners of Pano's and Paul's is still one of the hottest restaurants in town, a shimmering faux-diner wrapped in luscious hues of neon. Inlaid wood, Italian leather, hand-cut marble and mellow lights establish a languorous ambience reminiscent of the Orient Express. The cuisine is anything but diner: salt-and-pepper squid, neo-Asian shrimp wonton, buffalo-milk mozzarella melted in fresh tomato coulis, veal-and-wild-mushroom meatloaf, and homemade banana-walnut ice cream are a sampling. Interesting wines are available by the glass. *3073 Piedmont Rd., tel. 404/262-3336. No reservations; expect a long wait. Dress: casual chic. AE, D, DC, MC, V.*

Kudzu Cafe. Come here for witty, updated southern food that includes everything from fresh vegetables to homemade peanut butter. Have someone here tell you the history of kudzu. *3215 Peachtree Rd., tel. 404/262-0661. No reservations. AE, MC, V.*

Pricci. The stamp of acclaimed designer Patrick Kuleto is apparent in the chic mirrored and windowed decor of this high style hot spot. Deceptively simple southern Italian fare is accompanied by Pricci's own freshly baked breads. The homemade spinach-filled tortellini is delicious. *500 Pharr Rd., tel. 404/237-2941. Reservations advised. Dress: casual chic. AE, D, DC, MC, V. Closed weekend lunch.*

$$ **Basil's Mediterranean Cafe.** Tucked Down a side street, in renovated bungalow, this restaurant is handsomely decorated with original art. In good weather you can dine on the front deck. The food—mostly seafood—is well-seasoned, and each plate is an artistic masterpiece. The Greek-style shrimp with artichoke hearts, sundried tomatoes, olives, and feta cheese is superb. *2985 Grandview, tel. 404/233-9755. Reservations accepted. Dress: casual. AE, D, DC, MC, V. Closed Sun.*

$ ★ **Azalea.** East meets West on the menu at this see-and-be-seen restaurant, with its black-on-white contemporary decor. Try the potato-crusted salmon with a wild mushroom cream sauce. *3167 Peachtree Rd., tel. 404/237-9939. No reservations. Dress: casual chic. AE, D, DC, MC, V. No lunch.*

OK Café. Go "back to the future" in this witty take-off on small-town eateries. The cheeky waitresses, whimsical art, and roomy, comfortable booths make this a favorite hangout for Atlanta's artsy crowd—and lots of ordinary folk besides. The fried chicken with ginger salad, vegetables, and almonds is popular, as is the appetizer of sweet potato chips with blue cheese dip. Mammoth breakfasts, old-fashioned blue-plate specials, and chocolate shakes satisfy that high-cholesterol craving in all of us. It's open all night, too. *1284 W. Paces Ferry Rd., tel. 404/233–2888. No reservations. Dress: casual. AE, MC, V. Open 24 hours.*

Rocky's Brick Oven Pizzeria. It's a find in a city where good pizza is hard to come by. The bustling kitchen turns out thick, square Sicilian pizzas and thin-crusted Neapolitan pies with the city's most appealing combination of toppings. Clientele includes well-heeled parents with tots in tow, art school students, and rocker Mick Jagger, who frequented it while filming a movie. *1770 Peachtree St., tel. 404/876–1111. No reservations. Dress: casual. AE, MC, V.*

Lodging

One of America's three most popular convention destinations, Atlanta offers a broad range of lodgings. More than 12,000 rooms are in the compact downtown area, close to the Georgia World Congress Center, Atlanta Civic Center, Atlanta Merchandise Mart and Apparel Mart, and Omni Coliseum. Other clusters are in the affluent Buckhead corporate and retail area, and around Hartsfield International Airport.

Category	Cost*
$$$$	over $135
$$$	$90–$135
$$	$60–$90
$	under $60

**double room; add 11% for taxes*

Downtown and Midtown *$$$$*

Atlanta Marriott Marquis. Immense and coolly contemporary, the Marquis seems to go on forever as you stand under the lobby's huge fabric sculpture that appears to float from the sky-lit roof 50 stories above. Each guest room—of average-size and with standard-issue hotel decor— opens onto this atrium. *265 Peachtree Center Ave., 30303, tel. 404/521–0000 or 800/228–9290. 1,671 rooms, 71 suites. Facilities: 5 restaurants, 4 bars and lounges, health club, indoor/outdoor pool. AE, D, DC, MC, V.*

Colony Square Hotel. Theatricality and opulence are epitomized by the dimly lit lobby with overhanging balconies, piano music, and fresh flowers. Rooms are modern and done in muted tones—those on higher floors have nice city views. The hotel is one block from MARTA's Art Center station, across from the Woodruff Arts Center and the High Museum of Art, and it anchors the Colony Square office/residential/retail complex. *Peachtree and 14th Sts., 30361, tel. 404/892–6000 or 800/422–7895. 428 rooms, 33 suites. Facilities: lobby lounge, restaurant, access (for a fee) to the Colony Club health club, racquetball courts, outdoor pool. AE, D, DC, MC, V.*

Omni Hotel at CNN Center. The hotel is adjacent to the CNN Center, home of Ted Turner's Cable News Network. The lobby combines Old World and modern accents, with marble floors, Oriental rugs, exotic floral and plant arrangements, and contemporary furnishings. Rooms are large and decorated in shades of mauve. *100 CNN Center, near MARTA's Omni station stop, 30305, tel. 404/659–0000 or 800/843–6664. 465 rooms. Facilities: 2 restaurants, lounge, access to the Downtown Athletic Club. AE, D, DC, MC, V.*

★ **The Ritz-Carlton, Atlanta.** The mood here is set by traditional afternoon tea served in the intimate, sunken lobby beneath an 18th-century chandelier. Notice the 17th-century Flemish tapesty when you enter from Peachtree St. Spacious guest rooms are luxuriously decorated with marble writing tables, plump sofas, four-poster beds, and white marble bathrooms. The Cafe's Sunday brunch spread is spectacular. In the evenings the Jerry Lambert Jazz Trio performs at The Bar upstairs. Service is discreet but snappy. *181 Peachtree St., 30303, tel. 404/659–0400 or 800/241–3333. 447 rooms. Facilities: 2 restaurants, bar with live jazz trio, fitness center, ballroom. AE, D, DC, MC, V.*

Westin Peachtree Plaza. Every photograph of Atlanta's skyline taken in the last 10 years features this cylindrical glass tower, one of the tallest hotels in North America. The five-story atrium lobby was designed by John Portman. The hotel was recently renovated top to bottom to the tune of $35 million. For the best views, ask for the 45th floor or higher. *210 Peachtree St. at International Blvd., 30303, tel. 404/659–1400 or 800/228–3000. 1,074 rooms. Facilities: 3 restaurants, 3 bars, a rooftop indoor/outdoor pool, health club, sauna, shopping gallery, kosher kitchen. AE, D, DC, MC, V.*

$$$ **Ansley Inn.** Above a sloping lawn a block from Piedmont Park and in the heart of Ansley Park, one of Atlanta's most beautiful neighborhoods, stands this handsome three-story brick Tudor mansion. A 1987 restoration produced oversize guest rooms with private baths and common areas furnished with Chinese porcelains, antiques, and original art. The mediocre Continental breakfast is a disappointment. *253 15th St., 30309, tel. 404/872–9000. 11 rooms, 1 suite. Facilities: free use of athletic club. AE, D, DC, MC, V.*

Hyatt Regency Atlanta. The Hyatt's 23-story lobby (built in 1965) launched the chain's "atrium look." The rooms were renovated in honor of the hotel's 20th anniversary. Most guests are conventioneers. *265 Peachtree St. (connected to MARTA's Peachtree Center Station), 30303, tel. 404/577–1234. 1,278 rooms, 58 suites. Facilities: 4 restaurants, outdoor pool, health club, sauna, 2 ballrooms. AE, D, DC, MC, V.*

$ **Barclay Hotel.** This quiet, older downtown hotel was renovated in 1994. The teal-carpeted lobby is dominated by two modern chandeliers; the walls are hung with works by black artists. Done in mauve with floral accents, each room has a view of downtown; some rooms have balconies. The Celebrity Cafe is known for its waffles and fried chicken. *Directly behind the Peachtree Center at 89 Luckie St. NW, 30303, tel. 404/524–7991. 73 rooms. Facilities: pool and sun deck, 2 restaurants. AE, DC, MC, V.*

Buckhead

$$$$ **Hotel Nikko.** A dual-height lobby facing a courtyard with Japanese garden and cascading 35-foot waterfall is the opening statement of this towering hotel, opened in 1990. The understated decor features mainly hues of black, gray, and purple. Rooms are spacious and comfortable, with a style that's more American than Japanese. Japanese and Mediterranean cuisine are featured in the hotel's two restaurants. *3300 Peachtree Rd., 30305, tel. 404/365–8100 or 800/645–5687, fax 404/233–5686. 439 rooms, 32 suites. Facilities: 2 restaurants, health club, pool, library bar, lounge, ballroom, 14 meeting rooms. AE, D, DC, MC, V.*

JW Marriott. This elegant 25-story hotel, opened in Lenox Square in 1988, is traditionally decorated with reproduction furniture, hunter green and floral hues, and accents of brass and crystal. Irregularly shaped rooms have spacious baths with separate shower stall and tub. *3300 Lenox Rd., 30326, tel. 404/262–3344 or 800/228–9290. 371* *rooms, 30 suites. Facilities: restaurant, 2 lounges, indoor pool, health club, ballroom, meeting rooms. AE, D, DC, MC, V.*

★ **Ritz-Carlton, Buckhead.** Decorated with the Ritz's signature 18th- and 19th-century antiques, this elegant gem bids a discreet welcome to locals and visitors alike. Shoppers from nearby Lenox Mall and Phipps Plaza often revive here over afternoon tea or cocktails in the richly paneled Lobby Lounge; the Café, Café Bar, and the Bar offer other spots to relax within luxurious surroundings. The Dining Room (*see* Dining, *above*) is the city's finest restaurant. The spacious rooms are furnished with traditional reproductions and have luxurious white-marble baths. From the hotel's Club Floors you get a view of the financial district and an understanding of why Atlanta is known as a city of trees. *3434 Peachtree Rd., 30326, tel. 404/237–2700 or 800/241–3333. 524 rooms, 29 suites. Facilities: The Café, with live music and dance floor; The Dining Room; The Bar, with evening entertainment; indoor pool and deck; Jacuzzi, health center. AE, D, DC, MC, V.*

Swissotel. Sleek and efficient, this stunner boasts a chic contemporary glass-and-white-enamel exterior and sophisticated Biedermeier-style interiors. Comfortable sofas and chairs beckon in common areas. Handy to Lenox Square, a prime location for shopping and dining, the hotel is a favorite with business travelers. *3391 Peachtree Rd., 30326, tel. 404/365–0065 or 800/253–1397. 362 rooms, 15 suites. Facilities: indoor pool, health club, 2 lounges, 2 restaurants, ballroom, meeting rooms. AE, D, DC, MC, V.*

$$ **Embassy Suites.** This contemporary high-rise in Buckhead, on a major thoroughfare, is just blocks from Phipps Plaza and Lenox Square. A variety of suites ranging from deluxe presidential (with wet bars) to more basic sleeping- and sitting-room combinations are available, as are a limited number of double-bed rooms. *3285 Peachtree Rd., 30326, tel. 404/261–7733 or 800/362–2779. 313 suites, 15 rooms. Facilities: restaurant, lounge, indoor and outdoor pools, fitness room. AE, D, DC, MC, V.*

Wyndham Garden Hotel. A modest high-rise in the shadow of Hotel Nikko, this hotel was completely renovated in 1994. The neat rooms are spacious and decorated with botanical prints, and rates are reasonable given the excellent location. Service is not up to par with the luxury establishments in the area. *3340 Peachtree Rd., 30326, tel. 404/231–1234 or 800/822–4200. 221 rooms. Facilities: restaurant, outdoor pool, access to health club. AE, D, DC, MC, V.*

The Arts

For the most complete schedule of cultural events, check the "Leisure" tabloid section of Saturday's *Atlanta Journal & Atlanta Constitution.* Also check *Creative Loafing*, a lively community weekly distributed at Atlanta restaurants, bars, and stores. You can also call the 24-hour **Arts Hotline** (tel. 404/853-3ART).

TicketMaster (tel. 404/249–6400) and **Tic-X-Press, Inc.** (tel. 404/231–5888) handle tickets for the Fox Theatre, Atlanta Civic Center, and other large houses. However, most companies sell tickets through their own box offices.

Theater Consistently one of the region's best, the **Alliance Theatre** performs everything from Shakespeare to the latest Broadway and off-Broadway shows in the Woodruff Arts Center (*see* Exploring, *above*). The **Horizon Theatre Co.** (1083 Austin Ave., tel. 404/584–7450) in Little Five Points produces new works by contemporary playwrights.

Theatrical Outfit (1012 Peachtree at 10th St., tel. 404/872–0665) produces original and nationally known contemporary works.

Actor's Express (887 W. Marietta St., tel. 404/607–7469) formerly based in Little Five Points, opened its new theater last year at the King Plow Arts Center, a stylish artists' complex. An eclectic selection of productions takes place in the 150-seat theater, hailed by local critics as a showplace of industrial chic.

Touring Broadway musicals, pop music, and dance concerts are presented in **The Atlanta Civic Center** (395 Piedmont Ave., tel. 404/523–6275), **Center Stage** (1374 W. Peachtree St., tel. 404/873–2500), and at the **Fox Theatre** (660 Peachtree St., tel.404/881–2100; *see* Exploring, *above*).

Concerts The world-class **Atlanta Symphony Orchestra (ASO)** (tel. 404/892–2414), under the musical direction of Yoel Levi, performs its fall–spring subscription series in the 1,800-seat Symphony Hall at Woodruff Arts Center. (1280 Peachtree St.). Despite its international reputation, the ASO fails to sell out most local performances and suffers from financial problems and an acoustically flawed performance space. Executive director Allison Vulgamore, now in her second season with ASO, hopes to turn things around. During the summer, the orchestra accompanies big-name artists in Chastain Park. The acoustically magnificent little **Spivey Hall** (tel. 404/898–1189), located at Clayton State College 15 miles south of Atlanta, is widely considered to be one of the finest concert venues in the country. Artists of international renowned perform everything from choral works to chamber music to jazz.

Modeled after the Vienna Boys' Choir, the **Atlanta Boys' Choir** (tel. 404/378–0064) performs frequently at Atlanta locations and makes national and international tours. The long-established **Atlanta Chamber Players** (tel. 404/651–1228) perform classical works at various Atlanta locations.

Opera **The Atlanta Opera Association** (tel. 404/355–3311), made up of local singers and musicians, is augmented by internationally known artists.

Dance **The Atlanta Ballet Company** (tel. 404/873–5811), founded in 1929, has received international recognition for its high-quality productions of classical and contemporary works. Performances are at the Fox Theatre and Atlanta Civic Center. Artistic director Robert Barnett recently retired a year early after 32 years with the company, citing unacceptable budget cuts and lack of support from the ballet's board. At press time, no director had been named to succeed him, and the company's future direction remains wide open.

Nightlife

The pursuit of entertainment—from Midtown to Buckhead—is known as the "Peachtree Shuffle." Atlanta's vibrant nightlife can mean anything from coffee bars to sports bars, from country line dancing to high-energy dance clubs. Atlanta has long been known for having more bars than churches, and in the South, that's saying something.

Most bars and clubs are open seven nights, until 2–4 AM. Those with live entertainment usually have a cover charge. Consult *Creative Loafing* and the "Leisure" section of Saturday's newspaper.

Country Hot spots for boot-scoot and boogie include the **Buckboard Country Music Showcase** (2080 Cobb Parkway in Windy Hill Plaza, tel. 404/

955–7340) and the **Crystal Chandelier** (1750 North Roberts Rd., Kennesaw, tel. 404/436–5006), both north of the city.

Jazz and Blues New Orleans–style blues sends jam-packed crowds into a frenzy at **Blind Willie's** (828 N. Highland Ave., tel. 404/873–2583), a storefront club in Virginia-Highland.

Cafe 290 (290 Hilderbrand Ave. N.E. tel. 404/256–3942) showcases talented local jazz bands in a casual neighborhood restaurant/bar setting.

Dante's Down the Hatch's venues (3380 Peachtree Rd., tel. 404/266–1600 and Underground Atlanta, Lower Pryor St., tel. 404/577–1800) are two of the city's most popular nightspots. In Buckhead, The Paul Mitchell Trio conjures silky-smooth jazz sounds in the "hold" of a make-believe sailing ship. Downtown, jazz entertainers perform nightly. Swiss fondue and a large wine selection are part of the Dante's experience.

Just Jazz (2101 Tula St., tel. 404/355–5423; closed Mon.–Tues.), in an old warehouse off Bennett Street, features live performances by headline musicians.

Rock **The Cotton Club** (1021 Peachtree St., tel. 404/874–9524) is a loud, usually packed, Midtown club that features local and national performers in a variety of musical styles.

The Masquerade (695 North Ave., tel. 404/577–8178), a tri-level grunge hangout, features just about everything in popular music, from disco to techno to industrial. Crowds are an odd mix that reflects the club's three separate spaces, dubbed Heaven, Hell, and Purgatory.

The Point (420 Moreland Ave., tel. 404/577–6468) in Little Five Points—Atlanta's sanitized version of the East Village—showcases up-and-coming rock and progressive music groups in a small club setting.

Rupert's (3330 Piedmont Rd., tel. 404/366–9834) attracts the Buckhead after-work crowd with its 10-piece orchestra playing big band and contemporary dance music. The club's multitiered balcony overlooks the large dance floor.

More than one generation dances to the beat at **Axys** (1150-B Peachtree St., tel. 404/607–0922), an upscale, high-tech dance club in Midtown.

Bars **Limerick Junction** (822 N. Highland Ave., tel. 404/874–7147) is a lively Irish pub.

The antithesis of hip-and-trendy, 33-year-old **Manuel's Tavern** (602 N. Highland Ave. N.E., tel. 404/525–3447)—ancient by Atlanta standards—is a neighborhood saloon in the truest sense. Families, politicians, writers, students, professionals, and blue-collar workers enjoy drinks, bar food (chili dogs, french fries, strip steaks), and conversation.

Prince of Wales (1144 Piedmont Ave, tel. 404/876–0227) is a cozy, authentic English pub with live music, from alternative rock to jazz.

For great burgers, try **The Vortex** (1041 W. Peachtree St., tel. 404/875–1667). The atmosphere is friendly and the beer list is long.

Savannah

By Honey Naylor

Updated by Echo and Kevin Garrett

The very sound of the word Savannah conjures up misty images of mint juleps, live oaks dripping with Spanish moss, handsome mansions, and a somewhat decadent city moving at a lazy Southern pace. Why, you can hardly say "Savannah" without drawling.

Well, brace yourself. The mint juleps are there all right, along with the moss and the mansions and the easygoing pace, but this Southern belle rings with surprises.

Take, for example, St. Patrick's Day: Why on earth does Savannah, of all places, have a St. Patrick's Day celebration second only to New York's? The greening of Savannah began more than 164 years ago and nobody seems to know why, although everybody in town talks a blue (green) streak about St. Patrick's Day. Everything turns green on March 17, including the faces of startled visitors when green scrambled eggs and green grits are put before them. One year, some well-oiled revelers even tried to dye the Savannah River green.

Savannah's beginning was February 12, 1733, when English General James Edward Oglethorpe and 120 colonists arrived at Yamacraw Bluff on the Savannah River to found the 13th and last colony in the New World. As the port city grew, Englishmen, Scottish Highlanders, French Huguenots, Germans, Austrian Salzburgers, Sephardic Jews from Spain and Portugal, Moravians, Italians, Swiss, Welsh, and the Irish all arrived to create what could be called a rich gumbo.

In 1793, Eli Whitney of Connecticut, who was tutoring on a plantation near Savannah, invented a mechanized means of "ginning" seeds from cotton bolls. Cotton soon became king, and Savannah, already a busy seaport, flourished under its reign. Waterfront warehouses were filled with "white gold," and brokers trading in the Savannah Cotton Exchange set world prices. The white gold brought in solid gold, and fine mansions were built in the prospering city.

In 1864, Savannahians surrendered their city to Union General Sherman rather than see it torched. Following Reconstruction and the collapse of the cotton market, the city itself virtually collapsed, and languished for more than 50 years. Elegant mansions were either razed or allowed to decay, and cobwebs replaced cotton in the dilapidated riverfront warehouses.

But in 1955, Savannah's spirits rose again. News that the exquisite Isaiah Davenport home (324 E. State St.) was to be destroyed prompted seven outraged ladies to raise enough money to buy the house. They saved it the day before the wrecking ball was to swing.

Thus was born the Historic Savannah Foundation, the organization responsible for the restoration of downtown Savannah, where more than 1,000 restored buildings form the 2.5-square-mile Historic District, the nation's largest. Many of these buildings are open to the public during the annual tour of homes, and today Savannah is recognized as one of the top 10 cities in the U.S. for walking tours.

John Berendt's wildly popular *Midnight in the Garden of Good and Evil*, published in 1994, has dispatched many new visitors to Savannah. A nonfiction account of a notorious murder that took place in the city during the 1980s, the book brings to life such Savannah sites as Monterey Square, Mercer House, and Bonaventure Cemetery.

Arriving and Departing

By Plane Savannah International Airport (tel. 912/964–0514), 8 miles west of downtown, is served by **American, Delta, United,** and **USAir.** Despite the name, international flights are nonexistent.

Between the Airport and Center City **Vans** operated by **McCalls Limousine Service** (tel. 912/966–5364 or 800/673–9365) leave the airport daily 6 AM–10 PM, after the arrival of each flight, bound for downtown locations. The trip takes 15 minutes, and the one-way fare is $12.

Taxi fare from the airport to downtown is $15 for one person, $3 for each additional person.

By car, drive south on Dean Forest Drive to I–16, then east on I–16 into downtown Savannah.

By Train **Amtrak** (tel. 800/872–7245) has regular service along the Eastern Seaboard, with daily stops in Savannah. The Amtrak station (2611 Seaboard Coastline Dr., tel. 912/234–2611) is 4 miles southwest of downtown. Cab fare into the city is $5–$10.

By Bus The **Greyhound/Trailways** station (tel. 912/233–7723) is downtown at 610 W. Oglethorpe Avenue.

By Car I–95 slices north–south along the Eastern Seaboard, intersecting 10 miles west of town with east–west I–16, which dead-ends in downtown Savannah. U.S. 17, the Coastal Highway, also runs north–south through town. U.S. 80, which connects the Atlantic to the Pacific, is another east–west route through Savannah.

Getting Around

Despite its size, the downtown Historic District should be explored on foot. Its grid shape makes getting around a breeze, and you'll find any number of places to stop and rest.

By Bus Buses require 75¢ in exact change, and 5¢ extra for a transfer. **Chatham Area Transit (CAT)** (tel. 912/233–5768) operates buses in Savannah and Chatham County Monday–Saturday from 6:15 AM to 11:30 PM, Sunday 7 AM to 7 PM.

By Taxi Taxis start at 60¢ and cost $1.20 for each mile. **Adam Cab Co.**(tel. 912/927–7466) is a reliable, 24-hour taxi service.

Important Addresses and Numbers

Tourist Information For trip planning information, write to the **Savannah Area Convention & Visitors Bureau** (222 W. Oglethorpe Ave., Savannah 31499, tel. 912/944–0456 or 800/444–2427). The **Savannah Visitors Center** (301 Martin Luther King Jr. Blvd., tel. 912/944–0455) has free maps and brochures, lots of friendly advice, and an audiovisual overview of the city. The center is also the starting point for a number of guided tours. *Open Mon.–Fri. 8:30–5, weekends and holidays 9–5.*

Emergencies Dial 911 for **police** and **ambulance** in an emergency.

Hospitals Area hospitals with 24-hour emergency rooms are **Candler General Hospital** (5353 Reynolds St., tel. 912/354–9211) and **Memorial Medical Center** (4700 Waters Ave., tel. 912/350–8000).

24-hour Pharmacy **Revco Discount Drug Center** (Medical Arts Shopping Center, 4800 Waters Ave., tel. 912/355–7111).

Guided Tours

Orientation

Gray Line Tours (tel. 912/234–8687) is the official tour organization for the Historic Savannah Foundation. Knowledgeable and enthusiastic guides whisk you about in 20-passenger, climate-controlled vans. Tours of the Historic District and of the Victorian District take about two hours each. **Colonial Historic Tours** (tel. 912/233–0083) will take you on a two-hour tool around town on minibuses or on an "Old Time Trolley."

Special-interest

In April, the **Garden Club of Savannah** (tel. 912/238–0248) takes you into private gardens tucked behind old-brick walls and wrought-iron gates. For groups of five or more, the **Black Heritage Trail Tour** (tel. 912/234–8000), tracing the city's 250-year black history, provides a knowledgeable guide who will tell you about the Gullah culture of the Georgia and Carolina sea islands. Tours commence at the Black Heritage Museum.

Carriage Tours of Savannah (10 Warner St., tel. 912/236–6756 or 800/442–5933) show you the Historic District by day or by night at a 19th-century clip-clop pace, with coachmen spinning tales and telling ghost stories along the way. A romantic evening champagne tour in a private carriage will set you back $50–$60, plus $16 per bottle of bubbly. Regular tours are a more modest $9.50 adults, $4.50 children 11 and under.

Lowcountry

The **Associated Guides of the Low Country** (tel. 912/234–4088 or 800/627–5030; closed Mon.), and **Gray Line** (tel. 912/234–8687) make four-hour excursions to the fishing village of Thunderbolt; the Isle of Hope, with stately mansions lining Bluff Drive; the much-photographed Bonaventure Cemetery on the banks of the Wilmington River; and Wormsloe Plantation, with its mile-long avenue of arching oaks.

Walking Tours

Historic Walking Tours of Savannah (702 E. 50th St., tel. 912/355–1740 or 800/791-9393) offers two-hour walks of the historic district, as well as architectural tours. Cost: $12 a person.

The **Square Roots** (tel. 912/232–6866 or 800/868–6867) offers strolls through the Historic District and along Tybee Beach. The in-town tour focuses on the city's architecture and gardens. Tours usually last two hours and cost from $9.50 to $17.

Exploring Savannah

Numbers in the margin correspond to points of interest on the Savannah Historic District map.

Georgia's founder, General James Oglethorpe, designed the original town of Savannah and laid it out in a perfect grid. The Historic District is neatly hemmed in by the Savannah River, Gaston Street, and East and West Broad streets. Streets are arrow-straight, public squares of varying sizes are tucked into the grid at precise intervals, and each block is sliced in half by an alley. Bull Street, anchored on the north by City Hall and the south by Forsyth Park, charges down the center of the grid and lunges around the five public squares that stand in its way. (Maneuvering a car around Savannah's squares is a minor art form.)

The Historic District

Make your first stop the **Savannah Visitors Center** (*see* Important Addresses and Numbers, *above*), to pick up the maps and brochures
1 you'll need for exploring, and to look at the structure that houses the Center. The big redbrick building with its high ceilings and sweep-

Andrew Low House, **19**
Cathedral of St. John the Baptist, **17**
Chippewa Square, **15**
Colonial Park Cemetery, **16**
Emmet Park, **9**
Factors Walk, **5**
Forsyth Park, **25**
Great Savannah Exposition, **2**
Green-Meldrim House, **21**
Isaiah Davenport House, **10**
Johnson Square, **4**
Juliette Gordon Low Birthplace, **14**
King-Tisdell Cottage, **26**
Lafayette Sq., **18**
Madison Sq., **20**
Massie Heritage Interpretation Center, **24**
Owens-Thomas House & Museum, **11**
River Street, **6**
River Street Train Museum, **7**
Savannah Visitors Center, **1**
Scarbrough House, **3**
Ships of the Sea Museum, **8**
Telfair Mansion and Art Museum, **13**
Temple Mickve Israel, **22**
Wesley Monumental Church, **23**
Wright Sq., **12**

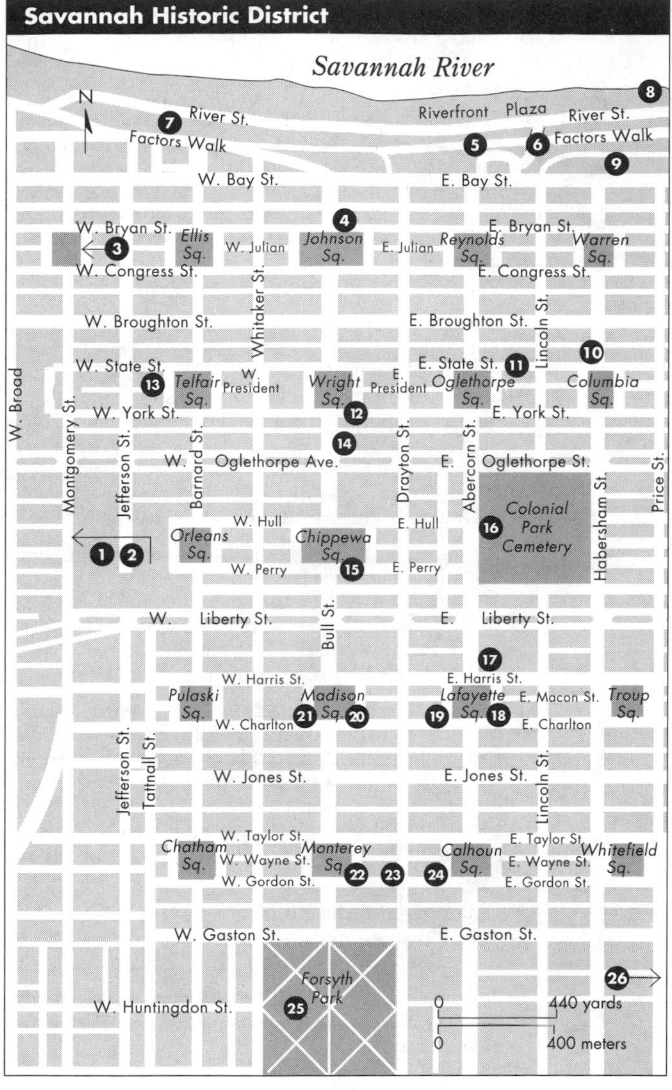

ing arches was the old Central of Georgia railway station, completed in 1860.

The Visitors Center lies just north of the **site of the Siege of Savannah.** In 1779, the Colonial forces, led by Polish Count Casimir Pulaski, laid siege to Savannah, in an attempt to retake the city from the Redcoats. They were beaten back, and Pulaski was killed while leading a cavalry charge against the British. On the battle site, adjacent
2 to the Visitors Center, the **Great Savannah Exposition,** in a restored shed of the railway station, offers an excellent introduction to the city. Two theaters present special-effects depictions of Oglethorpe's landing and of the siege. Exhibits range from old locomotives to a tribute to Savannah-born songwriter Johnny Mercer. There are two restored dining cars that aren't going anywhere, but you can climb

aboard for a bite to eat. *303 W. Broad St., tel. 912/238–1779. Admission: $3 adults, $2.50 senior citizens, $1.75 children 6–12, under 6 free. Open weekdays 8:30–5, weekends 9–5.*

3 Turn left on Broad Street and walk two blocks to the **Scarbrough House.** The exuberant Regency mansion was built during the 1819 cotton boom for Savannah merchant prince William Scarbrough and designed by English architect William Jay. A Doric portico is capped by one of Jay's characteristic half-moon windows. Four massive Greek Doric columns form a peristyle in the atrium entrance hall. Three stories overhead is an arched, sky-blue ceiling with sunshine filtering through a skylight. *41 Martin Luther King Dr., tel. 912/233–7787. Admission: free. Open Mon.–Sat. 10–4.*

Continue east across Franklin Square and stroll through City Market, which includes an art center with working studios of 35 area artists, along with sidewalk cafés, jazz joints, and shops. Now head
4 east on St. Julian Street to **Johnson Square.** Laid out in 1733 and named for South Carolina Governor Robert Johnson, this was the earliest of Oglethorpe's original 24 squares. The square was once a popular gathering place, where Savannahians came to welcome President Monroe in 1819, to greet the Marquis de Lafayette in 1825, and to cheer for Georgia's secession in 1861.

As you stand at the foot of Bull Street, the building to the north with the glittering dome (regilded in 1987) is **City Hall,** dating from 1905. Its lower stories face the spot from which the SS *Savannah* set sail in 1819, the first steamship to cross an ocean. Just west of City Hall, on Yamacraw Bluff, is a marble bench, appropriately called **Oglethorpe's Bench,** marking the site of the general's field tent.

5 Cobblestone ramps lead from Bay Street down to **Factors Walk** and,
6 below it, to **River Street.** Cars can enter Factors Walk via the ramps, and so can pedestrians. (These are serious cobblestones, and you will suffer if you wear anything but the most comfortable shoes you own.) There is also a network of iron walkways connecting Bay Street with the multistoried buildings that rise up from the river level, and iron stairways descend from Bay Street down to Factors Walk.

7 Children enjoy the **River Street Train Museum** (315 West River St., tel. 912/233–6175; admission: $1.50 adults, 50¢ children), which offers guided tours of antique train displays and railroad memorabilia.

Foreign vessels still call at the Port of Savannah, the largest port between Baltimore and New Orleans. Paper and other products have replaced the cotton exports, and in 1977 a multimillion-dollar riverfront revitalization transformed the decayed warehouses into a nine-block marketplace housing unique boutiques alongside musty taverns.

Benches line **Riverfront Plaza,** where you can watch a parade of freighters and pug-nosed tugs; youngsters can play in the tugboat-shaped sandboxes here. Each weekday, Dixieland music can be heard from the cabin of the ***River Street Rambler,*** a brightly painted freight train that rumbles down River Street to the port. River Street is the main venue for many of the city's celebrations, including the First Saturday festivals when flea marketeers, artists, and craftspeople display their wares and musicians entertain the crowds.

Even landlubbers can appreciate the fine craftsmanship of the ship
8 models in the **Ships of the Sea Museum.** The four floors of the museum contain models of steamships, nuclear subs, China clippers with

their sails unfurled, Columbus's ships, a showcase filled with ships-in-bottles, and a collection of fine Royal Doulton porcelain seafarers. *503 East River St. and 504 East Bay St., tel. 912/232–1511. Admission: $3 adults, $1.50 children 7–12, under 7 free. Open daily 10–5.*

If you entered the museum at the River Street entrance and worked your way up all four floors, you'll be topside again on Bay Street.
9 The tree-shaded park along Bay Street is **Emmet Park,** named for Robert Emmet, a late 18th-century Irish patriot and orator. Walk west along Bay Street and turn left onto Abercorn Street. In **Reynolds Square** you'll see the statue of John Wesley, who preached in Savannah and wrote the first English hymnal here in 1736. The monument to the founder of the Methodist Church is shaded by greenery and surrounded by park benches. On the square is the **Olde Pink House** (23 Abercorn St.). Built in 1771, it is one of the oldest buildings in town. The porticoed pink stucco Georgian mansion has been a private home, a bank, and headquarters for a Yankee general during the war. It is now a restaurant (*see* Dining, *below*).

From Reynolds Square walk south on Abercorn Street, turn left onto Broughton Street, and two blocks down turn right onto
10 Habersham Street. Ahead stands the **Isaiah Davenport House.** Semicircular stairs with wrought-iron trim lead to the recessed doorway of the redbrick Federal mansion that master builder Isaiah Davenport built for himself in 1815, using architectural texts available in his day. Three dormer windows poke through the sloping roof of the stately house, and inside there are polished hardwood floors, fine woodwork and plasterwork, and a soaring elliptical staircase. The furnishings are Hepplewhite, Chippendale, and Sheraton, and in the attic there is a collection of antique dolls and a dollhouse with tiny 19th-century furnishings. *324 E. State St., tel. 912/236–8097. Admission: $4 adults, $3 children 6–18. Open Mon., Tues., Wed., Fri., Sat. 10–4, Sun. 1:30–4.*

11 Walk west on State Street two blocks to the **Owens-Thomas House & Museum.** This was William Jay's first Regency mansion in Savannah, built in 1816, and it is the city's finest example of that architectural style. The thoroughly English house was built largely with local materials, including tabby—a mixture of oyster shells, sand, and water that resembles concrete. The entry portico is of Doric design with curving stairs leading to a recessed door topped by a fanlight. Of particular note are the curving walls of the house, Greek-inspired ornamental molding, Jay's half-moon arches, stained-glass panels, and Duncan Phyfe furniture. You'll see hoopskirt chairs (whose short arms accommodated the circular skirts of many Southern belles), canopied beds, a pianoforte, and displays of ornate silver. From a wrought-iron balcony, in 1825, the Marquis de Lafayette bade a two-hour au revoir to the crowd below. *124 Abercorn St., tel. 912/233–9743. Admission: $5 adults, $3 students, $2 children 6–12, under 6 free. Open Sun.–Mon. 2–4:30; Tues.–Sat. 10–4:30.*

Stroll through **Oglethorpe Square,** across State Street, and continue
12 two blocks west to **Wright Square.** The square was named for James Wright, Georgia's last Colonial governor. Centerpiece of the square is an elaborate monument erected in honor of William Washington Gordon, founder of the Central of Georgia Railroad. A slab of granite from Stone Mountain marks the grave of Tomo-Chi-Chi, the Yamacraw chief who befriended General Oglethorpe and the colonists.

Continue west on State Street, strolling through **Telfair Square** to
13 reach the **Telfair Mansion and Art Museum.** The South's oldest public art museum is housed in yet another of Jay's Regency creations, this one designed in 1819. Within its marbled halls are American, French, and Dutch Impressionist paintings; German Tonalist paintings; a large collection of works by Kahlil Gibran; plaster casts of the Elgin Marbles, the Venus de Milo, and the Laocoön, among other classical sculptures; and a room that contains some of the Telfair family furnishings, including a Duncan Phyfe sideboard and Savannah-made silver. *121 Barnard St., tel. 912/232–1177. Admission: $3 adults, $1 students, 50¢ children 6–12; free on Sun. Open Tues.–Sat. 10–5, Sun. 2–5.*

At the next corner, turn left onto Oglethorpe Avenue and cross Bull
14 Street to reach the **Juliette Gordon Low Birthplace.** This majestic Regency mansion is attributed to William Jay and in 1965 was designated Savannah's first National Historic Landmark. "Daisy" Low, founder of the Girl Scouts, was born here, and the house is now owned and operated by the Girl Scouts of America. Mrs. Low's paintings and other artworks are on display in the house, restored to the style of 1886, the year of Mrs. Low's marriage. *142 Bull St., tel. 912/233–4501. Admission: $4 adults, $3.75 senior citizens, $3 children under 18; discounts for Girl Scouts. Open Mon.–Sat. 10–4, Sun. 12:30–4:30. Closed Wed. and Sun. in Dec. and Jan.*

15 **Chippewa Square** is a straight shot south on Bull Street. There you can see Daniel Chester French's imposing bronze statue of the general himself, James Edward Oglethorpe. Also note the Savannah Theatre, the longest continuously operated theater site in North America.

From Chippewa Square, go east on McDonough Street to reach the
16 **Colonial Park Cemetery.** Savannahians were buried here from 1750 to 1853. Shaded pathways lace through the park, and you may want to stroll through and read some of the old inscriptions. There are several historical plaques in the cemetery, one of which marks the grave of Button Gwinnett, a signer of the Declaration of Independence.

17 The **Cathedral of St. John the Baptist** soars like a hymn over the corner of Abercorn and Harris streets, two blocks south of the cemetery. The French Gothic cathedral, with the pointed arches and free-flowing traceries characteristic of the style, is the seat of the Diocese of Savannah. It is the oldest Roman Catholic church in Georgia, having been founded in the early 1700s. Fire destroyed the early structures, and the present cathedral dates from 1876. Most of the cathedral's impressive stained-glass windows were made by Austrian glassmakers and imported around the turn of the century. The high altar is of Italian marble, and the Stations of the Cross were imported from Munich.

18 Across from the cathedral is **Lafayette Square,** named for the Marquis de Lafayette. The graceful three-tier fountain in the square was donated by the Georgia chapter of the Colonial Dames of America.

19 Across the square is the **Andrew Low House.** The house was built for Andrew Low in 1849, and later belonged to his son William, who married Juliette Gordon. After her husband's death, "Daisy" Low founded the Girl Scouts in this house on March 12, 1912. Robert E. Lee and William Thackeray were both entertained in this mansion. In addition to its historical significance, the house boasts some of the finest ornamental ironwork in Savannah. Members and friends

of the Colonial Dames have donated fine 19th-century antiques and stunning silver to the house. *329 Abercorn St., tel. 912/233–6854. Admission: $2 adults, $1 students, 75¢ children and Girl Scouts. Open daily 10:30–4:30.*

20 Two blocks to the west is **Madison Square,** laid out in 1839 and named for James Madison. The statue depicts Sergeant William Jasper hoisting a flag and is a tribute to his bravery during the Siege of Savannah. Though mortally wounded, he rescued the colors of his regiment in the assault on the British lines.

21 On the west side of the square is the **Green-Meldrim House,** designed by New York architect John Norris and built about 1850 for cotton merchant Charles Green. The house was bought in 1892 by Judge Peter Meldrim, whose heirs sold it to St. John's Episcopal Church, for which it is now the parish house. It was here that General Sherman lived after taking the city in 1864—in the splendid Gothic Revival mansion, complete with crenellated roof and oriel windows. The gallery that sweeps around three sides of the house is awash with filigreed ironwork. The mantels are Carrara marble, the woodwork is carved black walnut, and the doorknobs and hinges are silver-plated. There is a magnificent skylight above a gracefully curved staircase. The house is furnished with 16th- and 17th-century antiques. *1 West Macon St. on Madison Sq., tel. 912/233–3845. Admission: $3. Open Oct.–Feb. Tues., Thurs., Fri., and Sat. 10–4; Mar.–Sept., Mon. and Wed. 1–4.*

Time Out Students from the Savannah College of Art and Design buy art supplies and books at **Design Works Bookstore.** There is also a soda fountain and tables in this old Victorian drugstore, where you can get short orders, burgers, and deli sandwiches. *Corner of Bull and Charlton Sts., tel. 912/238–2481. Open Mon.–Thurs. 8–7:30, Fri. 9–4, Sat. 10–4.*

The fifth and last of Bull Street's squares is **Monterey Square,** which commemorates the victory of General Zachary Taylor's forces in Monterrey, Mexico, in 1846. The square's monument honors General Casimir Pulaski, the Polish nobleman who lost his life in the Siege of Savannah during the Revolutionary War.

22 On the east side of the square stands **Temple Mickve Israel,** which was consecrated in 1878. Five months after the founding of Savannah, a group of Spanish and German Jews arrived, bringing with them the prized "Sephar Torah" that is in the present temple. The splendid Gothic Revival synagogue contains a collection of documents and letters pertaining to early Jewish life in Savannah and Georgia. *20 E. Gordon St., tel. 912/233–1547. Admission free. Open weekdays 10–noon.*

A block east of the temple is a Gothic Revival church memorializing
23 the founders of Methodism. The **Wesley Monumental Church,** patterned after Queen's Kirk in Amsterdam, celebrated a century of service in 1968. The church is noted for its magnificent stained-glass windows. In the Wesley Window there are busts of John and Charles Wesley.

24 At the **Massie Heritage Interpretation Center,** in addition to a scale model of the city, maps and plans, and architectural displays, is a "Heritage Classroom" that offers schoolchildren hands-on instruction about early Colonial life. *207 E. Gordon St., tel. 912/651–7380. Admission free, but a donation of $1.50 is appreciated. Open weekdays 9–4:30.*

25 The southern anchor of Bull Street is **Forsyth Park,** with 20 luxuriant acres. The glorious white fountain, dating from 1858, was restored in 1988. In addition to its Confederate and Spanish-American War memorials, the park contains the Fragrant Garden for the Blind, a project of Savannah garden clubs. There are tennis courts and a tree-shaded jogging path. The park is often the scene of outdoor plays and concerts.

26 The **King-Tisdell Cottage,** perched behind a picket fence, is a museum dedicated to the preservation of African-American history and culture. The Negro Heritage Trail (*see* Special-interest Tours in Guided Tours, *above*) begins here, in this little Victorian house. Broad steps lead to a porch that's loaded with gewgaws, and dormer windows pop up through a steep roof. The interior is furnished to resemble an African-American coastal home of the 1890s. *514 E. Huntingdon St., tel. 912/234–8000. Admission: $2.50 adults, $1 children. Open weekdays 10:30–4:30, Sat. 1–4.*

Other houses of interest in the Victorian district are at **118 E. Waldburg Street** and **111 W. Gwinnett Street.** A stroll along **Bolton Street** will be especially rewarding for fans of fanciful architecture. Of particular note is the entire 200 block, 114 W. Bolton Street, 109 W. Bolton Street, and 321 E. Bolton Street.

Day-tripping to Tybee Island

Tybee Island, which lies 18 miles east of Savannah on the Atlantic Ocean, offers all manner of water and beach activities. Take Victory Drive (U.S. 80), which sometimes takes the alias of Tybee Road. There are two historic forts to visit on the way.

Fort Pulaski National Monument is 14 miles east of downtown Savannah. You'll see the entrance on your left just before U.S. 80E reaches Tybee Island. A must for Civil War buffs, the fort was built on Cockspur Island between 1829 and 1847 and named for General Casimir Pulaski, a Polish count who was a Revolutionary War hero. Robert E. Lee's first assignment after graduating from West Point was as an engineer here. During the Civil War the fort fell on April 12, 1862, after a mere 30 hours of bombardment by newfangled rifled cannons. It was the first time such cannons had been used in warfare—and the last time a masonry fort was thought to be impregnable. The restored fortification, operated by the National Park Service, is complete with moats, drawbridges, massive ramparts, and towering walls. The visitor center includes museum exhibits and an audiovisual program. The park has self-guided trails and ample picnic areas. *U.S. 80, tel. 912/786–5787. Admission: $2 adults, children 16 and under free. Open daily 8:30–5.*

Three miles farther along U.S. 80 is **Tybee Island.** "Tybee" is an Indian word meaning salt. The Yamacraw Indians came to the island to hunt and fish, and legend has it that pirates buried their treasure here. The island is about 5 miles long and 2 miles wide, with a plethora of seafood restaurants, chain motels, condos, and shops, most of which sprung up during the 1950s and haven't changed much since. The entire expanse of white sand is divided into a number of public beaches, where visitors go shelling and crabbing, play on waterslides, charter fishing boats, swim, and build sand castles. Contact Tybee Island Beach Visitor Information (Box 1628, 31402, tel. 800/868–2322).

The **Tybee Museum and Lighthouse** are at the island's tip. In the museum you'll see Indian artifacts, pirate pistols, powder flasks, old prints tracing the history of Savannah, even some sheet music of Johnny Mercer songs. The Civil War Room has old maps and newspaper articles pertaining to Sherman's occupation of the city. On the second floor there are model antique cars and ship models, and a collection of antique dolls. The lighthouse across the road is Georgia's oldest and tallest, dating from 1773, with an observation deck 145 feet above the sea. Bright red steps—178 of them—lead to the deck and the awesome Tybee Light. The view of the ocean will take away whatever breath you have left after the climb. *30 Meddin Dr. and the jumping off place, tel. 912/786–4077. Admission to both lighthouse and museum: $2.50 adults, $1.50 senior citizens, 75¢ children 6–12. Both open daily in summer 10–6; weekdays noon–4, in winter weekends 10–4. Closed Tues.*

Time Out **Spanky's Pizza Galley & Saloon** has fried shrimp, burgers, chicken fingers, and salads. *317 E. River St., tel. 912/236–3009. AE, MC, V. Open daily 11 AM–midnight; happy hour 4:30–7.*

Heading west back to Savannah, take the Islands Expressway, which becomes the President Street Extension. About 3½ miles outside the city you'll see a sign for **Fort Jackson,** located on Salter's Island. The Colonial fort was purchased in 1808 by the federal government and is the oldest standing fort in Georgia. It was garrisoned in 1812 and was the Confederate headquarters of the river batteries. The brick fort is surrounded by a tidal moat, and there are 13 exhibit areas. Battle reenactments, blacksmithing demonstrations, and programs of 19th-century music are among the fort's schedule of activities. The Trooping of the Colors and military tattoo take place at regular intervals during summer. *1 Ft. Jackson Rd., tel. 912/232–3945. Admission: $2.50 adults, $2 students, senior citizens, and military personnel. Open daily 9–5.*

Savannah for Free

Beach at Tybee Island (*see* Day-tripping, *above*). Savannah celebrates eight international theme festivals in addition to St. Patrick's Day, plus 69 annual events. Most of the celebrations take place on River Street. Arts-and-crafts displays, music, and entertainment are always part of such special events as the February Georgia Day Festival, Oktoberfest, the Great American 4th of July, the SeafoodFest, and First Saturday festivals every month. About 40,000 greenish folk flock to Riverfront Plaza after the St. Patrick's Day parade. Contact the Savannah Visitors Center (*see* Important Addresses and Numbers, *above*) or the **Artsline** (tel. 912/233–2787).

For great **people watching** in the summer months, grab a picnic lunch and head to Johnson Square in the heart of Savannah's financial district. Free concerts are Wed. and Fri. noon–2.

Oatland Island Education Center. This 175-acre maritime forest, 15 minutes from downtown, is not only a natural habitat for coastal wildlife (including timber wolves and panthers), it also offers environmental education for visitors. The center also houses the coastal offices of the Georgia Conservancy. *711 Sandtown Rd., tel 912/897–3773. Open weekdays 8:30–5; Special events and programs take place Oct.–May, on the 2nd Sat. of each month 11–5.*

Skidaway Island Marine Science Complex. On the grounds of the former Modena Plantation, the complex features a 12-panel, 12,000-gallon aquarium with marine and plant life of the Continental Shelf. Other exhibits highlight coastal archaeology and fossils of the Georgia coast. Nature trails overlook marsh and water. *30 Ocean Science Circle, Skidaway Island, tel. 912/598–2325. Open weekdays 9–4, Sat. noon–5.*

Telfair Mansion and Art Museum charges no admission on Sundays (*see* Exploring, *above*).

Watch the **parade of ships** on the Savannah River.

What to See and Do with Children

Forts Pulaski and **Jackson** (*see* Day-tripping, *above*).

Juliette Gordon Low Girl Scout National Center (*see* Exploring, *above*).

Oatland Island Education Center (*see* Savannah for Free, *above*).

Exhibits at the **Savannah Science Museum** include a plexi-glass "crawl through" which allows kids to view reptiles and amphibians, a discovery room, a 32-ft., two deck boat, an 800 gallon aquarium, Indian artifacts, plans, and planetarium shows. *4405 Paulsen St., tel. 912/355–6705. Admission: $3 adults; $2 senior citizens, students, and children 12 and under. Open Mon.–Sat. 10–5, Sun. 2-5; planetarium shows Sun. at 3 PM. Every second Sunday is free.*

Tybee Island Museum and Lighthouse (*see* Day-tripping, *above*).

Off the Beaten Track

If your tastebuds crave down-home barbecue, head for **Wall's,** place your order at the counter, then wait at an orange plastic booth. Entertainment is provided by a small black-and-white TV set. Drinks are serve-yourself from the refrigerator case, and your food comes in Styrofoam cartons. A sign taped above the counter reads, "When I work, I works hard. When I sit, I sits loose—when I think, I falls asleep." Plain? Not really. Barbecued spare ribs, barbecued sandwiches, and deviled crabs–the only items on the menu–are plenty rich. A large carton of ribs costs $8.50. *515 E. York La., between Oglethorpe Ave. and York St., tel. 912/232–9754. Dress: bibs. No credit cards. Open Wed. 11–5, Thurs. 11–10, Fri. and Sat. 11–10.*

Shopping

Regional wares to look for are handcrafted items from the Low Country—handmade quilts and baskets; wreaths made from Chinese tallow trees and Spanish moss; preserves, jams, and jellies. The favorite Savannah snack, and a popular gift item, is the benne wafer. It's about the size of a quarter and comes in a variety of flavors.

Shopping Districts

Riverfront Plaza/River Street is nine blocks of shops housed in the renovated waterfront warehouses, where you can find everything from popcorn to pottery. **City Market,** located on West St. Julian Street between Ellis and Franklin squares, has sidewalk cafés, jazz haunts, shops, and art galleries. If you're in need of anything from aspirin to anklets, head for **Broughton Street** and wander through its many variety and specialty stores.

Oglethorpe Mall (7804 Abercorn St., tel. 912/354–7038) is an enclosed center with four department stores (Sears, JC Penney, Belk, and Rich's) and more than 140 specialty shops, fast-food and full-service restaurants. The **Savannah Mall** (14045 Abercorn St. and Rio Rd., tel. 912/927–7467) just off I–95 also has four major anchor stores (JB White's, Belks, Parisians, and Montgomery Ward), along with 100 specialty shops, fast-food and full-service restaurants. Kids delight in its old-fashioned carousel. **Savannah Festival Factory Stores** (11 Gateway Blvd., South, tel. 912/925–3089) has manufacturers' merchandise at 25%-75% off.

Specialty Shops

Antiques **Arthur Smith** (1 W. Jones St., tel. 912/236–9701) houses four floors of 18th- and 19th-century European furniture, porcelain, rugs, and paintings. At **Claire West** (413 Whitaker St., tel. 912/236–8163) you will find two buildings filled with fine linens, antiques, prints and engravings, old and new decorative tabletop objects, and a children's boutique with handmade bonnets and pinafores.

Artwork **Exhibit A Gallery** (342 Bull St., tel. 912/238–2480), the gallery of the Savannah College of Art and Design, has hand-painted cards, handmade jewelry, and paintings by regional artists. **Gallery 209** (209 E. River St., tel. 912/236–4583) is a co-op gallery with paintings, watercolors, pottery, jewelry, and sculpture by local artists. Original artwork, prints, and books by internationally acclaimed artist Ray Ellis are sold in the **Compass Prints, Inc. Ray Ellis Gallery** (205 W. Congress St., tel. 912/234–3537).

Benne Wafers You can buy boxed bennes in most gift shops, but **The Byrd Cookie Company, Inc.** (2233 Norwood Ave., tel. 912/355–1716) is where they originated in 1924. The popular cookies are sold in 50 gift shops around town or on site at **The Cooky Shanty.**

Books The 12 rooms of **E. Shaver's** (326 Bull St., tel. 912/234–7257) bookstore are stocked with books on architecture and regional history, as well as used and rare books. **The Book Lady** (17 W. York St., tel. 912/233–3628) specializes in used, rare, and out-of-print books; it also provides a search service.

Country Crafts At **Charlotte's Corner** (1 W. Liberty St., tel. 912/233–8061) browse through regional cookbooks, children's clothes and hand-made toys, and potpourris. **Georgia Gifts** (217 W. St. Julian St., tel. 912/236–1220) has handmade baskets, antique dolls, jams, jellies, preserves, and wreaths.

Participant Sports

Bicycling Pedaling is a breeze on these flatlands. Rental bikes are available at **The City Market Bicycle Shoppe** (211 W. Saint Julian St., tel. 912/233–9401.) for $14 a day.

Boating **Saltwater Charters** (111 Wickersham Dr., tel. 912/598–1814) operates everything from two-hour sightseeing tours to 13-hour deep-sea fishing expeditions. Pedal boats can be rented for tooling around **Lake Mayer** (Lake Mayer Park, Sallie Mood Dr. and Montgomery Crossroads Dr., tel. 912/652–6780). There are public boat ramps at **Bell's Landing** on the Forest River (Apache Rd. off Abercorn St.); **Islands Expressway** on the Wilmington River (Islands Expressway adjacent to Frank W. Spencer Park); and **Savannah Marina** on the Wilmington River in the town of Thunderbolt.

Golf Try the 27-hole course at **Bacon Park** (Shorty Cooper Dr., tel. 912/354–2625), and the 9-hole course at **Mary Calder** (W. Lathrop Ave., tel. 912/238–7100).

Health Clubs **Savannah Downtown Athletic Club** (7 E. Congress St., tel. 912/236–4874) has Nautilus and free-weight equipment, whirlpool, sauna, aerobics, and karate classes.

YMCA Family Center (6400 Habersham St., tel. 912/354–6223) offers a gymnasium, aerobics, racquetball, pool, and tennis.

Jewish Educational Alliance (5111 Abercorn St., tel. 912/355–8111). Racquetball courts, gymnasium, weight room, sauna, steam, whirlpool, outdoor Olympic-size pool, and aerobic dance classes are here.

Jogging Flat-as-a-benne wafer **Forsyth Park** and the beach at **Tybee Island** are favorites with runners. Suburbanites favor the jogging trails in **Lake Mayer Park** (Montgomery Crossroads Rd. at Sallie Mood Dr.) and **Daffin Park** (1500 E. Victory Dr.).

Tennis There are 14 lighted courts in **Bacon Park** (Skidaway Rd., tel. 912/351–3850); four lighted courts in **Forsyth Park** (Drayton and Gaston Sts., tel. 912/351–3852); and eight lighted courts in **Lake Mayer Park** (Montgomery Crossroads Rd. and Sallie Mood Dr., tel. 912/652–6780). Five other local parks have courts as well.

Dining

On a river, 18 miles inland from the Atlantic Ocean, Savannah naturally has excellent seafood restaurants. Locals also have a passion for spicy barbecue. The Historic District yields culinary treasures among its architectural diamonds—especially along River Street. Savannahians also like to drive out to eat in Thunderbolt and on Skidaway, Tybee, and Wilmington islands.

The most highly recommended restaurants in each price category are indicated by a star ★.

Category	Cost*
$$$$	over $30
$$$	$25–$30
$$	$15–$25
$	under $15

**per person without tax, service, or drinks*

American
$$$$
★
The Olde Pink House. The brick Georgian mansion was built for James Habersham, one of the wealthiest Americans of his time, in 1771. The elegant tavern, one of Savannah's oldest buildings, has original Georgia pine floors, Venetian chandeliers, and 18th-century English antiques. The new owners have taken great pains to research Colonial cooking style and have introduced it where appropriate. Signature dishes are a colonial version of crisp roast duck with a savory wild-berry compote, and black grouper stuffed with blue crab and finished with Vidalia onion sauce. The restaurant is graced with one of the largest wine cellars in the state of Georgia—fitting, as the Habersham family dominated the Madeira trade for years. Piano jazz (Tues.–Sun. 6–11) is played downstairs at Planters Tavern, where Martha Washington chairs and a Queen Anne settee are pulled up to the original cooking hearths on cool days. *23 Abercorn St., tel. 912/232–4286. Reservations advised. Jacket required at dinner. AE, MC, V.*

$$$
★
45 South. This popular southside eatery moved in 1988 to the sprawling Pirates' House complex. It's a small, stylish restaurant with contemporary decor in lush mauve and green (typical of Savannah) colors. The ever-changing menu includes contemporary American dinner entrées such as sliced breast of duck with au gratin potatoes

Dining
Bistro Savannah, **2**
Crystal Beer Parlor, **18**
Elizabeth on 37th, **24**
45 South, **11**
Garibaldi Cafe, **1**
Johnny Harris, **9**
Mrs. Wilkes Boarding House, **19**
The Olde Pink House, **13**
Pirates' House, **12**
River House, **4**
Seashell House, **25**
Shrimp Factory, **6**

Lodging
Ballastone Inn, **14**
Days Inn/ Days Suites, **3**
DeSoto Hilton, **16**
Eliza Thompson House, **20**
Foley House Inn, **15**
Forsyth Park Inn, **21**
The Gastonian, **22**
Hyatt, **5**
Jesse Mount House, **17**
The Mulberry, **10**
Olde Harbour Inn, **7**
Radisson Plaza, **23**
River Street Inn, **8**

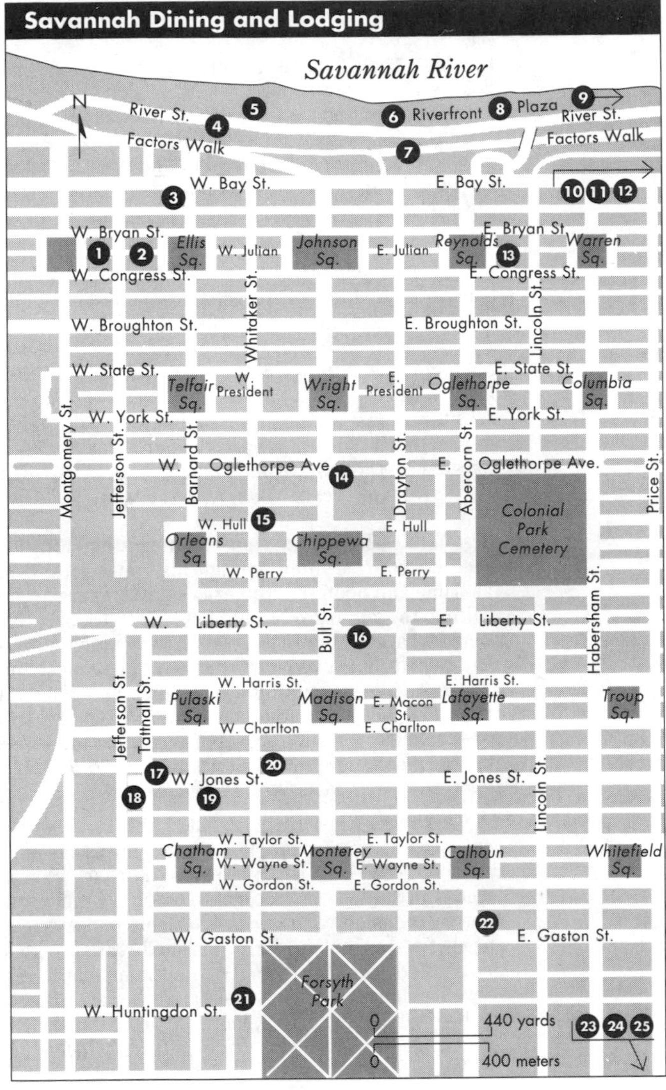

and yellowfin tuna with sautéed spinach and prosciutto. *20 E. Broad St., tel. 912/233–1881. Reservations and jacket advised. AE, MC, V. Closed Sun. No lunch.*

$$ **Bistro Savannah.** This Beaux-Arts–style gallery setting featuring new works by rising local artists is the place to see and be seen. Tucked in a historic building and featuring Savannah-gray brick walls, marble tables, and wicker chairs, this bistro has emerged as a favorite meeting and feeding spot among locals who love the Southern coastal cuisine. Items on the changing menu might include sweet onion-crusted North American red snapper with Madeira sauce and a 20-ounce "cowboy steak" with homemade smoked tomato-mustard barbecue sauce. Late-night cappuccino is popular here. *309 W. Con-*

gress St., tel. 912/233–6266. Reservations accepted. Dress: casual. AE, MC, V. No lunch.

Garibaldi Cafe. The 19th-century Savannah Germantown Firehouse houses this fanciful eatery with antique tin ceilings, handpainted murals depicting the African tropics, and original oil paintings. Here the emphasis is on fresh fish—caught daily by the restaurant's small fleet. Try the crisp local flounder with apricot-shallot glaze or the local lump blue crab fettucine with pepper cream. *315 W. Congress St., tel. 912/232–7118. Reservations accepted. Dress: casual. AE, MC, V. No lunch.*

$ **Crystal Beer Parlor.** This comfortable family tavern is famed for hamburgers, thick-cut french fries, onion rings, and frosted mugs of draft beer. The menu also offers fried oyster sandwiches, gumbo, and shrimp salad. *301 W. Jones St. at Jefferson St., tel. 912/232–1153. No reservations. Dress: casual. MC, V. Closed Sun.*

Johnny Harris. What started as a small roadside stand in 1924 has grown into one of the city's mainstays, with a menu that includes steaks, fried chicken, seafood, and a variety of barbecued meats spiced with the restaurant's famous sauce. *1651 E. Victory, tel. 912/354–7810. No reservations. Dress: casual. AE, DC, MC, V. Closed Sun.*

★ **Mrs. Wilkes Boarding House.** There's no sign out front, but you won't have any trouble finding this famed establishment. At breakfast time and noon (no dinner is served) there are long lines of folks waiting to get in for a culinary orgy. Charles Kuralt and David Brinkley are among the celebrities who have feasted on the fine Southern food, served family-style at big tables. For breakfast there are eggs, sausage, piping hot biscuits, and grits. At lunch, bowl after bowl is passed around the table. Fried or roast chicken, collard greens, okra, mashed potatoes, cornbread, biscuits—the dishes just keep coming. *107 W. Jones St., tel. 912/232–5997. No reservations. Dress: casual. No credit cards. No dinner.*

Seafood
$$$
★ **Elizabeth on 37th.** Elizabeth is the chef, and her namesake was recently toasted by *Food & Wine* magazine as one of the top 25 restaurants in America. Elizabeth and Michael Terry's restaurant is located in the city's Victorian District, in an elegant turn-of-the-century mansion with hardwood floors and spacious rooms. Among the chef's seasonal specialties is shad stuffed with sautéed shad roe and stuffed Vidalia onions. While the emphasis is on sea creatures served in delicate sauces, there are other excellent offerings, including beef tenderloin, quail, lamb, and chicken dishes. *105 E. 37th St., tel. 912/236–5547. Reservations advised. Jacket advised. AE, MC, V. Closed Sun. and lunch.*

Pirates' House. You'll probably start hearing about the Pirates' House about 10 minutes after you hit town. There are all sorts of legends about it involving shanghaied sailors and ghosts. It's a sprawling complex with nautical and piratical trappings, and 23 rooms with names like The Jolly Roger and The Black Hole; children love the place. The menu is almost as big as the building, with heavy emphasis on sea critters. For starters, try oysters, crab-stuffed mushrooms, or soft-shell crabs. The large portions of gumbo and seafood bisque come in iron kettles. Flounder Belle Franklin is crabmeat, shrimp, and fillet of flounder baked in butter with herbs and wines and a glaze of cheeses and toasted almonds. The Key lime pie is the best choice among the 40 listings on the dessert menu. Hard Hearted Hannah's Jazz Club is upstairs. *20 E. Broad St., tel. 912/233–5757. Reservations accepted. Dress: casual. AE, DC, MC, V. Sun. brunch 11–2:30.*

$$–$$$ **River House.** This stylish restaurant sits over the spot where the SS *Savannah* set sail for her maiden voyage across the ocean in 1819. A number of mesquite-grilled entrées, including swordfish topped with raspberry-butter sauce and grouper Florentine, served with creamed spinach and a fresh dill and lemon-butter sauce, are good. Entrées are served with freshly baked loaves of sourdough bread, and fish dishes come with homemade angel-hair pasta. *125 W. River St., tel. 912/234–1900. Reservations accepted. Dress: casual for lunch; jacket and tie required for dinner. AE, DC, MC, V.*

$–$$ ★ **Seashell House.** It may not look like much from the outside, but the steamed and fried seafood inside is regarded by many to be the city's best. Specialties are crab, shrimp, and oysters, as well as a Low Country Boil that includes shrimp, sausage, corn, and whatever else comes to mind that day. It also features a seafood platter second to none. The restaurant's pastry chef prepares a beautiful bananas Foster flambé. French-style coffee is brewed tableside. *3111 Skidaway Rd., tel. 912/352–8116. No reservations. Dress: casual. MC, V.*

Shrimp Factory. Like all of Savannah's riverfront restaurants, this was once an old warehouse. Now it's a light and airy place with exposed brick, wood paneling, beamed ceilings, and huge windows that let you gaze at the passing parade of ships. A house specialty is pine bark stew—five native seafoods simmered with potatoes, onions, and herbs, and served with blueberry muffins. Blackened dolphinfish fillet is smothered with herbs and julienned sweet red peppers in butter sauce. Baked deviled crabs are served with chicken-baked rice, and fish entrées come with angel-hair pasta. *313 E. River St., tel. 912/236–4229. Reservations accepted. Dress: casual. AE, DC, MC, V.*

Lodging

While Savannah has its share of chain hotels and motels, the city's most distinctive lodgings are the more than two dozen historic inns, guest houses, and bed-and-breakfasts gracing the Historic District.

If "historic inn" brings to mind images of roughing it in shabbily genteel mansions with slightly antiquated plumbing, you're in for a surprise. Most of the inns are in mansions with the prerequisite high ceilings, spacious rooms, and ornate carved millwork. Most have canopied, four-poster, or Victorian brass beds that dominate most quarters. And amid antique surroundings, modern luxury: enormous baths, many with whirlpools, hot tubs, or Jacuzzis; film libraries for in-room VCRs; and turn-down service with a chocolate, praline, or even a discreet brandy on your nightstand. Continental breakfast and afternoon refreshments are often included in the rate.

The most highly recommended properties in each price category are indicated by a star ★.

Category	Cost*
$$$$	over $100
$$$	$75–$100
$$	$50–$75
$	under $50

**double room; add taxes or service*

Inns and Guest Houses

$$$$

★

Ballastone Inn & Townhouse. This sumptuous inn within a mansion, dating from 1838, once served as a bordello. Notable for the wildly dramatic designs of its Scalamandre wallpaper and fabrics, each of its 17 rooms has a different theme. In Scarborough Fair, a vivid red and yellow room, the fabric pattern was adapted from a Victorian china serving platter in the Davenport House. This exquisite third-floor room has two queen-size Victorian brass beds, a Queen Anne lowboy and writing desk, and a Victorian slipper chair. On the garden level, rooms are small and cozy, with exposed brick walls, beamed ceilings, and, in some cases, windows at eye level with the lush courtyard. One such room is the Sorghum Cane, trimmed in the bronze color of sugarcane molasses; it has two queen-size brass beds, wicker furniture, and wall fabric patterned after the etched glass window of a restored local house. The townhouse, four blocks away, houses another five units (one room and four suites). Built in 1830, it's the oldest building south of Liberty Street. *14 E. Oglethorpe Ave,, 31401, tel. 912/236–1484 or 800/822–4553. 17 rooms with bath. Facilities: concierge, courtyard Jacuzzis, fireplaces, in-room VCRs, film library. AE, MC, V.*

Foley House Inn. In the parlor of this four-story, 1896 Victorian house, carved gargoyles flank the original fireplace and a graceful brass-and-crystal chandelier gleams overhead. An elaborate lamp on the newel post in the hall worked as an extra in *Gone with the Wind.* There are four rooms in the carriage house and 16 spacious rooms (five with Jacuzzis) in the main house, all with canopied or four-poster beds, polished hardwood floors covered with Oriental rugs, and 19th-century antiques. A splendid tapestry is the centerpiece in the Essex Room. Request a room with a balcony facing Chippewa Square, and ask about special package deals. *14 W. Hull St., 31401, tel. 912/232–6622 or 800/647–3708. 20 rooms with bath. Facilities: concierge, courtyard with hot tub, VCRs, film library. AE, MC, V.*

★ **The Gastonian.** Hugh and Roberta Lineberger's inn will probably, to put it modestly, knock your socks off. The mansion was built in 1868, and each of its 13 sumptuous suites is distinguished with vivid Scalamandre colors. The Caracalla Suite is named for the marble bath with an eight-foot whirlpool tub. The huge bedroom has a king-size canopy bed, working fireplace, and a lounge with a mirrored wet bar. The French Room, resembling a 19th-century French boudoir, is done in blues and whites, with Oriental rugs and flocked wallpaper. All rooms have working fireplaces and antiques from the Georgian and Regency periods. In the morning, a full breakfast is served in the formal dining room—or you can opt for a Continental breakfast in your room. Each guest receives a fruit basket and split of wine upon arrival. *220 E. Gaston St., 31401, tel. 912/232–2869, fax 912/232–0710. 13 rooms, 6 with oversized Jacuzzis. Facilities: concierge, courtyard, sun deck with hot tub. AE, MC, V.*

$$$–$$$$ **Olde Harbour Inn.** The building dates from 1892, when it was built on the riverfront as an oil warehouse, but the old inn is actually a thoroughly modern facility that housed condos until 1987. Each suite has a fully equipped kitchen, including dishwasher and detergent. All suites overlook the river and have wall-to-wall carpeting, exposed brick walls painted white, and a four-poster bed. There are studio suites; regular suites with living room, bedroom, kitchen, and bath; and loft suites. (The latter are lofty indeed, with 25-foot ceilings, balconies overlooking the water, huge skylights, and ample room to sleep six.) Each evening a dish of ice cream is brought to your room and placed in the freezer. Cereal, hot muffins and biscuits, juice, tea, and coffee are served in a cozy breakfast room each

morning. *508 E. Factors Walk, 31401, tel. 912/234–4100 or 800/553–6533; fax 912/233–5979. 24 housekeeping suites with bath. Facilities: concierge, cable TV, valet laundry, parking. AE, DC, MC, V.*

$$$ ★ **Eliza Thompson House.** This 25-room guest house, on one of the Historic District's prettiest tree-lined streets, was originally built in 1847 for "Miss Eliza." There are king- and queen-size four-poster and canopied beds; some rooms with wall-to-wall carpeting, others with Oriental rugs covering the Georgia pine floors. The choice rooms overlook the large brick courtyard, which is a popular place for wedding receptions. In nice weather the complimentary breakfast is served at tables around a tiered fountain in the courtyard. *5 W. Jones St., 31401, tel. 912/236–3620 or 800/348–9378. 25 rooms with bath. Facilities: concierge. AE, MC, V.*

★ **Forsyth Park Inn.** Rooms in this Victorian mansion across the street from Forsyth Park are outfitted with 19th-century furnishings, including king- and queen-size four-poster beds, and have working fireplaces and large marble baths (some with whirlpools). The carriage house, just off the courtyard, has a suite with bath, complete kitchen, and a screened porch. In the foyer is a grand piano, and afternoon wines and cheeses are served here. *102 W. Hall St., 31401, tel. 912/233–6800. 9 rooms with bath, 1 private guest cottage. AE, MC, V.*

Bed-and-breakfasts
$$$ ★

Jesse Mount House. The Georgian home of Sue Dron has two-bedroom suites, a garden suite with a kitchen and whirlpool, and a one-bedroom suite. All units have their own fireplace with gas logs. Continental breakfast is served in your room or in the formal dining room. *209 W. Jones St., 31401, tel. 912/236–1774. 4 suites with bath. Facilities: cable TV. V.*

Hotels and Motels
$$$–$$$$

DeSoto Hilton. Three massive chandeliers glisten over the jardinieres, fresh flowers, and discreetly placed conversation areas of the spacious lobby. The chandeliers are from the historic DeSoto Hotel that stood on this site long ago. Guest rooms are on the cushy side, in Savannah peach and green, with wall-to-wall carpeting, traditional furniture, and king, queen, or two double beds. (The best view is from the corner king rooms, which have the added attraction of coffeemakers.) Suites have refrigerators in small kitchens and custom-made contemporary furnishings in the bedroom, sitting room, and dining area. *15 E. Liberty St., 31401, tel. 912/232–9000 or 800/4266–8483, fax 912/232–6018. 254 rooms, 9 suites with bath. Facilities: concierge, 2 restaurants, lounge, outdoor heated pool with sundeck, golf and tennis privileges at area clubs. AE, DC, MC.*

Hyatt. When this riverfront hotel was built in 1981, preservationists opposed a seven-story modern structure in the historic district. Although it doesn't blend well with its surroundings, the hotel has some points to recommend it. The main architectural features are the towering atrium and a pleasant central lounge, as well as glass elevators. Rooms have mauve furnishings and balconies overlooking the atrium, the Savannah River, or Bay St. MD's Lounge is the ideal spot to have a drink and watch the river traffic drift by. *2 W. Bay St., tel. 912/238–1234 or 800/233–1234, fax 912/944–3678. 346 rooms with bath. Facilities: restaurant, lounge, indoor pool, gift shop. AE, DC, MC, V.*

★ **The Mulberry.** So many objets d'art fill the public rooms that the management has obligingly provided a walking tour brochure. Treasures include 18th-century oil paintings, an English grandfather clock dating from 1803, Chinese vases from the Ching Dynasty, and an ornate Empire game table. The restaurant is a sophisticated affair, with crystal chandeliers and mauve velvet Regency furniture. The spacious courtyard is covered with a mosquito net, which keeps it about 10 degrees cooler in the summer. The guest rooms are in a traditional motif; suites have king-size beds and wet bars. *601 E. Bay St., 31401, tel. 912/238–1200 or 800/554–5544 (in GA 800/465–4329), fax 912/236–2184. 122 rooms, 25 suites with bath. Facilities: concierge, bar, restaurant, outdoor pool, rooftop deck with Jacuzzi and riverview, accommodations for nonsmokers and the handicapped. AE, DC, MC, V.*

Radisson Plaza. This modern hotel is Savannah's newest. Located in the Historic District, the eight-story property with rounded balconies facing the river occupies a choice spot on the city's riverfront, adjacent to River Street and Factor's Walk. *100 Gen. McIntosh Blvd., 31401, tel. 912/233–7722 or 800/333–3333, fax 912/233–3765. 386 rooms, 46 suites with bath. Facilities: 2 restaurants, lobby lounge, indoor and outdoor pools, Jacuzzi, fitness club. AE, D, DC, MC, V.*

River Street Inn. This elegant hotel offers panoramic views of the Savannah River. Rooms are furnished with antiques and reproductions from the era of King Cotton. Amenities include turn-down service. The interior is so lavish, it's difficult to believe it was only recently a vacant warehouse dating back to 1830. One floor includes charming shops, another a New Orleans–style restaurant and blues club. *115 E. River St., tel. 912/234–6400 or 800/253–4229. 44 rooms with bath. Facilities: restaurant, lounge, shops. AE, MC, V.*

$$ **Days Inn/Days Suites.** This downtown hotel is located in the Historic District near the City Market, only a block off River Street. Its compact rooms have modular furnishings and most amenities, including HBO/ESPN on the tube and valet service. Interior corridors and an adjacent parking garage minimize its motel qualities. *201 W. Bay St., tel. 912/236–4440 or 800/325–2525. 235 rooms with bath. Facilities: restaurant, pool, health club, gift shop. AE, DC, MC, V.*

Nightlife

Savannah's nightlife is a reflection of the city's laid-back, easy-going personality. Some clubs feature live reggae, hard rock, and other contemporary music, but most stay with traditional blues, jazz, and piano bar vocalists. After-dark merrymakers usually head for watering holes on Riverfront Plaza or the southside.

Jazz Clubs

The Crossroads (219 W. Saint Julian St., tel. 912/234–5438) is Savannah's sole blues nightclub, featuring live performances from local and national talent Monday through Saturday.

Hard-Hearted Hannah's (*see* Pirate's House in Dining *above*) showcases local talents.

Bars and Nightclubs

City Slickers (9 W. Bay St., tel. 912/233–6999; open Wed.–Sat.) is the place for country music and dancing, from the achy breaky to the two-step.

Congress Street Station (121 W. Congress St., tel. 912/236–6266) is the city's liveliest music hall, featuring a variety of name performers in rock, blues, jazz, reggae, folk, country, and comedy. The age of the crowd on the tiny dance floor depends on who's on the bandstand.

Kevin Barry's Irish Pub (117 W. River St., tel. 912/233–9626), a cozy pub with a friendly bar and traditional Irish music, is *the* place to be on St. Patrick's Day. The rest of the year there's a mixed bag of tourists and locals, young and old.

The Golden Isles and Okefenokee Swamp

The Golden Isles are a string of lush, subtropical barrier islands meandering lazily down Georgia's Atlantic coast from Savannah to the Florida border. They have a long history of human habitation; Indian relics have been found on these islands that date to about 2500 BC. According to legend, the Indian nations agreed that no wars would be fought there and that tribal members would visit only in a spirit of friendship. In a latter-day spirit of friendship today, all of Georgia's beaches are in the public domain.

Each Golden Isle has a distinctive personality, shaped by its history and ecology. Three of them–Jekyll Island, Sea Island, and St. Simons Island—are connected to the mainland by bridges in the vicinity of Brunswick; these are the only ones accessible by automobile. The Cumberland Island National Seashore is accessible by ferry from St. Mary's. Little St. Simons Island, a privately owned retreat with a guest lodge, is reached by a private launch from St. Simons.

About 50 miles inland is the Okefenokee Swamp National Wildlife Refuge, which has a character all its own.

Getting There and Getting Around

By Plane The Golden Isles are served by **Glynco Jetport,** 6 miles north of Brunswick, which is served in turn by Delta affiliate **Atlantic Southeast Airlines** (tel. 800/282–3424), with flights from Atlanta, and by **USAir** (tel. 800/428–4322), with flights out of Charlotte, North Carolina.

By Car From Brunswick by car, take the Jekyll Island Causeway ($2 per car) to Jekyll Island, and the Torras Causeway to St. Simons and Sea Island. You can get by without a car on Jekyll Island and Sea Island, but you'll need one on St. Simons. You cannot bring a car to Cumberland Island or Little St. Simons.

By Ferry Cumberland Island and Little St. Simons are accessible only by ferry (*see below*).

Cumberland Island National Seashore

Numbers in the margin correspond to points of interest on the Golden Isles map.

The largest, most southerly, and most accessible of Georgia's primi-
1 tive coastal islands is **Cumberland,** a 16-by-3-mile sanctuary of marshes, dunes, beaches, forests, lakes and ponds, estuaries and inlets. Waterways are home to gators, sea turtles, otters, snowy egrets, great blue herons, ibis, wood storks, and more than 300 other species of birds. In the forests are armadillos, wild horses, deer, raccoons, and an assortment of reptiles.

After the ancient Guale Indians came 16th-century Spanish missionaries, 18th-century English soldiers, and 19th-century planters. During the 1880s, Thomas Carnegie of Pittsburgh built several lavish homes here, but the island remained largely as nature created it. In the early 1970s, the federal government established the Cumberland Island National Seashore and opened this natural treasure to the public.

The only public access to the island is by *The Cumberland Queen*, a reservations-only, 146-passenger ferry based near the National

Golden Isles

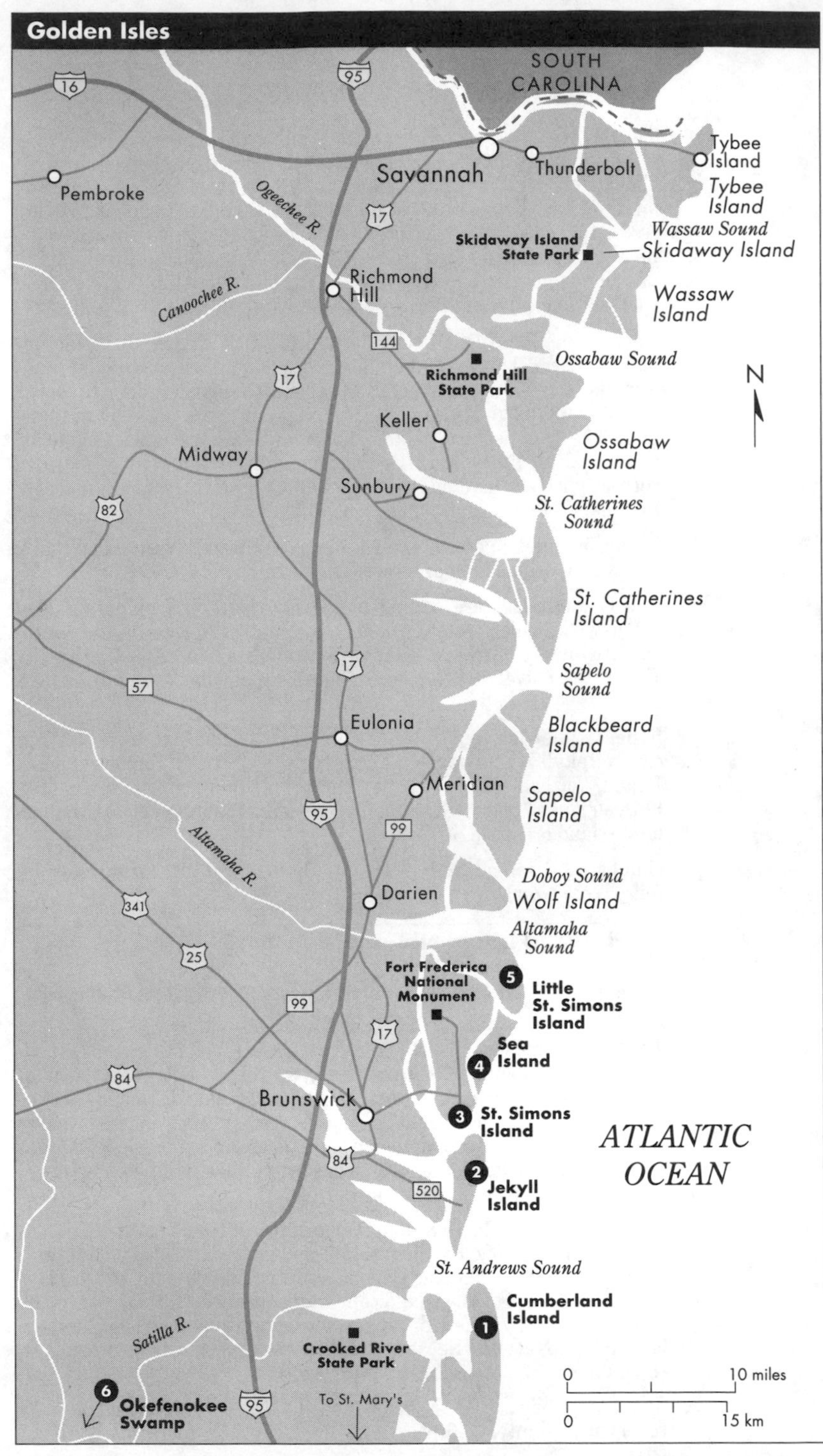

Park Service Information Center at St. Mary's (Cumberland Island National Seashore, Box 806, 31558, tel. 912/882–4335.) From mid-May through September, the ferry departs from St. Mary's daily at 9AM and 11:45AM and departs from Cumberland at 10:15AM and 4:45PM. From October through May 14, there is no ferry Tues.–Wed.) Ferry bookings are heavy in summer, but cancellations and no-shows often make last-minute space available. Adults pay $10.07 roundtrip; children 12 and under $5.99; and senior citizens, $7.95. *There is no transportation on the island.*

Exploring From the Park Service docks at the island's southern end, you can follow wooded nature trails, swim and sun on 18 miles of undeveloped beaches, go fishing and bird-watching, and view the ruins of Carnegie's great estate, **Dungeness.** You can also join history and nature walks led by Park Service rangers. Bear in mind that summers are hot and humid, and that you must bring your own food, soft drinks, sunscreen, and a reliable insect repellent. All trash must be transported back to the mainland by campers and picnickers. *Nothing can be purchased on the island.*

Lodging
Island

Greyfield Inn. The island's only accommodations are in a turn-of-the-century Carnegie family home. Greyfield's public areas are filled with family mementoes, furnishings, and portraits (you may feel as though you've stepped into one of Agatha Christie's mysterious Cornwall manors). Prices include all meals, transportation, tours led by a naturalist, and bike rentals. *Box 900 Fernandina Beach, FL 32035, tel. 904/261–6408. 11 rooms, 1 suite. MC, V. $$$$ (over $150).*

Novice campers usually prefer **Sea Camp,** a five-minute walk from the *Cumberland Queen* dock, with rest rooms and showers adjacent to campsites. The beach is just beyond the dunes. Experienced campers will want to hike 3–10 miles to several areas where cold-water spigots are the only amenities.

Mainland

The Charter House. Two miles from the Cumberland ferry dock is a 120-room motel, whose accommodations are spartan but air-conditioned. Rooms also have kitchenettes with microwaves for those who like to haul their own grub. Or the on-site restaurant serves reasonably priced breakfasts, lunches, and dinners and presents live evening entertainment in the lounge. *2710 Osborne St., St. Mary's 31588, tel. 800/768–6250. 120 rooms. Facilities: restaurant, lounge, swimming pool. AE, D, DC, MC, V. $*

Jekyll Island

For 56 winters, between 1886 and 1942, America's rich and famous
2 faithfully came south to **Jekyll Island.** Through the Gilded Age, the Great War, the Roaring '20s, and the Great Depression, Vanderbilts and Rockefellers, Morgans and Astors, Macys, Pulitzers, and Goodyears shuttered their Fifth Avenue castles and retreated to the serenity of their wild Georgia island. There they built elegant "cottages," played golf and tennis, and socialized. Early in World War II, the millionaires departed for the last time. In 1947, the state of Georgia purchased the entire island for the bargain price of $650,000.

Tourist Information The Jekyll Island Convention and Visitors Bureau (901 Jekyll Island Causeway, Jekyll Island 31520, tel. 912/635–3636), at the end of the causeway, is open daily 9–5. Ninety-minute open-air trolley tours of the Jekyll Island Club Historic Landmark District originate at the Museum Orientation Center on Stable Road. Sites include several restored homes and buildings in the 240-acre historic district: Indian Mound; William Rockefeller's shingled cottage; and Faith Chapel, illuminated by Tiffany stained-glass windows and open for meditation Sun.–Fri. 2–4. Audiovisual orientations are presented a half-hour before each tour departs. Go north on 95 to Exit 6/South on 95 to Exit 8, tel. 912/635–2762 or 800/841–6586. Admission: $7 adults, $5 students 6–18. Tours daily 10–3.

Exploring Jekyll Island is still a 7½-mile playground, but no longer restricted to the rich and famous. The golf, tennis, fishing, biking, jogging, water park, and picnic grounds are open to all. One side of the island is flanked by nearly 10 miles of hard-packed Atlantic beaches; the other, by the Intracoastal Waterway and picturesque salt marshes. Deer and wild turkeys inhabit interior forests of pine, magnolia, and moss-veiled live oaks. Egrets, pelicans, herons, and sandpipers skim the gentle surf.

Jekyll's clean, mostly uncommercialized public beaches are free and open year-round. Bathhouses with rest rooms, changing areas, and showers are open at regular intervals along the beach. Beachwear, suntan lotion, rafts, snacks, and drinks are available at the **Jekyll Shopping Center,** facing the beach at Beachview Drive.

Participant Sports

Golf Jekyll's 63 holes of golf include three 18-hole courses with a main clubhouse on Capt. Wylly Rd. (tel. 912/635–2368) and a 9-hole course on Beachview Dr. (tel. 912/635–2170).

Tennis Eight courts include J. P. Morgan's indoor court (tel. 912/635–2600, ext. 1060).

Water Park **Summer Waves,** the 11-acre water park, has an 18,000-square-foot wave pool; eight water slides; a children's activity pool with two slides; and a 1,000-foot river for tubing and rafting. *210 S. Riverview Dr., tel. 912/635–2074. Admission: $11.95 adults, $9.95 children under 48 inches. Open Sun.–Fri. 10–6, Sat. 10–8 May 28–Sept. 5.*

Dining **The Grand Dining Room.** In the Jekyll Island Club Hotel the dining room sparkles with silver and crystal. Low-country cuisine by the hotel's young chef includes delicately flavored fresh seafood, beef, veal, and chicken. *371 Riverview Dr., tel. 912/635–2600, ext. 1002. Reservations advised. Jacket requested at dinner. AE, DC, MC, V. $$$*

Chelsea on the Water. Opened in 1989 as the Golden Isles' only over-the-water dining, this restaurant provides a saltwater marsh view from its dock location. Fresh seafood is featured nightly in the dining room and screened-porch raw bar. Cocktails are served in the lounge. *One Pier Rd., tel. 912/635–3800. Dress: casual. AE, MC, V. $–$$*

Lodging **Jekyll Island Club Hotel.** Built in 1887, the four-story clubhouse with wraparound verandas and Queen Anne–style towers and turrets once served as the winter hunting retreat for wealthy financiers. In 1985, a group of Georgia businessmen spent $17 million restoring it to a splendor that would astonish even the Astors and Vanderbilts. The guest rooms and suites are custom-decorated with mahogany beds, armoires, and plush sofas and chairs. Some have flowery views of the Intracoastal Waterway, Jekyll River, and the hotel's croquet lawn. Several suites have Jacuzzis. The adjacent Sans Souci Apartments, built in 1896 by William Rockefeller, have been converted into spacious guest rooms. The hotel is operated as a Radisson resort. *371 Riverview Dr., Jekyll Island 31527, tel. 912/635–2600 or 800/333–3333, fax 912/635–2818. 134 units. Facilities: restaurant,* *outdoor pool, gift shops, 22 miles of bicycle trails, croquet lawn, free shuttle to beaches, 8 tennis courts. AE, DC, MC, V. $$$–$$$$*

Best Western Jekyll Inn. Located on a landscaped 15-acre site, these oceanfront units, the largest facility on the island, recently underwent a $2.5 million renovation. Rooms were redecorated with new lighting, carpeting, and saunas and Jacuzzis in some bathrooms. Island decor was added to the second-floor Ocean View lounge. Units include some villas with kitchenettes. *975 Beachview Dr., Jekyll Island 31520, tel. 912/635–2531 or 800/528–1234. 264 units. Facilities: restaurant, pool, playground. AE, DC, MC, V. $$–$$$$*

Holiday Inn Beach Resort. Nestled amid natural dunes and oaks in a secluded oceanfront setting, this hotel has a private beach, but its rooms with balconies still don't have an ocean view. Its recreational activities include outdoor pool and playground, tennis courts, and 63 holes of golf. *200 S. Beachview Dr., Jekyll Island 31520, tel. 912/635–3311 or 800-HOLIDAY. 205 rooms. Facilities: restaurant, lounge with live entertainment, satellite cinema, some in-room saunas and whirlpools, bike rentals. AE, D, DC, MC, V. $$$*

Rentals Jekyll's more than 200 rental cottages and condos are handled by **Jekyll Realty** (912/635–3301) and **Parker-Kaufman Realty** (912/635–2512).

St. Simons Island

As large as Manhattan, with more than 14,000 year-round residents,
3 **St. Simons** is the Golden Isles' most complete resort destination. Fortunately, the accelerated development in recent years has failed to spoil the natural beauty of the island's regal live oaks, beaches, and salt marshes. Visits are highlighted by swimming and sunning on hard-packed beaches, golf, biking, hiking, fishing, horseback riding, touring historic sites, and feasting on fresh local seafood at a growing number of restaurants.

Tourist Information **St. Simons Island Chamber of Commerce** (530 Beachview Dr., St. Simons Island 31522, tel. 912/638–9014 or 800/638–9014, fax 912/638–2172; closed Sun.) provides helpful information.

Exploring Many sights and activities are in **the village** area along Mallery Street at the more developed south end of the island, where there are shops, several restaurants, pubs, and a popular public pier. A quaint "trolley" takes visitors on a 1½-hour guided tour of the island, leaving from near the pier, several times a day in high season, less frequently in winter ($10 adults, $6 children).

Also at the island's south end is **Neptune Park,** which includes picnic tables, a children's play park, miniature golf, and beach access. A freshwater swimming pool, with showers and rest rooms, is open each summer in the **Neptune Park Casino** (tel. 912/638–2393), which also has a roller-skating rink, bowling lanes, and snack bars. Also in the park is **St. Simons Lighthouse,** a beacon since 1872. The **Museum of Coastal History** in the lightkeeper's cottage has a permanent exhibit of coastal history. *Tel. 912/638–4666. Admission (including the lighthouse): $3 adults, $1 children 6–12. Open Tues.–Sat. 10–5, Sun. 1:30–5.*

At the burgeoning north end of the island there's a marina, a golf club, and a housing development, as well as **Ft. Frederica National Monument.** Tabby ruins remain of a fort built by English troops in the mid-1730s as a bulwark against a Spanish invasion from Florida. Around the fort are the foundations of homes and shops. Start at the

National Park Service Visitors Center, which has a film and displays. *Tel. 912/638–3639. Admission: $4 per car. Open daily 9–5.*

On your way to Fort Frederica, pause at **Christ Episcopal Church** on Frederica Road. Consecrated in 1886 following an earlier structure's desecration by Union troops, the white frame Gothic structure is surrounded by live oaks, dogwoods, and azaleas. The interior is highlighted by beautiful stained-glass windows. Donations welcome.

Dining **Alfonza's Olde Plantation Supper Club.** Down-home versions of seafood, superb steaks, and plantation fried chicken are served in a gracious and relaxed environment. *Harrington La., tel. 912/638–9883. Reservations advised. Dress: casual. Closed Sun. and lunch. D, DC, MC, V. $$*

Blanche's Courtyard. In the village, this lively restaurant/nightclub is gussied up in "Bayou Victorian" dress, with lots of antiques and nostalgic memorabilia. True to its bayou decor, the menu features Cajun-style seafood as well as basic steak and chicken. A ragtime band plays for dancers on Saturday. *440 Kings Way, tel. 912/638–3030. Reservations accepted. Dress: casual. AE, DC, MC, V. $$*

CJ's. This tiny village-area restaurant serves the island's best Italian food. Deep-dish and thin-crust pizzas, pastas, and all of the menu's sandwiches draw a faithful local clientele. The limited seating capacity creates lengthy waits, but the cuisine is worth your patience, and take-out is available. *405 Mallory St., tel. 912/634–1022. No reservations. Dress: casual. No credit cards; personal checks accepted. No lunch. $*

Crab Trap. One of the island's most popular spots, the Crab Trap offers a variety of fried, blackened and broiled fresh seafood, oysters on the half shell, clam chowder, heaps of batter fries, and hush puppies. The atmosphere is rustic-casual—there's a hole in the middle of every table to deposit corn cobs and shrimp shells. *1209 Ocean Blvd., tel. 912/638–3552. No reservations. Dress: casual. MC, V. No lunch. $*

Lodging **King and Prince Hotel and Villas.** This hotel faces the beach. Guest rooms are spacious, and villas offer two or three bedrooms. *Box 20798, 201 Arnold Rd., St. Simons Island 31522, tel. 912/638–3631 or 800/342–0212. 125 rooms, 45 villas. Facilities: restaurant, lounge, indoor/outdoor pool, tennis, golf, bike rentals. AE, DC, MC, V. $$$*

Sea Palms Golf and Tennis Resort. A contemporary resort complex with fully furnished villas nestles on an 800-acre site. *5445 Frederica Rd., St. Simons Island 31522, tel. 912/638–3351. 200 rooms. Facilities: 2 pools, 27-hole golf course, tennis, children's recreation programs. AE, DC, MC, V. $$$*

Days Inn of America. This facility opened in 1989 on an inland stretch of the island's main thoroughfare. Each room has a built-in microwave and refrigerator. Continental breakfast is included in the rate. *1701 Frederica Rd., St. Simons Island 31522, tel. 912/634–0660, fax 912/638–7115. 101 rooms. Facilities: pool, cable TV. AE, MC, V. $$*

Island Inn. On wooded land just off one of the island's main streets, this newer antebellum-style motel offers convenience and privacy with its efficiency accommodations. Continental breakfast is included, and complimentary wine and cheese are served nightly 5:30–6:30. *301 Main St., tel. 912/638–7805, fax 912/638–2983. 74 rooms. Facilities: cable TV, pool, hot tub, meeting facilities. AE, MC, V. $$*

Queen's Court. This family-oriented complex in the village has clean, modest rooms with shower-baths, some with kitchenettes.

The grounds are beautiful. *437 Kings Way, St. Simons Island 31522, tel. 912/638–8459. 23 rooms. Facilities: cable TV, pool. MC, V. $$*

Sea Island

4 **Sea Island** has been the domain of the **Cloister Hotel** since 1928. Separated from St. Simons Island by a narrow waterway and a good many steps up the social ladder, this famed resort lives up to its celebrity status. Guests lodge in spacious, comfortably appointed rooms and suites in the Spanish Mediterranean hotel. The owners of the 500 or so private cottages and villas treat the hotel like a country club, and their tenants may use the hotel's facilities. Contact **Sea Island Cottage Rentals** (tel. 912/638–5112) to arrange to rent one.

For recreation, there's 54 holes of golf, tennis, swimming in pools or at the beach, skeet shooting, horseback riding, sailing, biking, lawn games, and surf and deep-sea fishing. After dinner, guests dance to live music in the lounge.

Like a person of some years, the Cloister has its eccentricities. Guest rooms were only recently equipped with TVs. Credit cards are not honored, but personal checks are accepted. Gentlemen must cover their arms in the dining rooms, even at breakfast. A complete and superb spa facility opened in 1989 in a beautiful building of its own by the pool and beach and features a fully equipped workout room, daily aerobics classes, personal trainers, facials and massages, and other beauty treatments.

There is no admission gate, and nonguests are free to admire the beautifully planted grounds and to drive past the mansions lining Sea Island Drive. Space permitting, they may also play at the Sea Island Golf Course (on St. Simons) and on the tennis courts and dine in the main dining room. *The Cloister, Sea Island 31561, tel. 912/638–3611, reservations 800/732–4752. 263 rooms. Facilities: 4 restaurants, 2 pools, golf, tennis, fitness center and spa; van service to Jacksonville, Savannah, and Brunswick airports. Breakfast, lunch, and dinner included in rate. No credit cards, but personal checks are accepted. $$$$ ($220–$448 for 2 in high season).*

Little St. Simons Island

Six miles long, 2 to 3 miles wide, skirted by Atlantic beaches and
5 salt marshes teeming with birds and wildlife, **Little St. Simons** is custom-made for Robinson Crusoe–style getaways. The island has been owned by one family since the early 1900s, and the only development is a rustic but comfortable guest compound.

The island's forests and marshes are inhabited by deer, armadillos, horses, raccoons, gators, otters, and over 200 species of birds. Guests are free to walk the 6 miles of undisturbed beaches, swim in the mild surf, fish from the dock, and seine for shrimp and crabs in the marshes. There are also horses to ride, nature walks with experts, and other island explorations via boat or the back of a pickup truck. From June through September, up to 10 nonguests per day may visit the island by reservation; the $60 cost includes the ferry to the island, an island tour by truck, lunch at the lodge, and a beach walk.

Dining and Lodging

River Lodge and **Cedar House.** Up to 24 guests can be accommodated in the lodge and house. Each has four bedrooms with twin or king-size beds, private baths, sitting rooms, and screened porches. Two other lodges have two bedrooms each; one with private and the other with shared baths. None of the rooms are air-conditioned, but ceiling fans make sleeping comfortable. The rates include all meals and dinner wines (cocktails available at additional cost). Meals, often featuring fresh fish, pecan pie, and home-baked breads, are served family-style in the lodge dining room. *Box 1078, Little St. Simons Island 31522, tel. 912/638-7472. Facilities: stables, pool, beach, transportation from St. Simons Island, transportation on the island, fishing boats, interpretive guides. Minimum 2-night reservations. Full American Plan. AE, MC, V. $$$$ ($300–$350 for 2). Mar.–May open to groups only; closed mid-Nov.–Feb.*

Okefenokee Swamp National Wildlife Refuge

Covering more than 700 square miles of southeast Georgia and spilling over into northeast Florida, the mysterious rivers and lakes of
6 the **Okefenokee Swamp** bristle with seen and unseen life. Scientists agree that Okefenokee is not duplicated anywhere else on earth. The swamp is actually a vast peat bog, remarkable in geologic origin and history. Once part of the ocean floor, it now rises more than 100 feet above sea level.

As you travel by canoe or speedboat among the water-lily islands and the great stands of live oaks and cypress, be on the lookout for otters, egrets, muskrats, herons, cranes, and gators cruising the dark channels like iron-clad subs. The Okefenokee Swamp Park, 8 miles south of Waycross, is a major visitor gateway to the refuge. The Swamp Park is a nonprofit development operating under a long-term lease. There are two other gateways to the swamp: an eastern entrance in the Suwanee Canal Recreation Area, near Folkston; and a western entrance at Stephen C. Foster State Park, outside the town of Fargo.

Seminole Indians, in their migrations south toward Florida's Everglades, once took refuge in the Great Okefenokee. Noting the many floating islands, they provided its name—"Land of the Trembling Earth."

Exploring

Okefenokee Swamp Park. South of Waycross, via U.S. 1, the park offers orientation programs, exhibits, observation areas, wilderness walkways, an outdoor museum of pioneer life, and boat tours into the swamp that reveal its ecological uniqueness. A boardwalk and 90-foot tower are excellent places to glimpse cruising gators and a variety of birds. Gate admission includes a guided boat tour and all exhibits and shows. You may also arrange for lengthier explorations with a guide and a boat. *Waycross 31501, tel. 912/283-0583. Admission: $8 adults, $6 children 5–11. Open daily summer, 9–6:30; spring, fall, and winter, 9–5:30.*

Suwanee Canal Recreation Area. This area, 8 miles south of Folkston, via GA 121/23, is administered by the U.S. Fish and Wildlife Service. Stop first at the Visitor Information Center, which has an orientation film and exhibits on the Okefenokee's flora and fauna. A boardwalk takes you over the water to a 40-foot observation tower. At the concession building you may purchase snacks and sign up for guided boat tours into an 11-mile waterway, which resulted from efforts to drain the swamp a century ago. Hikers, bicyclists, and private motor vehicles are welcome on the Swamp Island Drive; several interpretive walking trails may be taken along the way. Picnicking is allowed. *Park Supt., Box 336, Folkston 31537, tel. 912/496-7156. Admission to the park is free (there's a $3 charge per car). 1-hr tours: $6.75 adults, $3.50 children 5–11, $2.25 children 1–4; 2-hr* *tours: $13.50 adults, $7 children 5–11, $4.50 children 1–4. Refuge open daily 7 AM–7:30 PM Mar. 1–Sept. 10; 8–6 Sept. 11–Feb.*

Stephen C. Foster State Park. Eighteen miles from Fargo, via GA 11, is an 80-acre island park entirely within the Okefenokee Swamp National Wildlife Refuge. The park encompasses a large cypress and black gum forest, a majestic backdrop for one of the thickest growths of vegetation in the southeastern United States. The lush terrain and the mirrorlike black waters of the swamp provide at least a part-time home for more than 225 species of birds, 41 species of mammals, 54 species of reptiles, 32 species of amphibians, and 37 species of fish. Park naturalists leading boat tours will spill out a wealth of swamp lore as riders observe gators, many bird species, and native trees and plants. You may also take a self-guided excursion in rental canoes and fishing boats. Camping is also available here (*see* Lodging, *below*). *Fargo 31631, tel. 912/637–5274. Admission free. Open daily 6:30 AM–8:30 PM Mar. 1–Sept. 1; 7 AM–7 PM Sept. 2–Feb. 29. Admission: $3 to National Wildlife Refuge.*

Lodging
Camping

Stephen C. Foster State Park. The park has furnished two-bedroom cottages ($50 a night Sun.–Thurs.; $60 weekends) and campsites with water, electricity, rest rooms, and showers ($10 a night). Because of roaming wildlife and poachers, the park's gates close between sunset and sunrise. If you're staying overnight, stop for groceries in Fargo beforehand. *Park Supt., Fargo 31631, tel. 912/637–5274. $–$$*

Laura S. Walker State Park. Nine miles from Okefenokee Swamp Park are campsites ($10) with electrical and water hookups. Be sure to pick up food and supplies on the way to the park. *Park Supt., Waycross 31503, tel. 912/287–4900. Facilities: playground, fishing docks, pool, picnic areas. $*

Elsewhere in the State

Alpine Helen. The idea is an Alpine village in the Georgia mountains; the look is Bavaria; the attractions are mostly of the fun-and-fudge variety. The town's annual Oktoberfest draws crowds. *Rte. 385N from Atlanta to U.S. 129N to Cleveland, then Rte. 75N to Helen.*

Andersonville National Historic Site. Andersonville, which opened in 1864, was the Civil War's most notorious prisoner-of-war site: 13,000 prisoners died here, and at war's end the commandant was tried, convicted, and hanged. Earthworks, palisades, and some structures remain. Today it is the site of a memorial to prisoners of war. *I-75S from Macon to Rte. 26, then east to Oglethorpe, then Rte. 49 to Andersonville, tel. 912/924-0343. Admission free. Open daily 8–5.*

Athens. The home of the University of Georgia, this college town has an appeal that's a cross between Mayberry R.F.D. and M.T.V.—the latter owing to its reputation as a breeding ground for new and alternative music. Athens has several splendid Greek Revival buildings, including, on campus, the **University Chapel** (built in 1832) and the **University President's House,** built in the late 1850s (570 Prince Ave., tel. 706/354-4096; open by appointment). The **Taylor-Grady House** (634 Prince Ave., tel. 706/549-8688; admission: $2.50; open Tues.–Fri. 10–3:30), down the street, was constructed in 1844. The **Franklin Hotel** (480 E. Broad St.), also built in 1844, was recently restored and reopened as an office building. Contact the **Athens Convention and Visitors Bureau** (tel. 706/546–1805).

Barnsley Gardens, near Adairsville. The Civil War halted construction of Godfrey Barnsley's 26-room Italianate house, and in 1988 the estate and its gardens lay in ruins. A German prince, Hubertus Fugger-Babenhausen, and his wife, Princess Alexandra, bought it and started work on restoration. Today there are 30 acres of shrubbery, trees, ponds, fountains, and flowers, designed in the style of Mr. Barnsley's time. At press time, a restaurant was planned. *Barnsley Gardens Rd. off Hall Station Rd., tel. 404/773-7480. Admission: $6.50 adults, $5.50 senior citizens, children under 11 free. Open Tues.–Sat. 10–6, Sun. noon–6.*

Callaway Gardens, near Pine Mountain. This 14,000-acre family-style golf and tennis resort is best known for its impressive gardens and its not-to-be-missed butterfly conservatory. The gardens were developed in the 1930s by a wealthy couple determined to breathe new life into the area's dormant cotton fields. On the grounds are four nationally recognized golf courses, 17 tennis courts, bicycling trails, and a lakefront beach. The **Day Butterfly Center** contains more than 1,000 varieties flying free. Mountain Creek Lake is well-stocked with large-mouth bass and bream. If you visit here in the height of the spring season or during the garden's annual holiday light spectacular in December, you may find yourself in a traffic jam in the middle of rural Georgia. *U.S. 27S, tel. 706/663-2281 or 800/282-8181. Admission: $7.50 adults, $1.50 children 6–11, children under 6 free. Open daily 7–6.*

Chickamauga and Chattanooga National Battlefield Military Park. Established in 1890 and the nation's first military park, this was the site of one of the Civil War's bloodiest battles; casualties totaled more than 30,000. Though the Confederates routed the Federals early, Gen. Ulysses Grant eventually broke the siege of Chattanooga and secured the city as a base for Sherman's march through Atlanta and on to the sea. Monuments, battlements, and weapons adorn the road that traverses the 8,000-acre park, with markers explaining the action. *U.S. 27 off I-75, south of Chattanooga, tel. 706/866-9241. Admission free. Open daily 8–4:45.*

Clayton. This unassuming mountain town is near spectacular Tallulah Gorge, the deepest canyon in the U.S. besides the Grand Canyon, and a popular turn-of-the-century destination for Atlantans. The state of Georgia recently acquired the site for a state park, and vast improvements are planned. In Clayton, the **Main Street Gallery** (tel. 706/782–2440), one of the state's best sources for folk art, features works by local artists such as Tubby Brown and Sarah Rakes, and North Carolina's reclusive James Harold Jennings. About 10 miles north of Clayton on U.S. 441 is the **Dillard House,** justifiably famous for its spread of country food served family-style. *Tel. 706/746-5348 or 800/541-0671. Open daily for 3 meals; Sun. 11:30–8:30.*

Dahlonega. Gold was mined here before the Civil War, and a U.S. mint operated in this modest boom town from 1838 to 1861. In the present-day courthouse on the town square is the Gold Museum, with coins, tools, and a 5½-ounce nugget. The square is ringed with a mixture of tourist-oriented boutiques and old small-town businesses. *About 55 mi northeast of Atlanta, tel. 706/864–2257. Admission: $1.50 adults, 75¢ children under 18. Open daily.*

Fort Mountain State Park. Amid the deep woods and spectacular views in this out-of-the-way park in the Chattahoochee National Forest, nature is the main attraction, with a wide variety of trees and other flora. *Rte. 52 east of Chatsworth, tel. 706/695–2621. Admission: $2 per vehicle, free on Wed. Open daily 8–5, Fri. 8–10.*

Macon. This antebellum town features more than 70,000 cherry blossom trees. The Hay House (1861), considered one of the South's finest Italianate villas, contains 19 marble mantlepieces and other fine architectural detailing. *934 Georgia Ave., tel. 912/742–8155. Admission: $6.30 adults, $5.25 senior citizens, $2.10 children 12–18, $1.05 children 5 –12. Open Mon.–Sat. 10–5, Sun. 1–5; last tour 4:30.*

The **Harriet Tubman Museum** is a tribute to the former slave who led more than 300 people to freedom as one of the "conductors" on the Underground Railroad. A mural that spans two walls and several centuries depicts black history and culture. The museum also has an African artifacts gallery. *340 Walnut St., tel. 912/743–8544. Admission: $1. Open Mon.–Sat. 10–5,.*

Madison. This town remains virtually unchanged architecturally from the 1830s. The **Madison-Morgan Cultural Center** is housed in a turn-of-the-century schoolhouse built in Romanesque Revival style. Besides a restored classroom of the period, the center contains artifacts and information and printed guides for other historic sites in town. *434 S. Main St., tel. 706/342–4743. Admission: $2 adults, $1 students. Open Tues.–Sat. 10–4:30, Sun. 2–5.*

New Echota State Historic Site. From 1819 to 1832, New Echota was the capital of the Cherokee nation, whose constitution was patterned after that of the United States. There was a courthouse, a Supreme Court building, and the *Cherokee Phoenix*, a newspaper that utilized the Cherokee alphabet developed by Sequoyah. The buildings have been reconstructed. *Rte. 225, 1 mi east of I–75N, near Calhoun, tel. 706/629–8151. Admission: $2 adults, $1 children 6–18, under 6 free. Open Tues.–Sat. 9–5, Sun. 2–5:30.*

Ocmulgee National Monument. This archaeological site, occupied for more than 10,000 years, was at its peak under the Mississippian peoples who lived there between 900 and 1100. There's a reconstructed earth lodge and displays of pottery, effigies, and jewelry of copper and shells discovered in the burial mound. *Rte. 80 just east of Macon, tel. 912/752–8257. Admission free. Open daily 9–5.*

Spring Place. Chief James Vann, a leader of the Cherokee Nation around 1800, hired Moravian artisans to build this two-story brick house in 1805. The interior is intricately carved and beautifully restored. *Rte. 52A just west of Chatsworth, tel. 706/695–2598. Admission: $2 adults, $1.50 children under 12. Open Tues.–Sat. 9–5, Sun. 2–5:30.*

Summerville. Paradise Garden is the vision-come-to-life of the Rev. Howard Finster, preacher and folk artist. His artwork has been used for album covers by Talking Heads and R.E.M., and his eccentric visions are also in the collection of Atlanta's High Museum of Art. The garden, which occupies several city blocks, is dominated by the chapel built by Finster and members of his family. A tower built of old bicycle parts serves as a sentry for the spectacle. Artwork is for sale in the shop. *Off U.S. 27, near Pennville, tel. 706/857–2926. Admission free, donations accepted. Open daily noon–6.*

Warm Springs. President Franklin Delano Roosevelt first visited here in 1924 and in 1932 built the "Little White House," a simple, three-bedroom house where he stayed when taking the therapeutic hot waters of the area. Now restored and operated as a museum, it contains two hand-operated automobiles among his personal effects. *Rte. 85W, tel. 706/655–3511. Admission: $4 adults, $2 children 6–18, under 6 free. Open daily 9–5.*

3 North Carolina

By Carol Timblin

Updated by Susan Ladd

North Carolina may not have it all, but don't try telling that to a North Carolinian. Any native will point to its mountains, some of the tallest in the east, which are laced with waterfalls cascading over rocky cliffs into gorges thick with evergreens. He or she will tell you about Cape Hatteras and Cape Lookout national seashores, where tides wash over the wooden beams of ancient shipwrecks, and lighthouses have stood for 200 years. You'll be invited to Charlotte, the state's largest city, where banking and pro-basketball draw national attention, and to the University of North Carolina research center, at which the technology of virtual reality got a trial run.

North Carolina geography has carved out three distinct regions: The mountains, the Piedmont, and the coast. The Great Smoky and Blue Ridge mountain ranges create the rough, slanted border of western North Carolina. The mountains taper off into foothills and then into the Piedmont, a gently rolling landscape characterized by rich farmlands to the north, red clay soil in the center, and sandy pine forests to the south. Most major cities have grown up in the center of the state, built primarily by the textile, furniture, and tobacco industries. The rolling hills of the Piedmont level off into the rich soil of the coastal plain. Much of eastern North Carolina remains agricultural and sparsely populated. Wilmington is a bustling port city, in sharp contrast to the tranquil villages along the Outer Banks.

Golf is the recreational focus in the Sandhills, while skiing has taken hold in the High Country (Alleghany, Ashe, Avery, Mitchell, and Watauga counties). Asheville has maintained its status as a resort city for more than 100 years and continues to grow in popularity.

North Carolina has courted visitors since the first English settlers arrived in 1584. Since the Depression of the 1930s, when the state began to realize the importance of tourism, the welcome mat has been out. The Blue Ridge Parkway was built largely by the CCC (Civilian Conservation Corps), as were many state park facilities. Cape Hatteras was declared a national seashore—the country's first—in 1953. A good highway system and several airports were built, and now eight welcome centers greet visitors at state borders. People come to North Carolina for its historic sites and natural wonders, its sports, resorts, and down-home cooking, not to mention its legendary barbecue. And tourism today, after tobacco and textiles, is the state's largest industry.

Charlotte

Charlotte, once a sleepy Southern crossroads, has grown up to be quite a sophisticated city—with luxury hotels, excellent restaurants, sporting events, and varied cultural activities. The acquisition of a professional football franchise is the city's most recent achievement, and Carolina Panthers mania is already sweeping the state even though the team's first game will probably be played in Charlotte in 1996. The Charlotte Hornets basketball team has been setting NBA attendance and merchandise sales records since the team was formed in 1989.

Though Charlotte dates to Revolutionary War times (it is named for King George III's wife, Queen Charlotte), its Uptown is distinctively New South. The NationsBank Corporate Center, a 60-story skyscraper designed by Cesar Pelli, dominates the skyline. The Queen City is the largest city in the Carolinas, the third largest banking center in the nation, and a major trade and distribution center.

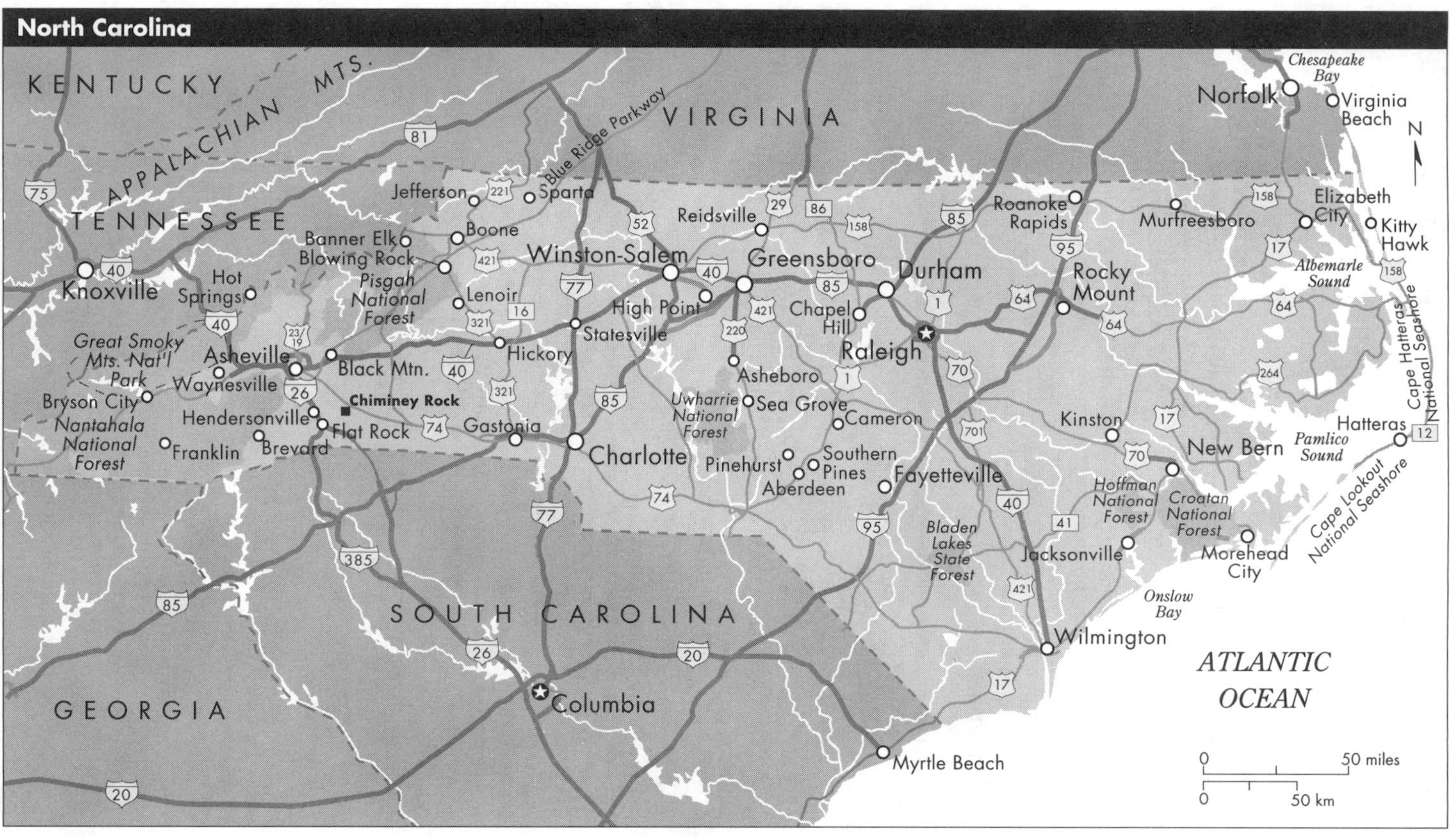
North Carolina
KENTUCKY
APPALACHIAN MTS.
TENNESSEE
VIRGINIA
Blue Ridge Parkway
SOUTH CAROLINA
GEORGIA
ATLANTIC OCEAN
Chesapeake Bay
Albemarle Sound
Pamlico Sound
Onslow Bay
Cape Hatteras National Seashore
Cape Lookout National Seashore
Norfolk
Virginia Beach
Elizabeth City
Kitty Hawk
Hatteras
Murfreesboro
Roanoke Rapids
Rocky Mount
Kinston
New Bern
Morehead City
Croatan National Forest
Hoffman National Forest
Jacksonville
Wilmington
Durham
Raleigh
Chapel Hill
Greensboro
Reidsville
Winston-Salem
High Point
Statesville
Asheboro
Sea Grove
Cameron
Southern Pines
Aberdeen
Pinehurst
Fayetteville
Bladen Lakes State Forest
Myrtle Beach
Uwharrie National Forest
Charlotte
Gastonia
Hickory
Lenoir
Sparta
Boone
Jefferson
Banner Elk
Blowing Rock
Pisgah National Forest
Black Mtn.
Chiminey Rock
Flat Rock
Hendersonville
Brevard
Asheville
Waynesville
Hot Springs
Knoxville
Great Smoky Mts. Nat'l Park
Bryson City
Franklin
Nantahala National Forest
Columbia
N
0 50 miles
0 50 km

Heavy development has created some typical urban problems. Outdated road systems make traffic a nightmare during rush hour, and virtually all the city's restaurants are packed on weekends. But the southern courtesy of the locals is contagious, and people still love the traditional pleasures of picnicking in Freedom Park or munching on barbecue at Mallard Creek Church.

Arriving and Departing

By Plane

Airports and Airlines **Charlotte-Douglas International Airport** (tel. 704/359–4013), is west of the city off I–85. Carriers include American, Delta, TWA, United, USAir, and their local affiliates. Direct service is available to London, Frankfurt, Nassau, and Puerto Rico.

Between the Airport and Center City Taxis cost about $11 ($2 each additional person), and airport vans are approximately $4 per person. Most major hotels provide complimentary transportation. By car, take the Billy Graham Parkway, then Wilkinson Boulevard (U.S. 74) east to I–277, which leads to the heart of Uptown.

By Train **Amtrak** (1914 N. Tryon St., tel. 704/376–4416 or 800/872–7245) offers daily service to Washington, DC, to Atlanta, GA, and points beyond and there's daily service to Raleigh.

By Bus **Greyhound Lines** (601 W. Trade St., tel. 800/231–2222) serves the Charlotte area.

By Car Charlotte is a transportation hub; I–85 and I–77, north–south routes, run through, and I–40, east–west, is 40 miles to the north. U.S. 74, a major east–west route, also serves the city. I–277 and Charlotte 4 are inner-city loops.

Getting Around

By Bus **Charlotte Transit** (tel. 704/336–3366) provides public transportation throughout the city. The Transit Mall has bus shelters on Trade and Tryon streets in Uptown. Fares are 80¢ for local rides and $1.15 for express service; senior citizens with ID cards pay 35¢ between 9 and 3, after 6, and on weekends. Free bus service is available between Mint and Kings Drive on Trade and between Stonewall and 11th on Tryon weekdays 9–3.

By Taxi **Yellow Cab** (tel. 704/332–6161) has cars and airport vans. **The University Shuttle** (tel. 704/553–2424 or 800/951–2424) caters to business travelers. Passengers pay a set flat rate.

Important Addresses and Numbers

Tourist Information **The Visitor Information Center** (122 E. Stonewall St., tel. 704/371–8700 or 800/231–4636) is open weekdays 8:30–5, Sat. 10–4, and Sun. 1–4. Parking is available. **The N.C. Welcome Center** (on I–77 north at the South Carolina line, tel. 704/588–2660) is open daily 8–5 except Christmas Eve, Christmas Day, New Year's Day, and Thanksgiving. **The Charlotte-Douglas International Airport** has a welcome center in the baggage claim area that's open daily, 7 AM–11 PM.

Emergencies Dial 911 for **police** and **ambulance** in an emergency.

Doctor **Care Connection,** operated by Presbyterian Hospital, will give physician referrals and make appointments (tel. 704/384–4111, open weekdays 8:30–4:30). **Healthfinder,** run by Mercy Hospital, is a similar operation (tel. 704/379–6100, open Tues. and Thurs. 8:30–noon).

The **Mecklenburg County Medical Society** also gives physician referrals (tel. 704/376–3688, open weekdays 9–1).

24-Hour Pharmacy **Eckerd Drugs** (Park Road Shopping Center, tel. 704/523–3031; and 3740 E. Independence Blvd., tel. 704/536–3600).

Guided Tours

Guided tours are given by **Gray Line** (tel. 704/332–8687), **Adam's Stage Lines** (tel. 704/537–5342), and **Queens Carriages** (tel. 704/391–1232). The ***Catawba Queen*** paddlewheeler (tel. 704/663–2628) gives dinner cruises and tours on Lake Norman.

Several balloon companies give aerial tours, which end with champagne: **Balloons Over Charlotte** (tel. 704/541–7058), **Adventures Aloft of Charlotte** (tel. 704/545–6418), and **Fantasy Flights** (tel. 704/552–0469).

Exploring Charlotte

Numbers in the margin correspond to points of interest on the Charlotte map.

Uptown Charlotte Walking Tour **Uptown Charlotte** is ideal for walking, and buses are adequate for getting around within the city limits; otherwise, you will need a car. The city was laid out in four wards from The Square, at Trade and Tryon streets. Stop first at the **Visitor Information Center,** on Stonewall Street, for information on a self-guided walking tour of Fourth Ward and a historic tour of Uptown, as well as maps and brochures. Then head for Uptown where you can park your car in an open lot a few blocks east of the Square, where Trade and Tryon intersect.

Take a stroll down **Tryon Street** and enjoy the ambience of this revitalized area, noting the outdoor sculptures on the plazas and the creative architecture of some of the newer buildings, among them the
1 **NationsBank Corporate Center,** a 60-story structure with a crownlike top designed by Pelli, which opened in late 1992. Its main attraction is three philosophical frescoes by Ben Long that symbolize the city's past, present, and future. Also housed in the tower are the **North Carolina Blumenthal Center for the Performing Arts** and **Founders Hall,** a complex of restaurants and shops.

2 From the bank, head north on North Tryon Street to **Discovery Place,** the city's premier attraction. Make the wonderful hands-on Science Museum a priority, and allow at least two hours for the aquariums, the rain forest, the Omnimax theatre, and Kelly Space Voyager Planetarium. Check the schedule for special exhibits. *301 N. Tryon St., tel. 704/372–6261 or 800/935–0553. Admission: $5–$8 adults, $4–$7 senior citizens and students, $2.50–$5 children 3–5. Open daily.*

3 **Fourth Ward,** Charlotte's new "old" city, which lies just north of Discovery Place, offers a refreshing change from the newly developed parts of town. The self-guided tour points to 18 historic sites in the area. Be sure to stop by **Old Settlers Cemetery,** behind the **First Presbyterian Church,** which contains stones that date to the 1700s. The church, which takes up a city block and faces W. Trade Street, reflects the prosperity of the early settlers and their descendants. By the turn of the last century, they had built this Gothic Revival complex with stained glass to replace a much simpler meeting house. **Fourth Ward Park** is an oasis in the middle of the city. **Alexander Michael's** (401 W. Ninth St.) is a favorite eatery. **Poplar Street**

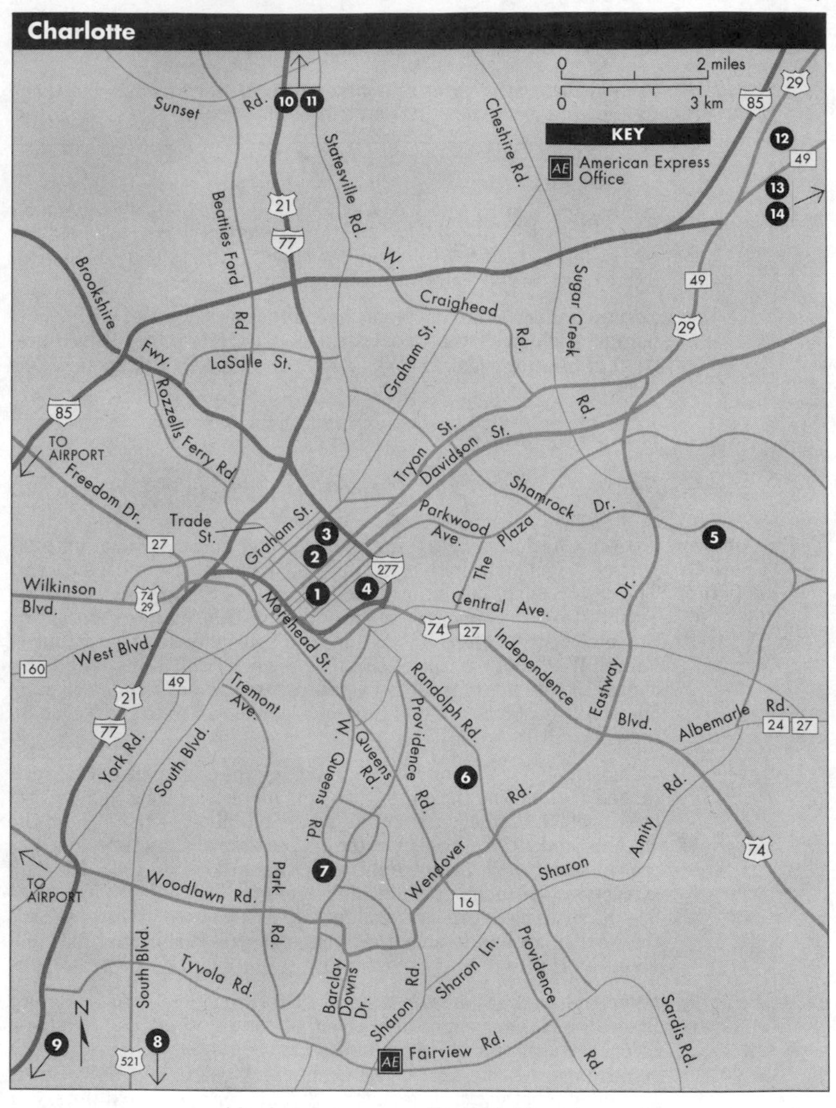

Afro-American Cultural Center, **4**
Backing Up Classics Memory Lane Motor Car Museum, **14**
Charlotte Motor Speedway, **13**
Discovery Place, **2**
Energy Explorium, **11**
Fourth Ward, **3**
Hezekiah Alexander Homesite and History Museum, **5**
James K. Polk Memorial, **8**
Latta Plantation Park, **10**
Mint Museum of Art, **6**
NationsBank Corporate Center, **1**
New Heritage USA, **9**
UNC Charlotte Botanical Garden and Sculpture Garden, **12**
Wing Haven Gardens and Bird Sanctuary, **7**

Books is housed in the Victorian Young-Morrison House (226 W. Tenth St.). U.S. President Taft spent the night in the **Liddell-McNinch House,** now a restaurant (511 N. Church St.) when he visited Charlotte in 1909. **Spirit Square** (345 N. College St.), in a former church, includes galleries, a performing arts center, and classrooms that used to be the sanctuary for the First Baptist Church. The **Public Library,** which contains a mural reproducing a Romare Bearden painting, is open weekdays 9–9, Saturday 9–6, and Sunday 2–6.

Other Area Attractions

You can reach the Afro-American Cultural Center, Hezekiah Alexander Homesite, Mint Museum, and Charlotte Nature Museum by city bus; for visits elsewhere, a car is needed.

From Uptown Charlotte, follow Seventh Street east to N. Myers
4 Street. The **Afro-American Cultural Center,** an arts center that has galleries and a theater, is housed in the former Little Rock AME Zion Church. *Tel. 704/374–1565. Admission free. Open Tues.–Sat. 10–6, Sun. 1–5.*

From Seventh Street, go east on Central Avenue to Eastway Drive,
5 north to Shamrock Drive, and east to the **Hezekiah Alexander Homesite and History Museum.** The stone house, built in 1774, is the oldest dwelling in the county. Here, Alexander and his wife, Mary, reared 10 children and farmed the land. Costumed docents give guided tours, and seasonal events commemorate the early days. *3500 Shamrock Dr., tel. 704/568–1774. Admission: $2 adults, $1 children 6–16. Open Tues.–Fri. 10–5, weekends 2–5.*

Follow Eastway Drive (Charlotte 4) south to Randolph Road and
6 turn right to the **Mint Museum of Art.** Built in 1837 as a U.S. Mint, it has served as a home for art since 1936, attracting such visiting exhibits as "Classical Taste in America." *2730 Randolph Rd., tel. 704/337–2000. Admission: $6 adults, $5 senior citizens, children under 12 free. Open Tues. and Fri. 10–10, Wed., Thurs., and Sat. 10–5, Sun. noon–6. Closed Christmas and New Year's Day.*

7 Continue on Charlotte 4 (Wendover Rd.) for a visit to **Wing Haven Gardens and Bird Sanctuary** in Myers Park, one of Charlotte's loveliest neighborhoods. The 3-acre garden, developed by the Clarkson family, is home to more than 135 species of birds. *248 Ridgewood Ave., tel. 704/331–0664. Admission free. Open Sun. 2–5, Tues.–Wed. 3–5 or by appointment.*

8 The **James K. Polk Memorial,** now a state historic site, marks the humble 1795 birthplace of the 11th president. Guided tours of the log cabins are available, and exhibits in the center depict early life in Mecklenburg County. *U.S. 521, Pineville, tel. 704/889–7145. Admission free. Open Mon.–Sat. 9–5, Sun. 1–5 Apr.–Oct.; Tues.–Sat. 10–4, Sun. 1–4 Nov.–Mar.*

9 Head south on I–77 for about 12 miles to **New Heritage USA,** on the South Carolina line, the 2,200-acre Christian theme park once owned by Jim and Tammy Bakker's PTL television ministry. It has reopened after being bought by a group of Malaysian businessmen, and nowadays, with no tacky solicitation, it's a very pleasant place, with an elaborate water park (open mid-May–Labor Day), paddleboats, farm animals, bike rentals, horseback riding, and shops. You can also visit Billy Graham's boyhood home, which was moved to the site. *3000 Heritage Pkwy., Fort Mill, SC, tel. 803/548–7800 or 800/374–1234. Free admission to the park and Graham house, attractions cost $1–$13.*

10 **Latta Plantation Park,** northwest of town (off I–77, near Huntersville), centers on Latta Place, a Catawba River plantation

house built by merchant James Latta in the early 1800s. Costumed guides give tours of the house. The park also has farm animals, an equestrian center, and the Carolina Raptor Center, a unique nonprofit facility where injured raptors are rehabilitated and then released. Those unable to return to the wild are cared for and used to educate visitors about the importance of bald eagles, owls, and other birds of prey. *5225 Sample Rd., Huntersville, tel. 704/875–2312 for Latta Place, 704/875–1391 for park, 704/875–6521 for Carolina Raptor Center. Admission: house tours $2 adults, $1 children. Park open daily 7* AM *to dark. House tours Tues.–Sun. at 2, 3, and 4. Carolina Raptor Center open Tues.–Sun. 10–5.*

11 Continue on I–77N to the **Energy Explorium,** operated by Duke Power Company on Lake Norman. Hands-on exhibits let you simulate the creation of nuclear power and other kinds of energy. A wildflower garden and picnic area offer diversion of a different kind. *McGuire Nuclear Plant, off I–77 and NC 73, Cornelius, tel. 704/875–5600 or 800/777–0003. Admission free. Open Mon.–Sat. 9–5, Sun. noon–5. Closed major holidays.*

12 **The UNC Charlotte Botanical Garden and Sculpture Garden,** on Route 49 off I–85, has a rhododendron garden and greenhouse with a rain forest, orchids, carnivorous plants, and cacti. Sculptures are constantly being added to the adjoining Sculpture Garden. *Rte. 49, tel. 704/547–4286. Admission free. Gardens open daylight–dark; greenhouse open weekdays 8–5 and weekends by appointment.*

13 Northeast of town on Route 29, you'll come to the **Charlotte Motor Speedway.** Learn all about racing at this state-of-the-art facility (which has condos overlooking the first turn), and take a ride in the pace car when the track is free. *Rte. 29 at Concord, tel. 704/455–3204. Admission: $3 (children under 3 free). Open Mon.–Sat. 9–4, Sun. 1–4.*

14 At the **Backing Up Classics Memory Lane Motor Car** (we're not making this up), **Museum** you can see up close some of the '50s race and muscle cars that have been the workhorses of stock-car racing. *4545 Hwy. 29, Harrisburg, tel. 704/788–9494. Admission: $4 adults, $3 senior citizens and students. Open weekdays 9–5:30, Sat. 9–5, Sun. noon–5.*

What to See and Do with Children

At **Celebration Station,** a commercial park, you can play miniature golf, ride in go-carts and bumper boats, try your skill at arcade games, stuff yourself, and watch mechanical cartoon characters entertain you. *10400 Cadillac St., Pineville, tel. 704/552–7888. Admission: $3–$4 per attraction. Open Sun.–Thurs. 10–10, Fri.–Sat. 10–midnight. Closed Thanksgiving and Christmas.*

Paramount's Carowinds, off I–77, an 83-acre theme amusement park on the South Carolina state line, has taken on a new image since its acquisition by the movie studio and the addition of new attractions based on films. Costumed movie characters and actors greet visitors to the park, and the Paladium offers musical concerts with star entertainers. *Carowinds Blvd., tel. 704/588–2600 or 800/888–4386. Admission: $24.95 adults; $13.50 senior citizens over 60 and children 4–6. Open daily June–late Aug.; weekends only Mar.–Apr., late Aug.–early Oct.*

The Nature Museum has live animals and nature exhibits. *1658 Sterling Rd. (next to Freedom Park), tel. 704/372–6261 or 800/935–0553.*

Admission: $1 (under 3 free). Open weekdays 9–5, Sat. 10–5, Sun. 1–5. Closed major holidays.

Reed Gold Mine, east of Charlotte in Cabarrus County, is where America's first gold rush began following Conrad Reed's discovery of a 17-pound nugget in 1799. Visitors may explore the underground mine shaft and gold holes, pan for gold during the summer months, learn about the history of gold mining, or enjoy a picnic. *Take NC 24/27 to Locust and follow the signs, tel. 704/786–8337. Gold panning is $3 (group rate $1 per person), but admission is free. Open Mon.–Sat. 9–5, Sun. 1–5 Apr.–Oct.; Tues.–Sat. 10–4, Sun. 1–4 Nov.–Mar.*

At the **N.C. Transportation Museum,** north of Salisbury, once a railway repair facility, a restored train takes passengers on a 45-minute ride over the 57-acre complex, with a stop at the round house. The museum, a state historic site, traces the development of transportation in North Carolina from Indian times to the present. The gift shop sells some unique train memorabilia. *Off I–85 at Spencer, tel. 704/636–2889. Admission free. Train rides $2.50–$3.50. Open Mon.–Sat. 9–5, Sun. 1–5 Apr. 1–Oct. 10; Tues.–Sat. 10–4, Sun. 1–4 Nov.–Mar.*

Shopping

Charlotte is the largest retail center in the Carolinas, with the majority of stores in suburban malls. Villages and towns in outlying areas offer some regional specialties. Uptown shops are open 10–5:30 daily except Sunday. Malls are open Monday–Saturday 10–9 and Sunday 1–6. Sales tax is 6%.

Shopping Districts You can buy well-known brands at a discount in outlets in **Midtown Square** near Uptown; **Cotswold Mall,** 1 mile east of Uptown; **Windsor Square** near Matthews; **Outlet Marketplace,** off I–77 near Carowinds; and **Cannon Village** at Kannapolis.

Carolina Place at Pineville is the newest mall in the area, with Belk, Dillard's, Hecht's, and JC Penney as anchors. Next, SouthPark, in the most affluent section of the city, caters to upscale customers. Belk, Dillard's, Hecht's, Montaldo's, and Sears are here. **Specialty Shops on the Park,** across from Southpark, is another cluster of expensive shops. **The Arboretum,** also on the south side, offers upscale mall shops and restaurants. **Eastland Mall,** on the east side of town, features an ice-skating rink, plus Dillard's, Belk, JC Penney, Sears, and other retail stores.

Specialty Stores

Antiques The towns of Waxhaw, Pineville, and Matthews are the best places to find antiques. Each has a number of shops, and Waxhaw sponsors an annual antiques fair each February. Shops are usually open Monday through Saturday in Pineville and Matthews. In Waxhaw, some shops are open on Sunday but closed on Monday. You can also find a good selection of antiques at the **Metrolina Expo** (off I–77N at 7100 Statesville Rd.) on the first and third weekends of the month.

Books There are some excellent bookshops in Charlotte. Sure bets are the **Little Professor Book Center** in the Park Road shopping center, **Barnes & Noble Bookstore** (5837 E. Independence Blvd., Charlotte, and 10701 Centrum Pkwy., Pineville) and **Poplar Street Books** in Fourth Ward. **The International News stand** (5636 E. Independence Blvd) carries publications from around the world.

Crafts The best buys are in the **Metrolina Expo** (*see* Antiques, *above*). At the **Carolina Craft Shows,** held in the fall and spring at the Convention Center, as well as the **Southern Christmas Show** and the **Southern Spring Show** at the Merchandise Mart, you can buy a wide variety.

Food and Plants Try the **Charlotte Regional Farmers Market** (1715 Yorkmount Rd.) for fresh produce and fish, plants, and crafts. The **Harris-Teeter** grocery store in Morrocroft Village (6701 Morrison Blvd., tel. 704/364–1245) is a white-columned showplace with a staff chef who oversees an elaborate dine-in deli and the two other stores.

Participant Sports

Bicycling North Carolina has designated bike tours stretching from the coast to the mountains. There is one between Southpark and Uptown Charlotte. Route maps are available from the NC Department of Transportation (Box 25201, Raleigh 27611).

Camping Near Charlotte, try McDowell Park and Nature Reserve, Carowinds and Duke Power State Park. Close by, in South Carolina, try Kings Mountain State Park.

Canoeing Inlets on Lake Norman and Lake Wylie are ideal for canoeing, as are some spots of the Catawba River. The Pee Dee River east of Charlotte and the New River in the mountains offer other options.

Fishing There's good fishing in Charlotte's neighboring lakes and streams. A mandatory state license can be bought at local bait and tackle shops or over the phone (with a credit card) from the North Carolina Wildlife Commission (tel. 919/715–4091).

Golf Charlotte has several good public golf courses, among them Crystal Springs, Renaissance, and Pebble Creek. The Visitor Information Center (tel. 704/371–8700) can provide a complete list.

Hiking Crowder's Mountain and Kings Mountain near Gastonia and the Uwharrie Mountains east of Charlotte offer plenty of varied terrain and challenge for hikers.

Jogging Jogging trails and tracks can be found in most city and county parks and at many local schools. Contact the Mecklenburg County Park and Recreation Department (tel. 704/336–3854).

Swimming The **Mecklenburg County Aquatic Center** (800 E. 2nd St., tel. 704/336–3483) has a 50-meter lap pool, a hydro-therapy pool, fitness room, and whirlpool. It is open daily to local residents and visitors. *Admission: $4 nonresident adults, $3 children under 19.*

Tennis Courts are available in several city parks, including Freedom, Hornet's Nest, Park Road, and Veterans. A growing number of hotels and motels provide courts as well. For details, call the Charlotte Park and Recreation Department (tel. 704/336–2464).

Spectator Sports

Baseball The Charlotte Knights play April–August at Knights Castle, I–77 and Gold Hill Road, in South Carolina (tel. 704/332–3746 or 803/548–8051).

Basketball The Charlotte Hornets play from November to April at the Charlotte Coliseum on Tyvola Road, off the Billy Graham Parkway (tel. 704/357–0489).

Racing NASCAR races, such as the **Coca-Cola 600** and **Winston Champion Spark Plug 300,** draw huge crowds at the Charlotte Motor Speedway near Concord. For tickets, call 704/455–3200.

Dining

There are many good places to eat in Charlotte, including various foreign restaurants. Local specialties include barbecued pork and chicken, fresh seafood, fried chicken, and country ham. Hush puppies, made from cornmeal batter and deep-fried in fat, almost always accompany fish and barbecue. Grits is another Southern specialty widely served in North Carolina, usually with breakfast. There is also a good selection of places that feature steaks and prime ribs of beef. The number of ethnic restaurants is increasing.

The most highly recommended restaurants in each price category are indicated by a star ★.

Category	Cost*
$$$$	over $20
$$$	$15–$20
$$	$10–$15
$	under $10

**per person without tax (6% in Charlotte), service, or drinks*

American
$$–$$$ ★ **Longhorn Steaks Restaurant and Saloon.** Longneck beers, buckets of roasted peanuts, and Margaritas will help you make it through the wait, which stretches to an hour on weekends at this popular watering hole. The menu concentrates on steaks, including a filet mignon as thick and tender as any you'll ever order. Other Longhorns are in Crown Pointe in Matthews and on Highway 51 near Pineville. *700 E. Morehead St., tel. 704/332–2300. No reservations. Dress: informal. AE, MC, V.*

Providence Café. Many of the dishes (especially the sandwiches) served in this chic, contemporary eatery, center around the foccacia that is baked daily on the premises. The eclectic menu also includes chicken, steaks, and seafood grilled over green hickory wood. It's a great place for Sunday brunch and after-hours desserts with cappuccino or espresso. *110 Perrin Pl., tel. 704/376–2008. No reservations on weekends. Dress: casual. AE, DC, MC, V.*

$–$$ ★ **Grady's American Grill.** Packed every night of the week, this restaurant has earned praise from patrons for its friendly service and excellent food. Favorites are the greenhouse salad served with honey-mustard dressing, the mesquite-grilled chicken or fish, and the hot chocolate bar cake. There's usually a wait of 30 minutes to an hour, but the time passes quickly at the lively bar. *5546 Albemarle Rd., tel. 704/537–4663. No reservations. Dress: informal. AE, DC, MC, V.*

Newmarket Grille. You can enjoy a variety of moderately priced dishes, including soups, sandwiches, salads, pastas, steak, and fish, within the rich mahogany walls of this restaurant in the Arboretum Shopping Center on the south side. Outdoor dining is also an option, and there's a cozy, dark bar for getting together with friends. *8136 Providence Rd., tel.704/543–4656. No reservations. Dress: informal. AE, DC, MC, V.*

$ **Landmark Restaurant-Diner.** This New York–style eatery in the Eastland Mall neighborhood is a cut above most inexpensive restaurants, and it's open until 3 AM on weeknights and 24 hours on weekends. Decorated in contemporary colors, this spacious restaurant is a good place for an informal breakfast, lunch, dinner, or after-hours des-

sert. (Ask for the New York–style cheesecake from the in-house bakery.) *4429 Central Ave., tel. 704/532–1153. Reservations accepted for parties of 8 or more. Dress: casual. AE, MC, V. Closed Christmas Day.*

Chinese *$$* **The Ginger Root.** Relaxation is guaranteed the moment you step into the quiet, peaceful atmosphere of this Uptown restaurant, convenient to the art centers and galleries. Ideal for lunch or dinner, the restaurant offers pork, chicken, beef, and seafood dishes, served Hunan, Szechuan, Yu Shawn, or Kao Pao style. There's also a comfortable bar. *201 E. Fifth St., tel. 704/377–9429. Reservations advised. Dress: casual. AE, DC, MC, V.*

Continental *$$$$* ★ **The Lamplighter.** You don't have to go abroad to find gourmet cuisine served in an elegant setting. Just step into the softly lit, sophisticated atmosphere of The Lamplighter, in an old Dilworth home. The trio combination entrées (beef, veal, and lamb, or different seafoods) are exceptional, and the wine list is extensive. There's a quiet, intimate lounge for cocktails. *1065 E. Morehead St., tel. 704/372–5343. Reservations advised. Jacket advised. AE, DC, MC, V.*

$$ **Pewter Rose Bistro.** In a renovated textile mill in historic Dilworth, 5 minutes from Uptown, the Pewter Rose Bistro is a favorite hangout for Charlotte's young professionals. Lace curtains and plants decorate the dining room, and the kitchen specializes in fresh seasonal foods, plus a variety of chicken and seafood dishes. *1820 South Blvd., tel. 704/332–8149. No reservations. Dress: informal. AE, D, MC, V. Closed Sun., Mon.*

Italian *$$$$* **Bravo!** Authentic classic Italian cuisine is served in a Mediterranean-style atmosphere at this hotel restaurant, the "in" place for special celebrations and Sunday brunches. A fixed-price dinner, including an appetizer, salad, entrée, dessert, and coffee for $18.95, plus tax and gratuity, is offered Monday–Thursday. The professionally trained singing waitresses and waiters never seem to tire of performing or graciously serving. *Adams Mark Hotel, 555 S. McDowell St., tel. 704/372–5440. Reservations advised. Jacket advised. AE, D, MC, V.*

$–$$ **PizZarrelli Trattoria.** The secret to the unique flavor of the made-from-scratch pizzas is in the wood-burning brick ovens, built by Italian masons. The menu also features calzone, lasagna, spaghetti, and other Southern Italian dishes—all family recipes and especially good when served with the mellow house wine. The tables are covered with red-checked gingham, and the walls are adorned with posters and photographs that chronicle the professional singing career of owner Neal Zarrelli, a former opera star who often sings for his customers. *9101 Pineville-Matthews Rd., Pineville, tel. 704/543–0647. Reservations not required. Dress: casual. No credit cards.*

Japanese *$$–$$$* **Kabuto Japanese House of Steaks.** The chef's preparation and cooking of food tableside is all the entertainment you need at this restaurant. Fish, chicken, and steak are prepared along with fresh vegetables. Sushi and sashimi are also available. *446 Tyvola Rd., tel. 704/529–0659; in Town Center Plaza, U.S. 49 near UNC–Charlotte, tel. 704/548–1219. Reservations advised. Dress: informal. AE, D, DC, MC, V. Closed major holidays.*

Lodging

Approximately 16,000 hotels rooms are available in the Charlotte area, from economy motels to convention hotels or bed-and-breakfast houses. Most of the major chains are represented, from Hilton, Hyatt, and Sheraton, to EconoLodge, Days Inn, and Motel 6. Some hotels offer great weekend packages. A 6% accommodations tax and 6% sales tax are added to every room charge. Pick up the "Charlotte Visitors Guide" for a more comprehensive list.

The most highly recommended properties in each price category are indicated by a star ★.

Category	Cost*
$$$$	over $100
$$$	$60–$100
$$	$30–$60
$	under $30

**double room; add 12% for taxes*

Hotels
$$$
★

The Dunhill. Charlotte's oldest and most historic hotel (built in 1929) features artwork by Philip Moose and 18th- and 19th-century reproduction furniture in the lobby, restaurant, and guest rooms. The restaurant, **Monticello's,** gets rave reviews for its beautifully presented California cuisine. A complimentary Continental breakfast is served here as well. *237 N. Tryon St., 28202, tel. 704/332–4141 or 800/354–4141, fax 704/376–4117. 59 rooms and 1 penthouse with Jacuzzi. Facilities: restaurant, lounge. AE, D, DC, MC, V.*

Embassy Suites. An eight-story atrium distinguishes this all-suite hotel, near the airport and the Coliseum. Guests have the option of regular suites (which have two rooms, plus a coffee maker, refrigerator, microwave, and regular amenities) or 12 upgraded suites, four of which have Jacuzzis. Guests are served a cooked-to-order full breakfast and are treated to an afternoon reception. *4800 S. Tryon St., 28217, tel. 704/527–8400 or 800/362–2779, fax 704/527–7035. 274 suites. Facilities: indoor pool, whirlpool, sauna, health club, restaurant, lounge, meeting rooms, airport transportation. AE, D, DC, MC, V.*

Hilton at University Place. This high-rise with a three-story atrium dominates the European-style shopping and entertainment village near the University of North Carolina at Charlotte. Movies, restaurants, shops, a bank, and even a hospital are just a few steps from the hotel door. Dining is offered in the Lakefront Café. *8629 J.M. Keynes Blvd., 28262, tel. 704/547–7444 or 800/445–8667, fax 704/548–1081. 243 rooms and suites. Facilities: restaurant, bar, fitness center, outdoor lap pool, beach club, paddleboats, meeting rooms, airport transportation. AE, D, DC, MC, V.*

Hyatt Charlotte SouthPark. The focal point of the four-story atrium is a Mexican water fountain surrounded by 25-foot olive trees. Meeting rooms and the lower lobby give onto the open-air courtyard. Scalini's restaurant serves Northern Italian cuisine; The Club piano bar is a favorite with the after-hours crowd. Guest rooms are equipped with data ports for lap-top computers and fax machines. *5501 Carnegie Blvd., 28209–3462, tel. 704/554–1234 or 800/233–1234, fax 704/554–8319. 267 rooms and suites. Facilities: restaurant, indoor pool, Jacuzzi, sauna, whirlpool, health club, meeting rooms, airport transportation. AE, D, DC, MC, V.*

Omni Charlotte Hotel. The pink marble used in the public rooms makes this one of Charlotte's classiest Uptown hotels. Guests can enjoy the ambience of C. Banknight's Bistro and Bar and then work out with Charlotte's movers and shakers in the adjoining 50,000-

square-foot YMCA, which includes an indoor track and a lap pool. For special pampering, stay on the Club levels or in the Presidential Suite. *222 E. 3rd St. 28202, tel. 704/377–6664 or 800/843–6664, fax 704/377–4143. 410 rooms. Facilities: restaurant, bar, indoor pool, health club, meeting rooms, airport transportation. AE, D, DC, MC, V.*

Radisson Plaza Hotel. Convenience and contemporary elegance are yours at this property just steps from The Square and the center of Uptown. It's also connected to the Overstreet Mall, a complex of shops and restaurants. Try dining at the Azaleas American Grill. All guests get complimentary newspapers and free parking. *1 Radisson Plaza, 101 S. Tryon St., 28280, tel. 704/377–0400 or 800/333–3333, fax 704/347–0649. 368 rooms and suites. Facilities: restaurant, bar, outdoor pool, health club, sauna, meeting rooms, airport transportation. AE, D, DC, MC, V.*

$ **Comfort Inn–Lake Norman.** This economy motel, north of Charlotte on I–77 near Lake Norman, offers complimentary breakfast and rooms with refrigerators and coffee makers. Some rooms also have VCRs, microwaves, and whirlpool baths. *20740 Torrence Chapel Rd., Davidson 28036, tel. 704/892–3500 or 800/221–2222, fax 704/892–6473. 90 rooms. Facilities: pool, health club privileges, laundry. AE, D, DC, MC, V.*

Bed-and-Breakfasts
$$–$$$

The Inn on Providence. Darlene and Dan McNeill offer luxurious bedrooms with private baths, plus a home-cooked breakfast. Guests enjoy the spacious grounds and swimming pool in this quiet southeast Charlotte neighborhood. *6700 Providence Rd., 28226, tel. 704/366–6700. 5 rooms. AE, MC, V.*

$$ ★ **The Homeplace.** This spotless turn-of-the-century Victorian gem is now a bed-and-breakfast inn filled with antiques and memorabilia from yesteryear. The inn's guest rooms all have private baths, and breakfast is prepared by owners Peggy and Frank Darien. The Homeplace is in a residential neighborhood. *5901 Sardis Rd., 27270, tel. 704/365–1936. 4 rooms. AE, MC, V.*

The Morehead Inn. Though it's a commercial venture catering to corporate clients, this Dilworth inn has all the comforts of a beautiful home. Wedding parties find it ideal. A Continental breakfast comes with the room. *1122 E. Morehead St., 28204, tel. 704/376–3357, fax 704/335–1110. 11 rooms. Facilities: meeting rooms. AE, DC, MC, V.*

Nightlife

Bailey's Billiard and Bar (5873 Albemarle Rd., tel. 704/532–1005 and 8500 Pineville-Matthews Rd., tel. 704/541–0794) offers billiards in an upscale setting and deli-style food.

Beau's (The Park Hotel, tel. 704/364–8220) is a popular spot for the young set to see and be seen.

Blockbuster Pavilion (707 Blockbuster Blvd., tel. 704/549–1292) and the **Paladium Amphitheater** at Paramount's Carowinds (14523 Carowinds Blvd., tel. 704/588–2600 or 800/888–4386) present stars in concert mid-spring through mid-fall. Ticket prices vary.

Comedy Zone (5317 E. Independence Blvd., tel. 704/568–4242) showcases live comedy nightly except Mondays, with two shows nightly on weekends.

Giorgio's Northern Italian Ristorante & Piano Bar (5301 E. Independence Blvd., tel. 704/535–7525), with nightly entertainment, is a great place to get together with friends.

Lizzie's (4809 S. Tryon St., tel. 704/527–3064), a restaurant on the south side, is best known for its piano bar, occasionally featuring owner Liz King.

The Triangle

The cities of Raleigh, Durham, and Chapel Hill make up "The Triangle," so called because together they form a triangle, with Raleigh to the east, Durham to the north, and Chapel Hill to the west, and because of the Research Triangle Park—a complex of public and private research facilities between the three cities which attracts scientists from all over the world. Although the cities lie within 30 miles of each other and all three can be cursorily visited in one day, plan to spend at least a day in each because of their unique character.

Raleigh is Old South and New South, down-home and upscale, all in one. Named for Sir Walter Raleigh (who established the first English colony on the coast in 1585), Raleigh is the state capital and the largest and busiest of the three cities. The state's largest and best museums are here, as are North Carolina State University and six other universities and colleges.

Durham, a tobacco town for decades (and once called Bull Durham, after one of the many brands of tobacco manufactured here), is now known as the City of Medicine, for the nationally known medical and research centers at Duke University. With more than 20,000 employees, Duke is not only the largest employer in Durham, it's one of the largest employers in the state.

Chapel Hill may be the smallest city in The Triangle, but its reputation as a seat of learning—and of liberalism—looms large indeed. The home of the state's first college, the University of North Carolina, Chapel Hill remains a quiet, tree-shaded small town that is crowded with students and retirees.

Politics and basketball are always hot topics throughout The Triangle. The NCAA basketball championship has been won by one of the area's three schools three of the past six years.

Arriving and Departing

By Plane The **Raleigh–Durham International Airport** (RDU, tel. 919/840–2123), between the two cities off I–40, is the regional hub for American Airlines and connects the area with Paris, Cancun, Bermuda, Puerto Rico, Nassau, and the U.S. Virgin Islands. American, Delta, TWA, United, and USAir and their regional affiliates together offer approximately 250 daily flights. If you're driving to Raleigh, take I–40 east to Exit 285; for Chapel Hill, take I–40 west; for Durham, also take I–40 west to NC 147. It takes about 20 minutes to get to any of the three cities.

By Train **Amtrak** (320 W. Cabarrus St., tel. 919/833–7594 or 800/872–7245) has one daily train northbound and one southbound, with stops in Raleigh and Durham. Service to Charlotte is also offered daily.

By Bus **Greyhound Lines** (tel. 800/231–2222) serves Raleigh, Durham, and Chapel Hill.

By Car I-40 and U.S. 401 form something of a perimeter route around Raleigh. I-40 runs west of downtown (to Durham and Chapel Hill), joining I-85 on the west side and I-95 on the east side. U.S. 1, which runs north and south, also links to I-85 going northeast. U.S. 64 and U.S. 70 run east-west through Raleigh.

Getting Around

By Bus **Capital Area Transit** (tel. 919/828-7228) is Raleigh's public transport system. Fares are 50¢ (25¢ for senior citizens). Children under 4 ride free.

Chapel Hill Transit (tel. 919/968-2769) buses serve the city.

Triangle Transit Authority (tel. 919/549-9999), which links downtown Raleigh with the Research Triangle Park, Durham, and Chapel Hill, runs weekdays except major holidays. Fares: $1 for a 10-mile trip, $1.50 for 15 miles, and $2 for 20 miles. Senior citizens and riders with disabilities pay half fare.

By Taxi Approximately 28 taxi companies serve The Triangle. Fares are calculated by the mile.

By Trolley The **Trolley Through Raleigh** makes six stops around the city, including City Market and the Capital Area Visitor Center. *Tel. 919/833-5701. Trolley runs weekdays, 10-2. Fare: 10¢.* On the third Saturday of each month, Mordecai Historic Park (*see below*) runs a **historic trolley tour** of Raleigh (12:30-4 PM, $3 adults, $1 children 7-17), with a pickup at the Amtrak station by advance arrangement.

Important Addresses and Numbers

Tourist Information **The Greater Raleigh Convention and Visitors Bureau** offers information on the area. *225 Hillsborough St., Suite 400, tel. 919/834-5900 or 800/849-8499.*

The Durham Convention & Visitors Bureau provides information on that city. *101 E. Morgan St., Durham 27701, tel. 919/688-2855 or 800/772-2855.*

Chapel Hill/Orange County Visitors Bureau (Box 600, Chapel Hill 27514, tel. 919/968-2060).

Emergencies Dial 911 for **police** or **ambulance** in an emergency.

Doctor Hospital emergency rooms are open 24 hours a day. For minor emergencies, the city has 10 urgent-care centers. **The Wake County Medical Society** (tel. 919/821-2227) can refer you to a doctor.

Pharmacies **Kerr Drug Store** (Lake Boone Shopping Center, 2462 Wyclif Rd., Raleigh, tel. 919/781-4070), is open 24 hours. **Eckerd Drugs** (3527 Hillsborough Rd., Durham, tel. 919/383-5591) is open 7 AM-midnight.

Guided Tours

Capital Area Visitor Center provides maps, brochures, and free tours of the executive mansion, state capitol, legislative building, and other government buildings. *301 N. Blount St., tel. 919/733-3456. Open weekdays 8-5, Sat. 9-5, Sun. 1-5.*

Exploring the Triangle

Raleigh Raleigh is spread out, so a car is almost a necessity unless you limit your sightseeing to downtown, where the streets are laid out in an orderly grid fashion with the State Capitol as the hub. Most of the attractions in the downtown Raleigh walking tour are state government and historic buildings and are free to the public. You'll need several hours just to hit the high spots, even more time if you tend to get hooked on museums.

State Capitol Walking Tour

After stopping in at the Capital Area Visitor Center to pick up maps and brochures, begin your tour at the **State Capitol,** a beautifully preserved example of Greek Revival architecture, which once housed all the functions of state government. Finished in 1840 and restored during the 1976 Bicentennial, its rich wood furnishings and elaborate decoration give it a special warmth not found in the more contemporary 1960s State Legislative Building. *Capitol Sq., tel. 919/733–4994. Open weekdays 8–5, Sat. 9–5, Sun. 1–5. Closed certain holidays.*

The **State Legislative Building,** on the corner of Salisbury and Jones streets, sits one block north of the capitol. When the legislature is in session, it hums with lawmakers and lobbyists, and it's fun to watch from the gallery. A free guided tour is available through the Visitor Center (*see above*). *Salisbury and Jones Sts., tel. 919/733–7928. Open weekdays 8–5, Sat. 9–5, Sun. 1–5.*

A half block away is the **North Carolina Museum of Natural Sciences,** where you can check out the massive skeletons of whales and dinosaurs or watch volunteers cleaning fossil bones. The gift shop sells some unusual souvenirs. *102 N. Salisbury St., tel. 919/733–7450. Open Mon.–Sat. 9–5, Sun. 1–5.*

Adjacent to the Museum of Natural Sciences, on Bicentennial Plaza, is the **North Carolina Museum of History.** Opened in 1994, the museum combines artifacts, audiovisual programs, and interactive exhibits to bring the state's history to life. Exhibits include the N.C. Sports Hall of Fame, N.C. Folklife, and Women Making History. *1 East Edenton St., tel. 919/715–0200. Open Tues.–Sat. 9–5, Sun. 1–6.*

The **Executive Mansion** (200 N. Blount St., tel. 919/733–3456), is a brick turn-of-the-century Queen Anne cottage-style structure with gingerbread trim. Tour hours vary; check with the Capital Area Visitor Center. A stroll through the nearby **Oakwood Historic District** will introduce you to more fine examples of Victorian architecture.

The revitalized **City Market** (Martin St. and Moore Sq.) is home to specialty shops, art galleries, restaurants, and **Playspace,** a children's educational play center. Trolleys shuttle between downtown and the market at lunchtime; the fare is only 10¢. *Tel. 919/828–4555. Stores open Mon.–Sat. 10–5:30; restaurants, Mon.–Sat. 7 AM–1 AM and Sun. 11:30–10.*

Fayetteville Street Mall extends from the State Capitol to the Raleigh Civic and Convention Center. Open to pedestrians only, it has a variety of shops, a couple of restaurants, and a bronze statue of Sir Walter Raleigh.

The **North Carolina Museum of Art** (Hillsborough St. west) exhibits art from ancient Egyptian times to the present, from the Old World and the New. The **Museum Café** is open for lunch Tuesday–Sunday, with live entertainment Friday evening. *2110 Blue Ridge Blvd., tel. 919/833–1935 (restaurant tel. 919/833–3548). Free guided tours daily at 1:30 PM. Open Tues.–Thurs. and Sat. 9–5, Fri. 9–9, Sun. 11–6.*

From downtown, follow Hargett St. east to the **Wakefield/Joel Lane House.** The oldest dwelling in Raleigh and the home of the landowner "father of Raleigh" dates to the 1760s. *728 W. Hargett & St. Mary's Sts., tel. 919/833–3431. Admission free. Open Mar.–mid-Dec., Tues., Thurs., and Fri. 10–2.*

Return on Hargett Street through downtown to Person Street and then take it north to **Mordecai Historic Park** to see some early buildings that were moved within the park, including a house dating to 1785 and the house where President Andrew Johnson was born. One-hour guided tours are given. *One Mimosa St., tel. 919/834–4844. Tour: $3 adults, $1 children 7–17. Open weekdays 10–3, weekends 1:30–3:30.*

Durham From Raleigh, take I–40 west to the Durham Freeway (NC 147), which brings you into downtown Durham and **Duke University.** A stroll along the beautiful tree-lined streets of the campus, which are dominated by Gothic-style buildings, is a lovely way to spend a few hours.

A right onto Anderson Street from the Durham Freeway brings you to the 55-acre **Sarah P. Duke Gardens,** complete with a wisteria-draped gazebo and a Japanese garden with a lily pond teeming with fat goldfish. *Main entrance on Anderson St., West Campus, tel. 919/684–3698. Open daily 8 AM to dusk.*

Head west on Campus Drive to Chapel Drive. The Gothic-style **Duke Chapel,** built in the early 1930s, is the centerpiece of the campus. Modeled after Canterbury Cathedral, it has 77 stained glass windows and a 210-foot bell tower. *West Campus, tel. 919/684–3214. Open during daylight hours.*

Time Out Return to Anderson Street, head north on Anderson to Hillsborough Road, and take Hillsborough east to 9th Street. At **McDonald's Drug Store** (732 9th St., tel. 919/286–2770), an old-fashioned soda fountain serves up the best milkshakes in town.

African-American art is showcased at the **North Carolina Central University Art Museum,** south of the Durham Freeway on Fayetteville Street. *1801 Fayetteville St., tel. 919/560–6211. Admission free. Open Tues.–Fri. 9–5, Sun. 2–5.*

From the Durham Freeway, take U.S. 501N (Roxboro Rd.) to **West Point on the Eno.** On the banks of the Eno River, this city park has a restored mill. *5000 Roxboro Rd., tel. 919/471–1623. Admission free. Open daily 8 AM–sunset (historic buildings open weekends only).*

West of the park on Cole Mill Road, the 2,064-acre **Eno River State Park** has hiking trails, historic homes and mills, and Class II rapids. *Rte. 2, Box 436-C, 27705, tel. 919/383–1686. Admission free. Open daily 8 AM–sunset.*

Chapel Hill U.S. 15–501 takes you from Durham into Chapel Hill. **Morehead Planetarium,** where the original Apollo astronauts and many since have trained, was the first planetarium in the state. Visitors can learn about the constellations and take in laser light shows. *East Franklin St., tel. 919/549–6863. Admission: $3 adults, $2.50 children, students, and senior citizens. Open Sun.–Fri. 12:30–5 and 7 PM–9:45 PM, Sat. 10–5 and 7 PM–9:45 PM.*

After leaving the planetarium, walk left on East Franklin Street a couple of blocks, into the heart of downtown Chapel Hill. **Franklin Street,** lined with bicycle shops, bookstores, clothing stores, restaurants and coffee shops, and flower vendors on the sidewalk, runs along the northern edge of the **University of North Carolina** campus, which is dotted with oak-shaded courtyards and stately old buildings.

Follow U.S. 15–501S to the **N.C. Botanical Garden.** Two miles of nature trails wind through a 300-acre Piedmont forest; there's also a legendary herb garden, one of the southeast's largest. *CB 3375, Totten Center, 27599, tel. 919/962–0522. Admission free. Open weekdays 8–5, daily 8–5 March–mid-Nov.*

What to See and Do with Children

Pullen Park (520 Ashe Ave., near NCSU, tel. 919/831–6468 or 919/831–6640) attracts large crowds during the summer to its 1911 Dentzel carousel and train ride. You can swim here, too, and enjoy an arts and crafts center and the Theater in the Park.

At the **North Carolina Museum of Life and Science,** you can create a 15-foot tornado, pilot an Apollo capsule, encounter near life-size models of dinosaurs on the nature trail, and ride a train through a 78-acre wildlife sanctuary. The nature center has such native North Carolina animals as flying squirrels. *433 Murray Ave., off I–85 in Durham, tel. 919/220–5429. Admission: $5 adults, $3.50 senior citizens and children 3–12, under 3 free. Open Mon.–Sat. 10–6, Sun. 1–6.*

Off the Beaten Track

Bennett Place. In this farmhouse in Durham in April 1865, Confederate General Joseph E. Johnston disobeyed President Jefferson Davis's order to retreat and instead surrendered to U.S. General William T. Sherman. The two generals then set forth the terms for a "permanent peace" between the South and the North. Historic reenactments are held annually. *4409 Bennett Memorial Rd., Durham 27705, tel. 919/383–4345. Admission free. Open Apr.–Oct., Mon.–Sat. 9–5, Sun. 1–5; Nov.–Mar. Tues.–Sat. 10–4, Sun. 1–4.*

Shopping

Shopping Districts

Fearrington Village, a planned community 8 miles south of Chapel Hill on U.S. 15–501, has a number of upscale shops selling art, garden items, handmade jewelry, and more. **Franklin Street** in Chapel Hill has a wonderful collection of shops, including bookstores, art galleries, crafts shops, and clothing stores. Durham's **9th Street** has funky shops and restaurants that cater to the hip student crowd.

Shopping Malls

Brightleaf Square (905 W. Main St., Durham) is an upscale shopping-entertainment complex housed in old tobacco warehouses in the heart of downtown.

Cameron Village Shopping Center (1900 Cameron St.), Raleigh's oldest shopping center and one of the first in the Southeast, is anchored by JC Penney and Hecht's and contains a Talbot's and Fresh Market.

Crabtree Valley Mall (Glenwood Ave.; U.S. 70) is Raleigh's largest enclosed mall. Stores include Belk, Sears, and Hecht's.

North Hills Mall (Six Forks Rd. and Beltline) offers the latest in high fashion. Stores include Montaldo's, Tyler House, and Dillard's.

Specialty Stores

Art/Antiques

City Market (Martin St. at Moore Sq., tel. 919/828–4555) is a revitalized shopping area with a number of shops selling antiques and art. Check out Artspace, a gallery where you can watch artists at work in their glassed-in studios.

Books

The Intimate Bookshop (119 E. Franklin St., Chapel Hill, tel. 919/929–0411), a town mainstay for years, recently re-opened after a fire destroyed the building and many rare books collected by owner Wallace Kuralt (brother of former CBS commentator Charles Kuralt, one of UNC's most famous graduates).

At **McIntyre's Fine Books** (Fearrington Village, tel. 919/542–3030), you can curl up and read in an armchair by the fire in one of the cozy library rooms.

Flea Markets

North Carolina State Flea Market. You can find anything and everything here—from fine antiques to "early attic" furniture. *Hillsborough St. and Blue Ridge Rd., tel. 919/832–0361. Open weekends 9–5.*

Another option is the **Raleigh Flea Market Mall.** *1924 Capital Blvd., tel. 919/839–0038. Open weekends 9–5.*

Food

Farmer's Market. This 60-acre market includes a garden center and a "down-home"-style restaurant. *Lake Wheeler Rd. and I–40, tel. 919/733–7417 (market) or 919/833–7973 (restaurant). Open 24 hrs, June–Sept.; 5 AM–6 PM Mon.–Sat. and 1–6 Sun., Oct.–May.*

9th Street Bakery (776 9th St., Durham, tel. 919/286–0303) is earning a reputation throughout the state for its baked goods.

A Southern Season (Eastgate Mall, Chapel Hill, tel. 919/929–7133 or 800/253–3663) offers such Tar Heel treats as cheese, wine, barbecue sauces, peanuts, turkeys, and hams.

Wellspring Grocery (737 9th St., Durham, tel. 919/286–2290) has outstanding fresh produce and the widest selection of health foods in town.

Men's Clothing

Julians College Shop (140 E. Franklin St., Chapel Hill, tel. 919/942–4563) is owned by the parents of designer Alexander Julian, a Chapel Hill native.

Participant Sports

Bicycling

Raleigh has more than 25 miles of greenways for biking, and maps are available at Raleigh Parks and Recreation (tel. 919/890–3285). Chapel Hill is a great town for biking; for a bicycling map, contact the Chapel Hill/Orange County visitors Bureau (*see* Tourist Information *above*).

Camping

Try the North Carolina State Fairgrounds, William B. Umstead State Park, Eno River State Park at Durham, Clemmons State Forest near Clayton, or Jordan Lake between Apex and Pittsboro. Other options are Lake Gaston and Kerr Lake near the Virginia line. *For details, call the Raleigh Convention and Visitors Bureau, tel. 919/834–5900 or 800/849–8499, or the North Carolina Division of Travel and Tourism, tel. 919/733–4171 or 800/VISIT–NC.*

Canoeing

Lake Wheeler and Shelley Lake are the best places for canoeing. The Eno River State Park near Durham is another option. The Haw River is popular as well, but can be treacherous after a heavy rain.

Fishing

You can buy a fishing license at local bait-and-tackle shops or over the phone (with a credit card) from the North Carolina Wildlife Commission (tel. 919/715–4091).

Golf The Raleigh area has about 10 golf courses open to the public, including **Wildwood Green Golf Club** and **Wake Forest Country Club.** A complete list of courses is available from the Raleigh Convention and Visitors Bureau (tel. 919/834–5900 or 800/849–8499).

Finley Golf Course (Chapel Hill, tel. 919/962–2349), on the UNC campus, is open to the public; greens fees range from $16 to $32. For a list of Durham's public courses, contact the Durham Convention and Visitors Bureau (tel. 919/687–0288 or 800/446–8604).

Hiking Jordan Lake, Lake Wheeler, and William B. Umstead State Park in Raleigh, and Eno River State Park and Duke Forest in Durham, offer thousands of acres for hiking. For trail information, call the North Carolina Division of Travel and Tourism (tel. 919/733–4171 or 800/VISIT–NC).

Jogging Runners frequent Shelley Lake, the track at NCSU, and the Capitol Area Greenway system.

Physical Fitness The YMCA (1601 Hillsborough St., tel. 919/832–6601) will permit visitors to use their facilities for $3–$10, provided they have a YMCA membership elsewhere. The Y also accepts guests staying at certain local hotels. Hotels with fitness centers are noted in the accommodations listings.

River Rafting You can shoot the rapids at Eno River State Park (*see* Exploring Durham, *above*).

Skiing (*See* the North Carolina High Country and Asheville sections, *below*).

Tennis More than 80 courts in Raleigh city parks are available for use. Millbrook Exchange Park (1905 Spring Forest Rd.) holds city tournaments. (For more details on tennis courts in Raleigh, call 919/876–2616.) For information on Durham's six public courts, call the Parks and Recreation Department (tel. 919/560–4355).

Spectator Sports

Baseball The **Durham Bulls** play at the Durham Athletic Park (426 Morris St., Durham, tel. 919/688–8211).

Basketball The Triangle is basketball heaven with three Atlantic Coast Conference teams: Duke's **Blue Devils** (tel. 919/681–2583), the University of North Carolina's **Tarheels** (tel. 919/962–2296), and North Carolina State University's **Wolfpack** (tel. 919/515–2106).

Ice Hockey The **Raleigh Ice Caps** compete in Dorton Arena at NC State Fairgrounds (tel. 919/755–0022).

Tennis The **Raleigh Edge** professional tennis team plays in the Raleigh Civic & Convention Center (tel. 919/878–7788).

Dining

Dining in The Triangle is both sophisticated and down-home. There are many upscale restaurants, as well as informal places where barbecue, Brunswick stew, fried chicken, and lots of country vegetables are served in great quantities for very low prices. Dress is usually casual.

Category	Cost*
$$$$	over $25
$$$	$15–$25
$$	$8–$15
$	under $8

**per person without tax (6%), service, or drinks*

Chapel Hill *$$–$$$* **Aurora.** In a historic cotton mill on the edge of downtown Chapel Hill, Aurora specializes in northern Italian cuisine. The changing menu sometimes includes succulent sea scallops and shiitake mushrooms sautéed in rosemary and white wine, fresh chive pasta stuffed with four cheeses and tossed with walnut sauce, and veal sautéed with Golden Delicious apples. *Carr Mill Mall, Carrboro, tel. 919/942–2400. Reservations accepted. Dress: neat but casual. MC, V.*

Pyewacket Restaurant. What began as a hole-in-the-wall vegetarian restaurant in 1977 has become one of Chapel Hill's most popular restaurants. Now in bigger digs and offering courtyard dining, Pyewacket has added seafood and pasta specialties to its former vegetarian repertoire. Appetizers include smoked trout paté; entrées range from Southwest grilled seafood to spinach lasagne. *431 West Franklin St., tel. 919/929–0297. Reservations accepted. Dress: casual. AE, DC, MC, V.*

$$ **Crook's Corner.** If there's such a thing as chic Southern cooking, Crook's produces it. Particularly famous for its barbecue, the restaurant also turns out such regional Southern specialities as hoppin' John, hot pepper jelly, collards, crab gumbo, cheese grits, and buttermilk pie. One of the joys of summer is lunching on Crook's patio, under the huge pig sculpture that sparked a local debate when erected but is now a beloved local landmark. *610 West Franklin St., tel. 919/929–7643. Reservations accepted. Dress: casual. AE, MC, V.*

Durham *$$* **Bullock's Bar-B-Cue (Durham).** If you want to experience local cuisine, try the Brunswick stew, barbecue, southern fried chicken, and hush puppies at this casual eatery that offers eat-in or carry-out service. *3330 Wortham St., tel. 919/383–3211. First-come, first-served (come early). Dress: casual. No credit cards. Closed Sun.*

Parizäde. This new restaurant in Erwin Square gets high marks for its food, service, and atmosphere (soft lighting and white tablecloths give the place an elegant feel, even at lunch. Start with grilled bread soaked in garlic oil, fresh tomatoes and eggplant relish, or fried calamari with jalapeno-tomato salsa. Then choose among such entreés as fettucine with fresh salmon and black pepper dill cream, sesame pasta with scallops, and roasted duck with fresh vegetables. *2200 West Main St., tel. 919/286–9712. Reservations accepted. Dress: neat but casual. Closed Sun. AE, MC, V.*

Raleigh *$$$* **Angus Barn, Ltd.** This Raleigh tradition is housed in a huge rustic barn. Gingham- and denim-clad waiters and waitresses add authenticity to the farmlike scene. The astonishing wine and beer list covers 35 pages of the menu. The restaurant serves the best steaks, baby back ribs, and prime rib, plus fresh seafood for miles around. Desserts are heavenly. *U.S. 70W at Airport Rd., tel. 919/781–2444. Reservations advised; Sat., first come, first served. Dress: informal. Live jazz Wed.–Sat. evenings. AE, DC, MC, V.*

42nd St. Oyster Bar. This much talked-about restaurant is the place to see and be seen in Raleigh. Politicians, businessmen, and laborers sit side by side downing succulent oysters and other seafood.

There's live jazz on Friday and Saturday evenings. *West and Jones Sts., tel. 919/831–2811. Reservations not necessary. Dress: casual. AE, DC, MC, V.*

$$–$$$ **Jean Claude's Café.** Casual and chic, this restaurant on the north side features authentic French cuisine, including such specials as veal sweetbreads, braised scallops, and smoked salmon. *6111 Falls of Neuse Rd., tel. 919/872–6224. No reservations. Dress: casual. MC, V.*

$$ **Est Est Est Trattoria.** The best place in town for authentic northern Italian pasta. *19 W. Hargett St., tel. 919/832–8899. Reservations not required. Dress: informal. AE, MC, V. Closed Sun.*

$ **Big Ed's City Market Restaurant.** A must for breakfast, this Raleigh favorite in the City Market serves three home-cooked meals. *220 Wolfe St., tel. 919/836–9909. Reservations not required. Dress: casual. No credit cards. Closed Sun.*

Greenshields Brewery & Pub. Enjoy beer and ale brewed on the spot with your soups, salads, sandwiches, and such entrées as fish and chips, shepherd's pie, and steak in this English-type pub in the City Market. *214 E. Martin St., City Market, tel. 919/829–0214. Reservations not necessary. Dress: casual. AE, D, MC, V.*

Irregardless Café. This eatery is a delight to vegetarians and weight-conscious eaters, and to nonsmokers, too. There's also live music. *901 W. Morgan St., tel. 919/833–8898. Reservations not required. Dress: casual. MC, V. Sat. dinner only. Sun. brunch.*

Lodging

The Triangle has lodgings in all price ranges—from convention hotels to bed-and-breakfast houses to economy chains. Major hotel chains represented here are Holiday Inn, Hilton, Radisson, Marriott, Embassy Suites, and Sheraton. Inexpensive lodging is offered by Comfort Inn, EconoLodge, Crickett Inn, Days Inn, and Hampton Inn. Since Raleigh is a business town, many hotels and motels advertise special weekend rates.

The most highly recommended hotels in each price category are indicated by a star ★.

Category	Cost*
$$$$	over $100
$$$	$60–$100
$$	$30–$60
$	under $30

**double room; add 8% for taxes*

Chapel Hill *$$$$* ★ **Fearrington House.** This French-style country inn is a member of Relais & Chateaux. Its restaurant serves regional food prepared in a classic manner. *8 mi south of Chapel Hill on U.S. 15–501 (postal address: Fearrington Village Center, Pittsboro 27312), tel. 919/542–2121 or 800/227–0130. 19 rooms. MC, V.*

Durham *$$$* ★ **The Blooming Garden Inn.** This B&B is truly a bright spot in the Holloway Historic District. With yellow paint on the exterior, the inn explodes inside with color and warmth, thanks to exuberant hosts Dolly and Frank Pokrass. For breakfast you might have walnut crepes with ricotta cheese and warm raspberry sauce. *513*

Holloway St., 27701, tel. 919/687–0801. 5 rooms with private baths. Full breakfast. AE, MC, V.

Washington Duke Hotel & Golf Club. On the campus of Duke University, this luxurious inn overlooks the Robert Trent Jones golf course. On display in the public rooms are memorabilia belonging to the Duke family for whom the hotel and university are named. The bar is called the Bull Durham. *3001 Cameron Blvd., 27706, tel. 919/490–0999 or 800/443–3853, fax 919/688–0105. 171 rooms. Facilities: outdoor pool, jogging trails, restaurant, bar, golf course. AE, D, DC, MC, V.*

$$ **Arrowhead Inn.** This bed-and-breakfast inn, in an 18th-century white clapboard farmhouse with black shutters has brick chimneys and tall Doric columns. It's a few miles outside Durham and offers a homelike setting with antiques, old plantings, and a log cabin in the garden. Guests are served a hearty breakfast. *106 Mason Rd., 27712, tel. 919/477–8430. 8 rooms, some with private baths. Closed Christmas week. AE, D, MC, V.*

Raleigh
$$$ **Courtyard by Marriott–Airport.** Convenient to the airport and the Research Triangle Park, this chain offers many luxuries, including a Continental breakfast, without hefty rates. Some rooms have refrigerators. *2001 Hospitality Ct., 27560, tel. 919/467–9444 or 800/321–2211, fax 919/476–9336. 152 rooms. Facilities: dining room, pool, whirlpool, exercise room, laundry, airport shuttle. AE, D, DC, MC, V.*

North Raleigh Hilton and Convention Center. This is a favorite capital city spot for corporate meetings. The Tower Suites offer a complimentary Continental breakfast, free hors d'oeuvres, concierge, newspapers, and secretarial service if wanted. Guests enjoy dining in Lofton's restaurant and listening to the piano afterward in the lobby bar. Bowties is one of the city's hottest nightspots. *3415 Wake Forest Rd., 27609, tel. 919/872–2323 or 800/445–8667, fax 919/833–0223. 337 rooms and suites. Facilities: indoor pool, health club, complimentary airport shuttle, meeting rooms. AE, D, DC, MC, V.*

Oakwood Inn. In Historic Oakwood, one of the city's oldest downtown neighborhoods, this is an alternative to hotel/motel living. Built in 1871 and now on the National Register of Historic Places, the inn is furnished with Victorian period pieces. Guests are served a sumptuous complimentary breakfast and assisted with dinner reservations and evening entertainment plans. *411 N. Bloodworth St., 27604, tel. 919/832–9712. 6 rooms with bath. AE, MC, V.*

Raleigh Marriott Crabtree Valley. This is one of the city's most luxurious hotels. Fresh floral arrangements adorn the elegantly decorated public rooms. Guests enjoy the intimacy of the Scotch Bonnets restaurant, the family atmosphere of Allie's, and Champions Sports Bar. The concierge floor offers complimentary Continental breakfast and hors d'oeuvres. *4500 Marriott Dr. (U.S. 70W near Crabtree Valley Mall) 27612, tel. 919/781–7000 or 800/228–9290, fax 919/781–3059. 375 rooms and suites. Facilities: indoor/outdoor pool, whirlpool, exercise room, game room, golf and racquetball nearby, complimentary airport shuttle. AE, D, DC, MC, V.*

Velvet Cloak Inn. This hotel is in a class of its own. Local brides have wedding receptions in the tropical garden around the enclosed pool, and politicians frequent the bar at Baron's Restaurant and Nightclub. The Charter Room, an elegant restaurant, often has live entertainment. Afternoon tea and cookies are served in the lobby. Rooms in the brick structure, decorated with delicate wrought iron, are frequently refurbished. *1505 Hillsborough St., 27605, tel. 919/828–0333 or 800/334–4372, in NC, 800/662–8829, fax 919/828–2656. 172 rooms and suites. Facilities: 2 restaurants, complimentary coffee* *and newspaper in the lobby, guest privileges at the YMCA next door, airport shuttle, meeting rooms. AE, D, DC, MC, V.*

$$ **Quality Suites Hotel.** Minutes from downtown, this hotel offers luxurious two-room suites equipped with VCRs, cassette stereos, microwaves, wet bars, and refrigerators. The manager's evening reception and the cooked-to-order breakfast are included in the tariff. *4400 Capital Blvd., 27604, tel. 919/876–2211 or 800/228–5151, fax 919/876–2211. 114 suites. Facilities: restaurant, outdoor pool, exercise room, meeting rooms, complimentary airport shuttle. AE, D, DC, MC, V.*

Ramada Inn Crabtree. This hotel gets the award for being the friendliest motel in town. It's also where football and basketball teams like to stay when they're here for a game, as evidenced by the helmet collection and other sports memorabilia in the Brass Bell Lounge. The Colonnade Restaurant is known for its Sunday buffets. *3920 Arrow Dr. (U.S. 70 and Beltline), 27612, tel. 919/782–7525 or 800/272–6232. 177 rooms and suites. Facilities: restaurant, lounge, outdoor pool, jogging trail, meeting rooms, airport shuttle. AE, DC, MC, V.*

$ **Hampton Inn North Raleigh.** This budget motel offers inexpensive rates without sacrificing quality. A Continental breakfast, local calls, and in-room movies are available at no extra charge. *1001 Wake Towne Dr., 27609, tel. 919/828–1813 or 800/426–7866, fax 919/834–2672. 131 rooms. Facilities: outdoor pool, meeting rooms, and airport shuttle. AE, D, DC, MC, V.*

The Arts

The **North Carolina Theatre** (One E. South St., Raleigh, tel. 919/831–6916), the state's only professional nonprofit theater, produces five Broadway shows a year. Durham's newly renovated, 1926 Beaux Arts **Carolina Theatre** (Morgan St., tel. 919/560–3060) hosts the city's symphony and opera company, as well as the International Jazz Festival in March and the American Dance Festival in June. The **North Carolina Symphony** (2 E. South St., Raleigh, tel. 919/733–2750) gives more than 200 concerts in the area annually.

Nightlife

Much of the nightlife is centered in the larger hotels, such as the Hilton or the Marriott. **Bowties** (North Raleigh Hilton, 3415 Wake Forest Rd., tel. 919/878–4917) is a popular after-hours spot. **Charlie Goodnight's Comedy Club** (861 W. Morgan St., tel. 919/828–5233) combines dinner with a night of laughs. Another option is **Comedy Sportz** (329 Blake St., City Market, Raleigh, tel. 919/829–0822; Omni Europa, U.S. 15–501, Chapel Hill, tel. 919/968–4900). At the **Triangle Dinner Theatre** at Radisson Governors Inn (tel. 919/549–8951) you can combine dinner with a comedy or musical show, offered Thursday, Friday, and Saturday evenings.

The Southern Pines and Pinehurst Sandhills

Because of their sandy soil—once the beaches of the Atlantic Ocean—the Sandhills weren't of much use to early farmers, most of whom switched to lumbering and making turpentine for a livelihood. Since the turn of the century, however, this area has proven ideal for golf and tennis. Today promoters call it the Golf Capital of the World, and there's even a museum here that honors the sport. First-class resorts are centered around more than three dozen golf courses, including the famed Pinehurst Number 2 and several spectacular new courses.

The Highland Scots, who settled the area, left a rich heritage perpetuated through festivals and gatherings. In Colonial times English potters were attracted to the rich clay deposits in the soil, and today their descendants and others turn out beautiful wares that are sold in more than 40 local shops.

Getting There

By Plane Visitors arrive via US Air Express (tel. 800/428–4322) from **Charlotte–Douglas International Airport** or they fly into the **Raleigh-Durham Airport** or the **Piedmont Triad International Airport** and rent a car.

By Car U.S. 1 runs north-south through the Sandhills and is the recommended route from the Raleigh-Durham area, a distance of about 70 miles. Another alternate is U.S. 15-501 from Chapel Hill. Route 27 leads east from Charlotte and intersects U.S. Southern Pines. U.S. 74 from Charlotte intersects U.S. 1 at Rockingham, about 25 miles south of Southern Pines.

By Train **Amtrak** (tel. 910/692–6305 or 800/872–7245) southbound and northbound trains, one daily from each direction, stop in Southern Pines.

Important Addresses and Numbers

Tourist Information **Pinehurst Area Convention and Visitor Bureau** (1480 Hwy. 15–501 N, Box 2270, Southern Pines 28288, tel. 910/692–3330 or 800/346–5362). For details on local events, call 910/692–1600.

Emergencies Dial 910/692–7031 in Southern Pines, or go to the **Sandhills Urgent Care Clinic** (1990 Hwy 15–501 South, Southern Pines, tel. 910/692–5555). Dial 910/295–3141 in Pinehurst, or go to the emergency room of the **Moore Regional Hospital** (Memorial Dr., Pinehurst, tel. 910/215–1111).

Exploring

Southern Pines **Southern Pines,** the center of the Sandhills, is a good place to start a tour. **The Shaw House,** the oldest structure in town (circa 1770), serves as headquarters for the Moore County Historical Association. *W. Broad St. and Morganton Rd., tel. 910/692–2051. Open Wed.–Sun. 1–4.*

Weymouth Center, former home of author James Boyd, hosts numerous music, lecture, and holiday events. *E. Vermont Ext., tel. 910/692–6261. Call ahead to arrange tours. Open weekdays 10–noon, 2–4.*

Weymouth Woods Nature Preserve, on the eastern outskirts of town, is a 667-acre wildlife preserve with a state-operated museum. *Off U.S. 1, 2 mi from downtown, tel. 910/692–2167. Admission free. Open Mon.–Sat. 9–6, Sun. noon–5.*

Pinehurst **Pinehurst** lies 8 miles west of Southern Pines via U.S. 15–501, or Midland Road. The New England–style village, with its quiet, shaded streets and immaculately kept cottages, was laid out in the late 1800s in a wagon-wheel fashion, by landscape genius Frederick Law Olmsted. It is a mecca for sports enthusiasts, retirees, and tourists. The **PGA/World Golf Hall of Fame** traces the history of golf from the 1600s to the present day. *PGA Blvd., tel. 910/295–6651. Admission: $3 adults, $2.50 senior citizens, $2 students 10–18. Open daily 9–5. Closed Mid-Dec.–mid-Feb.*

Aberdeen In **Aberdeen,** a town of Scottish ancestry south of Pinehurst, there's a beautifully restored turn-of-the-century train station, and on Bethesda Road east of town, the **Bethesda Presbyterian Church,** founded in 1778. The present wooden structure, which is used for weddings, funerals, and reunions, was built in the 1860s. The cemetery, where many early settlers are buried, is always open. Continue on Bethesda Road to the **Malcolm Blue Farm,** where people gather in September for a festival that recalls life here in the 1800s.

Asheboro Follow U.S. 220 north to NC 159, which leads to the **North Carolina Zoological Park** at Asheboro. This 1,400-acre natural habitat for animals is one of the up-and-coming zoos of the late 20th century. The park includes the African Pavilion, an aviary, a gorilla habitat, and a new Sonora Desert habitat, with snakes and scorpions. *Tel. 910/879–7000. Admission, including tram ride: $6 adults, $4 senior citizens and children 2–12. Open weekdays 9–5, weekends 10–6.*

Shopping

Antiques Shop for antiques in **Cameron,** which hasn't changed much since the 19th century. Approximately 60 antiques dealers operate out of several stores. The town itself has been declared a historic district. *Tel. 910/245–7001. Most shops open Wed.–Sat. 10–5, Sun. 1–5.*

Herbs and Wildflowers **Sandhill Farms,** 12 miles east of Cameron off Highway 24, is a one-of-a-kind operation offering herbs, wildflowers, wreaths, crafts, and oils. *Tel. 919/499–4753. Open weekdays 1–5. Closed Jan.–Feb.*

Pottery Mugs, bowls, pitchers, platters, and sometimes clay voodoo heads can be found in about 40 shops scattered along and off Route 705 and U.S. 220. The work of some local potters is exhibited in national museums, including the Smithsonian. A map locating the various potteries is available at most shops and at the North Carolina Pottery Museum on Rte. 705 in downtown Seagrove. *For information, tel. 910/873–7887. Most shops open Tues.–Sat. 10–5. Admission free. Museum hours are Thurs.–Sat. 10–3.*

Participant Sports

Golf More than three dozen courses await you in this golfers' paradise, including **Pinehurst, Pine Needles,** and **Mid-Pines.** Several Southern Pines courses are open to the public, including **Hyland Hills** (tel. 910/692–3752), **Knollwood Fairways** (tel. 910/692–3572), **The Pit** (tel. 910/944–1600), **Longleaf Country Club** (tel. 910/692–6100), **Beacon Ridge Country Club** (tel. 910/673–2950), **Country Club of Whispering Pines** (tel. 910/949–2311), **Legacy Golf Links** (tel. 910/944–8825 or 800/344–8825), **Talamore at Pinehurst** (tel. 910/692–5884), **Whisper-**

ing Woods Golf Club (tel. 910/949–4653), and **Oakwood Hills** (tel. 910/281–3169). A complete list of golf courses and their fee ranges is available from the Pinehurst Area Convention and Visitors Bureau (*see above*). New to the area is **Mini Pines** (tel. 910/692–4332), which offers miniature golf on an 18-hole course and the area's only softball and baseball batting cages.

Horseback and Carriage Riding Riding instruction and carriage rides are available by appointment at **Pinehurst Stables** (Hwy. 5, tel. 910/295–8456) and **Candlewood Carriage Rides** (Southern Pines, tel. 910/692–3447).

Tennis Facilities are available at the **Lawn and Tennis Club of North Carolina.** Pinehurst, Mid-Pines, Pine Needles Resort, Country Club of Whispering Pines, and the **Holiday Inn** at Southern Pines are known for their clinics. Public courts can be found in **Aberdeen, Carthage, Pinebluff,** and **Southern Pines** and at **Sandhills Community College.** For details, contact the Pinehurst Area Convention and Visitors Bureau.

Dining and Lodging

Dining No particular local cuisine typifies the Sandhills, but the area has a number of sophisticated restaurants.

Category	Cost*
$$$$	over $25
$$$	$15–$25
$$	$8–$15
$	under $8

**per person without tax (6%), service, or drinks*

Lodging Most lodging options in the Sandhills are in the luxury resort category, featuring full amenities and services. However, there are a few chain motels in Southern Pines, as well as several bed-and-breakfasts in the area.

Category	Cost*
$$$$	over $100
$$$	$60–$100
$$	$30–$60
$	under $30

**double room; add 8% for taxes*

Aberdeen *Lodging* **The Inn at the Bryant House.** Downtown, one block off U.S. 1, this charming B&B is like a home away from home. The inn offers golf packages and arranges tennis and horseback riding. *214 N. Poplar St., 28315, tel. 910/944–3300. 9 rooms, most with private bath. AE, MC, V. $$*

Cameron *Dining* **The Dewberry Deli.** Housed in the Old Hardware, this eatery is a wonderful place for a sandwich or salad after shopping for antiques. *Carthage St., tel. 910/245–3697. Reservations not required. Dress: casual. MC, V. Open Wed.–Sat. 10–5, Sun. 12:30–5. $*

Eagle Springs *Lodging* **The Inn at Eagle Springs.** A private girls' school during the 1920s, this B&B, amid the pines in a remote area 15 miles from Pinehurst, is great for golfers who want rest and quiet. The action-oriented might be bored, however. A full breakfast is always provided, and other meals can be arranged ahead. *Box 56, Samarcand Rd., 27242, tel. 910/673–2722. 6 rooms. No credit cards. $$*

Pinehurst
Dining

Pinehurst Playhouse Restaurant & Yogurt. This casual eatery housed in an old theater is in the heart of the village and is *the* place to meet for soups and sandwiches. *Theater Bldg., W. Village Green., tel. 910/295–8873. No reservations. Dress: casual. No credit cards. Lunch only. Closed Sun. $$*

Dining and Lodging

The Pinehurst Resort and Country Club. This venerable resort hotel, in operation since the turn of the century, has never lost the charm that founder James Tufts intended it to have. Civilized decorum rules in the spacious public rooms, on the rocker-lined wide verandas, and amid the lush gardens of the surrounding grounds. Guests can play lawn croquet, shoot skeet, or tee off on one of seven premier golf courses. The Carolina Dining Room is known for its gourmet cuisine. *Carolina Vista, Box 4000, 28374, tel. 910/295–6811 or 800/487–4653, fax 910/295–8503. 310 rooms and 125 condos. Facilities: pool, golf, tennis, croquet, riding instruction, sailing, fishing, boating, wind surfing, biking, trap and skeet shooting, meeting rooms. AE, D, DC, MC, V. $$$$*

Holly Inn. This renovated wooden inn, built in 1895, is testimony to James Tufts' success as an hotelier. It was so popular that he was forced to build a bigger structure—now the Pinehurst Resort. Guests at the inn enjoy their own pool, retaurant, and lounge. *Cherokee Rd., Box 2300, 28374, tel. 910/295–2300 or 800/682–6901 in NC, fax 910/295–0988. 77 rooms and suites. AE, D, MC. $$$*

The Magnolia Inn. Once just a hangout for golfing buddies, this Old South inn has sprung back to life under new ownership. Rooms sparkle with white and pink paint and wallpaper, and the inn's dining room serves superb grilled Norwegian salmon and roasted herb-crusted rack of lamb, among other delectables—there's also an English pub, where you can discuss your golf game. *Magnolia and Chinquapin Rds., Box 818, 28374, tel. 910/295–6900 or 800/526–5562, fax 910/215–0858. 12 double rooms. Facilities: pool, golf privileges, restaurant, English pub, full breakfast and gourmet dinner. AE, MC, V. $$$*

Pine Crest Inn. After an extensive remodeling, this small village inn, once owned by golfing great Donald Ross, sports chintz and mahogany in its rooms. Chefs Carl and Peter Jackson whip up some great dishes, including homemade soups; fresh seafood dishes; and the house special, stuffed pork chops. Mr. B's Bar is the liveliest nightspot in town. Guests have golf and tennis privileges at local clubs. *Dogwood Rd., Box 879, 28374, tel. 910/295–6121. 43 rooms and suites. Rates include 2 meals per day. AE, D, MC, V. $$*

Southern Pines
Dining

The Lob Steer Inn. Come hungry for broiled seafood and prime rib dinners, complemented by salad and dessert bars. The restaurant is upscale. *U.S. 1, Southern Pines, tel. 910/692–3503. Reservations advised on weekends. Dress: casual. AE, DC, MC, V. Closed lunch. $$–$$$*

Mannie's Dinner Theater. Guests can see musicals here on Saturday evenings, after a dinner of prime rib or shrimp scampi. *W. Penn. Ave., tel. 910/692–8400. Reservations required for dinner theater. Dress: casual. AE, MC, V. Closed Sun. $21.95 per person Sat., other times $$*

Silver Bucket Restaurant. You can order just about any kind of fish—plus steaks, ribs, barbecue, and some Italian dishes—for a tasty and satisfying meal. The atmosphere is très casual. *S.E. Broad St., tel.*

910/692–6227. Reservations accepted. Dress: casual. AE, MC, V. Closed lunch and Sun. and Mon. $–$$

Whiskey NcNeill's Restaurant. Diners fill up on soups, sandwiches, salads, and a variety of entrées (from grilled sirloin to pork chops) over what used to be a grease pit of a downtown filling station but is now a fabulous spot for lunch and dinner. Stare closely at the building, and you can practically imagine pulling up to the pump in your '57 Chevy. *Northeast Blvd., tel. 910/692–5440. Reservations accepted. Dress: casual. MC, V. $*

Lodging **Mid Pines Resort.** This resort community, a Clarion property, includes an 18-hole golf course designed by Donald Ross that has been the site of numerous tournaments. *1010 Midland Rd., Southern Pines 28388, tel. 910/692–2114 or 800/323–2114, fax 910/692–4615. 118 rooms. Facilities: pool, lighted tennis courts, golf, airport transportation, restaurant, meeting rooms. AE, D, DC, MC, V. $$$–$$$$*

Pine Needles Resort and Country Club. One of the bonuses of staying at this informal lodge is the chance to meet Peggy Kirk Bell, a champion golfer and golf instructor. She built the resort with her late husband, and she continues to help run it. The rooms of the spacious lodge are done in a rustic style, with exposed beams in many rooms. *Box 88, Southern Pines 28388, tel. 910/692–7111, fax 910/692–5349. 67 rooms, Facilities: pool, sauna, whirlpool, grass tennis courts, steam baths, golf, airport transportation, restaurant. AE, MC, V. $$$–$$$$*

Winston-Salem

The manufacture of cigarettes, textiles, and furniture built a solid economic base in the Winston-Salem area; major area employers today also include USAir, Wachovia Bank, the Bowman Gray School of Medicine, and N.C. Baptist Hospital. Winston-Salem residents' donations to the arts are the highest per capita in the nation, and the North Carolina School of the Arts commands international attention. Wake Forest University, where writer Maya Angelou teaches, is also here. Old Salem, a restored 18th-century Moravian town within the city of Winston-Salem, has been drawing tourists since the early 1950s.

Arriving and Departing

By Plane Five major airlines serve the **Piedmont Triad International Airport** (tel. 910/665–5666): American, Delta, Continental, United, and USAir.

By Bus Contact **Greyhound Lines** (tel. 910/723–3663 or 800/231–2222).

By Train **Amtrak** serves Greensboro (tel. 910/855–3382 or 800/872–7245), about 25 miles away.

Getting Around

By Trolley Trolleys run between the Winston-Salem Visitor Center and Old Salem, weekdays 9:40–5:30. *Fare: 25¢.*

Important Addresses and Numbers

Tourist Information **Winston-Salem Convention & Visitors Bureau** (Box 1408, Winston-Salem 27102, tel. 910/725–2361 or 800/331–7018). A visitors **recep-**

tion center in the City Market (601 N. Cherry St., Suite 100, tel. 910/777–3796) is open daily.

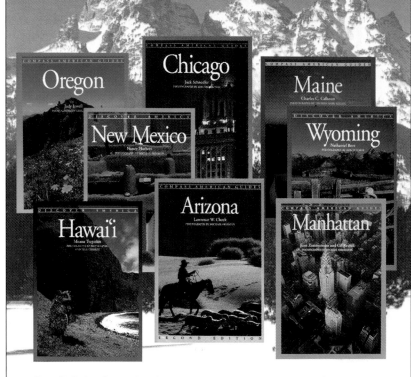

Emergencies Dial 911 for **police** and **ambulance** in an emergency.

Guided Tours

Contact **Carolina Treasures and Tours** (1031 Burke St., Winston-Salem 27101, tel. 910/631–9144) or **Margaret Glenn Tours** (Box 11342, Winston-Salem 27116, tel. 910/724–6547).

Exploring Winston-Salem

Begin your tour of the city at the **Winston-Salem Visitor Center** (*see above*), where you'll see a 12-minute film on the area.

Old Salem is just a few blocks from downtown Winston-Salem and only a stone's throw from I–40 (take the Old Salem/Salem College exit). The 1700s live again in this village of 80 original brick and wooden structures. The aromas of freshly baked bread, sugar cakes, and ginger snaps mix with those of beeswax candles and newly dyed flax. Tradesmen work in their shops making pewterware, cooking utensils, and other items, while the womenfolk embroider and weave cloth. There are African-American interpretations at each site. The Moravians, a Protestant sect, fled to Georgia to find religious freedom; from there they went to Bethlehem, Pennsylvania, finally settling here. In 1753, they built Bethabara (on Bethabara Rd., off University Pkwy.) and in 1766 built Salem. Tour tickets will get you into several restored buildings at Old Salem, but you may wander through the streets free of charge. Old Salem will undergo expansion over the next few years. *600 S. Main St., tel. 910/721–7300 or 800/441–5305. Admission: $10 adults, $5 children ages 6–14; families $25; combination ticket with MESDA* (see below). *Open Mon.–Sat. 9:30–4:30, Sun. 1:30–4:30.*

Time Out **Winkler Bakery** will satisfy your craving for hot, freshly baked Moravian sugar cake. *525 S. Main St., tel. 910/721–7302. Open Mon.–Sat. 9–5, Sun. 1:30–5.*

Another way to step back into time is to enter the **Museum of Early Southern Decorative Arts (MESDA).** Six galleries and 19 rooms are decorated with period furnishings. *924 S. Main St., tel. 910/721–7360. Admission: full tour $6 adults, $3 children, ages 6–14; combination tickets to MESDA and Old Salem: $13 adults, $6 children. Open Mon.–Sat. 10:30–4:30, Sun. 1:30–4:30.*

Stroh Brewery, approximately 5 miles south of downtown via U.S. 52, rolls out 5.5 million barrels of beer a year as the second-largest brewery in the country. A single machine can fill and seal up to 1,500 12-ounce cans of beer per minute. You can see it made and enjoy a complimentary drink. *Schlitz Ave., U.S. 52S at S. Main St., tel. 910/788–6710. Admission free. Open spring–fall, weekdays 11–4:30; winter, noon–3.*

R. J. Reynolds Whitaker Park is one of the world's largest and most modern cigarette manufacturing centers. On the guided tour you see how 8,000 are produced every minute. *1100 Reynolds Blvd., tel. 910/741–5718. Admission free. Open weekdays 8–6, 8–8 late May–early Sept.*

Historic **Bethabara Park** is another vision from the 1700s. You can explore the foundations of the town, as well as the three remaining buildings. Kids love the reconstructed Indian fort. A greenway now connects the park to another restoration of a 1700s mill, fort, and village. *2147 Bethabara Rd., tel. 910/924–8191. Admission free. Open weekdays 9:30–4:30, weekends 1:30–4:30. Guided tours Apr.–Nov. or by appointment. Brochures for a self-guided walking tour are available year-round at the visitor center.*

The **Museum of Anthropology,** the only one in the state, displays objects from cultures around the globe. *Wake Forest University, tel. 910/759–5282. Admission free. Open Tues.–Fri. 10–4:30, Sat. 2–4:30.*

Reynolda House Museum of American Art, formerly the home of tobacco magnate R. J. Reynolds, contains an outstanding collection of American art, a costume collection, and clothing and toys used by the Reynolds children. In Reynolda Village, on the estate, there are shops and restaurants. *Reynolda Rd., tel. 910/725–5325. Admission: $6 adults, $3 students, $5 senior citizens. Open Tues.–Sat. 9:30–4:30, Sun. 1:30–4:30.*

SECCA (the Southeastern Center for Contemporary Art), near Reynolda House, is the place to see the latest in Southern painting, sculpture, and printmaking. *750 Marguerite Dr., tel. 910/725–1904. Admission: $3 adults, $2 students and senior citizens, children under 12 free. Open Tues.–Sat. 10–5, Sun. 2–5.*

The manor house at **Tanglewood Park,** the former home of the late William and Kate Reynolds, has just been spruced up with antiques and furnishings of the 1920s and now takes overnight guests. The public park has riding, golf, tennis, boating, camping, and PGA golf. *Hwy. 158 off I-40, Clemmons, tel. 910/766–0591. Admission: $2 per car, plus separate fees for each activity.*

What to See and Do with Children

SciWorks. Look at the stars, handle live starfish in the tidal pool, pet the lambs and goats, and make discoveries at this hands-on museum. *Museum Dr., Winston-Salem, tel. 910/767–6730. Admission: $3.50 adults, $2.50 students and senior citizens, children under 3 free. Open Mon.–Sat. 10–5, Sun. 1–5.*

Shopping

Crafts *The New York Times* called the **Piedmont Craftsmen's Shop and Gallery** a "showcase for Southern crafts." *1204 Reynolda Rd., tel. 910/725–1516. Open Tues.–Sat. 10–6, Sun. 1–5.*

Outlets This is a textile center, so there are many clothing outlets clustered along the interstates. **Marketplace Mall** (2101 Peters Creek Pkwy., tel. 910/759–9889) and **Hanes Mill/Sara Lee Outlet** (Ricks Dr., tel. 910/744–3306) are good options. The 100 stores in **Burlington Manufacturers Outlet Center** (tel. 910/227–2872) and **Waccamaw Pottery and the Burlington Outlet Mall** (tel. 910/229–0418) make the area off I–85 near Burlington a mecca for dedicated shoppers. *Most stores are open Mon.–Sat. 10–9, Sun. 1–6.*

Dining

Traditional dining in these parts is Southern—fried chicken, ham, vegetables, biscuits, fruit cobblers, and the like. Chopped or sliced pork barbecue is also a big item. Nowadays, however, there's a growing number of gourmet restaurants.

Category	Cost*
$$$	$15–$25
$$	$8–$15
$	under $8

**per person without tax (6%), service, or drinks*

$$$ **La Chaudiere.** Elegantly prepared French country dishes of pheasant, rabbit, veal, and other delicacies are served here in a country French atmosphere. Soft white walls, original paintings, and fresh flowers set off this restaurant in Reynolda Village. *120 Reynolda Rd., tel. 910/748–0269. Reservations strongly advised. Jacket and tie advised. AE, DC, MC, V. Closed Mon.*

Leon's Café. This casual eatery in a renovated building near Old Salem serves some of the best gourmet food in town—fresh seafood, chicken breasts with raspberry sauce, lamb, and other specialties. The restaurant's dark colors are set off by artworks and lacy window treatments. *924 S. Marshall St., tel. 910/725–9593. Reservations advised. Dress: casual. MC, V. No lunch.*

$$–$$$ **Old Salem Tavern Dining Room.** Eat Moravian food in a Moravian setting served by waiters in Moravian costumes. Standard menu items are chicken pie (excellent choice!), ragout of beef, and rack of lamb. From April through October you can dine outside under the arbor. *736 S. Main St., tel. 910/748–8585. Reservations advised. Dress: casual. Sun. brunch. AE, MC, V.*

$$ **Café Piaf.** Inside the Stevens Center, a restored Art Deco performing-arts space, the café offers pasta primavera, chicken Piaf, and other French entrées. Dessert and coffee follow performances. *401 W. 4th St., tel. 910/750–0855. Reservations advised. Dress: casual. AE, DC, MC, V.*

Newmarket Grille. Fresh vegetables and meats, plus homemade breads and desserts, make this establishment a winner. The varied menu includes fresh grilled fish, poultry, beef, and pork dishes, as well as some stir-fry items, plus burgers and sandwiches. The bar is a popular gathering spot for the city's movers and shakers. *300 S. Stratford Rd., 27103, tel. 910/724–5220. No reservations. Dress: casual. AE, MC, V.*

Noble's Grille. This upscale French restaurant serves a variety of entrées grilled or roasted over an oak-and-hickory fire, including braised rabbit with black-pepper fettuccine and Carolina *poussin* with polenta. *380 Knollwood St., tel. 910/777–8477. Reservations advised. Jacket and tie advised. AE, DC, MC, V. Closed Sun.*

Lodging

Category	Cost*
$$$$	over $100
$$$	$60–$100
$$	$30–$60
$	under $30

**double room; add 8% for taxes*

$$$$ **Stouffer Winston Plaza Hotel.** Centrally located off I–40, this elegant hotel, Winston's premier lodging, has a marble lobby, tradi-

tional furnishings, and almost 10,000 square feet of meeting space. *425 N. Cherry St., 27101, tel. 910/725–3500 or 800/444–2326, fax 910/722–6475. 317 rooms. Facilities: 2 restaurants, bar, indoor/outdoor pool, steam room, sauna, game room, and gift shop. AE, D, DC, MC, V.*

$$$–$$$$ **Henry F. Shaffner House.** Accessible to downtown and Old Salem, this B&B is a favorite with business travelers and honeymoon couples. The rooms in the restored English Tudor house are furnished in 19th-century Victorian elegance. In addition to a complimentary Continental breakfast, there's afternoon tea and evening wine and cheese. *150 S. Marshall St., 27101, tel. 910/777–0052. 8 rooms with bath. AE, MC, V.*

Tanglewood Manor House. This former home of a branch of the Reynolds family has provided bed-and-breakfast guests with 10 rooms in the antiques-filled manor house, 18 lodge rooms, and four cottages on Mallard Lake in Tanglewood Park. Continental breakfast, admission to the park, swimming, and fishing are included in the cost. *Hwy. 158 off I–40, Clemmons, tel. 910/766–0591. 32 rooms. Facilities:* See *Exploring,* above, *for all park activities. AE, DC, MC, V. $$$–$$$$*

$$–$$$ **Brookstown Inn.** Sleep under a comfy handmade quilt in front of the fireplace or enjoy wine and cheese in the spacious lobby of this unusual bed-and-breakfast hotel, built in 1837 as one of the first textile mills in the South. Breakfast is Continental. *200 Brookstown Ave., 27101, tel. 910/725–1120 or 800/845–4262, fax 910/773–0147. 71 rooms. Facilities: some rooms with whirlpools, airport transportation, meeting rooms. AE, DC, MC, V.*

$$ **Comfort Inn–Cloverdale Place.** Off I–40 near downtown and Old Salem, this immaculately kept inn offers a free Continental breakfast. *110 Miller St., 27103, tel. 910/721–0220 or 800/221–2222, fax 910/723–2117. 122 rooms. Facilities: outdoor pool, health club, meeting room. AE, D, DC, MC, V.*

The Outer Banks

North Carolina's Outer Banks, a series of barrier islands, stretch from the Virginia state line south to Cape Lookout. Throughout history the nemesis of shipping, they have been called the "Graveyard of the Atlantic;" a network of lighthouses and lifesaving stations was built, which draw visitors today, and the many submerged wrecks attract scuba divers. English settlers landed here in 1587 and attempted to colonize the region, but the colony—known today as "The Lost Colony"—disappeared without a trace. The islands' coves and inlets offered privacy to pirates—the notorious Blackbeard lived and died here. For many years the Outer Banks remained isolated, home only to a few families who made their living by fishing. Today the islands, linked by bridges and ferries, have become popular tourist destinations. Much of the area is included in the Cape Hatteras and Cape Lookout national seashores. The largest towns are Kitty Hawk, Kill Devil Hills, Nags Head, and Manteo.

On the inland side of the Outer Banks is the historic Albemarle region, a remote area of small villages and towns surrounding Albemarle Sound. Edenton was the Colonial capital for a while, and many of its early structures are preserved.

Getting There and Getting Around

By Plane The closest commercial airports are the **Raleigh-Durham International Airport** (tel. 919/840–2123) and **Norfolk International** (tel. 804/857–3351), both of which are served by major carriers, including American, Continental, Delta, and USAir. Tiny Southeast Airlines (tel. 919/473–3222 or 800/927–3296) provides commuter service between Norfolk and the **Dare County Regional Airport** at Manteo.

By Train **Amtrak** service (tel. 800/872–7245) is available to Norfolk, VA, about 75 miles to the north.

By Car U.S. 158 links the Outer Banks with U.S. 17 leading to Norfolk and other places north. U.S. 64, 70, and 264 are western routes. Route 12 goes south toward Ocracoke Island and north toward Corolla. Toll ferries connect Ocracoke to Cedar Island and Swan Quarter. For reservations, call 919/225–3551 for departures from Cedar Island, 919/928–3841 from Ocracoke, and 919/926–1111 from Swan Quarter. There is a free ferry across Hatteras Inlet. On summer weekends, traffic waiting for the Hatteras Inlet ferry and the bridges to the mainland can be backed up for hours.

By Taxi **Beach Cabs** (tel. 919/441–2500), based in Nags Head, offers 24-hour service from Norfolk to Ocracoke and towns in between. Another option is **Outer Banks Limousine Service** (tel. 919/261–3133).

By Boat Seagoing visitors travel the Intracoastal Waterway through the Outer Banks and Albemarle region. Boats may dock at Elizabeth City, Manteo (the Salty Dawg Marina), and other ports.

Guided Tours

Historic Albemarle Tour, Inc. (Box 759, Edenton 27932, tel. 919/482–7325) offers guided tours of Edenton and publishes a brochure on a self-guided tour of the Albemarle Region.

Kitty Hawk AeroTours (tel. 919/441–4460) leave from the First Flight Airstrip or from Manteo for Kitty Hawk, Corolla, Cape Hatteras, Ocracoke, Portsmouth Island, and other areas along the Outer Banks. *Mar.–Labor Day.*

The **North Carolina Aquarium/Roanoke Island** (Box 967, Airport Rd., Manteo 27954, tel. 919/473–3493) sponsors summer boat tours of the estuary and the sound.

Ocracoke Trolley Tours (of Ocracoke Island) depart from Trolley Stop One, NC 12, Ocracoke, tel. 919/928–6711. *Easter–Labor Day, Mon.–Sat.*

Important Addresses and Numbers

Tourist Information **Dare County Tourist Bureau** (Box 399, Manteo, 27954, tel. 919/473–2138 or 800/446–6262). **Historic Albemarle Tour, Inc.** (Box 759, Edenton, 27932, tel. 919/482–7325). **Outer Banks Chamber of Commerce** (Box 1757, Kill Devil Hills, 27948, tel. 919/441–8144).

Emergencies Dial 911 for Oregon Inlet, Roanoke Island, and Hatteras Island; 919/928–4631 for Ocracoke. The **Outer Banks Medical Center** (tel. 919/441–7111) at Nags Head is open 24 hours a day.

Coast Guard Tel. 919/995–5881.

Exploring the Outer Banks

Numbers in the margin correspond to points of interest on the Outer Banks map.

You can tour the Outer Banks from the southern end or, as we do, from the northern end. Unless you're camping, overnight stays will probably be in Ocracoke or in the Nags Head–Manteo area, where motels and hotels are concentrated. You can drive the 70-mile stretch in a day, but be sure to allow plenty of time in summer to wait for the ferry to the mainland. Be aware that during major storms and hurricanes the roads and bridges become clogged with traffic. In that case, follow the blue-and-white evacuation signs.

The small settlements of Corolla and Duck are largely seasonal residential enclaves full of summer rental condominiums with, in Duck, a few restaurants and shopping outlets. **Kitty Hawk,** with 1,672 residents, qualifies as a metropolis, relatively speaking, and here such staples as gasoline, groceries, and laundromats can be found.

1 **Kill Devil Hills,** on U.S. 158 Bypass, is the windswept site of man's first motorized flight. The **Wright Brothers National Memorial,** a granite monument that resembles the tail of an airplane, stands as a tribute to Wilbur and Orville Wright, two bicycle mechanics from Ohio who took to the air on December 17, 1903. You can see a replica of *The Flyer* and stand on the exact spot where it made four takeoffs and landings, the longest being a distance of 852 feet. Exhibits and an entertaining, informative talk by a National Park Service ranger make the event come to life again. The Wrights had to bring in the unassembled airplane by boat and also all their food and supplies for building a camp. They made four trips to the site, beginning in 1900. The First Flight is commemorated annually. *Tel. 919/441–7430. Admission: $3 per car, $1 per person; under 16 and over 65 free. Open daily 9–5; extended hours in summer. Closed major holidays.*

A few miles south of Kill Devil Hills, via U.S. 158 Bypass, is **Jockey's Ridge State Park,** the tallest sand dune in the East and a popular spot for hang gliding and kite flying. You can join in the activities and have a picnic here. *Rte. 158 Bypass, Milepost 12, tel. 919/441–7132. Admission free. Open daily 8 AM–sunset.*

Nags Head got its name because Outer Bankers hoping for shipwrecks would tie lanterns around the heads of their horses to deceive merchant ships about the location of the shoals, thus profiting from the cargo that washed ashore. It is the most commercial area, with restaurants, motels, and hotels.

Take U.S. 64-264 from U.S. 158 Bypass to reach the appealing town
2 3 of **Manteo** on **Roanoke Island.** Clustered together on the other side of Manteo you'll find the lush **Elizabethan Gardens,** which were established as a memorial to the first English colonists. They are impeccably maintained by the Garden Club of North Carolina and are a fine site for a leisurely stroll. *U.S. 64, Manteo, tel. 919/473–3234. Admission: $2 adults, children under 12 free when accompanied by an adult. Open Mar.–Nov., daily 9–5; Dec.–Jan., weekdays 9–5.*

Fort Raleigh is a reconstruction of what is thought to be the original fort of the first Carolinian colonists. Be sure to see the orientation film and then take a guided tour of the fort. A nature trail leads to an outlook over Roanoke Sound. On special occasions, musicians play 16th-century music in the visitor center. *Tel. 919/473–5772. Admission free. Open Sept.–May, daily 9–5; June–Aug., Mon.–Sat. 9–8, Sun. 9–6.*

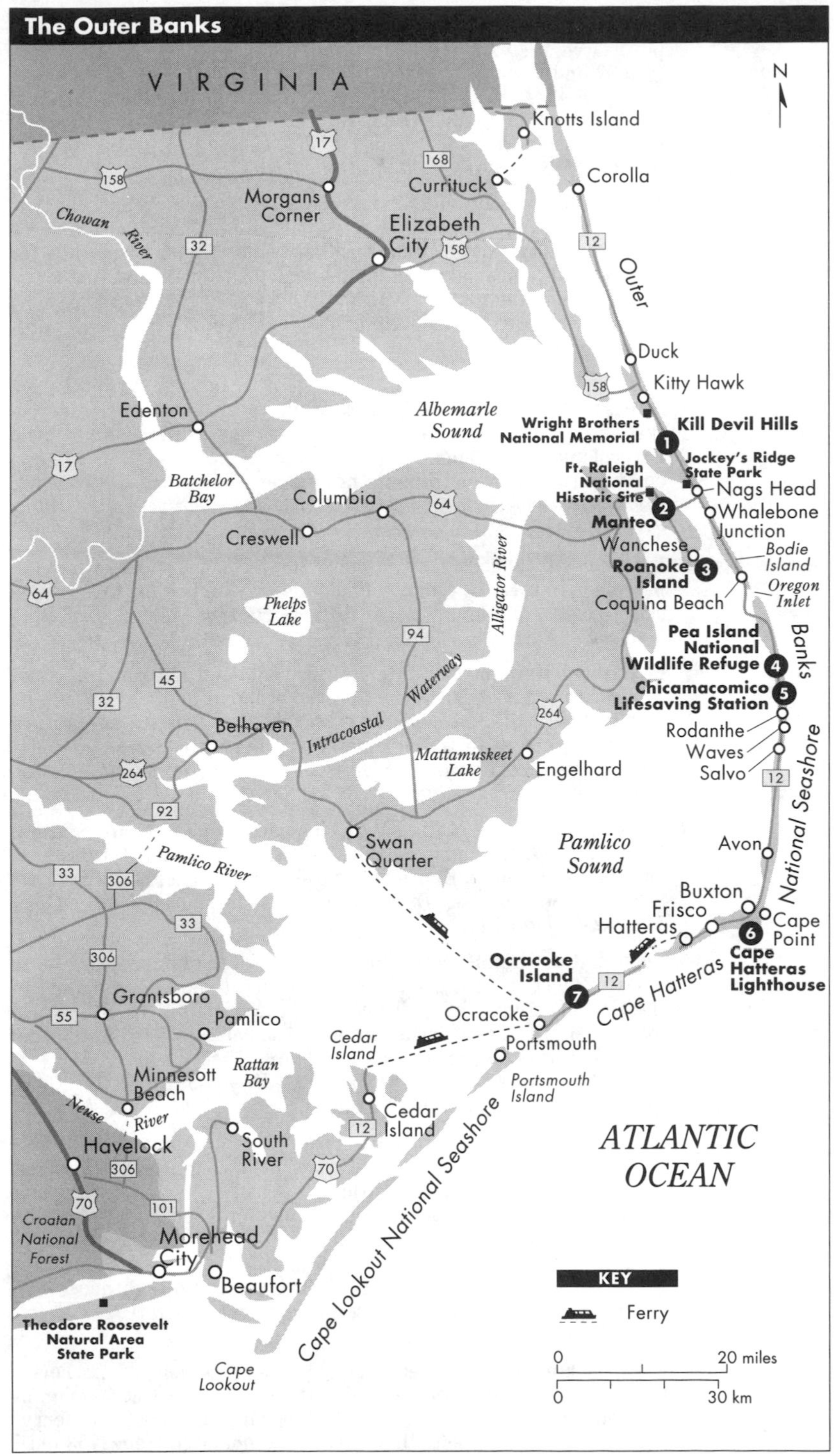
The Outer Banks
VIRGINIA
Knotts Island
Currituck
Corolla
Morgans Corner
Elizabeth City
Chowan River
Outer Banks
National Seashore
Duck
Kitty Hawk
Albemarle Sound
Wright Brothers National Memorial
Kill Devil Hills
Jockey's Ridge State Park
Nags Head
Whalebone Junction
Ft. Raleigh National Historic Site
Manteo
Wanchese
Roanoke Island
Bodie Island
Oregon Inlet
Coquina Beach
Edenton
Batchelor Bay
Columbia
Creswell
Phelps Lake
Alligator River
Pea Island National Wildlife Refuge
Chicamacomico Lifesaving Station
Rodanthe
Waves
Salvo
Intracoastal Waterway
Belhaven
Mattamuskeet Lake
Engelhard
Pamlico River
Swan Quarter
Pamlico Sound
Avon
Buxton
Frisco
Hatteras
Cape Point
Cape Hatteras Lighthouse
Cape Hatteras
Ocracoke Island
Ocracoke
Portsmouth
Portsmouth Island
Cedar Island
Grantsboro
Pamlico
Rattan Bay
Minnesott Beach
Neuse River
Havelock
South River
Croatan National Forest
Morehead City
Beaufort
Theodore Roosevelt Natural Area State Park
Cape Lookout National Seashore
Cape Lookout
ATLANTIC OCEAN
KEY
Ferry
0
20 miles
0
30 km

"The Lost Colony," an outdoor drama staged at the Waterside Amphitheatre, reenacts the story of the first colonists who settled here in 1587 and then disappeared. *Tel. 919/473–3414 or 800/488–5012. Admission: $10 adults, $4 children under 12. Reservations advised. Performances mid-June–late Aug., Mon.–Sat. at 8:30 PM. Backstage tours are offered afternoons, mid-June–Aug. (See the play first). Admission: $3 adults, $1.50 children under 12.*

A short drive away (right next to the Dare County Regional Airport) is the **North Carolina Aquarium/Roanoke Island,** one of three in the state. The aquarium is small but entertaining, especially for children, who especially love an unusual hands-on exhibit that is the aquatic equivalent of a petting zoo. *Airport Rd. (off U.S. 64), Manteo, tel. 919/473–3493. $2 donation requested. Open Mon.–Sat. 9–5, Sun.1–5.*

Back in Manteo, across a short bridge next to the Tranquil House Inn, is the **Elizabeth II State Historic Site,** a 16th-century vessel recreated to commemorate the 400th anniversary of the landing of the first colonists on Roanoke Island. Historical interpretations are given by costumed guides during the summer. *Downtown Manteo, tel. 919/473–1144. Admission: $3 adults, $2 senior citizens, $1.50 children. Open Nov.–Mar., Tues.–Sun. 10–4; Apr.– Oct., daily 10–6.*

Resume your journey southward on Route 12. On the way you will pass over **Herbert C. Bonner Bridge,** which arches for three miles over Oregon Inlet and carries traffic to Hatteras Island, the "Blue Marlin Capital of the World."

4 **Pea Island National Wildlife Refuge,** between Oregon Inlet and Rodanthe, is made up of more than 5,000 acres of marsh. On the Atlantic Flyway, it's a birder's paradise: More than 265 species are spotted regularly, including endangered peregrine falcons and piping plovers. *Pea Island Refuge Headquarters, tel. 919/473–1131. Open Apr.–Nov. weekdays 8–4.*

5 Rodanthe is the site of the 1911 **Chicamacomico Lifesaving Station.** Now restored, the museum tells the story of the 24 stations that once lined the Outer Banks. Living-history reenactments are performed June–August. *Tel. 919/987–2203. Admission free. Open May–Oct., Tues., Thurs., and Sat. 11–5.*

6 **Cape Hatteras Lighthouse,** about 30 miles south of Rodanthe, sits as a beacon to ships offshore. The 208-foot lighthouse is the tallest in the East. Offshore lie the remains of the *Monitor*, a Confederate ironclad ship that sank in 1862. The visitor center offers information on the national seashore. *Hatteras Island Visitor Center, tel. 919/995–4474. Admission free. Open Sept.–May 9–5, June–Aug. 9–6; lighthouse open June–Aug. 9–3:30.*

At Hatteras, board the free ferry to Ocracoke Island. Boats leave
7 every half-hour, and the journey takes 40 minutes. **Ocracoke Island** was cut off from the world for so long that native residents still speak in quasi-Elizabethan accents; today, however, the island is a refuge for tourists. There is a village of shops, motels, and restaurants around Silver Lake Harbor, which is where the infamous pirate Blackbeard met his death in 1718. The Ocracoke Lighthouse is a photographer's dream. *Ocracoke Visitor Center, Cedar Island, tel. 919/928–4531.*

Cape Lookout National Seashore extends for 55 miles from Portsmouth Island to Shackleford Banks. It includes 28,400 acres of uninhabited land and marsh, accessible only by boat or ferry. Portsmouth, a deserted village that was inhabited from 1753 until

1984, is being restored, and wild ponies roam the Shackleford Banks. *Tel. 919/728–2250.*

Off the Beaten Track

Merchants Millpond State Park. A 170-year-old millpond and an ancient Southern swamp comprises one of the state's rarest ecosystems. Cypress and gum trees hung with Spanish moss reach out of the still, dark waters, which are ideal for canoeing. Fishing, hiking, and camping are also available. *Rte. 1, Box 141-A, Gatesville, 27938, tel. 919/357–1191. Admission free. Open daily 8–8, until 9 June–Aug.*

Somerset Place. The Collins family kept meticulous records on the 300 slaves that worked this plantation on Albemarle Sound (now a state historic site) in the 1800s. The slaves' descendants still hold family reunions here. *Off U.S. 64 at Creswell, tel. 919/797–4560. Admission free. Open Apr.–Oct., Mon.–Sat. 9–5, Sun. 1–5; Nov.–Mar., Tues.–Sat. 10–4, Sun. 1–4.*

Beaches

More than 70 miles of unspoiled beaches stretch from Nags Head to Ocracoke Island. Preserved as Cape Hatteras National Seashore, this coastal area is ideal for swimming, surfing, windsurfing, diving, boating, and any number of water activities. If you want to swim, beware of strong tides and currents—there are no lifeguard stations. You can explore the *Laura Barnes* shipwreck site at Coquina Beach, considered the best swimming hole on the Outer Banks. Facilities here include picnic shelters, rest rooms, showers, and bath houses. "Ghost-fleet" maps locating the sunken wrecks are available at the Wright Brothers National Memorial and Cape Hatteras Lighthouse gift shops. Divers and surfers enjoy practicing their sports around Cape Hatteras.

Participant Sports

Fishing This area is a paradise for anglers who enjoy surf casting or deep-sea fishing. You can board a charter boat or head your own craft out of Oregon Inlet. (Call 919/441–6301 or 800/272–5199 for information on chartered trips.) You don't need a license for saltwater fishing.

Hang Gliding Only a few miles from where Wilbur and Orville Wright first took flight, you can try your hand at hang gliding. The giant sand dune at Jockey's Ridge State Park is where national champions gather every May for the Hang Gliding Spectacular. Lessons are given by **Kitty Hawk Kites** (U.S. 158 at Milepost 13, Nags Head, tel. 919/441–4124 or 800/334–4777), and by **Corolla Flight** (Box 1201, Kitty Hawk, 27949, tel. 919/453–4800).

Scuba Diving With over 600 known shipwrecks off the coast of the Outer Banks, diving opportunities are virtually unlimited. The *Monitor* is off-limits, however. The **USS Huron Historic Shipwreck Preserve,** which lies offshore between Mileposts 11 and 12, is a popular diving site. Dive shops include: **Hatteras Divers** (tel. 919/986–2557) and **Nags Head Pro Dive Shop** (tel. 919/441–7594).

Surfing and Windsurfing The Outer Banks offer ideal conditions for these sports. Contact **Kitty Hawk Sports** (U.S. 158 at Milepost 13, tel. 919/441–6800 or 800/334–4777).

Dining and Lodging

While you can find fancy restaurants catering to tourists in the major towns, by far the best fare around here is the fresh seafood. There are plenty of raw bars featuring oysters and clams on the half shell, and seafood houses offering fresh crabs (soft-shells in season, early in the summer) and whatever local fish—tuna, wahoo, dolphin (mahi-mahi, not Flipper)—has been hauled in that day. Competition keeps them on their toes, so the cooking is good. Dress is usually casual.

Category	Cost*
$$$$	over $25
$$$	$15–$25
$$	$8–$15
$	under $8

**per person without tax (6%), service, or drinks*

The majority of motels and hotels are clustered in the Nags Head–Manteo area, with a small number of rooms near Cape Hatteras. There are 60 cottages for rent on Ocracoke Island, plus a dozen or so motels and inns. The Outer Banks Chamber of Commerce (tel. 919/441–8144) can steer you in the direction of agencies to arrange weekly or monthly rentals.

Category	Cost*
$$$$	over $100
$$$	$60–$100
$$	$30–$60
$	under $30

**double room; add 8% for taxes*

Buxton
Dining

The Great Salt Marsh. A clean, well-lighted place with a black-and-white checkered Art Deco look, the restaurant serves lunch and dinner to regulars and the passers-through. Among the imaginative appetizers are fresh green beans sautéed and served with Parmesan cheese, and such entrées as Pamlico crab cakes with "absolutely no filler" and soft crabs served on a bed of garlic-laced spinach. It has a splendid wine list. *Osprey Shopping Center, Hwy. 12, tel. 919/995–6200. Reservations strongly advised. Dress: casual. AE, D, DC, MC, V. $$$*

Duck
Dining and Lodging

Sanderling Inn and Restaurant. If you enjoy being pampered, come to this inn on a remote beach north of Duck. Guests are treated to fruit and wine and complimentary hors d'oeuvres. For recreation you can play tennis, go swimming, or take a nature walk through the Pine Island Sanctuary and then curl up with a good book from the inn's library—or enjoy a videotape. Though it was built in 1985 and has all the contemporary conveniences, the inn has the stately, mellow look of old Nags Head. The ambitious but unexceptional restaurant is in a beautifully renovated lifesaving station. It serves three meals a day, and reservations are required for dinner. *1461 Duck Rd., 27949, tel. 919/261–4111. 60 rooms and 28 efficiencies. Facili-*

ties: pool, tennis, hot tub, health club, golf privileges, bicycles, meeting rooms. AE, MC, V. $$$$

Kill Devil Hills
Dining

Etheridge Seafood Restaurant. The fish comes straight from the boat to the kitchen at this family-owned, upscale seafood house, in operation for over half a century. It's decorated with Etheridge family memorabilia, depicting their successful fishing and warehousing operation. *U.S. 158 Bypass at Milepost 9.5, tel. 919/441–2645. No reservations. Dress: casual. MC, V. Open Mar.–Oct. $$–$$$*

Dining and Lodging

Ramada Inn. Rooms in this convention-style hotel have ocean views and come with refrigerators and microwave ovens. Peppercorns Restaurant, overlooking the ocean, serves breakfast and dinner, and lunch is available on the sun deck next to the pool. *U.S. 158, Milepost 9.5, Box 2716, 27948, tel. 919/441–2151 or 800/635–1824, fax 919/441–1830. 173 rooms. Facilities: pool, golf privileges, Jacuzzi, meeting rooms. AE, MC, V. $$–$$$*

Manteo
Dining

Elizabethan Inn. Enjoy "Pastime with Goode Companie," a show with an authentic 16th-century Elizabethan feast at this inn during the summer months, Tuesday–Friday. Cost: $25 adults, $14 children. *US 64, tel. 919/473–2101 or 800/346–2466. Reservations required. $$$*

Weeping Radish Brewery and Restaurant. Waiters dressed in Bavarian costumes serve German dishes while German music plays in the background. Tours of the brewery are given upon request. The beer is superb, but this isn't the place for seafood. *U.S. 64, tel. 919/473–1157. Reservations advised for parties of 6 or more. MC, V. Closed major holidays. $$*

Dining and Lodging

Tranquil House Inn. This 19th-century-style waterfront inn is only a few steps from shops, restaurants, and the Elizabeth II State Historic Site, but bikes are provided for adventures beyond. Guests receive fresh flowers and complimentary wine upon arrival. A Continental breakfast is also on the house. Guests often gather around the fireplace in the library to talk about the day's activities. *Queen Elizabeth Ave., the Waterfront, Box 2045, Manteo 27954, tel. 919/473–1404 or 800/458–7069. 28 rooms. Facilities: outdoor grill, observation deck. AE, D, DC, MC, V. $$$*

Nags Head
Dining

Owens' Restaurant. Housed in an old Nags Head–style clapboard cottage, Owens' has been in the same family since 1946. The seafood is outstanding—especially the coconut shrimp and lobster bisque. Nightly entertainment is offered in the brass and glass Station Keeper's Lounge. *U.S. 158, Milepost 17, tel. 919/441–7309. Reservations accepted for large parties only. AE, DC, MC, V. No lunch. Closed Dec.–Mar. $$$*

Lance's Seafood Bar & Market. You can contemplate the fishing and hunting memorabilia while you dine on steamed or raw seafood and then drop the shells through the hole in the table. *U.S. 158 bypass, Milepost 14, tel. 919/441–7501. MC, V. Closed Christmas. $$–$$$*

Lodging

First Colony Inn. The rooms in this historic inn near the ocean are furnished with four-poster and canopied beds, hand-crafted armoires, and English antiques. The suites have wet bars, kitchenettes, and Jacuzzis. A Continental breakfast and afternoon tea come with the room. *6720 S. Virginia Dare Trail, 27959, tel. 919/441–2343 or 800/368–9390. 26 rooms and 4 suites. Facilities: pool, laundry room, refrigerators in rooms. AE, D, MC, V. $$–$$$*

Ocracoke
Dining and Lodging

Island Inn and Dining Room. The inn was built as a private lodge back in 1901. It shows its age a bit, but is full of Outer Banks character and is being upgraded a step at a time. The large rooms in the

Crow's Nest on the third floor are the best; they have cathedral ceilings and look out over the island. The dining room is known for its oyster omelet, crab cakes, and hush puppies. Reservations are advised, particularly for dinner. *Rte. 12, Box 9, 27960, tel. 919/928–4351 (inn) or 919/928–7821 (dining room). 35 rooms. Facilities: heated pool. D, MC, V. Open year-round. $$–$$$*

Camping Camping is permitted in designated areas all along the Cape Hatteras National Seashore. All campgrounds in the park have cold showers, drinking water, tables, grills, and restrooms (except Ocracoke, which has pit toilets). Sanitary stations for recreational vehicles are at Oregon Inlet, Cape Point at Cape Hatteras, and Ocracoke. Oregon Inlet, Cape Point, and Ocracoke are open from mid-April through mid-October; Frisco, mid-June to late August. Be sure to take along extra-long tent stakes for sand, and don't forget the insect repellent. All sites are available on a first-come, first-served basis (except Ocracoke where reservations are required). *Contact Cape Hatteras National Seashore, Route 1, Box 675, Manteo 27954, tel. 919/473–2311.* There are also many private campgrounds scattered along the Outer Banks. *For information contact the North Carolina Travel and Tourism Division, tel. 800/847–4862.*

Wilmington and the Cape Fear Coast

The old seaport town of Wilmington has much to celebrate these days. Thanks to efforts led by the Downtown Area Revitalization Effort (DARE), the once-decadent downtown has been reborn. *Henrietta II*, a paddle wheeler similar to those that used to ply the waters of the Cape Fear River, has been put into service as a tourist vessel. Visitors are drawn to the Coast Line Convention Center complex, reminiscent of old railroad days, and to the charms of Chandler's, the Cotton Exchange, and Water Street Market, now shopping and entertainment centers. They also come to Wilmington for special annual events such as the Azalea Festival, North Carolina Jazz Festival, Christmas candlelight tours, and fishing tournaments. And on the surrounding Cape Fear Coast visitors tour old plantation houses and azalea gardens, study sea life at the state aquarium, and bask in the sun at nearby beaches.

Getting There and Getting Around

Visitors can get to Wilmington and the Cape Fear Coast via car, plane, bus, or boat. Several cruise lines dock here on their way to Bermuda or the Caribbean.

By Plane US Air (tel. 800/428–4322), American Eagle (tel. 800/433–7300), and ASA Delta Connection (to Atlanta) (tel. 800/282–3424) serve the **New Hanover International Airport** (tel. 910/341–4333), ½ mile from downtown Wilmington.

By Car U.S. Highways 421, 74, 76, 17, and 117 serve Wilmington. I-40 now links the city with I-95.

By Bus **Greyhound Lines** serves the Union Bus Terminal, at 201 Harnett Street (tel. 910/762–6625 or 800/231–2222). The **Wilmington Transit Authority** (tel. 910/343–0106) provides service every day except Sunday. There is also taxi service.

By Boat Public boat access is offered at Atlantic Marina, Carolina Beach State Park, Masonboro Boat Yard and Marina, Seapath Transient Dock, Wrightsville Gulf Terminal, and Wrightsville Marina. The Wilmington Hilton, Blockade Runner, Harbor Inn, and Summer Sands provide docking facilities for their guests. A river taxi runs (mid-June—Labor Day) across the Cape Fear River between the USS *North Carolina Battleship Memorial* and downtown Wilmington. The fare is $1 round-trip. A state-run car ferry connects Fort Fisher with Southport on the coast.

Guided Tours

The "Guide Map of Historic Wilmington and the Cape Fear Coast" is available from the Cape Fear Coast Convention and Visitors Bureau in the restored New Hanover County Courthouse (*see below*) and at the Visitor Information Booth at the foot of Market Street (in the summer). The bureau can suggest itineraries and arrange tours of local industries upon advance request.

The Wilmington Adventure Walking Tours, run by Bob Jenkins, will guide you around old Wilmington and other parts of the Lower Cape Fear Region year-round. *Tel. 910/763–1785. Admission: $10 adults, $5 children 6–12.*

Walk and Talk Tour, offered by the Lower Cape Fear Historical Society, covers 12 blocks in downtown Wilmington. *Tours operate Feb.–Dec., Wed. only. Depart from Latimer House. 126 S. 3rd St., tel. 910/762–0492. Admission: $5 ($6, including Latimer House).*

Sightseeing Tours by Horse Drawn Carriage, given by John and Janet Pucci of Springbrook Farms Tuesday–Sunday during the summer and on weekends off-season, depart from Water & Market streets. *Tel. 910/251–8889. Admission: $7 adults, $4 children under 12.*

Cape Fear Riverboats, Inc., operated by Capt. Carl Marshburn, offers a variety of cruises aboard a stern-wheel riverboat that departs from Riverfront Park. *Tel. 910/343–1611 or 800/676–0162. Sightseeing tours: adults $8, children $4. Entertainment/dinner cruises: $29–$32.50 per person. Sunset dinner cruises: adults $19.50, children $14. Moonlight cruises: adults $8, children $5 (call for boarding times).*

The Captain J. N. Maffitt Harbor Tour (tel. 910/343–1611 or 800/676–0162) runs cruises, and shuttles passengers between Riverfront Park and the USS *North Carolina Battleship Memorial. Shuttle: every 30 minutes 10–5 except during tours. Fare: $1. Cruises: $5 adults, $3 children.*

Cape Fear Tours (tel. 910/686–7744) offers walking and driving tours of the Wilmington Historic District, mansions, and the beaches for individuals and groups by reservation. Individual tours are $20 per hour.

Important Addresses and Numbers

Tourist Information **Cape Fear Coast Convention and Visitors Bureau** (24 N. 3rd St., Wilmington 28401, tel. 910/341–4030 or 800/222–4757).

Emergencies Tel. 911.

Coast Guard Tel. 910/343–4881.

Exploring Wilmington and the Cape Fear Coast

Wilmington USS ***North Carolina*** **Battleship Memorial,** a top tourist priority, can be reached by car or by taking the river taxi from Riverfront Park. The ship participated in every major naval offensive in the Pacific during World War II. The self-guided tour takes about two hours, and a 10-minute film is shown throughout the day. Narrated tours on cassette are available for rent, and a 70-minute sound-and-light spectacular "The Immortal Showboat," is presented nightly at 9 from early June until Labor Day. *Box 480, Wilmington 28402, tel. 910/251–5797. Admission: $6 adults, $3 children 6–11; sound-and-light show $3.50 adults, $1.75 children. Open daily 8–sunset.*

The **Wilmington Railroad Museum,** at the corner of Red Cross and Water streets, focuses on the days of the Wilmington and Weldon Railroad (about 1840) to the present. Children love climbing on the steam locomotive and caboose. *Tel. 910/763–2634. Admission: $2 adults, $1 children 6–11. Open Tues.–Sat. 10–5, Sun. 1–5.*

From the museum, follow Red Cross Street one block toward downtown and turn right on Front Street. On the second block is the **Cotton Exchange,** a shopping-dining complex housed in restored buildings that have flourished as a trading center since the pre-Civil War days. *Tel. 910/343–9896. Open Mon.–Sat. 10–5:30, some stores open Sun. 1–5.*

Continue east on Grace Street until you reach Third Street and then go south to Chestnut Street, to the **New Hanover County Public Library.** The North Carolina Room in the library attracts researchers and genealogists from all over the country. *201 Chestnut St., tel. 910/341–4394. Admission free. Open Mon.–Thurs. 9–9, Fri. 9–6, Sat. 9–5, Sun. 1–5.*

Follow Chestnut Street to 4th Street, then go two blocks to Market Street. On that corner is the **St. James Graveyard,** which contains the headstones of many early settlers. In the next block of South Fourth Street is the **Temple of Israel,** the oldest Jewish place of worship in the state.

Continue several blocks north on Market Street to the **Cape Fear Museum,** which traces the natural, cultural, and social history of Cape Fear River Country from its beginnings to the present day. *814 Market St., tel. 910/341–7413. Suggested donations: $2 adults, $1.50 military personnel and senior citizens, $1 children 5–17. Open Tues.–Sat. 9–5, Sun. 2–5. Closed holidays.*

Several blocks west on Market Street at the corner of Third, is the **Burgwin-Wright House,** built in 1770 on the foundations of a jail. This colonial restoration, which includes a period garden, is maintained by the National Society of the Colonial Dames of America and by the state of North Carolina. *224 Market St., tel. 910/762–0570. Admission: $3 adults, $1 children. Open Tues.–Sat. 10–3:30.*

Go two blocks south on Third Street, where you'll find the **Zebulon Latimer House,** built in 1852 in the Italianate style. *126 S. 3rd St., tel. 910/762–0492. Admission: $3 adults, $1 children. Open Tues.–Sat. 10–4.*

Wind up your tour at **Chandler's Wharf** on Water Street. Originally a complex of warehouses, it now contains shops and some good seafood restaurants like Elijah's. This is a great place to conclude your tour of downtown Wilmington.

Cape Fear Coast

Go three blocks east to U.S. 17. On the way out of town, stop at **Greenfield Lake and Gardens,** on South Third Street (U.S. 421). The park offers picnicking and canoe and paddle-boat rentals on a scenic 180-acre lake bordered by cypress trees laden with Spanish moss. *Tel. 910/763–9371. Admission free. Open daily.*

Follow U.S. 17 northeast for 9 miles until you reach **Poplar Grove Historic Plantation.** The home of the Foy family for generations, the 1850 Greek Revival plantation was opened to the public in 1980. You can tour the manor house and outbuildings, see craft demonstrations, shop in the country store, and pet the farm animals. *9 mi northeast of Wilmington on U.S. 17, tel. 910/686–9989 (restaurant 910/686–9503). Guided tours Feb.–Dec.: $6 adults, $5 senior citizens, $3 students and children 5–16. Open Mon.–Sat. 9–5, Sun. noon–5.*

Now head south on U.S. 17 until you reach Military Cut-off Road, which becomes Oleander Drive and leads to **Airlie Gardens** (8 mi east). The gardens are open from March through September. *Rte. 74/76, tel. 910/763–4646. Admission: $6 adults, $5 senior citizens ($1 less May–Oct.), children under 10 free.*

Take Route 76 west to Route 421 south and follow it to the **Southport–Fort Fisher Ferry** (tel. 910/458–3329), some 20 miles south of Wilmington. On the way, stop at **Fort Fisher State Historic Park** and its **aquarium** (*see* What to See and Do with Children, *below*). The car-ferry trip is an enjoyable river ride between Old Federal Point at the tip of the spit and the quaint town of Southport. You can see the "Old Baldy" lighthouse en route. *Ferries run year-round 8–6. Fare: $3 per car. (The privately owned passenger ferry to Bald Head Island runs from Southport 8–7; fare: $15 adults, $8 children.)*

After you get off the ferry in Southport, take Route 87 north to the **Carolina Power and Light Company Visitors Center.** Here you can learn about nuclear power through exhibits and movies and then use the picnic area. *Tel. 910/457–6041. Admission free. Open June–Aug., weekdays 9–4; Sun. and July 4, 1–4; Sept.–May, weekdays 9–4.*

Continue north on Route 87/133 and you will arrive at **Orton Plantation Gardens.** The house is not open to the public, but the gardens may be toured anytime. *Tel. 910/371–6851. Admission: $7 adults, $3 children 6–12. Open Mar.–Aug., daily 8–6, Sept.–Nov., daily 8–5.*

Take a short detour off Route 133 to **Brunswick Town State Historic Site,** where you can explore the excavations of a colonial town, see Fort Anderson, a Civil War earthworks fort, and have a picnic. *Tel. 910/371–6613. Admission free. Open Apr.–Oct., Mon.–Sat. 9–5, Sun. 1–5; Nov.–Mar., Tues.–Sat. 10–4, Sun. 1–4.*

What to See and Do with Children

Fort Fisher State Historic Site was the largest and one of the most important earthwork fortifications in the South during the Civil War. Visitors enjoy the reconstructed battery and Civil War relics and artifacts from sunken blockade-runners. *U.S. 421 at Kure Beach, tel. 910/458–5538. Admission free. Open Apr.–Oct., Mon.–Sat. 9–5, Sun. 1–5; Nov.–Mar., Tues.–Sat. 10–4, Sun. 1–4.*

The **North Carolina Aquarium at Fort Fisher,** one of three state aquariums, has a 20,000-gallon shark tank, a touch pool (where you can handle starfish, sea urchins and the like), a whale exhibit, and other attractions. The park is also a natural area where wildflowers, birds, and small animals thrive. You can also visit the World War II bunker that stood guard against sea attacks from the Atlantic. Field trips and workshops for groups can be arranged. *U.S. 421 at Kure Beach, tel. 910/458–8257. Admission free. Open Mon.–Sat. 9–5, Sun. 1–5. Closed major holidays.*

The **Wilmington Railroad Museum** (*see* Exploring, *above*).

Off the Beaten Track

Military history buffs get a bang out of **Moore's Creek National Battlefield,** where American patriots defeated the Loyalists in 1776. *20 mi northwest of Wilmington on Rte. 210, tel. 910/283–5591. Admission free. Open daily 8–5.*

A visit to **Tryon Palace at New Bern,** about 150 miles from the Outer Banks, 100 miles north of Raleigh, and 80 miles from Wilmington, is an ideal overnight trip. The reconstructed Georgian palace, considered the most elegant government building in the country in its time, was the colonial capitol and the home of Royal Governor William Tryon in the 1770s. It was rebuilt according to architectural drawings of the original palace and furnished in English and American antiques as listed in Governor Tryon's inventory. Costumed interpreters give tours of the house; tours of the 18th-century formal gardens are self-guided. During the summer, actors in period dress give monologues describing a day in the life of Governor Tryon. Special events are held periodically throughout the year, and craft demonstrations are given daily. The stately John Wright Stanly House (circa 1783), Dixon-Stevenson House (circa 1826), and the recently restored New Bern Academy (circa 1809) are a part of the Tryon Palace Complex. An audiovisual orientation is offered in the Visitor Reception Center. *610 Pollock St., New Bern 28560, tel. 919/638–1560. Admission (palace and gardens only): $8 adults, $4 K–12 students. Combination tour of all buildings and gardens: $12 adults, $6 students. Garden tour only: $4 adults, $3 students. Open Mon.–Sat. 9:30–4, Sun. 1–4. Closed major holidays.*

Shopping

Visitors will find it easy to restrict their shopping to Chandler's Wharf, the Cotton Exchange, and the Water Street Market, but the city also offers many unique shops in the Historic District, as well as shopping malls and discount outlets.

Beaches

Three beaches—**Wrightsville, Carolina,** and **Kure**—are within a short drive from Wilmington, and miles and miles of sand stretch northward to the Outer Banks and southward to South Carolina. The beaches offer a full gamut of activities, from fishing to sunbathing to scuba diving, and a choice of accommodations, including weathered cottages, resorts, condos, and motels. Wrightsville, about 5 miles east of Wilmington, is a posh and popular beach with a number of outstanding restaurants nearby. Carolina and Kure beaches, about 12 miles south, cater to families. Camping and picnicking are permitted at Carolina Beach State Park. There are approximately 100 points of public access along the shoreline. Marked by orange-and-blue signs, these points offer parking, restrooms, and outdoor showers. Some of the smaller beaches have lifeguards on duty, and many are accessible to people with disabilities. A number of fishing piers are also open to the public.

Participant Sports

Fishing Surf fishing is popular on the piers that dot the coast. Charter boats and headboats are available for off-shore fishing. Four major fishing tournaments, for substantial prize money, are held each year—the **Cape Fear Marlin Tournament,** the **Wrightsville Beach King Mackerel Tournament,** East Coast Open King Mackerel Tournament, and the **U.S. Open King Mackerel Tournament.** For more information on these tournaments, contact the Cape Fear Coast Convention and Visitors Bureau (*see* Tourist Information, *above*).

Golf The city has an 18-hole course designed by Donald Ross. In addition, there are 10 public and semi-private courses in the Greater Wilmington area, including the breathtaking Bald Head Island Golf Course, a George Cobb design. For more information on golf, call the Cape Fear Coast Convention and Visitors Bureau (*see* Tourist Information, *above*).

Sailboat Racing The Wrightsville Beach Ocean Racing Association sponsors sailboat races for yachts from April through October.

Surfing and Board Sailing These sports are popular at area beaches, and rentals are available at shops in Wilmington, Wrightsville Beach, and Carolina Beach.

Scuba Diving Wrecks such as the World War II tanker *John D. Gill* make for exciting diving off the coast. **Aquatic Safaris** (5751–4 Oleander Dr., Wilmington, tel. 910/392–4386) rents equipment and leads trips.

Triathlon Those who enjoy jogging, swimming, and bicycling can join in the annual **Wilmington Triathlon** in the fall. Participants swim across Banks Channel to Wrightsville Beach, then bicycle to Carolina Beach and back to Wilmington, and then run from there back to Wrightsville Beach.

Spectator Sports

College Sports Local fans support the University of North Carolina at Wilmington's Seahawk basketball, baseball, and swimming teams. The school belongs to the NCAA Division I Colonial Athletic Association. *For tickets, tel. 910/395–3232.*

Rugby The Cape Fear Rugby Tournament is an annual July 4th event, held at UNC-W. *Tel. 910/395–3233.*

Dining and Lodging

Dining Local cuisine is simply seafood. Shrimp (this is where the shrimp boats come in), oysters, Atlantic blue crab, and king mackerel—and lots of it—are prepared in a variety of ways. Homegrown fruits and vegetables, too, are used extensively in local cooking. Barbecued pork is another popular dish. International cuisines—from Mexican to Japanese to German—are also represented. Dress at these restaurants is neat but casual.

Category	Cost*
$$$$	over $25
$$$	$15–$25
$$	$8–$15
$	under $8

**per person without tax (6%), service, or drinks*

Lodging Visitors to Wilmington and Cape Fear Coast can choose among 6,000 rooms. The selection includes a variety of chains, condos and resorts overlooking the ocean, and in-town guest houses. In addition to in-town properties, there are many accommodations at Carolina, Kure, and Wrightsville beaches. A complete list is included in the *Accommodations Guide*, available from the Convention and Visitors Bureau.

Category	Cost*
$$$$	over $100
$$$	$60–$100
$$	$30–$60
$	under $30

**double room; add 9% for taxes*

Dining *$$–$$$* **Ocean Terrace Restaurant.** Part of the Blockade Runner Resort (*see* Lodging, *below*), this restaurant attracts large crowds to its Saturday seafood-buffet and Sunday brunch. Regular dishes here include grilled New York strip steak with bourbon-shallot butter; sautéed almond-breaded flounder with shrimp; and sautéed chicken breast with toasted pecans, pears, and apples. *Blockade Runner Resort Hotel and Conference Center, 275 Waynick Blvd., Wrightsville Beach, tel. 910/256–2251 or 800/541–1161. Reservations advised. AE, D, DC, MC, V.*

$$ **Market Street Casual Dining.** This always busy eatery offers a wide variety of sandwiches and entrées, including seafood and steaks, served in a casual atmosphere. There's also a bar on the premises. *6309 Market St., tel. 910/395–2488. No reservations. AE, D, MC, V.*

Oceanic Restaurant and Grill. Its Oceanic Pier location gives patrons the top panoramic view of the Atlantic for miles around—a wonderful backdrop for the fresh seafood, steaks, and chicken served here. *703 S. Lumina St., Wrightsville Beach, tel. 910/256–5551. Reservations advised for large parties. AE, MC, V.*

The Pilot House. At this Chandler's Wharf restaurant, known for its seafood, pastas, and fresh vegetables, you can now dine outdoors overlooking the Cape Fear River. The Sunday Brunch (April–October), featuring Low Country Southern food, is the most popular in town. *2 Ann St., tel. 910/343–0200. Reservations advised. AE, D, MC, V.*

$–$$ **Ken and Art's Studio Café** is where you might spot a star when they're filming on location in Wilmington. The menu features a mixture of California, New York, and Carolinas cuisine, served amid movie memorabilia. *North Carolina Film Studios, 1223 N. 23rd St., tel. 910/343–3708. Reservations advised. No credit cards. Open for lunch.*

$ **Water Street Restaurant and Sidewalk Café.** Housed in a restored two-story brick waterfront warehouse that dates to 1835, this outdoor café and restaurant serves up Greek, Mexican, Middle Eastern, and other ethnic cooking. *5 Water St., tel. 910/343–0042. Reservations not required. MC, V.*

Lodging *$$$$* **Bald Head Island Resort.** Accessible only by ferry from Southport, this resort offers privacy in a luxurious isolated setting. Despite the quiet surroundings, there's always something to do on the resort island: Activities include golf, tennis, sailing, and fishing. Other favorite pastimes are watching the loggerhead turtles, and taking a tour led by a naturalist. Guests have their own rental condo or beach house. *Bald Head Island, 28461, tel. 910/457–5000 or 800/234–1666, fax 910/457–9232. Over 100 rental condos and beach houses. Facilities: pool, marina, restaurants, and shops. AE, DC, MC, V. Three-night minimum. Ferry $15 adults, $8 children, tel. 910/457–5003.*

$$$ **Catherine's Inn.** Built in 1883 and in the historic district, this two-story Italianate home, now a B&B, has hardwood floors, a sunken garden, four-poster and canopy beds, and claw-foot tubs—many items collected by the innkeepers over the years. *410 South Front St., 28401, tel. 910/251–0863 or 800/476–0723. 3 rooms. MC, V.*

The Docksider Inn. In a class of its own, this waterfront hotel in the heart of Kure Beach is nautical both outside and in. Gray with navy shutters, the inn is furnished in light-colored beachy furniture and enhanced with marine art and artifacts, including a set of 1930s British Admiralty signal flags. Each bathroom has an original watercolor. The third floor is being converted into "Captain's Cabins" for those seeking a romantic getaway. *202 Fort Fisher Blvd. (U.S. 421), 28449, tel. 910/458–4200, fax 910/458–6468. 34 rooms. Facilities: wooden-deck pool, golf, tennis. DC, D, MC, V.*

The Inn at St. Thomas Court. Guests are pampered yet enjoy total privacy at this small luxurious apartment-type house, which has studios and one- and two-bedroom suites, furnished in a traditional style in keeping with the surrounding historic district. Guests may opt for sailing lessons with the owners. *101 S. 2nd St., 28401, tel. 910/343–1800 or 800/525–0909, fax 910/251–1149. 30 units. Complimentary Continental breakfast for suite occupants. AE, DC, MC, V.*

Wilmington Hilton Inn. Overlooking the Cape Fear River on one side and the city on the other, this is one of the most convenient places to stay in town. The spacious inn has a dining room and lounge. *301 N. Water St., Wilmington 28401, tel. 910/763–5900 or 800/445–8667, fax 910/763–0038. 175 rooms and suites. Facilities: outdoor pool, meeting rooms, complimentary airport transportation. AE, DC, D, MC, V.*

$$ **Blockade Runner Resort Hotel and Conference Center.** This extensive complex is widely known for both its food (*see* Dining, *above*) and lodging. Rooms overlook either the inlet or the ocean. *275 Waynick Blvd., Wrightsville Beach 28480, tel. 910/256–2251 or 800/541–1161, fax 910/256–5502. 150 rooms and suites. Facilities: restaurant, pool, health spa, meeting rooms, sailing center, bike rentals, golf privileges. AE, D, DC, MC, V.*

$ **Hampton Inn.** This economy chain motel, 3 miles from downtown, is not luxurious but offers such extras as complimentary Continental breakfast, in-room movies, and free local calls. *5107 Market St., 28403, tel. 910/395–5045 or 800/426–7866, fax 910/799–1971. 118 rooms. Facilities: pool. AE, D, DC, MC, V.*

The Arts and Nightlife

The arts are very much a part of Wilmington life. Theatrical productions are staged by the **Thalian Association, Opera House Productions,** and **Tapestry Players.** The city has its own symphony orchestra, oratorio society, civic ballet and concert association; and the **North Carolina Symphony** makes four appearances here each year. The annual **Wilmington Jazz Festival,** held in February, and the **Blues Festival,** in August, draw big crowds.

The Arts **St. John's Museum of Art** is known for its 13 prints by Cassatt, as well as for its works by North Carolina artists. The museum is housed in three buildings, including the 1804 Masonic Lodge Building, the oldest such lodge in the state. There is also a sculpture garden. *114 Orange St., tel. 910/763–0281. Suggested donation: $1 per person, $3 per family. Open Tues.–Sat. 10–5, Sun. noon–4.*

The Museum of World Cultures (601 S. College Rd., tel. 910/395–3411 or 910/350–4007), at the University of North Carolina at Wilmington, exhibits its collections of African art, pre-Columbian textiles, Chinese ceramics, and Middle Eastern artifacts at various locations around the campus.

Thalian Hall, a magnificent opera house built in 1858 and refurbished to the tune of $5 million, is the site of theater, dance, and musical performances. *310 Chestnut St., tel. 910/343–3664 or 800/523–2820 in NC. The hall is open for self-guided tours Mon.–Sat. noon–8:30, pending performance schedules.*

Nightlife Wilmington nightlife is centered in hotel lounges. The **Ocean Terrace Restaurant** in the Blockade Runner Hotel (*see* Dining and Lodging, *above*) offers live entertainment Thursday through Sunday, with nationally known acts in the **Comedy Zone** March–November. **The Ice House Beer Garden** (115 S. Water St., tel. 910/251–1158 or 910/763–2084) serves food and beer and showcases a different music group nightly. **The Yellow Rose Saloon** (5025 Market St., tel. 910/791–2001) is known for country music.

North Carolina High Country, Including Asheville

The majestic peaks, meadows, and valleys of the Appalachian, Blue Ridge, and Smoky mountains characterize the High Country in the western corner of the state. National parks and forests and the Blue Ridge Parkway are the region's main attractions, providing prime opportunities for skiing, hiking, bicycling, camping, fishing, and canoeing, or just taking in the breathtaking views.

The largest and most cosmopolitan city in High Country, Asheville has been a retreat for the wealthy and famous for decades. In recent years this mountain city has been rated, among cities of its size, as America's number-one favorite place to live. It has scenic beauty, low levels of pollution, a good airport and road system, a moderate four-season climate, a variety of hotels and restaurants, and a thriving arts community. Banjo pickers are as revered as violinists, mountain folks mix with city slickers, and everyone loves where they live.

Cities like Boone, Blowing Rock, and Banner Elk have boomed in the 30 years since the introduction of snowmaking equipment. Luxury resorts now dot the valleys and mountaintops. Visitors to the hills take advantage of the many crafts shops, music festivals, theater offerings, and such special events as the Grandfather Mountain Highland Games. The passing of each season is a special visual event here, and autumn is the star.

Getting There and Getting Around

By Plane **Asheville Regional Airport** (tel. 704/684–2226) is served by American Eagle, Atlantic Southeast Airlines, ComAir, Delta, United–United Express, and USAir. USAir Express (tel. 800/428–4322) serves the **Hickory Airport,** about 40 miles from Blowing Rock.

By Car I–40 runs east and west through Asheville. I–26 runs from Charleston, SC, to Asheville. I–240 forms a perimeter around the city. U.S. 23-19A is a major north and west route. The Blue Ridge Parkway runs northeast from Great Smoky Mountains National Park to Shenandoah National Park in Virginia. U.S. 221 runs north from Little Switzerland to the Virginia border through Blowing Rock and Boone and intersects I–40 at Marion. U.S. 321 intersects I–40 at Hickory and heads to Blowing Rock/Boone.

By Bus **Greyhound Lines** (tel. 704/253–5353 or 800/231–2222) serves Asheville.

Guided Tours

Travel Professionals, Inc. (tel. 704/298–3438), **Western Carolina Tours** (tel. 704/254–4603), and **Young Transportation** (tel. 704/258–0084 or 800/622–5444) provide group tours of Asheville.

Important Addresses and Numbers

Tourist Information The **Visitor Information Center** (151 Haywood St., Asheville 28801, tel. 704/258–3858) and the **Asheville Travel and Tourism Office** (Box 1010, Asheville 28802, tel. 704/258–6111 or 800/257–1300) can answer questions and provide maps. **North Carolina High Country Host** (701 Blowing Rock Rd., Boone 28607, tel. 704/264–1299 or 800/438–7500).

Emergencies Dial 911.

Exploring North Carolina High Country, Including Asheville

Asheville Downtown Asheville is noted for its eclectic architecture. The **Battery Park Hotel,** built in 1924, is neo-Georgian; the **Flatiron Building** (1924) is neo-classical; the **Church of St. Lawrence** (1912) is Spanish Baroque; **Old Pack Library** (1925) is in Italian Renaissance–style; the **S & W Cafeteria** (1929) is Art Deco. In fact, the city has the largest collection of Art Deco buildings outside of Miami. A brochure entitled "Asheville Heritage Tour" (available at the Visitor Information Center) details six different historic districts in the city. **Tour Services of Historic Asheville** (tel. 704/255–1093) conducts 2-hour walking tours of downtown, April–October; tours leave from Pack Place. The Preservation Society of Asheville has produced a walking tour cassette ($10), available at Pack Place.

Pack Place, the newest addition to downtown, houses the Asheville Art Museum, Colburn Gem & Mineral Museum, Health Adventure, YMI Cultural Center, and a performing arts theater. *2 S. Pack Sq., tel. 704/252–3866. Admission fees vary. Open Tues.–Sat. 10–6, Sun. 1–5.*

The **Thomas Wolfe Memorial** (48 Spruce St.), built in 1880 in the Queen Anne style, is one of the oldest houses in downtown Asheville. Wolfe's mother ran a boarding house here for years, and he used it as the setting for his novel *Look Homeward, Angel.* Family pictures, clothing, and original furnishings fill the house, now a state historic site. Guided tours are available. *Tel. 704/253–8304. Admission: $1 adults, 50¢ students. Open Apr.–Oct. Mon.–Sat. 9–5, Sun. 1–5; Nov.–Mar. Tues.–Sat. 10–4, Sun. 1–4.*

From downtown, take U.S. 25 south. The entrance to the architecturally famous **Biltmore Estate** faces Biltmore Village, about three blocks from the interstate. Built as the private home of George Vanderbilt, the 255-room French Renaissance château is today a museum. Richard Morris Hunt designed it, and Frederick Law Olmsted landscaped the original 125,000-acre estate (now 8,000 acres). It took 1,000 men five years to complete the gargantuan project. On view are the priceless antiques and art collected by the Vanderbilts, and 17 acres of gardens. Visitors can also see the state-of-the-art winery and take Christmas candlelight tours of the house. *Tel. 704/255–1700 or 800/543–2961. Admission: $22.95 adults, $17.25 students ages 10–15, accompanied children under 10 free. Open daily 9–5 except Thanksgiving, Christmas, and New Year's.*

Weaverville Take U.S. 19-23 Bypass north about 18 miles to Weaverville and the **Zebulon B. Vance Birthplace** state historic site, with a two-story log cabin and several outbuildings, where North Carolina's governor during the Civil War grew up. Crafts and chores typical of his period are often demonstrated. Picnic facilities are available. *Reems Creek Rd. (Rte. 1103), tel. 704/645–6706. Admission free. Open Apr.–Oct., Mon.–Sat. 9–5, Sun. 1–5; Nov.–Mar., Tues.–Sat. 10–4, Sun. 1–4.*

Blue Ridge Parkway The most direct route from Asheville to the Boone/Blowing Rock area is the **Blue Ridge Parkway,** a 469-mile stunningly beautiful road which gently winds through mountains and meadows and crosses mountain streams on its way from Cherokee, North Carolina, to Waynesboro, Virginia. To get onto the Parkway from the Vance Birthplace, take U.S. 19-23 south, I–240 east, and then I–40 east. The Parkway is generally open year-round but often closes during heavy snows. Maps and information are available at visitor centers along the highway. *Superintendent, Blue Ridge Pkwy., BB & T Bldg., 1 Pack Sq., Asheville 28801, tel. 704/298–0398.*

The Folk Art Center (Milepost 382 on the Blue Ridge Pkwy.) sells authentic mountain crafts made by members of the Southern Highland Handicraft Guild. *Tel. 704/298–7928. Open daily except major holidays.*

About 65 miles north of the Folk Art Center, just off the parkway on U.S. 221, is **Linville Caverns,** the only caverns in the Carolinas. They go 2,000 feet underground and have a year-round temperature of 51 degrees. *Tel. 704/756–4171. Admission: $4 adults, $2.50 children 5–12. Open 9–6 March–Oct., 9–4:30 Nov.–Feb.*

About a mile further north along the Parkway is **Linville Falls** (Milepost 316.3), one of North Carolina's most frequently photographed waterfalls. An easy trail winds through evergreens and rhododendrons to overlooks where you can get wonderful views of the series of cascades tumbling into Linville Gorge. There's also a visitor center, a campground, and a picnic area.

Just off the parkway at Milepost 305 is **Grandfather Mountain,** famous for its Mile-High Swinging Bridge, a 228-foot-long bridge that sways over a 1,000-foot drop into the Linville Valley. Sweaty-palmed tourists have crossed it since 1952. A Natural History Museum has exhibits on native minerals, flora and fauna, and pioneer life. The annual Singing on the Mountain in June is an opportunity to hear old-time gospel music and preaching, and the Highland Games in July brings together Scottish clans from all over North America for athletic events and Highland dancing. There's also hiking, picnicking, and an environmental habitat. *Blue Ridge Pkwy. and U.S. 221, Linville 28646, tel. 704/733–4337. Admission: $9 adults, $5 children 4–12. Open Apr.–mid-Nov., 8–dusk; mid-Nov.–Mar., 9–4, weather permitting.*

Parks along the parkway include **Julian Price Park** (Mileposts 298–295.1), which offers hiking, canoeing on a mountain lake, trout fishing, and camping, and **Moses H. Cone Park** (Mileposts 292.7–295), which has a turn-of-the-century manor house that's now the **Parkway Craft Center.**

Blowing Rock Just north of the entrance to Moses H. Cone Park, take U.S. 221/321 to Blowing Rock, a tourist mecca since the 1880s, which has retained the flavor of a quiet mountain village. Only a few hundred people are permanent residents, but the population swells each summer. The **Blowing Rock,** considered the state's oldest tourist attraction, looms 4,000 feet over the Johns River Gorge. If you throw your hat over the sheer precipice, it may come back to you, should the wind gods be playful. The story goes that a Cherokee brave and a Chickasaw maiden fell in love. Torn between his tribe and his love, he jumped from the cliff, but she prayed to the Great Spirit and he was blown safely back to her. It's more or less a gimmick, but the view from the observation tower is nice, and there's a garden landscaped with mountain laurel, rhododendron, and other native plants. *Off U.S. 321, tel. 704/295–7111. Admission: $4 adults, $1 children 6–11. Open summer 8–8, winter 10–5.*

Head north toward Boone on U.S. 321, until you come to **Tweetsie Railroad,** a popular theme park where visitors can ride a train beset by train robbers and Indians. The park also has a petting zoo, country fair (May–October), rides, gold panning, a saloon show, and concessions. *Tel. 704/264–9061 or 800/526–5740. Admission: $12.95 adults, $10.95 children 4–12 and senior citizens 60 years and older. Open late-May–Labor Day daily 9–6; May weekends 9–6, July weekends until 8; Sept.–Oct. weekdays 9–5 and weekends 9–6.*

Boone Boone, named for frontiersman Daniel Boone, is a city of several thousand residents at the convergence of three major highways—U.S. 321, U.S. 421, and NC 105. **"Horn in the West,"** a project of the Southern Highlands Historical Association, is an outdoor drama that traces the story of Boone's life. *Amphitheater off U.S. 321, tel. 704/264–2120. Admission: $9 adults, $4.50 children under 13. 8:30 nightly except Mon. mid-June–mid-Aug.*

Boone's **Appalachian Cultural Museum** showcases the successes of such mountain residents as stock-car racer Junior Johnson and country singers Lula Belle and Scotty Wiseman, and exhibits a vast collection of antique quilts, fiddles, and handcrafted furniture. *University Hall near Greene's Motel, U.S. 321, tel. 704/262–3117. Admission: $2 adults, $1.75 senior citizens, $1 children 12–18. Open Tues.–Sat. 10–5, Sun. 1–5. Closed Mon.*

Banner Elk From Boone, take U.S. 321 west and NC 194 south to Banner Elk, a popular ski resort town surrounded by the lofty peaks of Grandfather, Hanging Rock, Beech, and Sugar mountains.

Ashe County North of Boone in Ashe County, past Blue Ridge Parkway Milepost 258.6, are the **Blue Ridge Mountain Frescoes.** North Carolina artist Ben Long painted four big-as-life frescoes in two abandoned churches here in the 70s. "The Last Supper" (measuring 17 × 19.5 feet) is in the Glendale Springs Holy Trinity Church. The others are in St. Mary's Episcopal Church at Beaver Creek, including "Mary, Great with Child," which won the Leonardo da Vinci International Award. *Tel. 910/982–3076, 9–1. Admission free. Open 24 hours a day. Guide service available with prior arrangements.*

What to See and Do with Children

Tour an underground mine or dig for gems of your own at **Emerald Village,** an old mine. *McKinney Mine Rd. at Blue Ridge Pkwy. Milepost 334, tel. 704/765–6463. Museum admission: $3.50 adults, $2.50 students, $3 senior citizens, plus cost of gem bucket chosen ($3–$100). A $50 bucket guarantees you a stone, which will be cut free of charge, $100 guarantees two. Open late May–early Sept. 9–6, early May and Oct. 9–5.*

Sliding Rock. In summer, you can skid 150 feet on a natural water slide in Pisgah National Forest. Wear old jeans and tennis shoes, and bring a towel. *Pisgah National Forest, north of Brevard, off U.S. 276, tel. 704/257–4200. Admission free. Open daily.*

Tweetsie Railroad (*see* Exploring, *above*).

Off the Beaten Track

At **Chimney Rock Park,** about 25 miles southeast of Asheville on U.S. 74/64, you can ride an elevator up through a 26-story shaft of rock for a staggering view of Hickory Nut Gorge and the surrounding Blue Ridge Mountains. Trails lead to 400-foot Hickory Nut Falls, where *The Last of the Mohicans* was filmed. *Tel. 704/625–2126 or 800/277–9611. Admission: $9 adults, $4.50 children 6–15. Open daily 8:30–4:30, until 5:30 May–mid-Oct.*

About 25 miles south of Asheville via I–26 is **Flat Rock,** the town to which the poet and Lincoln biographer Carl Sandburg moved with his wife, Lilian in 1945. Guided tours of their house, **Connemara,** where the Sandburg's papers still lie scattered on his desk, are given by the National Park Service. In summer, "The World of Carl Sandburg" and "Rootabaga Stories" are presented at the Flat Rock Playhouse by the Vagabond Players. *Tel. 704/693–4178. Admission: $1 ages 17–61, under 17 and over 61 free. Open daily 9–5.*

You'll find everything from ribbons and calico to brogans and overalls in the **Mast General Store,** ten miles northwest of Boone in the tiny town of Valle Crucis. Built in 1882, the store has plank floors worn to a soft sheen and a potbellied stove that's still fired up on chilly mornings. (The company operates a similar store in downtown Boone: Old Boone Mercantile, 104 E. King St., Boone, tel. 704/262–0000; open Mon.–Sat. 10–6, Sun. 1–6.) *NC 194, Valle Crucis, tel. 704/963–6511. Open Mon.–Sat. 6:30–6:30, Sun. 1–6.*

Shopping

Crafts

Biltmore Homespun Shop, on the grounds of the Grove Park Inn and established by Mrs. George Vanderbilt, sells woven goods, such as blankets, shawls, and baskets, made on the premises. *Macon St., Asheville, tel. 704/253–7651. Open Mon.–Sat. 10–5; June–Oct. also Sun. 1–5.*

Bolick Pottery sells mountain crafts and pottery, handcrafted on the spot by Glenn and Lula Bolick; Glenn will even throw in a mountain tale, a buck dance, or a tune on his saw free of charge. *Off U.S. 321, Rte. 8, Box 285–A, Lenoir, tel. 704/295–3862. Open Mon.–Sat. 9–5, Sun. 1–6.*

The **Goodwin Weavers** create bedspreads, tablecloths, and afghans on Civil War–era looms and then sell them in their shop. *Off U.S. 321 Bypass, Blowing Rock, tel. 704/295–3394. Open daily 9–5.*

Qualla Arts and Crafts has authentic Cherokee Indian crafts and items from other American tribes. *U.S. 441 and Drama Rd., Cherokee, tel. 704/497–3103. Open daily 9–5.*

Participant Sports

Canoeing/ Whitewater In the Asheville area, the Chattooga, Nolichucky, French Broad, Nantahala, Ocoee, and Green rivers offer Class I–V rapids. Outfitters include Carolina Wilderness (Box 488, Hot Springs 28743, tel. 704/622–3535 or 800/872–7437) and **Nantahala Outdoor Center** (13077 Hwy. 19W, Box 41, Bryson City, 28713, tel. 704/488–2175 or 800/232–7238).

Near Boone and Blowing Rock, the wild and scenic New River (Class I and II) provides hours of excitement, as do the Nolichucky River, the Watauga River, Wilson Creek, and Toe River. Outfitters include **Edge of the World Outfitters** (Banner Elk, tel. 704/898–9550) and **Wahoo's Adventures** (Boone, tel. 704/262–5774 or 800/444–7238).

Golf Western North Carolina offers many challenging courses. For a listing of public courses in Asheville, Black Mountain, Brevard, Hendersonville, Lake Lure, Old Fort, and Waynesville, contact Asheville's Visitor Information Center (tel. 704/258–3858). North Carolina High Country Host (tel. 704/264–1299 or 800/438–7500) has information on public courses in Boone, Seven Devils, Newland, and West Jefferson.

Hiking More than 100 trails lead off the Blue Ridge Parkway, from easy strolls to strenuous hikes. The **Bluff Mountain Trail** at Doughton Park (Milepost 238.5) is a moderately strenuous 7.5 mile trail winding through forests, pastures, and valleys, and along the mountainside. Moses H. Cone Memorial Park's (Milepost 292.7) **Figure 8 Trail** is an easy and beautiful trail which the Cones designed specifically for their morning walks. The half-mile loop winds through a tunnel of rhododendron and a hardwood forest lined with moss-covered rocks, wildflowers, and lush green ferns. Those who tackle the half-mile, strenuous **Waterrock Knob Trail** (Milepost 451.2), near the southern end of the parkway, will be rewarded with spectacular views from the 6,400-foot-high Waterrock Knob summit. For more information on parkway trails, contact the Blue Ridge Parkway (*see* Exploring, *above*). Another good source is *Walking the Blue Ridge: a Guide to the Trails of the Blue Ridge Parkway* by Leonard Adkins (UNC Press, $11.95), available at most parkway visitor center gift shops.

Trails abound in **Great Smoky Mountains National Park.** For trail maps, contact the Superintendent (Great Smoky Mountains National Park, Gatlinburg, TN 37738, tel. 615/436–5615). The park maintains an information bulletin board with basic trail information at the entrance at the junction of Milepost 469.1 and U.S. 441.

Serious hikers wishing to explore the **Appalachian Trail,** which runs along the crest of the Appalachian Mountains at the North Carolina–Tennessee border, can pick it up at several points, including at the Newfound Gap Parking Area in Great Smoky Mountains National Park (tel. 615/436–5615) and at Grandfather Mountain (tel. 704/733–4337), where you can get trail maps.

Horseback Riding and Trekking Trail rides are offered by several Asheville area stables, including **Pisgah View Ranch** (Rte. 1, Candler 28715, tel. 704/667–9100) and **Cataloochee Ranch** (Rte. 1, Box 500, Maggie Valley 28751, tel. 704/926–1401). And you can hike with llamas carrying your pack into the

Pisgah National Forest on day- and overnight trips with **Windsong Llama Treks, Ltd.** (120 Ferguson Rd., Clyde 28721, tel. 704/627–6111).

Rock Climbing One of the most challenging climbs in the country is the Linville Gorge (Milepost 317, Blue Ridge Pkwy.). Permits are available from the District Forest Ranger's Office in Marion (tel. 704/652–2144) or from the Linville Falls Texaco Station on U.S. 221. **Edge of the World Outfitters in Banner Elk** (tel. 704/898–9550) provides instruction and guided trips.

Skiing Ski resorts in the Asheville area include **Cataloochee** (Rte. 1, Box 500, Maggie Valley 28751, tel. 704/926–0285 or 800/768–0285), **Fairfield–Sapphire Valley** (4000 US 64W, Sapphire Valley 28774, tel. 704/743–3441), and **Wolf Laurel** (Rte. 3, Mars Hill, 28754, tel. 704/689–4111).

The Boone/Blowing Rock area offers downhill skiing at **Appalachian Ski Mountain** (Box 106, Blowing Rock 28605, tel. 704/295–7828 or 800/322–2372), **Ski Beech** (Box 1118, Beech Mountain 28604, tel. 704/387–2011 or 800/438–2093), **Hound Ears Club** (Box 188, Blowing Rock 28605, tel. 704/963–4321), **Sugar Mountain** (Box 369, Banner Elk 28604, tel. 704/898–4521 or 800/643–4370), and **Hawksnest Golf and Ski Resort** (1605 Skyland Dr., Banner Elk, tel. 704/963–6561 or 800/822–4295). For ski conditions, call 800/438–7500. Cross-country skiing is offered at **Moses H. Cone Park** and at **Linville Falls** on the Blue Ridge Parkway (tel. 704/295–7591), and **Roan Mountain** (tel. 615/772–3303). Tours and equipment are available from **High Country Ski Shop** in Pineola (tel. 704/733–2008).

Dining and Lodging

Dining Dining choices in Asheville are many: upscale gourmet restaurants, middle-of-the-road country fare, and fast-food eateries. In the past 30 years, High Country towns outside Asheville have seen a tremendous increase in restaurants. Fresh mountain trout, as well as such game meats as pheasant and venison, are regional specialties. Beer, wine, and liquor by the drink are permitted in Blowing Rock, Banner, Elk, and Beech Mountain; beer and wine only in Boone.

Category	Cost*
$$$$	over $25
$$$	$15–$25
$$	$8–$15
$	under $8

**per person without tax (6%), service, or drinks*

Lodging Lodging options range from posh resorts to mountain cabins, country inns, and economy chain motels. There's a bed for virtually every pocketbook.

Category	Cost*
$$$$	over $100
$$$	$60–$100

$$	$30–$60
$	under $30

**double room; add 8% for taxes*

Asheville
Dining

Market Place on Wall Street. Nouvelle cuisine is served in a relaxed atmosphere. Vegetables and herbs are regionally grown, and bread, pasta, and pastries are made on the premises. *20 Wall St., tel. 704/252–4162. Reservations advised. Dress: informal. No lunch. AE, DC, MC, V. Closed Sun. $$$$*

Black Forest Restaurant. Enjoy traditional German dishes in a Bavarian setting. Specialties include sauerbraten, knockwurst, schnitzel, and Kasseler Rippchen (cured pork ribs). The restaurant celebrates Oktoberfest in the fall. *2155 Hendersonville Hwy., U.S. 25, tel. 704/684–8160. Reservations advised. Dress: casual. AE, DC, MC, V. $$*

Blue Moon Bakery. Chris and Margaret Kobler offer a variety of pastries and breads made on site, as well as sandwiches and salads for lunch, at their European-style bakery. *60 Biltmore Ave., tel. 704/252–6063. No reservations. Dress: casual. MC, V. $$*

West Side Grill. Have a country-style breakfast or dine on meatloaf, turkey, roast beef, baked chicken, and all the trimmings at this '50s-style diner. Wine and beer are available. *1190 Patton Ave., tel. 704/252–9605. No reservations. Dress: casual. AE, MC, V. $$*

Windmill European Grill/Il Pescatore. As the name implies, the menu is international—this cool, dark, and cozy cellar restaurant even serves Asian dishes. There's also an extensive wine list. Dinner only is served. *85 Tunnel Rd., tel. 704/253–5285. Reservations advised. Dress informal. AE, MC, V. $$*

Dining and Lodging

Richmond Hill Inn. Once a private residence, this elegant Victorian mansion is on the National Register of Historic Places. **Gabrielle's,** the gourmet restaurant, is named for the former mistress of the house—wife of congressman and ambassador Richmond Pearson. *87 Richmond Hill Dr., 28806, tel. 704/252–7313 or 800/545–9238, fax 704/252–8726. 21 rooms. Facilities: meeting rooms, Jacuzzi, croquet court. Lunch, dinner, and Sunday brunch open to the public. Reservations advised. Dress: informal. AE, MC, V. $$$$*

Lodging

Grove Park Inn Resort. This is Asheville's premier resort, and it's just as beautiful and exciting as it was the day it opened in 1913. The guest list has included Henry Ford, Thomas Edison, Harvey Firestone, and Warren G. Harding. Novelist F. Scott Fitzgerald stayed here while his wife, Zelda, was in a nearby sanitorium. In the past five years the hotel has been completely renovated. The two newer wings are in keeping with the original design. *290 Macon Ave., 28804, tel. 704/252–2711 or 800/438–5800, fax 704/253–7053 (guests), fax 704/252–6102 (reservations). 510 rooms and suites. Facilities: 4 restaurants, meeting rooms, pool, sauna, whirlpool, putting green, fitness center, golf, tennis, racquetball, parking garage, airport shuttle, children's program, social program. AE, D, MC, V. $$$*

Haywood Park Hotel. Imagine yourself the star in "Are You Being Served?" at this downtown contemporary hotel that was once a department store. **23 Page,** the hotel's elegant restaurant, serves seafood and game, and a free Continental breakfast is delivered to your room. A shopping galleria adjoins the property. *One Battery Park Ave., 28801, tel. 704/252–2522, fax 704/253–0481. 33 rooms, some with refrigerators and whirlpool baths. Facilities: 2 restaurants, exercise room, sauna. AE, D, DC, MC, V. $$$*

Cedar Crest Victorian Inn. This beautiful cottage was constructed by Biltmore craftsmen as a private residence around the turn of the century. Lovingly restored as a bed-and-breakfast inn, it's filled with Victorian antiques. Guests are treated to afternoon tea, evening coffee or chocolate, and a breakfast of fruit, pastry, and coffee. *674 Biltmore Ave., 28803, tel. 704/252–1389 or 800/252–0310. 13 rooms. AE, MC, V. $$–$$$*

Quality Inn Biltmore. Built on the grounds of the old Biltmore Dairy, this hotel is especially convenient for Biltmore Estate visitors. It is attached to the **Biltmore Dairy Bar,** a popular restaurant that offers sandwiches and ice cream. *115 Hendersonville Rd., 28803, tel. 704/274–1800 or 800/221–2222, fax 704/274–5960. 160 rooms. Facilities: outdoor pool, jogging trail nearby, meeting rooms. AE, D, DC, MC, V. $$*

Hampton Inn. Guests can swim in the enclosed pool and then relax beside the fire in the lobby at this economy motel off I–26 that's convenient to downtown. Some guest rooms have whirlpool baths. *One Rocky Ridge Rd., tel. 704/667–2022 or 800/426–7860, fax 704/665–9680. 121 rooms. Facilities: pool, sauna, exercise room, airport shuttle. AE, D, DC, MC, V. $*

Banner Elk
Dining

Heidi's Swiss Inn. Authentic Swiss-German cuisine is served up at this unique mountain farmhouse-turned-restaurant. *Rte. 184, tel. 704/898–5020. Reservations required. Dress: casual. D, MC, V. Closed Sun.–Mon. $$$*

Stonewalls. This contemporary rustic restaurant enjoys one of the best views of Beech Mountain. Fare includes steak, prime rib, fresh seafood, chicken, and homemade desserts. *Hwy. 194, tel. 704/898–5550. Reservations required for groups of 7 or more. Dress: casual. MC, V. No lunch. $$*

Dining and Lodging

Beech Alpen Inn. Guests have a view of the slopes or the Blue Ridge Mountains at this friendly country inn. A continental breakfast is included in the tariff. *700 Beech Mountain Pkwy., Banner Elk 28604, tel. 704/387–2252. 25 rooms (4 with fireplaces). AE, MC, V. Open year-round. $$$*

Blowing Rock
Dining and Lodging

Hound Ears Club. This Alpine inn, overlooking Grandfather Mountain and a lush golf course, offers comfortable, well-kept rooms dressed in Waverly print fabrics. The room rate includes breakfast and dinner. *Off NC 105, 6 mi from Boone; Box 188, 28605, tel. 704/963–4321, fax 704/963–8030. 29 rooms. Facilities: restaurant, pool, golf, tennis. AE, MC, V. $$$$*

Chetola Resort. This small resort of about 70 acres grew out of a turn-of-the-century stone-and-wood lodge that overlooks Chetola Lake. The original building now houses the resort's restaurant and meeting rooms and is adjacent to the 1988 lodge, which contains the accommodations. (The best rooms have balconies facing the lake.) The property adjoins Moses Cone H. Park, part of the Blue Ridge Parkway system, with hiking trails and riding facilities. *Box 17, 28605, tel. 704/295–9301 or 800/243–8652, fax 704/295–5529. 37 rooms, 5 suites. Facilities: restaurant, indoor pool, sauna, racquetball, fitness center, hot tub, tennis, boating, hiking, meeting rooms, whirlpools in suites. AE, D, MC, V. $$$–$$$$*

Green Park Inn. This 100-year-plus Victorian charmer on the eastern continental divide offers spacious rooms, wide porches with rocking chairs, and large public rooms decorated in bright colors and wicker. The bilevel restaurant has won high ratings and is often the setting for dinner theater productions and murder mystery weekends. *U.S. 321, Box 7, 28605, tel. 704/295–3141. Open year-round; restaurant May–Oct.; golf and tennis available May–Oct.*

88 rooms. Facilities: pool, golf, tennis, meeting rooms. AE, MC, V. $$$–$$$$

Boone
Dining

Mike's Inland Seafood. Calabash-style or broiled, the seafood here couldn't taste better if it were served at the ocean. (There's another one in Banner Elk.) *U.S. 321, Boone, tel. 704/262–5605. Reservations not required. Dress: casual. AE, DC, MC, V. Closed Mon. $$*

Shadrack's. Barbecue and seafood are featured at this all-you-can-eat buffet. Patrons also love the live music and square dancing. Children are welcome. *U.S. 321, tel. 704/264–1737. Reservations not required. Dress: casual. AE, D, MC, V. Open Fri.–Sat. evenings only, Thurs. evenings during summer. $$*

Dining and Lodging

Broyhill Inn. Though primarily a conference center, this contemporary hotel on the ASU campus is attractive to individual travelers who enjoy a university atmosphere. The dining room offers a great view of the mountains. *96 Bodenheimer Dr., 29607, tel. 704/262–2204 or 800/951–6048, fax 704/262–2946. 76 rooms, 7 suites. Facilities: meeting rooms, restaurant. AE, MC, V. $$*

Smoketree Lodge. Enjoy grand views of Grandfather Mountain, indoor swimming, and great food at this mountain inn near the ski slopes with fully equipped efficiencies. *Hwy. 105, Box 3407, 28607, tel. 704/963–6505. 40 units. Facilities: restaurant, indoor pool, Jacuzzi, sauna, exercise room, game room, laundry, picnic tables. AE, D, MC, V. $$*

Linville
Dining and Lodging

Eseeola Lodge and Restaurant. Built in the 1880s, this lodge is the cornerstone of Linville. Rich chestnut paneling and stonework grace the interior rooms. *U.S. 221, tel. 704/733–4311. 28 rooms. Facilities: restaurant, lounge, golf, tennis, pool. Open June–Labor Day. MC, V. $$$$*

Little Switzerland
Dining and Lodging

Switzerland Inn and Chalet Restaurant. This Swiss-style lodge overlooking the mountains offers lodge rooms, parlor-bedroom suites, and a lovely honeymoon cottage with a fireplace, plus three meals a day. *Milepost 334, off Blue Ridge Pkwy., Box 399, Little Switzerland 28749, tel. 704/675–2658 or 800/654–4026. 66 rooms. Facilities: outdoor pool, tennis courts, shuffleboard, shopping. MC, V. Closed Nov.–Apr. $$–$$$*

Valle Crucis
Dining and Lodging

Mast Farm Inn. You can turn back the clock and still enjoy modern amenities at this charming pastoral inn. Guests have a choice of rooms in the farmhouse or in the log out-buildings. Breakfast and dinner are included in the tariff. *Box 704, Valle Crucis 28691, tel. 704/963–5857. Closed early Mar.–late Apr., early Nov.–late Dec. 12 rooms. MC, V. $$$*

4 South Carolina

By Edgar and Patricia Cheatham

Updated by Andrew Collins

From its Low Country shoreline, with wide sand beaches, spacious bays, and forests of palmettos and moss-strewn live oaks, South Carolina extends into an undulating interior region rich with fertile farmlands, then reaches toward the Blue Ridge Mountains, studded with scenic lakes, forests, and wilderness hideaways. What this smallest of Southern states lacks in land area it makes up for in diversity.

The historic port city of Charleston, lovingly preserved, links past with present. Many of its treasured double-galleried antebellum homes are now authentically furnished house museums. Culturally vibrant, the city nurtures theater, dance, music, and visual arts, showcased each spring during the internationally acclaimed Spoleto Festival USA.

Myrtle Beach is the hub of the Grand Strand, a 60-mile stretch of wide golden-sand beaches and recreational activities (especially golf, a top attraction throughout the state). To the south, tasteful, low-key Hilton Head—a sea island tucked between the Intracoastal Waterway and the ocean and divided into several sophisticated, self-contained resorts—also offers beautiful beaches and wonderful golf and tennis. Nearby is the port city of Beaufort (pronounced *Bew*fort), where the most rewarding activity is wandering the lovely streets dotted with preserved 18th-century homes, live oaks, and palmettos.

Columbia, the state capital, is a lively (and of course historic) city cleaved by a rushing river. In addition to several museums, and a good minor-league baseball team, the city has one of the country's top zoos. It is also home to the State Museum and the fine new Koger Center for Performing Arts. Nearby lakes and state parks offer abundant outdoor recreation and first-rate fishing.

Thoroughbred Country, centered around the town of Aiken, is a peaceful area of rolling pastures where top race horses are trained. It is also notable for magnificent mansions built by wealthy Northerners who vacationed here at the turn of the century. Upcountry South Carolina, at the northwestern tip of the state, is less visited than the rest of the state but well repays time spent there with dramatic mountain scenery, excellent hiking, and challenging whitewater rafting. Scattered along S.C. 11 are premier parks, some of which offer luxurious accommodations.

Since 1670, when the British established the first permanent European settlement at Charleston, the history of the Palmetto State has been characterized by periods of great prosperity contrasted with eras of dismal depression. This vibrant past is preserved in cherished traditions and an enduring belief in family, which give resonance to the optimism and vitality of today's South Carolina.

Charleston

At first glimpse, Charleston resembles an 18th-century etching come to life. Its low-profile skyline is punctuated with the spires and steeples of 181 churches, representing 25 denominations (Charleston was known for its religious freedom). Parts of the city appear stopped in time because block after block of old downtown structures have been preserved and restored for both residential and commercial use. Charleston has survived three centuries of epidemics, earthquakes, fires, and hurricanes, and it is today one of the South's best-preserved cities.

South Carolina

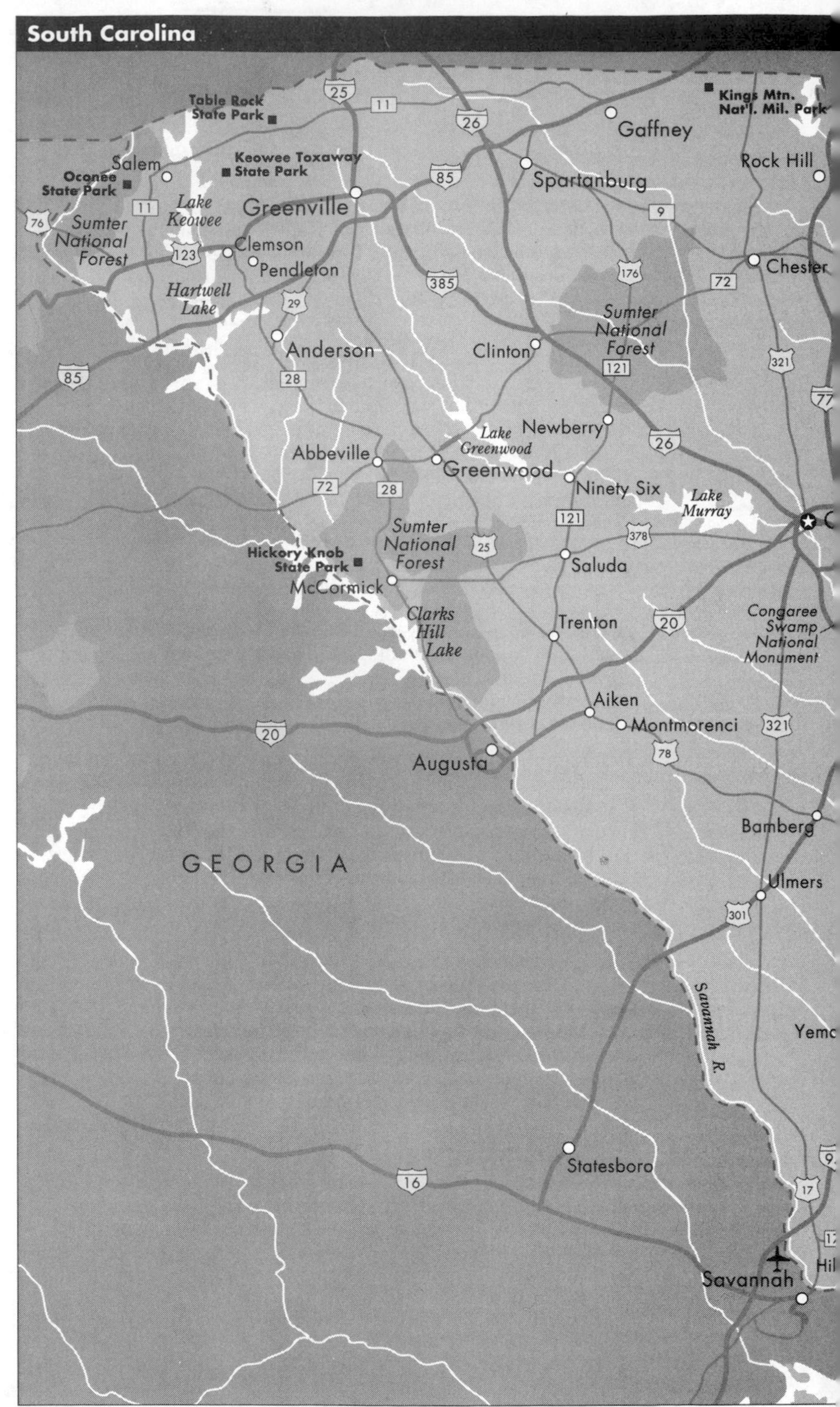

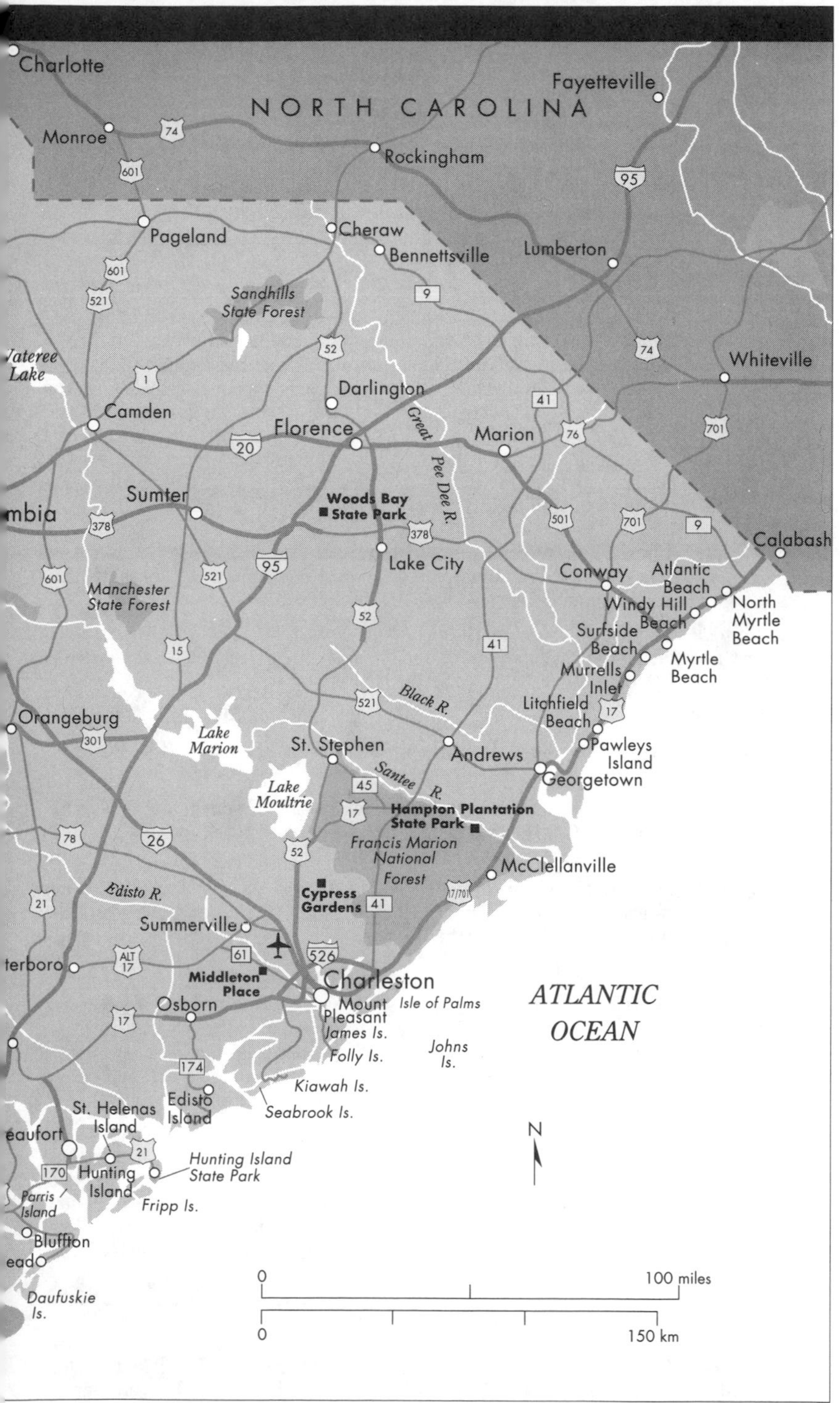
NORTH CAROLINA
Charlotte
Fayetteville
Monroe
Rockingham
Pageland
Cheraw
Bennettsville
Lumberton
Sandhills State Forest
Wateree Lake
Whiteville
Darlington
Camden
Florence
Marion
Great Pee Dee R.
Sumter
Woods Bay State Park
Lake City
Calabash
Conway
Atlantic Beach
North Myrtle Beach
Windy Hill Beach
Manchester State Forest
Surfside Beach
Myrtle Beach
Murrells Inlet
Black R.
Litchfield Beach
Orangeburg
Lake Marion
St. Stephen
Andrews
Pawleys Island
Georgetown
Santee R.
Lake Moultrie
Hampton Plantation State Park
Francis Marion National Forest
McClellanville
Edisto R.
Cypress Gardens
Summerville
Middleton Place
Charleston
Mount Pleasant
Isle of Palms
ATLANTIC OCEAN
Osborn
James Is.
Johns Is.
Folly Is.
Kiawah Is.
Edisto Island
Seabrook Is.
St. Helenas Island
Hunting Island
Hunting Island State Park
Fripp Is.
Parris Island
Bluffton
Daufuskie Is.
N
0
100 miles
0
150 km

Along the Battery, on the point of a narrow peninsula bounded by the Ashley and Cooper rivers, handsome mansions in the "Charleston style," surrounded by gardens, face the harbor. Their distinctive look is reminiscent of the West Indies, and for good reason. Before coming to the Carolinas in the late 17th century, many early British colonists had first settled on Barbados and other Caribbean islands where against the warm and humid climate they'd built houses with high ceilings and broad piazzas at each level, to catch the sea breezes. In Charleston, they adapted these designs for other practical reasons. One new type—narrow two-to four-story houses (called single houses) built at right angles to the street—emerged partly because buildings were taxed according to frontage length.

Each year, from mid-March to mid-April, the Festival of Houses conducts tours of private homes, gardens, and churches, and celebrates with symphony galas in stately drawing rooms, plantation oyster roasts, and candlelight tours. Each year in May and June, the renowned Spoleto Festival USA and Piccolo Spoleto take place, when hundreds of local and international artists, musicians, and other performers fill the city with sound and spectacle.

Arriving and Departing

By Plane **Charleston International Airport** (tel. 803/767–1100) on I–26, 12 miles west of downtown, is served by American, Continental, Delta, United, and USAir.

Between the Airport and Downtown **Airport Limousine Service** (tel. 803/767–7111 or 800/222–4771) charges $9 per person one-way to downtown Charleston, by reservation. By **car,** take I–26S into the city.

By Train **Amtrak** (4565 Gaynor Ave., N. Charleston, tel. 800/872–7245).

By Bus **Greyhound** (3610 Dorchester Rd., N. Charleston, tel. 800/231–2222).

By Car I–26 traverses the state from northwest to southeast and terminates at Charleston. U.S. 17, the coast road, passes through Charleston.

By Boat Boaters traveling the Intracoastal Waterway may dock at the **City Marina** (Lockwood Blvd., tel. 803/724–7357) in the Charleston Harbor or **Wild Dunes Yacht Harbor** (tel. 803/886–5100) on the Isle of Palms.

Getting Around

By Taxi Fares within the city average $2–$3 per trip. Companies include **Yellow Cab** (tel. 803/577–6565), **Safety Cab** (tel. 803/722–4066), and **Airport Limousine Service** (*see* Arriving and Departing *above*).

By Bus Regular buses run in most of Charleston from 5:35 AM till 10 PM and to North Charleston until 1 AM. The cost is 75¢ exact change (free transfers); at nonpeak hours (9:30–3:30), senior citizens and people with disabilities pay 25¢. **DASH** (Downtown Area Shuttle) trolley-style buses provide fast service in the main downtown areas. The fare is 75¢; $1 for an all-day pass. For schedule information for buses or DASH, call 803/747–0922.

Important Addresses and Numbers

Tourist Information **Charleston Trident Convention & Visitors Bureau** (Box 975, Charleston 29402, tel. 803/853–8000) has information also on Kiawah Island,

Seabrook Island, Mount Pleasant, North Charleston, and the Isle of Palms. **Historic Charleston Foundation** (Box 1120, Charleston 29402, tel. 803/723–1623) has information on house tours.

Emergencies The emergency rooms are open all night at **Charleston Memorial Hospital** (326 Calhoun St., tel. 803/577–0600) and **Roper Hospital** (316 Calhoun St., tel. 803/724–2000).

Guided Tours

Orientation **Adventure Sightseeing** (tel. 803/762–0088) and **Carolina Lowcountry Tours** (tel. 803/797–1045) offer van or motor-coach tours of the historic district. **Gray Line** (tel. 803/722–4444) offers similar tours, plus seasonal trips to gardens and plantations.

Special-Interest **Doin' the Charleston** (tel. 803/763–1233) combines its narration with audiovisuals and makes a stop at the Battery.

Carriage Tours **Charleston Carriage Co.** (tel. 803/577–0042), **Old South Carriage Tours** (tel. 803/723–9712), and **Palmetto Carriage Works** (tel. 803/723–8145) run approximately one-hour horse- and mule-drawn carriage tours of the historic district, some conducted by guides in Confederate uniforms.

Personal Guides Contact **Associated Guides of Historic Charleston** (tel. 803/724–6419); **Parker Limousine Service** (tel. 803/723–7601), which offers chauffeur-driven luxury limousine tours; or **Tours of Historic Charleston** (tel. 803/722–0026).

Walking Tours Guided tours are given by **Historic Charleston Walking Tours** (tel. 803/722–6460); **Charleston Strolls** (tel. 803/884–9505); and **Charleston Tea Party Walking Tour** (tel. 803/577–5896 or 803/722–1779), which includes tea in a private garden.

Boat Tours **Princess Gray Line Water Tours** (tel. 803/722–1112 or 800/344–4483) and **Charleston Harbor Tour** (tel. 803/722–1691) tour the harbor. **Fort Sumter Tours** (tel. 803/722–1691) includes a stop at Fort Sumter and also offers Starlight Dinner Cruises aboard a luxury yacht.

Exploring Charleston

Numbers in the margin correspond to points of interest on the Charleston map.

If you have just a day to spend in Charleston, you might begin with a carriage tour for the tidbits of history and humor that the driver-guides provide as they take you through the main streets of the historic district. This is the best way to decide where to go on your own. Next, browse through the shops of the Old Market area, where most of the carriage tours begin and end. After that, walk south along East Bay Street, past Rainbow Row (a row of pastel-painted houses near Tradd Street), or along any side streets on your way to your choice of the area's four house museums. Spend the rest of the day wandering the cool, palmetto-shaded streets, peeking into private gardens and churches of every stripe, discovering all the little surprises that reveal themselves only to those who seek them out.

If you have more time (and you really should), expand your itinerary by adding more sights within the same area; by adding an excursion to the Shops at Charleston Place or along King Street; by including the Marion Square area, which has an excellent art museum and a house museum; or by adding trips to magnificent plantations and gardens west of the Ashley River or to major historic sites east of the Cooper. There are also boat excursions and some very nice beaches.

For a good overview of the city before you begin touring, drop by the
1 **Visitor Information Center,** where there's parking (free for two hours; 50¢ per hour thereafter). Take time to see *Forever Charleston,* a multimedia presentation on the city. *375 Meeting St., tel. 803/853–8000. Admission: $2.50 adults, $2 senior citizens, $1 children 6–12, under 6 free. Shown daily 9–5 on ½ hour. Center open daily 8:30–5:30; Nov.–Feb., until 5 PM.*

The Historic District

On Meeting Street, housed in a $6 million contemporary complex, is the oldest city museum in the United States. The **Charleston Muse-**
2 **um,** founded in 1773, is especially strong on South Carolina decorative arts. The 500,000 items in the collection—in addition to Charleston silver, fashions, toys, snuff boxes, etc.—include objects relating to natural history, archaeology, and ornithology. Two historic homes—the Joseph Manigault Mansion *(see below)* and the Heyward-Washington House—are part of the museum. *360 Meeting St., tel. 803/722–2996. Admission: $6 adults, $3 children 3–12, under 3 free. Open Mon.–Sat. 9–5, Sun. 1–5. Combination ticket for museum and both houses: $15; for just the two houses: $10.*

Across John Street is one of Charleston's fine house museums, and a
3 National Historic Landmark, the **Joseph Manigault Mansion.** An outstanding example of Adam-style architecture, it was designed by Charleston architect Gabriel Manigault in 1803 and is noted for its carved-wood mantels and elaborate plasterwork. Furnishings are British, French, and Charleston antiques, including rare tricolor Wedgwood pieces. *350 Meeting St., tel. 803/723–2926. Admission: $6 adults, $3 children 3–12, under 3 free (for combination ticket* see *Charleston Museum,* above*). Open Mon.–Sat. 10–5, Sun. 1–5.*

Walk down Meeting Street to Marion Square. Facing the square is
4 the **Old Citadel Building,** built in 1822 to house state troops and arms. Here began the famed South Carolina Military College—The Citadel—now on the Ashley River.

Walk down a block, cross Meeting, and turn east to 110 Calhoun
5 Street to visit **Emanuel African Methodist Episcopal Church,** home of the South's oldest AME congregation, which had its beginnings in 1818. The church was closed in 1822 when authorities learned that Denmark Vesey used the sanctuary to plan his slave insurrection. It was reopened in 1865 at the present site. *Call 803/722–2561 in advance for tour. Open daily 9–4.*

If you've left your car at the visitor center, return now to retrieve it.
6 From here proceed to the lovely **College of Charleston** (founded in 1770), whose graceful main building (1828) was designed by Philadelphia architect William Strickland. Within the College is the **Avery Research Center for African-American History and Culture,** which traces the heritage of South Carolina Low Country African-Americans. *125 Bull St., tel. 803/727–2009. Admission free. Reading room/archives open weekdays 1–4:30 (or by appointment). Group tours weekdays 2–4 or by appointment.*

Next you can make a shopping tour of King Street, or go directly to the market area and head for one of the many parking garages. Now is the time for a carriage tour, many of which leave from here (*see*
7 Guided Tours, *above*). Our tour picks up again at **Congregation Beth Elohim** (90 Hasell St.), considered one of the nation's finest examples of Greek Revival architecture. It was constructed in 1840 to replace an earlier temple—the birthplace of American Reform Judaism in 1824—that was destroyed by fire. *Tel. 803/723–1090. Open weekdays 10–noon.*

American Military Museum, **20**
Calhoun Mansion, **24**
Charleston Museum, **2**
Circular Congregational Church, **13**
City Hall, **18**
College of Charleston, **6**
Congregation Beth Elohim, **7**
Dock Street Theatre, **16**
Edmondston-Alston House, **25**
Emanuel African Methodist Episcopal Church, **5**
Exchange Building/Provost Dungeon, **21**
French Huguenot Church, **17**
Gibbes Museum of Art, **10**
Heyward-Washington House, **22**
Joseph Manigault Mansion, **3**
Market Hall, **8**
Nathaniel Russell House, **23**
Old Citadel Building, **4**
Old City Market, **9**
Old Powder Magazine, **14**
St. John's Lutheran Church, **12**
St. Michael's Episcopal Church, **19**
St. Philip's Episcopal Church, **15**
Unitarian Church, **11**
Visitor Information Center, **1**
Waterfront Park, **26**

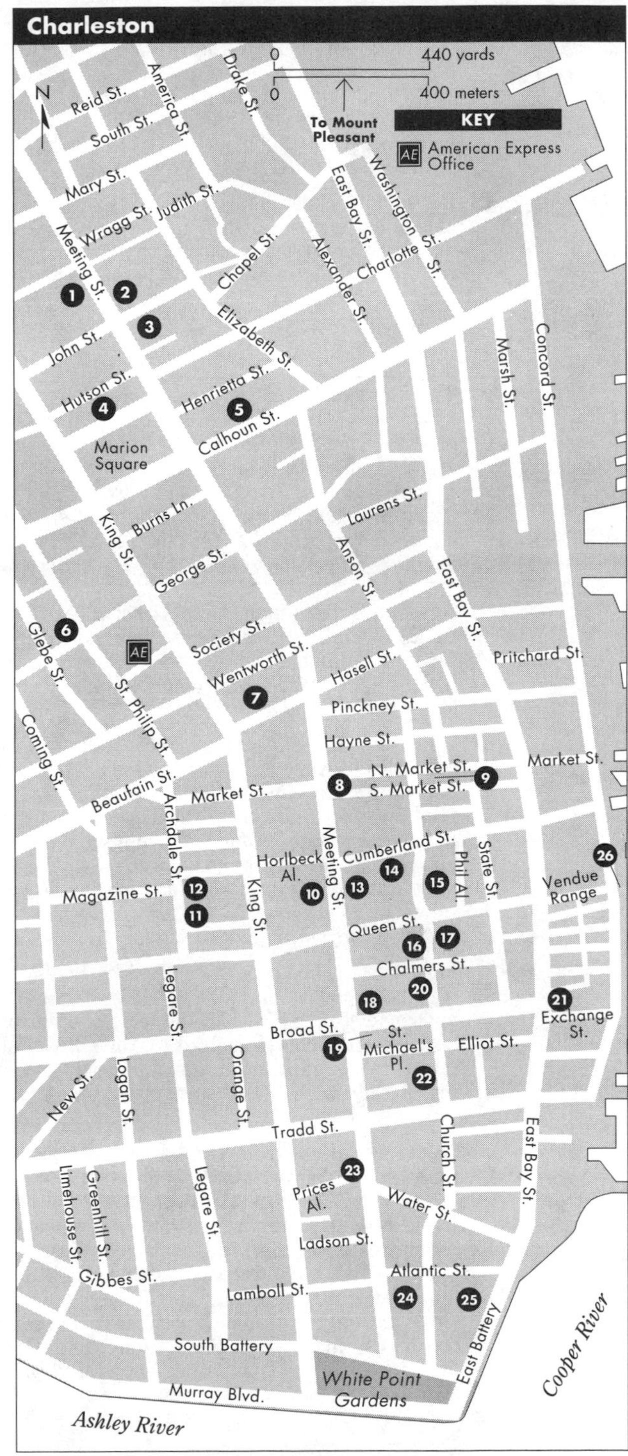

Follow Meeting Street south to Market Street, and at the intersec-
8 tion on the left you'll see **Market Hall,** a National Historic Landmark built in 1841 and modeled after the Temple of Nike in Athens. Here you'll find the **Confederate Museum,** where the Daughters of the Confederacy preserve and display flags, uniforms, swords, and other memorabilia. *188 Meeting St., tel. 803/723–1541. Admission: $1 adults, 25¢ children 6–12. Hours vary.*

9 Between Market Hall and East Bay Street is **Old City Market,** a series of low sheds that once housed produce and fish markets. The area now has restaurants and shops, along with the vegetable and fruit vendors and local "basket ladies" busy weaving and selling distinctive sweet-grass, pine-straw, and palmetto-leaf baskets—a craft inherited from their West African ancestors. *Usually open daily 9 AM–sunset.*

Time Out This is a great area for some serious time out. Pick up batches of Charleston's famed benne (sesame) seed wafers at **Olde Colony Bakery** (280 King St., tel. 803/722–2147). Choose from 12 gourmet food stands in **The Gourmetisserie** (tel. 803/722–4455) in the Market Square shopping complex across South Market Street. Or indulge the urge to munch on oysters on the half-shell, steamed mussels, and clams at **A.W. Shucks** (tel. 803/723–1151) in nearby State Street Market.

Across the street is the **Omni Hotel at Charleston Place** (130 Market St.). You might wander over to peer at the lobby or have cocktails or tea in the intimate Lobby Lounge. The city's only world-class hotel is flanked by a four-story complex of upscale boutiques and specialty shops (*see* Shopping, *below*).

10 Heading south on Meeting Street, see the **Gibbes Museum of Art.** Its collection of American art includes notable 18th- and 19th-century portraits of Carolinians and an outstanding group of more than 400 miniature portraits. Don't miss the miniature rooms—intricately detailed with fabrics and furnishings and nicely displayed in shadow boxes inset in dark-paneled walls—or the Tiffany-style stained-glass dome in the rotunda. *135 Meeting St., tel. 803/722–2706. Admission: $5 adults, $4 senior citizens, $3 children 6–18. Open Tues.–Sat. 10–5, Sun. and Mon. 1–5.*

For a detour, head south on Meeting Street to Queen Street, then
11 west to Archdale. At no. 8 is the **Unitarian Church,** begun in 1772 and completed in 1787. The building was remodeled in the mid-19th century after plans inspired by the Chapel of Henry VII in West minster Abbey, including the addition of a Gothic fan-tracery ceiling. *8 Archdale St., No regular visiting hours. Call 803/723–4617 weekdays 8:30–2:30.*

At the corner of Clifford and Archdale streets is the Greek Revival
12 **St. John's Lutheran Church,** built in 1817 for a congregation that celebrated its 250th anniversary in 1992. Notice the fine craftsmanship in the delicate wrought-iron gates and fence. Organ aficionados may be interested in the 1823 Thomas Hall organ case. The church is open weekdays 9:30–3 (tel. 803/723–2426 in advance). Back at Meeting Street, across from the Gibbes is the unusual Romanesque
13 **Circular Congregational Church,** its corners rounded off, it's said, so the devil would have no place to hide. The church is simple but pretty, with a beamed, vaulted ceiling. *Tel. 803/577–6400. Tours given Apr.–Oct., weekdays 9–1.*

On Cumberland Street, one of Charleston's few remaining cobble-
14 stone thoroughfares, is the **Old Powder Magazine,** built in 1713, used
during the Revolutionary War, and now a museum with costumes, furniture, armor, and other artifacts from 18th-century Charleston. Because The Historic Charleston Foundation will be restoring the building through 1995, visitors should call ahead for information on tours and opening hours. *79 Cumberland St., tel. 803/723–1623. Open by appointment.*

Around the corner at 146 Church Street you come to the graceful
15 late-Georgian **St. Philip's Episcopal Church** (tel. 803/722–7734), the
second on the site, built in 1838 and restored in 1994. In its serene graveyard are buried some legendary native sons, including statesman John C. Calhoun and DuBose Heyward, the author of *Porgy*. *Open by appointment.*

16 The **Dock Street Theatre,** across Queen Street, was built on the site of one of the nation's first playhouses. It combines the reconstructed early Georgian playhouse and the preserved Old Planter's Hotel (ca. 1809). *135 Church St., tel. 803/720–3968. Open weekdays 10–4 for free tours.*

17 Across the street is the Gothic-style **French Huguenot Church,** the only one in the country still using the original Huguenot liturgy, which can be heard in a special service held each spring. *Tel. 803/722–4385. Donations accepted. Open weekdays 10–12:30 and 2–4.*

The intersection of Meeting and Broad streets is known as the Four
Corners of Law, representing federal, state, city, and religious ju-
risdiction. Ignore the County Court House and the U.S. Post Office
18 and Federal Court, and turn to the graceful 1801 **City Hall,** on the
northeast corner, whose second-floor Council Chamber has interesting historical displays and fine portraits, including John Trumbull's 1791 portrait of George Washington and Samuel F. B. Morse's likeness of James Monroe. *Tel. 803/577–6970. Admission free. Open weekdays 10–5.*

19 On the last corner is **St. Michael's Episcopal Church,** modeled after London's St. Martin's-in-the-Fields. Completed in 1761, this is Charleston's oldest surviving church. Climb the 186-foot steeple for a panoramic view. *Tel. 803/723–0603. Open weekdays 9–5, Sat. 9–noon.*

From the Four Corners, head east down Broad Street to Church
20 Street. The **American Military Museum** displays hundreds of uni-
forms and artifacts from all branches of service, dating from the Revolutionary War. *Pinckney St., tel. 803/723–9620. Admission: $2 adults, $1 children under 12, uniformed military personnel free. Open Mon.–Sat. 10–6, Sun. 1–6.*

21 At the corner of East Bay Street stands the **Exchange Building/Provost Dungeon,** originally a customs house. The dungeon was used by the British during the Revolutionary War; today, a tableau of lifelike manikins recalls this era. *122 East Bay St., tel. 803/792–5020. Admission: $4 adults, $3.50 senior citizens, $2.50 children 7–12. Open daily 9–5.*

Return to Church Street and continue south to the neighborhood
known as Cabbage Row, the home of Dubose Heyward and an area
central to Charleston's African-American history. At 87 Church
22 Street is the **Heyward-Washington House,** built in 1772 by rice king
Daniel Heyward, which was also the setting for Dubose Heyward's *Porgy*. President George Washington stayed here during his 1791 visit. The mansion is full of fine period furnishings by the likes of

Thomas Elfe, and its restored 18th-century kitchen is the only one in Charleston open to visitors. *Tel. 803/722–0354. Admission: $6 adults, $3 children 3–12 (for combination ticket,* see *Charleston Museum,* above.*) Open Mon.–Sat. 10–5, Sun. 1–5.*

23 At 51 Meeting Street is the **Nathaniel Russell House,** headquarters of the Historic Charleston Foundation. Built in 1808, it is one of the nation's finest examples of Federal architecture. The interior is notable for its ornate detailing, its lavish period furnishings, and a "flying" circular staircase that spirals three stories with no apparent support. *Tel. 803/724–8481. Admission: $6 adults, children under 7 free. Open Mon.–Sat. 10–5, Sun. 2–5. Combination ticket with the Edmondston-Alston House: $10.*

Continuing south, you'll come into an area where somewhat more
24 lavish mansions reflect the wealth of a later era. The **Calhoun Mansion,** at 16 Meeting Street, is opulent by Charleston standards, an interesting example of Victorian taste. Built in 1876, it's notable for ornate plasterwork, fine wood moldings, and a 75-foot domed ceiling. *Tel. 803/722–8205. Admission: $10 adults, $5 children 6–16. Open Thurs.–Sun. 10–4. Closed Jan.*

25 The imposing **Edmondston-Alston House,** with commanding views of Charleston Harbor, was built in 1825 in the late Federal style and transformed into a Greek Revival structure during the 1840s. It is tastefully furnished with antiques, portraits, Piranesi prints, silver, and fine china. *Tel. 803/722–7171 or 803/556–6020. Admission: 6 adults, children under 7 free. Combination ticket with Nathaniel Russell House: $10. Open Tues.–Sat. 10–5, Sun.–Mon. 1:30–5.*

After all this serious sightseeing, relax in **White Point Gardens,** on Battery Point, facing the harbor, a tranquil spot, shaded by palmet-
26 tos and graceful oaks. Another option is **Waterfront Park,** on the Cooper River in the historic district. It offers beautiful river views, fountains, landscaped gardens, and a fishing pier.

East of the Cooper River

Across the Cooper River Bridges, via U.S. 17, is the town of **Mount Pleasant,** named not for anything in the area resembling so much as a hillock, but for a plantation in England from which a number of the area's settlers hailed. Here, along Shem Creek, where the area's fishing fleet brings in the daily catch, seafood restaurants attract visitors and locals alike. **Patriots Point,** the world's largest naval and maritime museum, is also in Mount Pleasant. Berthed here are the aircraft carrier *Yorktown,* the World War II submarine *Clamagore,* the destroyer *Laffey,* and the cutter *Ingham,* the most decorated ship in the U.S. fleet. Tours are offered in all vessels, and the film *The Fighting Lady* is shown regularly aboard the *Yorktown. Tel. 803/884–2727. Admission: $8 adults, $7 senior citizens and active military personnel, $4 children 6–12. Open daily 9–6:30, Apr.–Labor Day until 7:30.*

Fort Sumter Tours' boats leave from the docks here and from Charleston's Municipal Marina for 2¼-hour cruises that include a stop at **Fort Sumter National Monument,** on a manmade island in the harbor. *Tel. 803/722–1691. Cost: $9 adults, $4.50 children 6–11, under 6 free. Tours leave from Municipal Marina daily at 9:30, noon, and 2:30. Tours leave from Patriots Point daily at 10:45 and 1:30, as well as at 4 Apr.–Labor Day.*

It was at Fort Sumter that the first shot of the Civil War was fired on April 12, 1861, when Confederate forces at Fort Johnson (now defunct) across the way opened fire. After a 34-hour bombardment Union forces surrendered, and Confederate troops occupied Sumter, which became a symbol of Southern resistance. The Confederacy held the fort—despite almost continual bombardment—for nearly four years, and when it was finally evacuated it was a heap of rubble. Today, National Park Service rangers conduct free guided tours of the restored structure, which includes a museum (also free) with historical displays and dioramas. *Tel. 803/883–3123.*

Continuing north out of Mount Pleasant along U.S. 17, you'll find "basket ladies" at roadside stands. If you have the heart to bargain, you *may* be able to purchase the baskets at somewhat lower prices than in Charleston. SC 703 will take you to Sullivan's Island and **Fort Moultrie,** completed in 1809, the third fort on this site. Here Colonel William Moultrie's South Carolinians repelled a British assault in one of the first Patriot victories of the Revolutionary War. The interior has been restored. A film and slide show tell the history of the fort. *W. Middle St., Sullivan's Island, tel. 803/883–3123. Admission free. Open daily 9–5, Memorial Day–Labor Day until 6.*

Back on U.S. 17, about 8 miles out of Charleston, is the 1681 **Boone Hall Plantation,** approached via one of the South's most majestic avenues of oaks. The primary attraction is the grounds, with formal azalea and camellia gardens, as well as the original slave quarters—the only "slave street" still intact in the Southeast—and the cotton-gin house used in the film *North and South.* Visitors may also tour the first floor of the classic columned mansion, which was built in 1935 incorporating woodwork and flooring from the original house. *Tel. 803/884–4371. Admission: $7.50 adults, $6 senior citizens, $3 children 6–12. Open Apr.–Labor Day, Mon.–Sat. 8:30–6:30, Sun. 1–5; rest of year, Mon.–Sat. 9–5, Sun. 1–4.*

West of the Ashley River

Vestiges of the Old South—and Charleston's beginnings— beckon as you cross the Ashley River Bridge. Take SC 171 north to reach **Charles Towne Landing State Park,** commemorating the site of the original Charleston settlement, begun in 1670. There are a reconstructed village and fortifications, English park gardens with bicycle trails and walkways, and a replica 17th-century vessel moored in the creek. In the animal park roam species native to the region for three centuries. Bicycle and kayak rentals and cassette and tram tours are available. *1500 Old Towne Rd., tel. 803/852–4200. Admission: $5 adults, $2.50 senior citizens and children 6–14. Open daily 9–5, Memorial Day–Labor Day until 6.*

Nine miles west of Charleston via the Ashley River Road (SC 61) is **Drayton Hall,** built between 1738 and 1742. A National Historic Landmark, it is considered the nation's finest example of Georgian Palladian architecture. The mansion is the only plantation house on the Ashley River to have survived the Civil War and serves as an invaluable lesson in history as well as in architecture. It has been left unfurnished to highlight the original plaster moldings, opulent hand-carved woodwork, and other ornamental details. *Tel. 803/766–0188. Admission: $7 adults, $4 children 6–18. Guided tours daily 10–3, Mar.–Oct. until 4.*

A mile or so farther on SC 61 is **Magnolia Plantation and Gardens.** The 50-acre informal garden, begun in 1685, has a huge collection of azaleas and camellias and was proclaimed the "most beautiful garden in the world" by John Galsworthy. You can ride a tram for an overall tour with three stops. Nature lovers may canoe through the 125-acre Waterfowl Refuge, explore the 30-acre **Audubon Swamp Garden** along boardwalks and bridges, or walk or bicycle over 500 acres of wildlife trails. Tours of the manor house, built during the Reconstruction period, depict plantation life. You can also see the petting zoo and a mini-horse ranch. *Tel. 803/571–1266. Admission: $9 adults, $8 senior citizens, $7 children 13–19, $4 children 4–12 (house tour $4 extra, swamp tour $3 extra, tram tour $3 extra). Open daily 8–5:30.*

Middleton Place, 4 miles farther north on SC 61, has the nation's oldest landscaped gardens, dating from 1741. Design highlights of the magnificent gardens—ablaze with camellias, magnolias, azaleas, roses, and flowers of all seasons—are the floral *allées*, terraced lawns, and ornamental lakes. Much of the mansion was destroyed during the Civil War, but the south wing has been restored and houses impressive collections of silver, furniture, paintings, and historic documents. The stableyard is a living outdoor museum: here craftspeople, using authentic tools and equipment, demonstrate spinning, blacksmithing, and other domestic skills from the plantation era. Farm animals, peacocks, and other creatures roam free. *Tel. 803/556–6020 or 800/782–3608. Admission: $10 adults, $5 children 4–12. Open daily 9–5. House tours Tues.–Sun. 10–4:30, Mon. 1:30–4:30; $6 extra.*

On the banks of the Old Santee Canal in Moncks Corner is the new **Old Santee Canal State Park,** reached via I–26 and Highway 52. You can explore on foot or take a canoe. There's also an interpretive center. *Rembert C. Dennis Blvd., Moncks Corner, tel. 803/899–5200. Admission $3 per car. Open daily 9–5, spring and summer until 6.*

The picturesque town of **Summerville,** about 25 miles northwest of Charleston via I–26 (Exit 199), is a pleasant place for a drive or stroll. Built by wealthy planters as an escape from hot-weather malaria, it's a treasure trove of mid-19th-century and Victorian buildings—many of which are listed in the National Register of Historic Places—with colorful gardens of camellias, azaleas, and wisteria. Streets often curve around tall pines, since a local ordinance prohibits cutting them down. This is a good place for a bit of antiquing in attractive shops. Stop by the **Summerville Chamber of Commerce** (106 E. Doty Ave., Box 670, 29483, tel. 803/873–2931) to get oriented; they're open weekdays 8:30–12:30 and 1:30–5, and Saturdays 10–3.

About 24 miles north of Charleston via U.S. 52 is **Cypress Gardens,** a swamp garden created from what was once the freshwater reserve of a vast rice plantation. Explore the inky waters by boat, or walk along paths lined with moss-draped cypress trees, azaleas, camellias, daffodils, wisteria, and dogwood. *Tel. 803/553–0515. Admission Feb. 15–Apr. 30: $6 adults, $5 senior citizens, $2 children 6–16. Rest of year, $1 less. Open daily 9–5.*

Charleston for Free

The Citadel Corps of Cadets Dress Parade. Visitors are welcome at the military college's parade at Summerall Field (171 Moultrie St., by Hampton Park) every Friday at 3:45 PM during the school year.

The Citadel Memorial Military Museum. Military documents and relics relating to the Civil War, the college, and its graduates are on display at this on-campus museum. *Tel. 803/953–6846. Open Sun.–Fri. 2–5, Sat. noon–5.*

Hampton Park Concerts in the Park (tel. 803/724–7305). These free Sunday afternoon concerts are held April–May and September–October. **Monday Night Recital Series.** The College of Charleston (tel. 803/953–8228) presents guests and faculty artists in free musical performances during the school year.

What to See and Do with Children

American Military Museum (*see* The Historic District in Exploring Charleston, *above*).
Boat Ride to Fort Sumter (*see* East of the Cooper River in Exploring Charleston, *above*).
Charles Towne Landing State Park (*see* West of the Ashley River in Exploring Charleston, *above*). Birds, alligators, bison, pumas, bears, wolves, and many other animals roam in natural environments. Children's Days are held during the last two weeks of December.
Charleston Museum (*see* The Historic District in Exploring Charleston, *above*). The Discover Me Room, designed just for children, has computers and other hands-on exhibits.
Magnolia Plantation and Gardens petting zoo and mini-horse ranch (*see* West of the Ashley River in Exploring Charleston, *above*).
Middleton Place (*see* West of the Ashley River in Exploring Charleston, *above*).
Palmetto Islands County Park. This family-oriented nature park has a Big Toy playground, a two-acre pond, a canoe trail, an observation tower, and marsh boardwalks. Bicycles, pedal boats, and canoes can be rented in season. *On U.S. 17N, ½ mi past Snee Farm, turn left onto Long Point Rd., tel. 803/884–0832. Admission: $1. Open Apr., Sept., and Oct. daily 9–6; May–Aug., daily 9–7; Nov.–Mar., daily 10–5.*
Shelling. Kiawah Island has excellent shelling. If you're not staying at the private resort, you can shell at **Beachwalker Park,** the public beach at the west end of the island. *Tel. 803/762–2172. Parking fee: $3. Open June–Aug., daily 10–7; May and Sept., daily 10–6; Apr. and Oct., weekends 10–6.*

Off the Beaten Track

Angel Oak. Reportedly the oldest living thing east of the Rockies, this 1,500-year-old giant has a 25½-foot circumference and a 151-foot limb spread. *From SC 700 turn left onto Bohicket Rd.; after about ½ mi, turn right at sign and follow dirt road, tel. 803/559–3496. Daily 9–5.*

Francis Marion National Forest. About 40 miles north of Charleston via U.S. 52, this site comprises 250,000 acres of swamps, vast oaks and pines, and little lakes thought to have been formed by meteors—a good place for picnicking, camping, boating, and swimming (tel. 803/765–5222). At the park's **Rembert Dennis Wildlife Center** (off U.S. 52 in Bonneau, tel. 803/825–3387), deer, wild turkey, and striped bass are reared and studied.

At Goose Creek, about 19 miles north of Charleston, is the remarkably well preserved **St. James United Methodist Church,** built between 1708 and 1719. Not in use since 1808, it retains the original box pews, slave gallery, and pulpit. The British royal arms are still visible above the chancel. The sexton, who lives nearby, will open the church on request. *Off U.S. 78, tel. 803/553–3117. Donation. Open weekdays 9–noon.*

Shopping

Shopping Districts. Don't miss the colorful produce market in the three-block **Old City Market** at East Bay and Market streets and adjacent to it, the **open-air flea market,** with crafts, antiques, and memorabilia. **The Market** is a complex of specialty shops and restaurants. Other such complexes in the area are **The Shops at Charleston Place** adjoining the Omni Hotel, **Rainbow Market** (in two interconnected 150-year-old buildings), **Market Square,** and **State Street Market.** Also, some of Charleston's oldest and finest shops are on **King Street.**

Antiques King Street is the center. **Petterson Antiques** (201 King St., tel. 803/723–5714) offers books, furniture, porcelain, and glass. **Livingston & Sons Antiques,** dealers in 18th- and 19th-century English and Continental furniture, clocks, and bric-a-brac, has a large shop west of the Ashley (2137 Savannah Hwy., tel. 803/556–6162) and a smaller one at 163 King Street (tel. 803/723–9697). **Birlant & Co.** (191 King St., tel. 803/722–3842) offers a fine selection of 18th- and 19th- century English antiques, as well as the famous Charleston Battery Bench, identical to those on Charleston Green.

Art and Crafts The **Birds I View Gallery** (119-A Church St., tel. 803/723–1276) sells bird paintings and prints by Anne Worsham Richardson. At **Birds & Ivy** (235 King St., tel. 803/853–8534), which sells garden art and accessories of every type, there's a coffee shop in back where you can have a sandwich or a snack. **Charleston Crafts** (38 Queen St., tel. 803/723–2938) has a fine selection of pottery, quilts, weavings, sculptures, and jewelery fashioned mostly by local artists. The **Elizabeth O'Neill Verner Studio & Museum** (79 Church St., tel. 803/722–4246) in a 17th-century house is now open to the public. Prints of her pastels and etchings are on sale at adjacent **Tradd Street Press** (38 Tradd St., tel. 803/722–4246). The **Virginia Fouché Bolton Art Gallery** (127 Meeting St., tel. 803/577–9351) sells original paintings and limited-edition lithographs of Charleston and Low Country scenes.

Gifts **Charleston Collections** (233 King St., tel. 803/722–7267, at the Straw Market, Kiawah Island Resort, tel. 803/768–7487, Quadrangle Center, tel. 803/556–8911) has Charleston chimes, prints, and candies, T-shirts, and more. The **Charleston Catalog Company** (139 Market St., tel. 803/722–6121) also offers merchandise with a Charleston motif. Charleston's and London's own **Ben Silver,** (149 King St., tel. 803/577–4556), premier purveyor of blazer buttons, has over 800 designs, including college and British regimental motifs. He also sells British neckties, embroidered polo shirts, and blazers.

Period Reproductions **Historic Charleston Reproductions** (105 Broad St., tel. 803/723–8292) has superb replicas of Charleston furniture and accessories, all authorized by the Historic Charleston Foundation. Royalties from sales contribute to restoration projects. At the **Thomas Elfe Workshop** (56 Queen St., tel. 803/722–2130), you'll find excellent 18th-century reproductions and objets d'art, Charleston rice beds, handmade mirrors, and Charleston pieces in silverplate, pewter, or porcelain. At the **Old Charleston Joggling Board Co.** (652 King St., tel. 803/723–4331), these Low Country oddities (on which people bounce) can be purchased.

Sports and the Outdoors

Beaches South Carolina's climate allows swimming from April through October. There are public beaches at **Beachwalker Park,** on Kiawah Island; **Folly Beach County Park** and **Folly Beach,** on Folly Island; **Isle of Palms;** and **Sullivan's Island.** Resorts with extensive private beaches are **Fairfield Ocean Ridge,** on Edisto Island; **Kiawah Island Resort; Seabrook Island;** and **Wild Dunes Resort,** on the Isle of Palms.

Bicycling The **historic district** is ideal for bicycling, and many city parks have biking trails. **Palmetto Islands County Park** also has trails. Bikes can be rented at **The Bicycle Shoppe** (280 Meeting St., tel. 803/722-8168, or on Kiawah Island (tel. 803/768-9122); and at the **Charleston Carriage Co.** (96 N. Market St., tel. 803/577-0042), which also rents tandem bikes.

Golf Public courses include **Charleston Municipal** (tel. 803/795-6517), **Patriots Point Links** (tel. 803/881-0042), **Oak Point** (tel. 803/768-7431), **Plantation Pines** (9 par-3 holes; tel. 803/559-2009), and **Shadowmoss Plantation** (tel. 803/556-8251). **Kiawah Island** (tel. 803/768-2121) and **Wild Dunes** (tel. 803/886-6000) allow nonguests to play on a space-available basis.

Tennis Courts are open to the public at **Shadowmoss Plantation** (tel. 803/556-8251), **Kiawah Island** (tel. 803/768-2121), and **Wild Dunes** (tel. 803/886-6000).

Dining

By Eileen Robinson Smith

Updated by Andrew Collins

She-crab soup, sautéed shrimp and grits, variations on pecan pie, and other Low Country specialties are served all over the Charleston area, but local chefs whip up some creative contemporary dishes as well. Known for outstanding eateries—ranging from fresh seafood houses to elegant French restaurants—Charleston is a mecca for gastronomes. Sadly, the stellar and popular **Robert's of Charleston** closed indefinitely in May 1994 but may reopen in a new space by '95; for information, call 803/577-7565.

Across the East Cooper Bridge, in the trendy suburb of Mount Pleasant, there are a number of good restaurants.

The most highly recommended restaurants in each price category are indicated by a star ★.

Category	Cost*
$$$	over $30
$$	$20-$30
$	under $20

**per person without 5% tax, service, or drinks*

$$$
American

Anson. After an afternoon of strolling through the Old City Market, you can walk a couple hundred feet up Anson Street to one of the better, and newer, restaurants in town. The softly lit, gilt-trimmed dining room is framed by about a dozen magnificent French windows; booths are anchored by marble-top tables. Anson's serves up dependable American fare—mainly seafood, chicken, and steak selections—with the occasional foreign twist (like the Thai-influenced, cashew-crusted grouper). Desserts are of the rich, southern variety, so save room. *12 Anson St., tel. 803/577-0551. Reservations accepted. Dress: casual. AE, D, DC, MC, V. No lunch.*

French **Restaurant Million.** This restaurant serves French nouvelle cuisine on Limoges china in a building dating to 1788. The rack of lamb, the five-course ($50), and the three-course ($28) prix-fixe meals are outstanding. Downstairs at the casual and inexpensive **McCrady's** (tel. 803/853-8484), soup, salad, sandwiches, and grills are served. *2 Unity Alley, tel. 803/577-7472. Reservations required. Jacket and*

Dining
Anson, **19**
Barbadoes Room, **25**
California Dreaming Restaurant & Bar, **1**
Captain Guilds Cafe, **4**
Carolina's, **30**
82 Queen, **24**
Gaulart and Maliclet Cafe Restaurant, **28**
Louis's Charleston Grill, **16**
Magnolias Uptown/ Down South, **21**
McCrady's, **29**
Mike Calder's Deli & Pub, **12**
Moultrie Tavern, **22**
Restaurant Million, **29**
Shem Creek Bar & Grill, **2**
Slightly North of Broad, **23**

Lodging
Ansonborough Inn, **15**
Best Western King Charles Inn, **14**
Brasington House Bed & Breakfast, **9**
Cannonboro Inn, **11**
Comfort Inn Riverview, **5**
Days Inn Historic District, **20**
1837 Bed andBreakfast and Tearoom, **13**
Elliott House Inn, **25**
Hampton Inn – Historic District, **6**
Hawthorn Suites Hotel, **18**
Holiday Inn Charleston/ Mount Pleasant, **3**
John Rutledge House Inn, **27**
Maison DuPré, **10**
Mills House Hotel, **26**
Omni Hotel at Charleston Place, **16**
Planters Inn, **17**
Quality Inn–Heart of Charleston, **8**
Sheraton Inn Charleston, **7**
Two Meeting Street, **31**

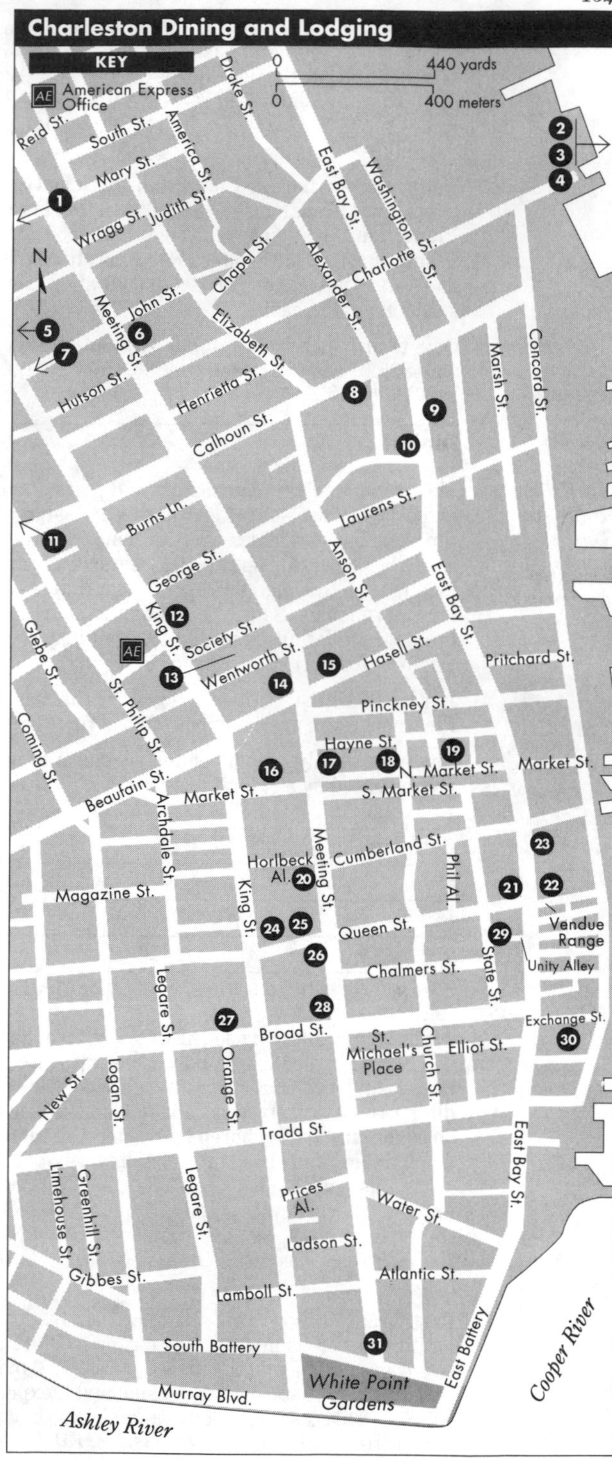

tie required. AE, DC, MC, V. Restaurant Million: No lunch. Closed Sun. McCrady's: No lunch Sat. Closed Sun.

Low Country ★ **Louis's Charleston Grill.** When owner-chef Louis Osteen took over the former Shaftesbury Room in the Omni, he created an elegant low-key ambience, with historic photographs of old Charleston on mahogany-panel walls and wrought-iron chandeliers reflected in gleaming crystal and china. The food is "local, not too fancy," and entrées match a variety of grilled meat and fish fillets with such exotic sauces as pear-walnut conserve and warm cumin vinaigrette. The staff is friendly, not stuffy, and will gladly help you choose from among the wines on its long and distinguished list. *224 King St. at Charleston Pl., tel. 803/577–4522. Reservations advised. Jacket advised. AE, MC, V. No lunch.*

$$ *American* ★ **82 Queen.** This popular restaurant, part of a complex of pink stucco buildings dating to the mid-1800s, is the unofficial headquarters for many of the city's annual events; during Spoleto, musicians perform in the courtyard garden. Low Country favorites such as crab cakes are served with sweet red pepper cream sauce. The traditional mingles with such innovations as roast duck with a blueberry-Cointreau glaze and oysters stuffed with Daufuskie crab. For dessert, choose Death by Chocolate or the healthy cheesecake. *82 Queen St., tel. 803/723–7591. Reservations advised for dinner. Dress: casual but neat. AE, MC, V.*

French **Gaulart and Maliclet Cafe Restaurant.** This casual, chic eatery serves Continental dishes—breads and pastries, soups, salads, and sandwiches, and evening specials like Seafood Normandy and chicken sesame. *98 Broad St., tel. 803/577–9797. Reservations accepted. Dress: casual. AE, DC, MC, V. Closed Sun. No lunch Mon.*

Low Country **Carolina's.** European chic with its black lacquer, white, and peach decor, Carolina's is the brainchild of German restaurateurs Franz Meier and Chris Weihs. Many come here for the "appeteasers" and the late-night (until 1 AM) offerings, which include everything from smoked baby back ribs to pasta with crawfish and tasso (spiced ham) in cream sauce. Dinner entrées are selections from the grill: Carolina quail with goat cheese, sun-dried tomatoes and basil; salmon with cilantro, ginger, and lime butter; and lamb loin with jalapeño chutney. *10 Exchange St., tel. 803/724–3800. Reservations advised. Dress: casual. D, MC, V. No lunch.*

Moultrie Tavern. This reconverted brick 1883 warehouse is filled with artifacts and artwork from the Civil War era. Chef/owner Robert Bohrn, who greets guests in a Confederate uniform, is a historian and unearths his own relics. The fife-and-drum music plays continuously and the food and spirits are authentically 1860s. Try an early Southern specialty: baked oyster and sausage pie with puff pastry. *18 Vendue Range, tel. 803/723–1862. Dinner reservations recommended. Dress: casual. AE, D, DC, MC, V.*

★ **Slightly North of Broad.** This high-ceilinged haunt with visible air ducts, brick and stucco walls, and red wooden floors opened early in 1994 to a packed house. The best seats are those looking directly into the exposed kitchen. From here you'll see chef Frank Lee laboring over his inventive—but hardly esoteric—dishes: Sautéed quail filled with herbed chicken mousse; pad Thai noodles with shrimp, pork, and an authentic fish sauce; and corn-and-crab soup with spinach ravioli. You can order almost every item as either an appetizer or an entrée. The wine list is extensive and moderately priced. *192 E. Bay St., tel. 803/723–3424. No reservations. Dress: Casual. AE, MC, V. Closed Sun. No lunch Sat.*

Seafood **Barbadoes Room.** This large, airy plant- and light-filled space has a sophisticated island look and a view out to a cheery courtyard garden. Entrées include sautéed jumbo shrimp and scallops served with creamy wild mushroom sauce on a bed of fresh spinach; linguini with an assortment of fresh shellfish in a light saffron sauce; and grilled breast of duck served with tarragon pear sauce. There's an elegant and extensive Southern-style breakfast menu and a popular Sunday brunch. *115 Meeting St., in the Mills House Hotel, tel. 803/577-2400. Reservations advised. Dress: casual but neat. AE, D, DC, MC, V.*

$ *American* **California Dreaming Restaurant & Bar.** The floor-to-ceiling windows of this heavy-volume restaurant, in an impressive stone fort on the Ashley River, look out at night on the lights of the harbor. The crowds come for the great view, low prices, and bountiful platters of food, such as grilled salmon, chicken salads, prime rib, and catch of the day. To make the wait bearable, take to the bar for a frothy piña colada. *1 Ashley Pointe Dr. (5 min from downtown), tel. 803/766-1644. No reservations. Dress: casual. AE, MC, V.*

Mike Calder's Deli & Pub. Soups, salads, sandwiches, daily specials, and 12 different draft beers are offered in an "Old World" setting, once a pharmacy in the historic district. *288 King St., tel. 803/577-0123. No reservations. Dress: casual. D, MC, V. Closed Sun.*

Low Country/Southern **Captain Guilds Cafe.** There are actually two restaurants here: The little downstairs storefront restaurant churns out inexpensive, expertly prepared southern food. The catfish with honey curry butter and the chicken breast breaded with parmesan cornmeal and lemon caper sauce are surprisingly light and tender given the regional tendency to deep fry. For dessert, sample the bread pudding with a brown-sugar cream sauce. Upstairs, formal, prix-fixe, four-course Continental meals ($29) are presented in a grand dining room—the menu changes daily and depends largely on what's fresh that day. *101 Pitt St., Mount Pleasant, tel. 803/884-7009. Downstairs: No reservations. Dress: casual. Upstairs: Reservations required. Jacket and tie advised. AE, MC, V. Downstairs: No dinner Sun. Closed Mon. Upstairs: No lunch. Closed Sun. and Mon.*

★ **Magnolias Uptown/Down South.** This popular place, in an 1823 warehouse on the site of the old customs house, is cherished by Charlestonians and visitors alike. The magnolia theme is seen throughout, and a custom-built circular bar overlooks the dining room. Specialties include grilled mahi-mahi fillet topped with succotash of shrimp, butter beans, yellow corn, and fresh spinach. Even the Black Angus strip steak is distinctive, served with fricassee of wild mushrooms, black-eyed peas, and Madeira sauce. Equally innovative appetizers include seared yellow grits cakes with Tasso gravy and yellow corn relish, and the salt-and-pepper fried shrimp with honey mustard-and-horseradish dip. *185 E. Bay St., tel. 803/577-7771. Reservations advised. Dress: casual. AE, MC, V.*

Seafood **Shem Creek Bar & Grill.** This pleasant dockside spot is perennially popular for its oyster bar and light fare (until 10 PM Sun.–Thurs., until 1 AM Fri.–Sat.). There's also a wide variety of seafood entrées, including a steam pot—lobsters, clams, oysters, and sausages with melted lemon butter or hot cocktail sauce—big enough for two. *508 Mill St., Mount Pleasant, tel. 803/884-8102. No reservations. Dress: casual. AE, D, DC, MC, V.*

Lodging

Rates tend to increase during the Spring Festival of Houses and Spoleto, when reservations are essential. The **Charleston Trident Convention and Visitors Bureau** (Box 975, Charleston 29402, tel. 803/853-8000) distributes a Courtesy Discount Card entitling the bearer to 10%–50% off at many accommodations, restaurants, tours, and shops between mid-November and mid-February. To find rooms in homes, cottages, and carriage houses, try **Charleston East Bed and Breakfast League** (1031 Tall Pine Rd., Mount Pleasant 29464, tel. 803/884-8208) and **Historic Charleston Bed and Breakfast** (60 Broad St., Charleston 29401, tel. 803/722-6606). For historic home rentals in Charleston, contact **Charleston Carriage Houses–Oceanfront Realty** (Box 6151, Hilton Head, SC 29938, tel. 803/785-8161). For condo and house rentals on the Isle of Palms—some with private pools and tennis courts—try **Island Realty** (Box 157, Isle of Palms 29451, tel. 803/886-8144).

The most highly recommended properties in each price category are indicated by a star ★.

Category	Cost*
$$$$	over $150
$$$	$90–$150
$$	$50–$90
$	under $50

**double room; add 7% for taxes*

Hotels and Motels

$$$$

Best Western King Charles Inn. This inn in the historic district has spacious rooms furnished with period reproductions. *237 Meeting St., 29401, tel. 803/723-7451 or 800/528-1234, fax 803/723-2041. 91 rooms. Facilities: pool, dining room, lounge. AE, D, DC, MC, V.*

Hawthorn Suites Hotel. The hotel's spacious suites, all decorated with 18th-century reproductions and canopied beds, include full kitchens or wet bars with microwave ovens and refrigerators. Across from the City Market, the hotel is popular with business people, families, and tour groups. *181 Church St., 29401, tel. 803/577-2644 or 800/527-1133, fax 803/577-2697. 164 suites. Facilities: lounge, restaurant, business and meeting services, fitness center, pool, whirlpool, complimentary full breakfast and afternoon refreshments. AE, D, DC, MC, V.*

$$$

★ **Mills House Hotel.** Antique furnishings and period decor give great charm to this luxurious Holiday Inn property, a reconstruction of an old hostelry on its original site in the historic district. There's a lounge with live entertainment, and excellent dining in the Barbadoes Room (*see* Dining, *above*). *115 Meeting St., 29401, tel. 803/577-2400 or 800/874-9600, fax 803/722-2712. 215 rooms. Facilities: restaurant, 2 lounges, pool. AE, D, DC, MC, V.*

★ **Omni Hotel at Charleston Place.** Among the city's most luxurious hotels, this graceful, low-rise structure in the historic district is flanked by upscale boutiques and specialty shops. The lobby features a magnificent hand-blown Venetian glass chandelier, an Italian marble floor, and antiques from Sotheby's. Rooms are furnished with period reproductions. *130 Market St., 29401, tel. 803/722-4900 or 800/843-6664, fax 803/722-4074. 348 rooms, 46 suites. Facilities: fitness center, heated pool, sauna, whirlpool, concierge floor with* *complimentary food and drink service, 2 restaurants, 2 lounges with entertainment, shopping arcade. AE, D, DC, MC, V.*

Sheraton Inn Charleston. Some rooms and suites in this 13-story hotel outside the historic district overlook the Ashley River. Spacious rooms and suites are highlighted with Queen Anne furnishings. There's also concierge service and live entertainment. *170 Lockwood Dr., 29403, tel. 803/723-3000 or 800/968-3569. 337 rooms. Facilities: lighted tennis, pool, jogging track, coffee shop, dining room, lounge, exercise room, meeting rooms. AE, D, DC, MC, V.*

$$–$$$ **Holiday Inn Charleston/Mount Pleasant.** This hotel just over the Cooper River Bridge is a 10-minute drive from the downtown historic district. Every thing has been gracefully done: brass lamps, crystal chandeliers, Queen Anne–style furniture. The "high-tech suites" offer PC cable hookups, large working areas, glossy ultramodern furniture, and refrigerators. *250 U.S. 17, Mount Pleasant 29464, tel. 803/884-6000 or 800/290-4004, fax 803/744-0942. 158 rooms. Facilities: outdoor pool, sauna, exercise room, meeting facilities, concierge floor, restaurant, raw bar, lounge with DJ. AE, D, DC, MC, V.*

$–$$ ★ **Comfort Inn Riverview.** Close to the Ashley River, the historic district, and restaurants, this 7-story contemporary inn offers free parking and complimentary Continental breakfast. *144 Bee St., 29401, tel. 803/577-2224 or 800/228-5150, fax 803/577-9001. 128 rooms. Facilities: pool. AE, DC, MC, V.*

Days Inn Historic District. This inn is well located and attractively furnished. *155 Meeting St., 29401, tel. 803/722-8411 or 800/325-2525, fax 803/733-5361. 124 units. Facilities: pool, dining room. AE, D, DC, MC, V.*

Hampton Inn–Historic District. This downtown property has hardwood floors in the lobby, extra-light guest rooms furnished in period reproductions, a courtyard garden, and pool. Guests also get a Continental breakfast. *345 Meeting St., 29403, tel. 803/723-4000 or 800/426-7866. 171 rooms. AE, DC, MC, V.*

Quality Inn–Heart of Charleston. A block from the Gaillard Auditorium, the inn is clean and run by a friendly staff. *125 Calhoun St., 29401, tel. 803/722-3391 or 800/845-2504, fax 803/577-0361. 126 rooms. Facilities: restaurant, lounge, pool. AE, D, DC, MC, V.*

Inns and Guest Houses

The charms of historic Charleston can be enhanced by a stay at one of its many inns, most in restored structures. Some are reminiscent of European inns; one is tastefully contemporary, tucked away on the grounds of a famous estate.

Historic District

★ **John Rutledge House Inn.** This 1763 house, built by John Rutledge, one of the framers of the U.S. Constitution, is one of Charleston's most luxurious inns. Ornate ironwork on the facade has a palmetto tree and eagle motif, signifying Rutledge's service to both his state and his nation. Wine and tea are served in the ballroom, and Continental breakfast and newspapers are delivered to your room. Two charming period carriage houses also accommodate guests. *116 Broad St., tel. 803/723-7999 or 800/476-9741, fax 803720-2615. 11 rooms in mansion, 4 in each carriage house. Facilities: cable TV, some rooms with whirlpool tubs. AE, MC, V. $$$$*

Ansonborough Inn. Formerly a turn-of-the-century stationer's warehouse, this spacious all-suite inn is furnished in antique reproductions. It offers hairdryers, irons, off-street parking, a morning newspaper, message service, wine reception, morning newspaper, and Continental breakfast, but it's best known for its friendly staff. *21 Hasell St., 29401, tel. 803/723-1655 or 800/522-2073, fax 803/527-6888. 37 suites. Facilities: meeting room. AE, MC, V. $$$*

Brasington House Bed & Breakfast. During afternoon tea or at the Continental breakfast, Dalton and Judy Brasington, educators by profession, will advise you on what to see and do in Charleston. The formal dining room of their restored Greek Revival "single house" in the historic district is filled with antiques and treasures from around the world. *328 E. Bay St., 29401, tel. 803/722–1274 or 800/722–1274, fax 803/722–6785. 4 rooms with private baths. MC, V. $$$*

Elliott House Inn. Listen to the chimes of St. Michael's Episcopal Church as you sip wine in the courtyard of this lovely old inn in the heart of the historic district. Then retreat to a cozy room with period furniture, including canopied four-posters and Oriental carpets. A Continental breakfast is included. *78 Queen St., 29401, tel. 803/723–1855 or 800/729–1855, fax 803/722–1567. 26 rooms. Facilities: cable TV, bicycles, Jacuzzi in courtyard, Continental breakfast. AE, D, MC, V. $$$*

Maison DuPré. A quiet retreat off busy East Bay Street, this 1801 inn was created out of three restored homes and two carriage houses. It is filled with antiques, and each room features an original painting by Lucille Mullholland, who operates the inn with her husband Robert. Enjoy a full Low Country–tea, Continental breakfast, and tickets to the Nathaniel Russell house museum—all complimentary. *317 E. Bay St., 29401, tel. 803/723–8691 or 800/844–4667. 12 rooms, 3 suites. AE, MC, V. $$$*

Planters Inn. Rooms and suites here are beautifully appointed with opulent furnishings, including mahogany four-poster beds and marble baths. There's a concierge and 24-hour room service. *112 N. Market St., 29401, tel. 803/722–2345 or 800/845–7082, fax 803/577–2125. 41 rooms and suites. AE, DC, MC, V. $$$*

★ **Two Meeting Street.** As pretty as a wedding cake and just as romantic, this turn-of-the-century inn near the Battery features Tiffany windows, carved English oak paneling, and a chandelier from Czechoslovakia. There are two very private honeymoon suites. Guests are treated to afternoon sherry and Continental breakfast. *2 Meeting St., 29401, tel. 803/723–7322. 9 rooms. No credit cards. $$$*

Cannonboro Inn. One of the most elegant inns in town, this B&B in the historic district has luxurious rooms, tastefully decorated in period furnishings by owners Bud and Sally Allen. Guests are treated to a complimentary full English breakfast, use of the bicycles, and afternoon sherry. *184 Ashley Ave., 29403, tel. 803/723–8572, fax 803/723–9080. 6 rooms with private baths. MC, V. $$–$$$*

1837 Bed and Breakfast and Tea Room. Though it's not as fancy as some of the B&Bs in town, this inn is long on hospitality. It even sets an afternoon tea that's open to the public for a nominal price. *126 Wentworth St., 29401, tel. 803/723–7166. 8 rooms with baths. AE, MC, V. $$*

Resort Islands

The semitropical islands dotting the South Carolina coast near Charleston are home to several sumptuous resorts. A wide variety of packages is sold. Peak-season rates (during spring and summer vacations) range from $100 to $250 per day, double occupancy. Costs drop considerably off-season.

Kiawah Island Resort. Choose from 150 inn rooms, 48 suites, and 300 completely equipped one- to four-bedroom villas in two luxurious resort villages on 10,000 wooded acres. The accommodations and much of the property were refurbished in 1994. There are 10 miles of fine broad beaches, four golf courses (the 1991 Ryder Cup was here), two tennis centers, jeep and water safaris, land sailing, canoeing, surfcasting, fishing, and children's programs. There's also a general store and shops. Dining options are many and varied: Low Country specialties in the Jasmine Porch and Veranda, Indigo House; Continental cuisine in the Charleston Gallery; lagoonside dining at the Park Cafe; casual dining in the Sand Wedge, Sundancers, Jonah's. *Kiawah Island, Box 12357, Charleston 29412, tel. 803/768–2121 or 800/654–2924, fax 803/768–9386. AE, DC, MC, V. $$$$*

Seabrook Island Resort. There are 360 completely equipped one- to three-bedroom villas, cottages, and beach houses. Beach Club and Island Club, open to all guests, are centers for dining and leisure activities. Amenities include championship golf, tennis and equestrian centers, bicycling, water sports, pools, children's programs. *1002 Landfall Way, Seabrook Island 29455, tel. 803/768–1000 or 800/845–2475, fax 803/768–4922. AE, D, MC, V. $$$$*

Wild Dunes. This breezy, 1,600-acre resort has 250 villas for rent, each with a kitchen and washer and dryer. There are two widely acclaimed golf courses, a racquet club, a yacht harbor on the Intracoastal Waterway, bicycling, nature trails, surfcasting, water sports, and children's programs. Beef specialties are served at The Club House and seafood at The Island House, where all dishes are created by a French master chef. There's a lounge with live entertainment. *Box 503, Isle of Palms 29451, tel. 803/886–6000 or 800/845–8880, fax 803/886–2916. AE, MC, V. $$$$*

The Arts

Pick up the Schedule of Events at the Visitors Center (375 Meeting St.) or at area hotels, inns, and restaurants. Also see "Tips for Tourists" each Saturday in *The News & Courier/The Evening Post.*

Arts Festivals

Spoleto Festival USA. Founded by the composer Gian Carlo Menotti in 1977, Spoleto has become one of the world's greatest celebrations of the arts. For two weeks, from late May to early June, opera, dance, theater, symphonic and chamber music performances, jazz, and the visual arts are showcased in concert halls, theaters, parks, churches, streets, and gardens throughout the city. For information: Spoleto Festival USA (Box 157, Charleston 29402, tel. 803/722–2764).

Piccolo Spoleto Festival. The spirited companion festival of Spoleto Festival USA showcases the best in local and regional talent from every artistic discipline. There are about 700 events—from jazz performances to puppet shows—held at 60 sites in 17 days, from mid-May through early June, and most performances are free. For a program, contact the Office of Cultural Affairs, Piccolo Spoleto Festival (133 Church St., Charleston 29401, tel. 803/724–7305).

During the **Festival of Houses and Gardens,** held during March and April each year, more than 100 private homes, gardens, and historic churches are open to the public. (Contact the Historic Charleston Foundation, Box 1120, 29202, tel. 803/723–1623.)

Moja Arts Festival. Theater, dance, and music performances, art shows, films, lectures, and tours celebrating the rich heritage of the African continent are held at sites throughout the historic district the first two weeks in October. For information: The Office of Cultural Affairs (133 Church St., Charleston 29401, tel. 803/724–7305).

Southeastern Wildlife Exposition. Held in mid-February, one of Charleston's biggest annual events features art by renowned wildlife artists. *211 Meeting St., 29401, tel. 803/723–1748.*

Concerts

The College of Charleston has a **Monday Night Recital Series** (*see* Charleston for Free, *above*). The **Charleston Symphony Orchestra** (tel. 803/723–7528) presents its Classics Concerts Series at Gaillard Municipal Auditorium (77 Calhoun St., tel. 803/577–4500). Its Brass

Quintet plays at the Charleston Museum Auditorium (360 Meeting St., tel. 803/722–2996) and the Garden Theatre (tel. 803/577–7400) and at other locations around the city.

Dance The **Charleston Ballet Theatre** (280 Meeting St., tel. 803/723–7334) performs everything from contemporary to classical dance. The **Charleston Civic Ballet** (tel. 803/722–8779 or 803/577–4502) performs at the Sotille Theater (tel. 803/953–6340). The **Robert Ivey Ballet Company** (tel. 803/556–1343), a student group at the College of Charleston, gives a fall and spring program of jazz, classical, and modern dance at the **Simons Center for the Arts.**

Theater Several groups, including the **Footlight Players,** perform at the Dock Street Theatre (135 Church St., tel. 803/577–7400). Performances by the College of Charleston's drama department and guest theatrical groups are presented during the school year at the **Simons Center for the Arts** (tel. 803/953–5600).

Nightlife

Music and Dancing **Windjammer** (tel. 803/886–8596), on the Isle of Palms, is an oceanfront spot featuring live rock music. In the market area, there's **Fannigans** (tel. 803/722–6916), where a DJ spins Top-40 hits, and the best of beach music. The shag, South Carolina's state dance, popularized in the early '60s, is alive and well here.

Film **Stage One Cinema** (30 Cumberland St. Courtyard, tel. 803/722–1900) offers films from around the world in an old livery stable, plus wine, beer, coffee, and pastries.

Hotel and Jazz Bars **The Best Friend Lounge** (115 Meeting St., tel. 803/577–2400), in the Mills House Hotel, has a guitarist playing light tunes Monday–Saturday nights. In the **Lobby Lounge** (130 Market St., tel. 803/722–4900) in the Omni Charleston, cocktails and appetizers are accompanied by piano. Live jazz is offered Friday and Saturday evenings at **Henry's Restaurant** (54 N. Market St., tel. 803/723–4363).

Restaurant/ Lounges **A.W. Shucks** (State Street Market, tel. 803/723–1151) is a popular spot for relaxed evenings set to taped easy-listening. **Cafe 99** (99 S. Market St., tel. 803/577–4499) has laid-back '60s and '70s music indoors and out by vocalists and guitarists. **East Bay Trading Co.** (161 E. Bay St., tel. 803/722–0722) has a small dance floor in its lively bar and a DJ playing Top 40s Friday and Saturday nights. You find authentic Irish music at **Tommy Condon's Irish Pub & Restaurant** (160 Church St., tel. 803/577–3818).

Dinner Cruise For an evening of dining and dancing, climb aboard the luxury yacht *Spirit of Charleston. Tel. 803/722–2628. Reservations required. Closed Sun. and Mon.*

Myrtle Beach and the Grand Strand

The kitschy and frenetic Grand Strand, a booming resort area along the South Carolina coast, is one of the Eastern Seaboard's megafamily-vacation centers. Myrtle Beach alone accounts for about 40% of the state's tourism revenue. The main attraction, of course, is the broad, beckoning beach—60 miles of it, stretching from the North Carolina border south to Georgetown, with Myrtle Beach at the hub. But the Strand has something for everyone: nearly 80 championship golf courses, designed by Arnold Palmer, Robert

Trent Jones, and Tom and George Fazio, among others; excellent seafood restaurants; giant shopping malls and factory outlets; amusement parks, water slides, and arcades; a dozen shipwrecks for divers to explore; fine fishing; campgrounds, most on the beach; plus antique-car and wax museums, the world's largest sculpture garden, a half dozen country music shows, an antique pipe organ and merry-go-round, and a museum dedicated entirely to rice.

Getting There and Getting Around

By Plane The **Myrtle Beach Jetport** (tel. 803/448–1589) is served by American, American's American Eagle affiliate; Delta and its Atlantic Southeast Airlines affiliate; and USAir.

By Car Midway between New York and Miami, the Grand Strand can be reached from all directions via Interstates 20, 26, 40, 77, 85, and 95, which connect with U.S. 17, the major north–south coastal route through the Strand.

By Train **Amtrak** (tel. 800/872–7245) service for the Grand Strand is available through a terminal in Florence. Buses connect with Amtrak there for the 65-mile drive to Myrtle Beach.

By Bus **Greyhound Bus Lines** (tel. 800/231–2222) serves Myrtle Beach.

By Boat Boaters traveling the Intracoastal Waterway may dock at **Hague Marina** (Hwy. 707, Myrtle Beach, tel. 803/293–2141).

By Taxi Service is provided by **Coastal Cab Service** in Myrtle Beach (tel. 803/448–3360 or 803/448–4444).

Guided Tours

Palmetto Tour & Travel (tel. 803/626–2660) and **Leisure Time Unlimited/Gray Line** (tel. 803/448–9483), both in Myrtle Beach, offer tour packages, guide services, and charter services. At the **Georgetown County Chamber of Commerce and Information Center** (102 Broad St., tel. 803/546–8436 or 800/777–7705), you can take tours of historic areas (Mar.–Oct.) by tram, by 1840 horse-drawn carriage, or by boat. You can also rent cassette walking tours and pick up free driving- and walking-tour maps. **Miss Nell's Tours** (tel. 803/546–3975) take you on 30- to 90-minute strolls through Georgetown's historic area.

Important Addresses and Numbers

Tourist Information **Georgetown County Chamber of Commerce and Information Center** (*see* Guided Tours, *above*). **Myrtle Beach Area Chamber of Commerce and Information Center** (1301 N. Kings Hwy., Box 2115, Myrtle Beach, 29578, tel. 803/626–7444 or 800/356–3016).

Emergencies Dial 911 for emergency assistance. The emergency room is open 24 hours a day at the **Grand Strand General Hospital** (off U.S. 17 at 809 82nd Pkwy., Myrtle Beach, tel. 803/449–4411).

Exploring the Grand Strand

Myrtle Beach—whose population of 26,000 explodes to about 350,000 in summer—is the center of activity on the Grand Strand. It is here that you find the amusement parks and other children's activities that make the area so popular with families, as well as most of the nightlife that keeps parents and teenagers happy into the wee hours. In 1993, the city put up dozens of colorful street-light displays around major intersections, adding yet a few more volts of energy to the already pulsating scene. On the North Strand, there is Little River, with a thriving fishing and charter industry, and the several communities that make up North Myrtle Beach. On the South Strand, Surfside Beach and Garden City have more summer homes and condominiums. Farther south are Murrells Inlet, once a pirate's haven and now a popular fishing port, and Pawleys Island, one of the East Coast's oldest resorts. Historic Georgetown forms the southern tip.

Our tour begins at the **Myrtle Beach Pavilion Amusement Park,** which underwent a major renovation and expansion in 1994. Here families while away the days enjoying thrill and kiddie rides, the Carolinas' largest flume, video games, a teen nightclub, specialty shops, antique cars, and sidewalk cafés. *Ninth Ave. N and Ocean Blvd., tel. 803/448–6456. Fees for individual attractions; family discount book available. Open Mar.–May and Sept.–Oct., weekdays 6 PM–midnight and weekends 1 PM–midnight; June–Sept., daily 1 PM–midnight.*

More of the unusual awaits at **Ripleys Believe It or Not Museum.** Among the more than 750 exhibits is an 8-foot, 11-inch wax replica of the world's tallest man. *901 N. Ocean Blvd., tel. 803/448–2331. Admission: $6.50 adults, $3.50 children 6–12. Open daily 10 AM–10 PM.*

Drama, sound, and animation highlight religious, historical, and entertainment sections in the **Myrtle Beach National Wax Museum.** *1000 N. Ocean Blvd., tel. 803/448–9921. Admission: $5 adults, $3 children 5–12, under 5 free. Open late Feb.–mid-Oct., daily 9 AM–11 PM, in summer until midnight.*

When your family's appetite for more raucous amusements has been sated, it's time to head out of town. Going south on Kings Highway, you'll come to **Murrells Inlet,** a picturesque little fishing village with popular seafood restaurants that's also a great place for chartering a fishing boat or joining a group excursion.

Three miles south, on the grounds of a Colonial rice plantation, is the largest outdoor collection of American sculpture, with works by such artists as Frederic Remington and Daniel Chester French. **Brookgreen Gardens** was begun in 1931 by railroad magnate/philanthropist Archer Huntington and his wife, Anna, herself a sculptor. Today, more than 500 works are set amid beautifully landscaped grounds, with avenues of live oaks, reflecting pools, and over 2,000 plant species. Also on the site is a wildlife park, an aviary, a cypress swamp, nature trails, and an education center. *18 mi south of Myrtle Beach off U.S. 17, tel. 803/237–4218. Admission: $6.50 adults, $3 children 6–12. Tape tours, $2.50 extra. Open daily 9:30–5:30.*

Across the highway is **Huntington Beach State Park,** the Huntingtons' 2,500-acre former estate. The park's focal point is Atalaya (ca. 1933), their Moorish-style, 30-room home, open to visitors in season. In addition to the splendid beach, there are surf fishing, nature trails, an interpretive center, a salt-marsh boardwalk, picnic areas, a playground, concessions, and a campground. *Tel. 803/237–4440. Admission free; parking fee in peak months. Open daily dawn to dusk.*

Farther south is **Pawleys Island,** 4 miles long and a half-mile wide, which began as a resort before the Civil War, when wealthy planters and their families summered here. It has mostly weathered old summer cottages nestled in groves of oleander and oak trees. You can watch the famous Pawleys Island hammocks being made here (*see* Shopping, *below*), but there's little else to do.

Bellefield Nature Center Museum, south on U.S. 17 near Georgetown, is at the entrance of Hobcaw Barony, on the vast estate of the late Bernard M. Baruch. Here such guests as Franklin D. Roosevelt and Winston Churchill came to confer with him. The museum, run by the Belle W. Baruch Foundation, is used for teaching and research in forestry and marine biology. There are aquariums, touch tanks, and video presentations. *Tel. 803/546–4623. Admission to museum free. Open weekdays 10–5, Sat. 1–5. A variety of nature tours and estate tours are given year-round; call at least 1 month in advance for schedules and fees.*

Georgetown, on Winyah Bay, founded in 1729 by a Baptist minister, soon became the center of America's Colonial rice empire. A rich plantation culture took root here and developed on a scale comparable to Charleston's. Today, oceangoing vessels still come to Georgetown's busy port, and the **Harbor Walk,** the restored waterfront, hums with activity. Georgetown's historic district—probably the prettiest in the state north of Charleston—encompasses more than 50 homes and other buildings and can be walked in a couple of hours.

The graceful market-meeting building in the heart of town, topped by an 1842 clock and tower, has been converted into the **Rice Museum,** with maps, tools, and dioramas. *Front and Screven Sts., tel. 803/546–7423. Admission: $2 adults, children under 18 and students free. Open Mon.–Sat. 9:30–4:30.*

Nearby, **Prince George Winyah Episcopal Church** (named after King George II) still serves the congregation established in 1721. It was built in 1737 with bricks brought from England. *Broad and Highmarket Sts., tel. 803/546–4358. Donation suggested. Open Mar.–Oct., weekdays 11:30–4:30.*

Overlooking the Sampit River from a bluff is the **Harold Kaminski House** (ca. 1760). It's especially notable for its collections of regional antiques and furnishings, its Chippendale and Duncan Phyfe furniture, Royal Doulton vases, and silver. *1003 Front St., tel. 803/546–7706. Admission: $4 adults, $2 children under 13. Open Mon.–Sat. 10–5, Sun. 1–4.*

Twelve miles south of Georgetown lies **Hopsewee Plantation,** surrounded by moss-draped live oaks, magnolias, and tree-size camellias, overlooking the North Santee River. The mansion has a fine Georgian staircase and hand-carved Adam candlelight moldings. *U.S. 17, tel. 803/546–7891. Admission to mansion: $5 adults, $2 children 5–17, under 5 free. Admission to grounds: $2 per car. Mansion open Mar.–Oct., Tues.–Fri. 10–4. Grounds, including nature trail, open year-round, daily dawn–dusk.*

Hampton Plantation State Park, at the edge of the Francis Marion National Forest (*see* Off the Beaten Track in Charleston section, *above*), preserves the home of Archibald Rutledge, poet laureate of South Carolina for 39 years until his death in 1973. The 18th-century plantation house is a fine example of a Low Country mansion. The exterior has been restored; cutaway sections in the finely crafted interior show the changes made through the centuries. The grounds are landscaped, and there are picnic areas. *Off U.S. 17, tel. 803/546–9361. Mansion admission: $2 adults. Admission to grounds free. Mansion open Apr.–Labor Day, Thurs.–Mon. 1–4, Labor Day–Mar., weekends 1–4. Grounds open Thurs.–Mon. 9–6.*

What to See and Do with Children

Brookgreen Gardens (*see* Exploring, *above*).

Myrtle Beach is the minigolf capital of the world, and **Hawaiian Rumble** is its crown jewel, featuring a smoking mountain that erupts fire and rumbles at timed intervals. *3210 33rd Ave. S, U.S. 17, Myrtle Beach, tel. 803/272–7812. Admission: $4 all day 9–5, $4 per round 5–midnight. Closed Jan.–Feb.*

Huntington Beach State Park (*see* Exploring, *above*).

Myrtle Beach Grand Prix. Auto-mania heaven, it offers Formula 1 race cars, go-carts, bumper boats, mini-go-carts, kiddie cars, and mini-bumper boats for adults and children age 3 and up. *Two locations: 3201 Hwy. 17, Myrtle Beach, tel. 803/238–2421, and Windy Hill, U.S. 17N, N. Myrtle Beach, tel. 803/272–6010. Rides priced individually, $2–$5.50. Open Mar. 10–Oct. 31, daily 10 AM–11 PM.*

Myrtle Beach Pavilion and Amusement Park (*see* Exploring, *above*).

Myrtle Waves Water Park. There's splashy family fun for all ages in 17 rides and activities. *U.S. 17 Bypass and 10th Ave. N, Myrtle Beach, tel. 803/448–1026 or 800/524–9283. Cost: $10.95, $8.45 after 3 PM, $5.95 spectators and over 54, children under 3 free. Open Memorial Day Weekend–Labor Day, daily 10–6 (Tues.–Thurs. until 8), May and Sept., weekends only.*

Shopping

Malls — **Myrtle Square Mall** (2501 N. Kings Hwy., Myrtle Beach, tel. 803/448–2513) has 71 upscale stores and restaurants, and a Food Court. **Barefoot Landing** in North Myrtle Beach (4898 S. Kings Hwy., tel. 803/272–8349) is a unique complex built over marshland and water. **Briarcliffe Mall** (10177 N. Kings Hwy., Myrtle Beach, tel. 803/272–4040) has 100 specialty shops. Malls are generally open Monday–Saturday 10–9, Sunday 1–6.

Discount Outlets — Off-price shopping outlets abound in the Grand Strand. At **Waccamaw Pottery and Outlet Park** (U.S. 501 at the Waterway, Myrtle Beach, tel. 803/236–1100) over 3 miles of shelves in several buildings are stocked with china, glassware, wicker, brass, pewter, and countless other items, and about 50 factory outlets sell clothing, furniture, books, jewelry, and more. The **Hathaway/Olga Warner** (tel. 803/236–4200), across from Waccamaw, offers menswear by Chaps, Ralph Lauren, Speedo, and Jack Nicklaus, and women's lingerie.

Specialty Stores — **The Hammock Shops at Pawleys Island** (tel. 803/237–8448) is a handsome complex of approximately 20 boutiques and gift shops built with old brick brought from England as ballast. In one shop, rope hammocks are being made as they have been since 1880. Others sell jewelry, toys, antiques, and designer fashions.

Beaches

All the Grand Strand beaches are family oriented, and almost all are public, with many stretches lifeguarded. The widest expanses are in North Myrtle Beach.

Participant Sports

Fishing The Gulf Stream makes fishing usually good from early spring through December. Anglers can fish from 10 piers and jetties for amberjack, sea trout, and king mackerel. Surfcasters may snare bluefish, whiting, flounder, pompano, and channel bass. In the South Strand, salt marshes, inlets, and tidal creeks yield flounder, blues, croakers, spots, shrimp, clams, oysters, and blue crabs. **Capt. Dick's** (U.S. 17 Bus., Murrells Inlet, tel. 803/651–3676), and **Hague Marina** (Hwy. 707, Myrtle Beach, tel. 803/293–2141) offer half- and full-day fishing and sightseeing trips. The annual **Grand Strand Fishing Rodeo** (tel. 803/626–7444, Apr.–Oct.) features a "fish of the month" contest, with prizes for the largest catch of a designated species.

Golf Many of the Grand Strand's nearly 80 public courses are championship layouts. Spring and fall, with off-season rates, are the busiest seasons, and there are many packages (call **Golf Holiday,** tel. 803/448–5942 or 800/845–4653). Popular courses include: in Myrtle Beach, **Arcadian Shores Golf Club** (tel. 803/449–5217) and **Myrtle Beach National Golf Club** (tel. 803/448–2308 or 800/344–5590); in North Myrtle Beach, **Bay Tree Golf Plantation** (tel. 803/249–1487 or 800/845–6191), **Gator Hole** (tel. 803/249–3543 or 800/447–2668), **Heather Glen Golf Links** (tel. 803/249–9000), and **Robbers Roost Golf Club** (tel. 803/249–1471 or 800/352–2384); near Surfside Beach, **Blackmoor Golf Club** (tel. 803/650–5555); in Cherry Grove Beach, the much touted **Tidewater** (tel. 803/249–6675); on Pawleys Island, **Litchfield by the Sea Resort** (tel. 803/237–3000), **Litchfield Plantation** (tel. 803/237–9121), and **Pawleys Plantation Golf & Country Club** (tel. 803/237–3451).

Scuba Diving In summer, a wide variety of warm-water tropical fish finds its way to the area from the Gulf Stream. Off the coast of Little River, rock and coral ledges teem with coral, sea fans, sponges, reef fish, anemones, urchins, arrow crabs, and stone crabs. Several outlying shipwrecks are home to schools of spadefish, amberjack, grouper, and barracuda. Instruction and equipment rentals are available from **Scuba Syndrome** (2718 Hwy. 501, Myrtle Beach, tel. 803/626–6740).

Tennis There are more than 150 courts on the Grand Strand. Facilities include hotel and resort courts, as well as free municipal courts in Myrtle Beach, North Myrtle Beach, and Surfside Beach. Among tennis clubs offering court time, rental equipment, and instruction are **Myrtle Beach Racquet Club** (tel. 803/449–4031), **Myrtle Beach Tennis and Swim Club** (tel. 803/449–4486), and **Litchfield Racquet Club** (tel. 803/237–3411).

Water Sports Surfboards, Hobie Cats, Jet Skis, Windsurfers, and sailboats are available for rent at **Downwind Sails** (Ocean Blvd. at 29th Ave. S, Myrtle Beach, tel. 803/448–7245) and **Driftwood Cruising** (Dock C2, Myrtle Beach Yacht Club, Coquina Harbor, N. Myrtle Beach, tel. 803/249–8036).

Dining

Coastal South Carolina serves traditionally prepared seafood in lavish portions, garnished with hush puppies, cole slaw, and fresh vegetables. Myrtle Beach's mile-long "Restaurant Row" stretches along U.S. 17 from the city's northermost limits. Here you'll find every type of cuisine imaginable, but you won't find the gourmet cooking of Charleston and Hilton Head; instead, expect family-style restaurants with predictable, but dependable, menus. The most highly recommended restaurants in each price category are indicated by a star ★.

Category	Cost*
$$$$	over $25
$$$	$15–$25
$$	$7–$15
$	under $7

**per person without 5% tax, service, or drinks*

Georgetown

★ **Rice Paddy.** This cozy Low Country restaurant is apt to be crowded at lunch, when local solons flock in for homemade vegetable soup, garden-fresh salads, and sandwiches. Dinner is more relaxed, and the menu might have broiled fresh seafood, crabmeat casserole, or veal scaloppine. *408 Duke St., tel. 803/546–2021. Reservations accepted. Dress: informal. AE, MC, V. Closed Sun. $$*

River Room. This restaurant on the Sampit River specializes in char-grilled fish, seafood pastas, and steaks. For lunch you can have shrimp and grits or a variety of sandwiches and salads. It's especially romantic at night when the oil lamps and brass fixtures cast a warm glow on the dark wood and brick interior of the turn-of-the-century building. *801 Front St., tel. 803/527–4110. No reservations. Dress: casual. AE, MC, V. Closed Sun. $$*

Murrells Inlet

★ **Planter's Back Porch.** Sip cool drinks in the spring house of a turn-of-the-century farmhouse, then have dinner in a garden setting. Black wrought-iron chandeliers are suspended from high white beams, and hanging baskets of greenery decorate white latticework archways separating the fireplace-centered main dining room and the airy, glass-enclosed porch. You can't go wrong with baked whole flounder, panned lump crabmeat, or the hearty Inlet Dinner with several types of fish. *U.S. 17 and Wachesaw Rd., tel. 803/651–5263. Reservations accepted. Dress: casual. AE, D, MC, V. Closed Dec.–mid-Mar. $$*

Myrtle Beach

Slug's Rib. A Carolinas institution, this immensely popular restaurant has a welcoming contemporary setting, with an outdoor lounge overlooking the Intracoastal Waterway. It features only aged prime ribs. There is also a children's menu. *9713 N. Kings Hwy., tel. 803/449–6419. No reservations. Dress: casual. AE, DC, MC, V. $$–$$$*

★ **Rice Planters.** Dine on fresh seafood, quail, or steaks grilled to order in a homey setting enhanced by candlelight, Low Country antiques, and rice-plantation tools and artifacts. Shrimp Creole is a house specialty; among the appetizers, don't miss the crab fingers! The bread and the pecan pie are home-baked. *6707 N. Kings Hwy., tel. 803/449–3456. Reservations accepted. Dress: casual. AE, D, MC, V. $$*

★ **Sea Captain's House.** At this picturesque restaurant with nautical decor, the best seats are in the windowed porch room, which overlooks the ocean. The fireplace in the wood-paneled dining room inside is warmly welcoming on cool off-season evenings. Menu highlights include she-crab soup, Low Country crab casserole, and avocado-seafood salad. The breads and desserts are baked here. *3002 N. Ocean Blvd., tel. 803/448–8082. Reservations not required. Dress: casual. AE, D, MC, V. $$*

Southern Suppers. Here's hearty family dining in a cozy farmhouse filled with country primitive art; handmade quilts line the walls. The menu features an all-you-can-eat seafood buffet and such down-home Southern specialties as fried chicken, country-fried steak, and country ham with red-eye gravy and grits. *5301 U.S. 17, midway between Myrtle Beach and Surfside Beach, tel. 803/238–4557. Reservations not required. Dress: casual. MC, V. Closed Oct.–Mar. $$*

North Myrtle Beach

Horst Gausthaus. Dine on knockwurst, bratwurst, sauerbrauten, and other traditional German foods at this Bavarian–style restaurant, where there's oom-pah-pah music every night but Sunday. *802 37th Ave. S, tel. 803/272–3351. Reservations advised. Dress: casual. AE, MC, V. $$*

Marina Raw Bar. This casual eatery overlooking Vereen's Marina is famous for fresh oysters, clams, and other seafood, served broiled, grilled, or fried. *1203 Hwy. 17 N., tel. 803/249–3972. Reservations not required. Dress: casual. AE, V. $$*

Afloat

Dinner cruises aboard the cruise ship *Hurricane* depart from Vereen's Marina (Hwy. 17 and 11th Ave., N. Myrtle Beach, tel. 803/249–3571).

Pawleys Island

Tyler's Cove. This restaurant specializes in such unusual Low Country fare as fried Carolina alligator, seasoned with buttermilk batter, and spicy Cajun chicken tossed in a salad of lettuce, cabbage, and jalapeño honey dressing. Sunday brunch is served. *The Hammock Shops, U.S. 17, tel. 803/237–4848. Reservations advised. Dress: casual. AE, D, MC, V. $$*

Lodging

With about 55,000 rooms available along the Grand Strand, it's never difficult to find a place to stay, and discounting is rampant. Package deals are offered year-round, the most attractive of them between Labor Day and spring break. Among other lodgings options, condominiums are popular, combining spaciousness and modern amenities and appealing especially to families. You can choose among cottages, villas, and hotel-style high-rise units. Maid service is frequently available. For the free directories *Grand Hotel and Motel Accommodations* and *Grand Condominium and Cottage Accommodations*, write to the Myrtle Beach Area Convention Bureau (710 21st Ave. N, Ste. J, Myrtle Beach, SC 29577, tel. 803/448–1629 or 800/356–3016). The most highly recommended properties in each price category are indicated by a star ★.

Category	Cost*
$$$$	over $100
$$$	$65–$100
$$	$45–$65
$	under $45

**double room; add 7% for taxes*

Georgetown *$$–$$$*

1790 House. This lovely restored house, redecorated in 1993 by new owners Patricia and John Wiley, is in the center of the historic district. Built after the Revolution, when Georgetown's rice culture was at its peak, it contains Colonial furnishings suitable to its age. Guests are treated to gourmet breakfasts, evening refreshments, and the use of bicycles. For a romantic hideaway, request the private carriage house. *630 Highmarket St., 29440, tel. 803/546–4821. 6 rooms. AE, MC, V.*

McClellanville *$$$*

Laurel Hill Plantation. This Low Country plantation bed-and-breakfast house, overlooking the marsh near the Intracoastal Waterway, has been rebuilt after its destruction by Hurricane Hugo (ask to see the scrapbooks of the storm). Owners Lee and Jackie Morrison have furnished it with country antiques. Guests can read a book in the hammock, go fishing or crabbing, take a boat ride, or watch the birds. The Morrisons serve a full breakfast and complimentary afternoon refreshments. *8913 N. Hwy. 17, Box 190, 29458, tel. 803/887–3708. 4 rooms with private baths. No credit cards.*

Myrtle Beach
$$$$
★
Radisson Resort Hotel at Kingston Plantation. The Grand Strand's most luxurious property, this 20-story glass-sheathed tower is part of a complex of shops, restaurants, hotels, and condominiums set amid 145 acres of oceanside woodlands. Guest rooms are highlighted by bleached-wood furnishings and attractive art. The balconied one-bedroom suites have kitchenettes. *9800 Lake Dr., 29577, tel. 803/449–0006 or 800/333–3333, fax 803/497–1110. 614 suites. Facilities: 2 restaurants, lounge, fitness center, tennis, pool. AE, D, DC, MC, V.*

$$$–$$$$
Best Western/The Landmark. The rooms in this high-rise oceanfront resort hotel are tastefully decorated in a modern style. Some have balconies and refrigerators. *1501 S. Ocean Blvd., 29577, tel. 803/448–9441 or 800/845–0658, fax 803/626–1501. 325 rooms. Facilities: pool, children's activity program, game room, dining rooms, lounges, nightclub. AE, D, DC, MC, V.*

Breakers Resort Hotel. The rooms in this recently renovated oceanfront hotel are airy and spacious, with contemporary decor. Many have balconies and refrigerators. *2006 N. Ocean Blvd., Box 485, 29578–0485, tel. 803/626–5000 or 800/845–0688, fax 803/626–5000. 247 rooms. Facilities: restaurant, 3 pools, 2 whirlpools, saunas, exercise room, lounge, laundry, children's programs. AE, D, DC, MC, V.*

Sheraton Myrtle Beach Resort. All rooms and suites have a fresh, contemporary look. Oceanfront Lounge, highlighted by tropical colors and rattan furnishings, is a lively evening gathering spot. *2701 S. Ocean Blvd., 29577, tel. 803/448–2518 or 800/992–1055, fax 803/449–1879. 219 units. Facilities: restaurant, health club, arcade, outdoor and indoor pools. AE, D, DC, MC, V.*

$$$
Chesterfield Inn. A remnant from the past, this oceanfront brick inn, hidden beneath the towers of Myrtle Beach's more glitzy hotels, has been in operation for over half a century. The rooms in the old part are simple and plain, but many guests prefer them to the ones in the newer wing. Family–style meals are served on starched white tablecloths in the paneled dining room. *700 N. Ocean Blvd., 29578, tel. 803/448–3177, fax 803/626–4736. 57 rooms, 6 kitchenettes. Facilities: pool, restaurant, shuffleboard. AE, D, DC, MC V.*

Driftwood on the Oceanfront. Under the same ownership for more than 50 years, this facility is popular with families. Some rooms are oceanfront; all are decorated in sea, sky, or earth tones. *1600 N. Ocean Blvd., Box 275, 29578, tel. 803/448–1544 or 800/942–3456, fax 803/448–2917. 90 rooms. Facilities: fitness center, game room, 2 pools. AE, D, DC, MC, V.*

Holiday Inn Oceanfront. This oceanfront inn is right at the heart of the action. The spacious rooms are decorated in cool sea tones. After beach basking, you can prolong the mood in the inn's spacious, plant-bedecked indoor recreation center, which comprises an indoor pool, exercise room, game room, and gift shop. *415 S. Ocean Blvd., 29577, tel. 803/448–4481 or 800/845–0313. 310 rooms. Facilities: outdoor and indoor pools, snack bar, sauna, whirlpool, game room, 2 restaurants, 2 lounges. AE, D, DC, MC, V.*

$$–$$$ **Comfort Inn.** This chain motel, 400 yards from the ocean, is clean, well furnished, and well maintained. *2801 S. Kings Hwy., 29577, tel. 803/626–4444 or 800/228–5150, fax 803/626–0753. 139 rooms, 14 suites. Facilities: outdoor pool, health club, restaurant. AE, D, DC, MC, V.*

North Myrtle Beach
$ **Days Inn at Waccamaw.** Relax by the pool or in the gazebo after a full day of shopping at the pottery and other outlets. *3650 Hwy. 501, 29577, tel. 803/236–1950 or 800/325–2525, fax 803/236–9415. 160 rooms. Facilities: restaurant, lounge, pool, whirlpool. AE, D, DC, MC, V.*

Pawleys Island
$$–$$$ **Litchfield by the Sea Resort and Country Club.** Contemporary gray-blue wood suite units on stilts, a short walk from the beach, nestle amid 4,500-acre gardenlike grounds, which include three private golf clubs open to guests. *U.S. 17, 2 mi north of Pawleys Island, tel. 803/237–3000 or 800/845–1897, fax 803/237–4282. 97 suites. Facilities: restaurant, lounge, exercise room, whirlpool, sauna, racquetball, tennis, indoor and outdoor pools, conference center. AE, MC, V.*

$$ **Ramada Inn Seagull.** This is a very well-maintained inn on a golf course (excellent golf packages are available). The rooms are spacious, bright, and airy. *U.S. 17S, Box 2217, 29585, tel. 803/237–4261 or 800/272–6232, fax 803/237–9708. 99 rooms. Facilities: pool, dining room, lounge. AE, DC, MC, V.*

The Arts

Theater productions, concerts, art exhibits, and other cultural events are regularly offered at the **Myrtle Beach Convention Center** (Oak and 21st Ave. N, Myrtle Beach, tel. 803/448–7166). **The Atalaya Arts Festival** at Huntington Beach State Park in the fall is a big draw. **Art in the Park,** featuring arts and crafts, is staged in Myrtle Beach's Chapin Park three times during the summer season (call 803/626–7444 for details).

Nightlife

Clubs offer varying fare, including beach music, the Grand Strand's unique '50s-style sound. During summer, sophisticated live entertainment is featured nightly at some clubs and resorts. Some hotels and resorts also have piano bars or lounges featuring easy-listening music.

In Myrtle Beach: **Sandals,** at the Sands Ocean Club (tel. 803/449–6461) is an intimate lounge with live entertainment. **Coquina Club,** at the Best Western Landmark Resort Hotel (tel. 803/448–9441), features beach-music bands. The shag (the state dance) is popular at **Studebaker's** (2000 N. Kings Hwy., tel. 803/448–9747) and **Duck's** (229 Main St., N. Myrtle Beach, tel. 803/249–3858). At The Breakers Hotel, **Atlantis Nightlife** (Hwy. 501, tel. 803/448–4200) is three nightclubs in one: a high-energy dance club, live entertainment and music, and a quiet patio lounge. At **The Afterdeck,** enjoy live bands, dancing, and comedy at an open-air club along the Intracoastal Waterway (Hwy. 17, Restaurant Row, tel. 803/449–1550).

In Murrells Inlet: **Drunken Jack's** (tel. 803/651–2044 or 803/651–3232) is a popular restaurant with a lounge overlooking the docks and fishing fleets.

Country-and-western music shows are popular along the Grand Strand, which is home to seven music halls: **the Dixie Jubilee** (701

Main St., N. Myrtle Beach, tel. 803/249-4444); **The Carolina Opry** (8901 U.S. 17,, Myrtle Beach, tel. 803/449-6779); the **Legendary Stars of Country Music** (600 U.S. 17, Surfside Beach, tel. 803/238-9100); **Southern Country Nights** (301 U.S. 17, Surfside Beach, tel. 803/238-8888); the **Myrtle Beach Opry** (1901 N. Kings Hwy., Myrtle Beach, tel. 803/448-6779); **Alabama** (4750 U.S. 17, Barefoot Landing, N. Myrtle Beach, tel. 803/272-1111 or 800/342-2262), which features the country music group by the same name and other top performers; and Dolly Parton's **Dixie Stampede** (8901-B U.S. 17 Business, Myrtle Beach, tel. 803/497-9700), a show that revolves around a four-course "country" dinner.

Hilton Head and Beyond

Anchoring the southern tip of South Carolina's coastline is 42-square-mile Hilton Head Island, named after English sea captain William Hilton, who claimed it for England in 1663. It was settled by planters in the 1700s and flourished until the Civil War. Thereafter, the economy declined and the island languished until Charles E. Fraser, a visionary South Carolina attorney, began developing the Sea Pines resort in 1956. Other developments followed, and today Hilton Head's casual pace, broad beaches, myriad activities, and genteel good life make it one of the East Coast's most popular vacation getaways.

Beaufort (locally pronounced "Bewfort") is a graceful antebellum town with a compact historic district preserving lavish 18th- and 19th-century homes. Southeast, on the ocean, lies Fripp Island, a self-contained resort with controlled access. And midway between Beaufort and Charleston is Edisto ("ED-is-toh") Island, settled in 1690 and once notable for its silky Sea Island cotton. Some of its elaborate mansions have been restored; others brood in disrepair.

Getting There and Getting Around

By Plane **Hilton Head Island Airport** (no phone) is served by American Eagle, USAir Express, and GP Express Airlines, which flies daily to and from Atlanta. Most travelers use the **Savannah International Airport** (tel. 912/964-0514), about an hour from Hilton Head, which is served by American, Delta, United, USAir, and ValuJet.

By Car The island is 40 miles east of I-95 (Exit 28 off I-95S, Exit 5 off I-95N).

By Taxi **Yellow Cab** (tel. 803/686-6666) and **Low Country Taxi and Limousine Service** (tel. 803/681-8294) provide service in Hilton Head.

By Boat Hilton Head is accessible via the Intracoastal Waterway, with docking available **Shelter Cove Marina** (tel. 803/842-7001), **Harbour Town Marina** (tel. 803/671-2704), and **Schilling Boathouse** (tel. 803/681-2628).

Guided Tours

Low Country Adventures (tel. 803/681-8212) offers tours of Hilton Head, Beaufort, and Charleston. **Discover Hilton Head** (tel. 803/842-9217) gives daily historical tours of the island. Hilton Head's **Adventure Cruises** (tel. 803/785-4558) offers dinner, sightseeing, and murder-mystery cruises. Several companies, including **Harbour Town Charters** (tel. 803/363-2628), run dolphin sightseeing and feeding trips. Call the **Greater Beaufort County Chamber of Com-**

merce (tel. 803/524–3163) to find out about self-guided walking or driving tours of Beaufort.

Important Addresses and Numbers

Tourist Information **Beaufort County Chamber of Commerce** (Box 910, 1006 Bay St., Beaufort, 29901, tel. 803/524–3163). In Hilton Head, your best bet for tourist information is to stop by the **Welcome Center and Museum of Hilton Head** (100 William Hilton Pkwy, tel. 803/681–7705), which opened in 1994. You can also write to the **Hilton Head Island Chamber of Commerce** (Box 5647, Hilton Head, 29938, tel. 803/785–3673). The two **Hilton Head Welcome Centers,** run by a private real estate firm, are on Route 278 next to the bridge to Hilton Head and at 6 Lagoon Road at the south end of the island. In addition to providing tourism information about the island, these centers attempt to entice you into purchasing real estate on Hilton Head.

Emergencies No appointment is necessary at **Family Medical Center** (South Island Square, U.S. 278, tel. 803/842–2900); open daily 8–5.

Exploring Hilton Head and Beyond

Lined by towering pines, wind-sculpted live oaks, and palmettos, Hilton Head's 12 miles of beaches are a major attraction, and the semitropical barrier island also has oak and pine woodlands and meandering lagoons. Choice stretches are occupied by various resorts, or "plantations," among them Sea Pines, Shipyard, Palmetto Dunes, Port Royal, and Hilton Head. In these (except Hilton Head, which has no rentals), accommodations range from rental villas and lavish private houses to luxury hotels. The resorts are also private residential communities, although many have public restaurants, marinas, shopping areas, and recreational facilities. All are secured, and visitors cannot tour them unless arrangements are made at the visitor office near the main gate of each plantation.

In the south of the island, at the **Audubon–Newhall Preserve,** you'll find unusual native plant life identified and tagged in a pristine 50-acre site. There are trails, a self-guided tour, and seasonal plant walks. *Palmetto Bay Rd., tel. 803/671–2008. Admission free. Open dawn to dusk.*

Also in the south is the **Sea Pines Forest Preserve,** a 605-acre public wilderness tract with walking trails, a well-stocked fishing pond, a waterfowl pond, and a 3,400-year-old Indian shell ring. Both guided and self-guided tours are available. *Tel. 803/671–6486. Admission to Sea Pines Plantation: $3 per car for nonguests; this allows free access to preserve. Open daily 7–4. Closed during the Heritage Golf Classic in April.*

The Museum of Hilton Head Island's permanent collection consists of a diorama depicting Indian life on Hilton Head in the 15th century AD; the museum also hosts changing exhibits. Beach walks are conducted on weekdays, and tours of Indian sites, forts, and plantations randomly in season. *100 William Hilton Pkwy., tel. 803/689–6767. Admission free. Open Mon.–Sat. 10–5, Sun. noon–4.*

Three miles west of the island, there's the **James M. Waddell, Jr., Mariculture Research & Development Center,** where methods of raising seafood commercially are studied. Visitors may tour its 24 ponds and research building to see work in progress. *Sawmill Creek Rd., near U.S. 278-SC 46 intersection, tel. 803/837–3795. Admission free. Tours weekdays at 10 AM and by appointment.*

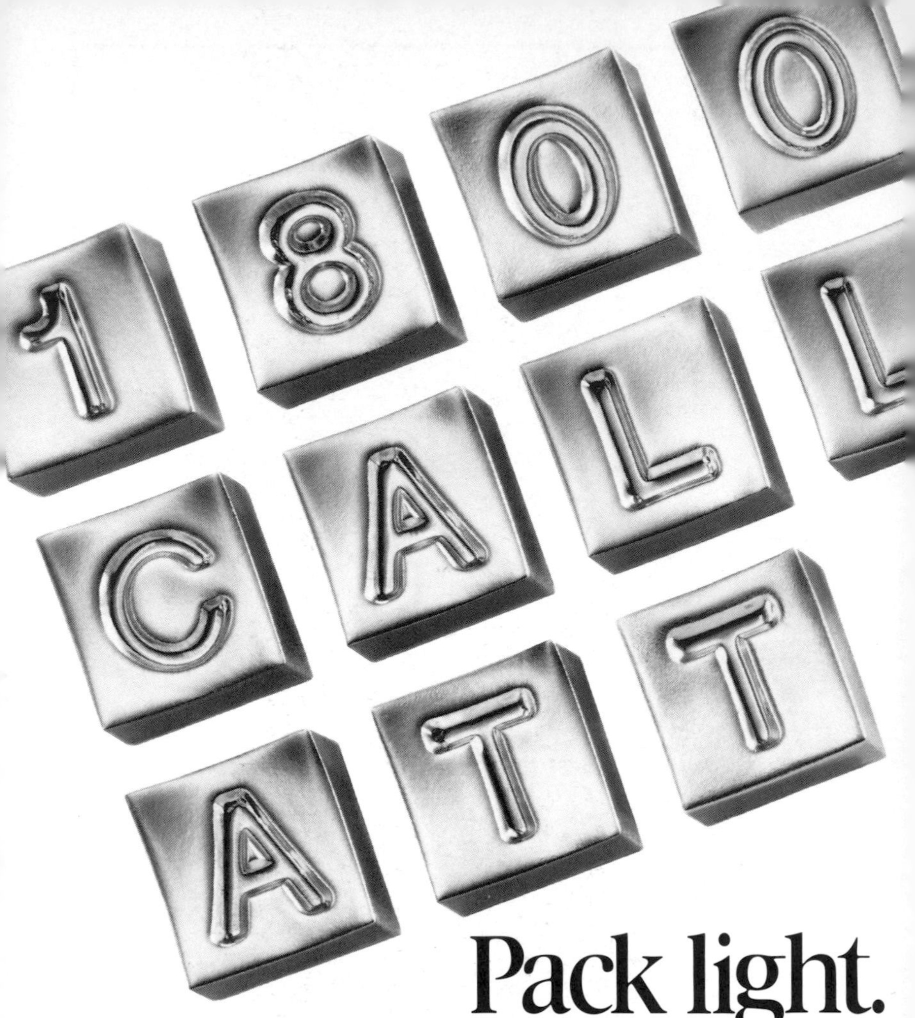

Beaufort North of here is the waterfront city of **Beaufort,** established in 1710. It achieved immense prosperity toward the close of the 18th century when Sea Island cotton was introduced, and many of its lavish houses—with wide balconies, high ceilings, and luxurious appointments—remain today. Although many private houses in **Old Point,** the historic district, are not usually open to visitors, some may be on the annual Fall House Tour in mid-October, and the Spring Tour of Homes and Gardens, in April or May. The rest of the year, you'll have to content yourself with appreciating the fine exteriors.

Across the street from the Chamber of Commerce is the **George Elliot House Museum,** which served as a Union hospital during the Civil War. It was built in 1840 in Greek Revival style, with leaded-glass fanlights, pine floors, and rococo ceilings. The furnishings include some fine early Victorian pieces. *1001 Bay St., tel. 803/524–6334. Admission: $3 adults, $2 children under 15. Open weekdays 11–3. Closed Jan.–early–Feb.*

Nearby, the **John Mark Verdier House Museum,** built about 1790 in the Federal style, has been restored and furnished as it would have been between 1790 and the visit of Lafayette in 1825. It was headquarters for Union forces during the Civil War. *801 Bay St., tel. 803/524–6334. Admission: $4 adults, $2 children under 15. Open Tues.–Sat. 11–4.*

Built in 1795 and remodeled in 1852, the Gothic-style arsenal that was home of the Beaufort Volunteer Artillery now houses the **Beaufort Museum,** with prehistoric relics, Indian pottery, and Revolutionary and Civil War exhibits. *713 Craven St., tel. 803/525–7077. Admission: $2 adults, 50¢ students and children 6–18. Open Mon.–Tues. and Thurs.–Sat. 10–5, Sun. 1–5.*

St. Helena's Episcopal Church, dating from 1724, was also touched by the Civil War: It was turned into a hospital and gravestones were brought inside to serve as operating tables. *501 Church St., tel. 803/522–1712. Open Mon.–Sat. 10–4.*

Before setting off to explore outlying areas, pause in the **Henry C. Chambers Waterfront Park** to rest and survey the scene. Its seven landscaped acres along the Beaufort River, part of the Intracoastal Waterway, include a seawall promenade, a crafts market, gardens, and a marina. Some events of the popular mid-July Beaufort Water Festival, as well as a seasonal farmers'/crafts market, take place here.

On the Coast Nine miles southeast of Beaufort via U.S. 21 is **St. Helena's Island,** site of the **Penn Center Historic District** and **York W. Bailey Museum.** Penn Center, established in the middle of the Civil War as the South's first school for freed slaves, today provides community services. The museum (formerly Dr. Bailey's clinic) has displays reflecting the heritage of sea island blacks. *Land's End Rd., St. Helena's Island, tel. 803/838–2432. Donation suggested. Open Tues.–Fri. 11–4 and by appointment.*

Nine miles farther east via U.S. 21 is **Hunting Island State Park,** a secluded domain of beach, nature trails, and varied fishing. The 1,120-foot fishing pier is the longest on the East Coast. If you climb the 181 steps of the photogenic 140-foot **Hunting Island Lighthouse** (built in 1859 and abandoned in 1933) you'll be rewarded with sweeping views. *Tel. 803/838–2011. Admission: $3 per car Mar.–Oct.; free rest of year. For cabin and camping reservations, write to Hunting Island State Park, 1775 Sea Island Pkwy., St. Helena, 29920.*

Heading north from Beaufort on U.S. 21 to Gardens Corner, take Rte. 17N and then S-7-21 to the ruins of the **Sheldon Church,** built in 1753 and burned in 1779 and 1865. Only the brick walls and columns remain beside the old cemetery. Get back on Rte. 17N and then follow Rte. 174 to **Edisto Island** (80 miles from Beaufort). Here, magnificent stands of age-old oaks festooned with Spanish moss border quiet streams and side roads, but the island is developing fast. Many of the island's inhabitants are descendants of former slaves. **Edisto Beach State Park** has 3 miles of beach with excellent shelling, housekeeping cabins by the marsh, and campsites by the ocean. For camping reservations, call 803/869–2156 or 803/869–3396.

What to See and Do with Children

On Hilton Head Island, all major hotels offer **summer youth activities,** some have full-scale youth programs. The Island Recreation Center (Wilborn Rd.) runs a summer camp that visiting youngsters can join. *Hilton Head Island Recreation Association, Box 22593, Hilton Head Island, 29925, tel. 803/681–7273. Camp open mid-June–late Aug., weekdays.*

Off the Beaten Track

From Hilton Head, you can go by boat to **Daufuskie Island,** the setting for Pat Conroy's novel *The Water Is Wide,* which was made into the movie *Conrack*. Most inhabitants, descendants of former slaves, live on small farms among remnants of churches, homes, and schools—reminders of prosperous antebellum times. With its unspoiled live oaks, pines, and palmettos, Daufuskie won't remain off the beaten track for long. Excursions to the island are run out of Hilton Head by **Adventure Cruises** (Shelter Cove Marina, tel. 803/785–4558), **Vagabond Cruises** (Harbour Town Marina, tel. 803/842–4155), and **Daufuski Seafari** (Broad Creek Marina, tel. 803/681–7925). You can arrange kayak nature trips at Shelter Cove Marina (tel. 803/384–8125) and South Beach Marina (tel. 803/671–2643).

At **Parris Island,** south of Beaufort, visitors are welcome to observe U.S. Marine Corps recruit training and take a guided tour. There's a replica of the Iwo Jima flag-raising monument on the base. The **Parris Island Museum** exhibits vintage uniforms, photographs, and weapons. *Tel. 803/525–2951. Admission free. Open daily 10–4:30, Thurs. until 7.*

Shopping

Malls and Outlets Major Hilton Head Island shopping sites include **The Mall at Shelter Cove** (Hwy. 278, ½ mi north of Palmetto Dunes Resort, tel. 803/686–3090), with 55 shops and four restaurants; and **Coligny Plaza** (Coligny Circle, tel. 803/842–6050), with 60-plus shops, restaurants, a movie theater, and a supermarket. **Shoppes on the Parkway** (Hwy. 278, 1 mi south of Palmetto Dunes Resort, tel. 803/686–6233), comprises nearly 30 outlets, including Dansk, Gorham, Aileen, and Van Heusen. **Low Country Factory Outlet Village** (Hwy. 278 at the island gateway, tel. 803/837–4339), has 40 outlets selling clothing, shoes, and housewares.

Antiques **Den of Antiquity** (Hwy. 170, Beaufort, tel. 803/842–6711), the area's largest antiques shop, carries a wide assortment of Low Country and nautical pieces. **Harbour Town Antiques** (Harbour Town, Hilton Head, tel. 803/671–5999) carries American and English furniture and unusual Oriental and English porcelain.

Art Galleries In Hilton Head, the **Red Piano Art Gallery** (220 Cordillo Pkwy., tel. 803/785–2318) showcases works by island artists and craftspeople. In Beaufort, the **Rhett Gallery** (901 Bay St., tel. 803/524–3339) sells Low Country art by members of the Rhett family and Stephen Webb.

Jewelry On Hilton Head, **The Bird's Nest** (Coligny Plaza, tel. 803/785–3737) sells locally made shell and sand-dollar jewelry. **The Goldsmith Shop** (3 Lagoon Rd., tel. 803/785–2538) features classic jewelry, island charms, custom designs, and repairs. **Touch of Turquoise** (The Mall at Shelter Cove, tel. 803/842–3880). In Beaufort, **The Craftseller** (813 Bay St., tel. 803/525–6104) showcases jewelry and other items by Southern craftsfolk.

Nature **The Audubon Nature Store** (The Village at Wexford, tel. 803/785-4311) and **The Hammock Company** (Coligny Plaza, tel. 803/686–3636 or 800/344–4264) sell gift items and other things with a nature theme.

Beaches

Although the resort beaches are reserved for guests and residents, there are four public entrances to Hilton Head's 12 miles of ocean beach. Two main parking and changing areas are at Coligny Circle, near the Holiday Inn, and on Folly Field Road, off U.S. 278. Signs along U.S. 278 point the way to Bradley and Singleton beaches, where parking space is limited. **Hunting Island State Park** and **Edisto Beach State Park** each have about 3 miles of public beach.

Participant Sports

Bicycling There are pathways in several areas of Hilton Head (many in the resorts), and pedaling is popular along the firmly packed beach. Bicycles can be rented at most hotels and resorts and at **Harbour Town Bicycles** (Heritage Plaza, tel. 803/785–3546), **South Beach Cycles** (Sea Pines Plantation, tel. 803/671–2453), and **Fish Landing Creek** (Palmetto Dunes, tel. 803/785–2021).

Fishing On Hilton Head, you can pick oysters, dig for clams, or cast for shrimp; supplies are available at **Shelter Cove Marina** at Palmetto Dunes (tel. 803/842–7001). Local marinas offer in-shore and deep-sea fishing charters. Each year a billfishing tournament and two king mackerel tournaments attract anglers.

Golf Many of Hilton Head's 30 championship courses are open to the public, including **Palmetto Dunes Plantation** (tel. 803/785–1138); **Sea Pines Plantation** (tel. 803/671–2446); **Port Royal and Shipyard Plantations** (tel. 803/689–5600); **Island West Golf Course** (Hwy. 278, tel. 803/686–8802); and **Old South Golf Links** (Hwy. 278, tel. 803/785-5353). Harbour Town Golf Links at Sea Pines Plantation hosts the MCI Heritage Golf Classic (tel. 803/671–2448) every spring.

Horseback Riding Many trails wind through woods and nature preserves. Some stables in and near Hilton Head are: **Lawton Stables** in Sea Pines (tel. 803/671–2586), **Rose Hill Plantation Stables** (Bluffton, tel. 803/757-3082), **Sandy Creek Stables** near Spanish Wells (tel. 803/689–3423).

Tennis There are more than 300 courts on Hilton Head. **Sea Pines Racquet Club** (tel. 803/842–8484), home of the Family Circle Tournament; **Shipyard Plantation** (tel. 803/686–8804); and **Port Royal** (tel. 803/686–8803) are highly rated. Clubs that welcome guests include **Palmetto Dunes** (tel. 803/785–1152) and **Van der Meer Tennis Center** (tel. 803/785–8388).

Windsurfing Lessons and rentals are available from **Outside Hilton Head** at Sea Pines Resort's South Beach Marina (tel. 803/671–2643) and at Shelter Cove Plaza (tel. 803/686–6996).

Spectator Sports

Polo There are matches every other Sunday during spring and fall at **Rose Hill Plantation** (Bluffton, tel. 803/757–4945).

Dining

Hilton Head serves South Carolina seafood, of course, but this cosmopolitan island has restaurants to suit every palate. Highly recommended restaurants in each price category are indicated by a star ★.

Category	Cost*
$$$$	over $25
$$$	$15–$25
$$	$7–$15
$	under $7

**per person without 5% tax, service, or drinks*

Beaufort
Low Country

The New Gadsby Tavern. Dine on fresh seafood and Low Country specials in any of three dining areas overlooking Beaufort's Waterfront Park and bay. The formal dining room and taproom are noted for Italian specialties and great European desserts. On the terrace, you can feast on tapas or selections from a fresh raw bar. *822 Bay St., tel. 803/525–1800. Reservations advised. Dress: casual. AE, D, MC, V. $$*

Edisto Island
Low Country
★

The Old Post Office. Try the Veal Edistonian, the Fussed Over Pork Chop, or the Blue Crab and Asparagus Pie, served with the house salad, vegetables, and freshly baked bread, at this island restaurant on Shore Creek. The house specialty is shrimp and grits. Originally Bailey's General Store and U.S. Post Office, the renovated building contains the original post office boxes and window. *Hwy. 174, 5 mi from Edisto Beach, tel. 803/869–2339. Reservations advised. Dress: casual. MC, V. Closed Sun. June–Sept., Sun. and Mon. Oct.–May. No lunch. $$–$$$*

Hilton Head
Continental

Harbourmaster's. With sweeping views of the harbor, this spacious, multilevel dining room offers such dishes as chateaubriand and New Zealand rack of lamb laced with a brandy demiglaze. Service is deft. Prix-fixe early dinners ($16.95) are offered daily except Sunday. *Shelter Cove Marina, off U.S. 278, tel. 803/785–3030. Reservations required. Jacket required at dinner. AE, DC, MC, V. Closed Sun. and Jan. No lunch. $$$$*

★ **The Barony Grill.** A series of softly lighted seating areas with upscale country French decor lead off the main dining room, which is centered with a display of drop-dead desserts, marzipan flowers, and exotic cheese and bread. Try an elegant low-calorie dish like: chilled coconut-pineapple soup, asparagus salad with quail eggs, poached fillet of Dover sole with seafood mousse, or macédoine of fresh fruit with raspberry sauce. *The Westin Resort, 135 S. Port Royal Dr., tel. 803/681–4000. Reservations required. Dress: casual but neat. AE, D, DC, MC, V. No lunch. $$$–$$$$*

Low Country

Old Fort Pub. Tucked away in a quiet site overlooking Skull Creek and beside the Civil War ruins of Fort Mitchell, this rustic restaurant specializes in such dishes as oyster pie, oysters wrapped in Smithfield ham, Savannah chicken-fried steak with onion gravy, and hoppin' john. *Hilton Head Plantation, tel. 803/681–2386. Reservations advised. Dress: casual. AE, D, DC, MC, V. No lunch Sun. $$*

Seafood

Crazy Crab. This casual eatery serves seafood as fresh as you can get it—steamed, fried, baked, or broiled—at two locations overlooking the water. They're famous for their steamed seafood pot and Crazy Crab boil. *U.S. 278, tel. 803/681–5021 (no lunch); Harbour Town Yacht Basin, tel. 803/363–2722. No reservations. Dress: casual. AE, D, MC, V. $$*

Hemingway's. This oceanfront restaurant serves pompano *en papillote,* trout amandine with herbed lemon-butter sauce, fresh grilled seafoods, and steaks, in a relaxed, Key West–type atmosphere. *Hyatt Regency Hilton Head, Palmetto Dunes Resort, tel. 803/785–1234. Reservations advised. Dress: casual but neat. AE, D, DC, MC, V. No lunch. $$*

Hudson's on the Docks and **Carmine's.** Hudson's on the Docks is a huge, airy, family-owned restaurant with its own fishing fleet; freshly caught fish is rushed straight to the kitchens. The dining room seems always to be full, but service is quick and friendly, and diners never feel rushed. There's also an oyster bar. Next door is Carmine's, which specializes in steaks and ribs, as well as serving seafood. A third branch, **Hudson's on the Beach,** nearby at Coligny Place, also emphasizes seafood. *Hudson's on the Docks and Carmine's: The Landing, tel. 803/681–2772. Hudson's on the Beach: Coligny Place, tel. 803/842–4888. All three: No reservations. Dress: casual. AE, MC, V. Carmine's: Closed Sun. No lunch. Hudson's on the Beach: No lunch Sun. $$*

Lodging

Sea Pines, the oldest and best-known of Hilton Head's resort developments, or plantations, occupies 4,500 thickly wooded acres with three golf courses, a fine beach, tennis clubs, stables, and shopping plazas. The focus of Sea Pines is **Harbour Town,** built around the charming marina, which has shops, restaurants, some condominiums, and the landmark Hilton Head lighthouse. Accommodations are in luxurious houses and villas facing the ocean or the golf courses.

The Crystal Sands–Crowne Plaza Resort is the oceanfront centerpiece of **Shipyard Plantation,** which also has villa condominiums, three nine-hole courses, a tennis club, and a small beach club. **Palmetto Dunes Resort** has the oceanfront Hyatt Regency Hilton Head, the Hilton Resort and other accommodations, the renowned Rod Laver Tennis Center, a good stretch of beach, three golf courses, and several oceanfront rental villa complexes. At **Port Royal Plantation** there's the posh Westin Resort, which is on the beach and has three golf courses and a tennis club.

Hilton Head Central Reservations (Box 5312, Hilton Head Island, 29938, tel. 803/785–9050 or 800/845–7018) represents almost every hotel, motel, and rental agency on the island. Other options are available through the **Hilton Head Condo Hotline** (tel. 803/785–2939 or 800/258–5852, ext. 53) and **Hilton Head Reservations and Golf Line** (tel. 803/444–4772). Rates drop appreciably in the off-season (Nov.–Mar.), and package plans are available year-round. The most highly recommended properties in each price category are indicated by a star ★.

Category	Cost*
$$$$	over $145
$$$	$95–$145
$$	$55–$95
$	under $50

**double room; add 7% for taxes*

Beaufort
$$$
★

Rhett House Inn. True southern hospitality can be had at this storybook inn in the heart of the historic district. Art and antiques fill the rooms, and guests are served breakfast and afternoon tea. The restaurant, which is open to the public by reservation, serves such excellent Continental fare as leek-and-goat cheese tarts, seared veal chops in a green peppercorn sauce, and chicken fricassee with quenelles. *1009 Craven St., 29902, tel. 803/524–9030, fax 803/524–1310. 9 rooms, 1 suite. Facilities: pool table, bicycles. MC, V.*

Two Suns Inn. Guests at this B&B, a restored 1917 Neoclassical house overlooking the Beaufort River, enjoy large rooms, afternoon tea-and-toddy hour, and a full breakfast. The inn also has an extensive business center and extremely down-to-earth and friendly hosts, making this a great spot for business travelers after companionship and computer modems. *1705 Bay St., 29902, tel. or fax 803/522–1122, tel. 800/552–4244. 5 rooms. AE, MC, V.*

$$

Best Western Sea Island Inn. At this well-maintained resort inn in the downtown historic district, rooms feature period decor. *1015 Bay St., Box 532, 29902, tel. 803/524–4121 or 800/528–1234, fax 803/524–9396. 43 rooms. Facilities: pool, cable TV, restaurant, lounge. AE, DC, MC, V.*

Edisto Island
$$$

Cassina Point Plantation. You can live out your fantasies about the antebellum days at this authentically restored plantation house, now a bed-and-breakfast inn, surrounded by fields that used to be planted in Sea Island cotton. Federal troops who occupied the house for three years left their graffiti in the basement. Guests may fish in the creek (watch for the playful porpoises), go crabbing or shrimping, watch birds, or take a stroll. A fruit bowl, beverages, and full breakfast come with the room. *1642 Clark Rd., Box 535, 29438, tel. 803/869–2535. 4 rooms with half baths (2 full hall baths). Facilities: lawn sports, boat docks. No credit cards.*

$$–$$$

Fairfield Ocean Ridge Resort. This is a good choice for vacationers seeking to combine all the resort amenities with a get-away-from-it-all setting. There are accommodations in well-furnished two- and three-bedroom villa units tastefully decorated in contemporary style. *1 King Cotton Rd., Box 27, 29438, tel. 803/869–2561 or 800/845–8500. 100 units. Facilities: pool, wading pool, beach, marina, fishing, tennis, golf, minigolf, nature trails, restaurant, lounge. AE, D, MC, V.*

Fripp Island
$$–$$$

Fripp Island Resort. The resort encompasses the entire island, and access is limited to guests only. The two- and three-bedroom villas are contemporary in decor. *19 mi south of Beaufort via U.S. 21, 1 Tarpon Blvd., 29920, tel. 803/838–3535 or 800/845–4100, fax 803/828–2733. 133 units. Facilities: pools, tennis, golf, marina, rental boats, bicycle and jogging trails, 3 restaurants. AE, MC, V.*

Hilton Head Island
$$$$

Hyatt Regency Hilton Head. The island's largest oceanfront resort hotel has beautifully decorated rooms, some with balconies. *U.S. 278, Box 6167, 29938, tel. 803/785–1234 or 800/233–1234. 505 rooms. Facilities: pools, health club, sailboats, concierge floor, convention facilities, Restaurants, lounges, access to Palmetto Dunes golf, tennis, and 3-mi beach. AE, DC, MC, V.*

★ **Westin Resort, Hilton Head Island.** This horseshoe-shaped hotel sprawls in a lushly landscaped oceanfront setting. The expansive guest rooms, most with ocean views, are furnished in a mix of period reproduction and contemporary furnishings. All have comfortable seating areas and desks. Public areas display fine Oriental porcelains, screens and paintings. *2 Grass Lawn Ave., 29928, tel. 803/681–4000 or 800/228–3000, fax 803/681–1087. 415 rooms, 38 suites. Facilities: pool, health club, 3 restaurants, 3 lounges. AE, DC, MC, V.*

$$$–$$$$

Crystal Sands–Crowne Plaza Resort. Holiday Inn Worldwide's first property of this caliber in the United States, this oceanfront resort (formerly Marriott's Hilton Head) opened in 1993. Decorated in a nautical theme and set in a luxuriant garden, it offers all the amenities of Shipyard Plantation. *130 Shipyard Dr., 29928, tel. 803/842–2400 or 800/465–4329, fax 803/785–8463. 313 rooms and 25 suites. Facilities: golf, tennis, indoor and outdoor pools, spa, health club, 2 restaurants, pub, business center, meeting space. AE, D, DC, MC, V.*

Hilton Resort. There's a Caribbean feel to this five-story resort hotel. The grounds are beautifully landscaped, and the rooms, all oceanside, are spacious and colorfully decorated in a modern style. *23 Ocean Ln., Box 6165, 29938, tel. 803/842–8000 or 800/221–2222. 324 rooms. Facilities: pool, health club, sauna, whirlpool, volleyball, canoeing, fishing, biking, sailing, restaurant, access to Palmetto Dunes golf and tennis. AE, DC, MC, V.*

Marriott's Grande Ocean Resort. Though built as a time-share property in Sea Pines Plantation, this beautiful oceanfront condo development, within walking distance of shops and restaurants, offers a limited number of rentals. The fully furnished two-bedroom, two-bath luxurious villas come with kitchens, large whirlpool tubs, and maid service. *51 S. Forest Beach Dr., 29929, 803/785–2000 or 800/473–6674, fax 803/842–3413. Facilities: golf, pools. AE, MC, V.*

$$$

Holiday Inn Oceanfront Resort. This handsome high-rise motor hotel is on a broad, quiet stretch of beach. The rooms are spacious and well furnished in a contemporary style. *S. Forest Beach Dr., Box 5728, 29938, tel. 803/785–5126 or 800/465–4329, fax 803/785–6678. 249 rooms. Facilities: outdoor pool, restaurant, 2 lounges, golf, tennis, marina privileges. AE, D, DC, MC, V.*

$–$$

Red Roof Inn. This two-story inn is especially popular with families. It's a short drive to the public beaches. *5 Regency Pkwy. (U.S. 278), 29928, tel. 803/686–6808 or 800/843–7663, fax 803/842–3352. 112 rooms. AE, D, DC, MC, V.*

The Arts

The Cultural Council of Hilton Head (tel. 803/686–3945) has details on Hilton Head arts events. **Community Playhouse** (Arrow Rd., tel. 803/785–4878) presents up to 10 musicals or plays each year and has a young people's theater program. In warm weather, free outdoor concerts are held at **Harbour Town** and **Shelter Cove.** Concerts, plays, films, art shows, theater, sporting events, food fairs, and minitournaments make up Hilton Head's **SpringFest,** (tel. 803/686-4944), which runs for the month of March.

Nightlife

Dancing **Club Indigo** (tel. 803/785-1234), a large cabaret downstairs at the Hyatt Regency Hilton Head, has dancing and two shows nightly Monday through Saturday. **Scarlett's** (tel. 803/842-8000), a sophisticated oceanfront night spot in the Hilton Resort, features smooth jazz nightly. **Tiki Bar** (tel. 803/785-5126), a locally popular lounge in the Holiday Inn Oceanfront Resort, has nightly entertainment, as does **Signals** (tel. 803/842-2400), in the Crystal Sands Crowne Plaza Resort.

Easy Listening **Cafe Europa** (tel. 803/671-3399), at the Lighthouse in Harbourtown, has nightly piano entertainment. **Hemingway's Lounge** (tel. 803/785-1234) at the Hyatt Regency Hilton Head has live entertainment in a casually elegant setting Tuesday through Saturday. **The Pelican Poolside** (tel. 803/681-4000), an oceanfront lounge at the Westin Resort, has informal entertainment every night but Sunday. **Playful Pelican** (tel. 803/681-4000), the pool bar at the same location, has a live calypso band Tuesday through Sunday from 1 to 4 PM.

The Heartland

South Carolina's Heartland, between the coastal Low Country and the mountains, is a varied region of swamps and flowing rivers, fertile farmland, and vast forests of pines and hardwoods. Lakes Murray, Marion, and Moultrie offer wonderful fishing, and the many state parks are popular for hunting, hiking, swimming, and camping. At the center of the region is the state capital, Columbia, an engaging contemporary city superimposed on cherished historic remnants. It's a city of restored mansions, several museums, a university, a variety of dining, a lively arts scene, and one of the country's best zoos.

In Aiken, the center of South Carolina's Thoroughbred Country, such champions as Kelso and Pleasant Colony were trained. The beautiful scenery is studded with the fine mansions of such wealthy Northerners as the Vanderbilts and Whitneys. Throughout the region, towns like Ninety Six, Sumter, and Camden preserve and interpret the past, with historic re-creations, exhibits, and restorations. Several splendid public gardens provide islands of color during much of the year.

Arriving and Departing

By Plane **Columbia Metro Airport** (tel. 803/822-5000) is served by American/American Eagle, Com Air/Delta, United/United Express, and USAir.

By Car I-77 leads into Columbia from the north. I-26, I-20 and U.S. 1 intersect at Columbia.

By Train **Amtrak** (tel. 800/872-7245) makes stops at Camden, Columbia, Denmark, Dillon, Florence, and Kingstree in the Heartland.

By Bus **Greyhound** (tel. 800/231-2222) serves all of South Carolina.

Important Addresses and Numbers

Tourist Information **Greater Abbeville Chamber of Commerce** (104 Pickens St., Abbeville 29620, tel. 803/459–4600). **Greater Aiken Chamber of Commerce** (400 Laurens St. NW, Box 892, Aiken 29802, tel. 803/641–1111). **Greater Columbia Convention and Visitors Bureau** (Gervais and Assembly Sts., Box 15, Columbia 29202, tel. 803/254–0479 or 800/264–4884). **Kershaw County Chamber of Commerce** (724 S. Broad St., Box 605, Camden 29020, tel. 803/432–2525). **Ninety Six Chamber of Commerce** (Box 8, tel. 803/543–2900).

Emergencies **Taylor Street Pharmacy** (1520 Taylor St. at Pickens in Columbia, tel. 803/256–1611), is open 7 AM–9 PM weekdays, 9–9 weekends.

Guided Tours

Historic Columbia Foundation (tel. 803/252–1770) runs guided tours and rents out historic properties. In Sumter, the charismatic former Mayor **"Bubba" McElveen** (tel. 803/775–2851) gives walking, bus, and auto tours of the area. The **Aiken Chamber of Commerce** runs a 90-minute tour of the historic district and will customize tours to suit individual interests. Customized tours of Camden are also available through either the **Kershaw County Chamber of Commerce** or from **Greenleaf Tours** (contact Louise Burns, tel. 803/432–1515).

Exploring the Heartland

Columbia In 1786, South Carolina's capital was moved from Charleston to Columbia, in the center of the state along the banks of the Congaree River. One of the nation's first planned cities, Columbia's streets are among the the widest in America—designed this way because it was then thought that stagnant air fostered the spread of malaria. The city soon grew into a center of political, commercial, cultural, and social activity. But in early 1865 General William Tecumseh Sherman invaded South Carolina with a destructive determination described by a New York newspaper as 50 times worse than the earlier march through Georgia. Two-thirds of Columbia was incinerated, though a few homes and public buildings were spared. Today the city is a sprawling blend of modern office blocks, suburban neighborhoods, and the occasional antebellum home.

Our tour begins at the **State House.** Started in 1855 and completed in 1950, the Capitol is made of native blue granite in the Italian-Renaissance style. Six bronze stars on the outer western wall mark direct hits by Sherman's cannons. The interior is richly appointed with brass, marble, mahogany, and artworks, and a replica of Jean Antoine Houdon's statue of George Washington is on the grounds. *Main and Gervais Sts., tel. 803/734–2430. Free guided tours every half-hour. Open weekdays 9–noon, 1:30–3:30.*

The **Fort Jackson Museum,** on the grounds of the U.S. Army Training Center, displays armaments, heavy equipment from the two world wars, and exhibits on the life of Andrew Jackson. *Bldg. 4442, Jackson Blvd., tel. 803/751–7419. Admission free. Open Tues.–Fri. 10–4, weekends 1–4.*

The **Columbia Museum of Art and Gibbes Planetarium** contains the Kress Foundation Collection of Renaissance and Baroque treasures, sculpture, decorative arts, and European and American paintings, with special emphasis on works by Southeastern artists. *1112 Bull St., tel. 803/799–2810. Admission free; planetarium shows: $2.50 adults, $1.50 children under 18 and senior citizens. Open Tues.–*

Fri. 10–5, weekends 12:30–5. Planetarium shows weekends at 2, 3, and 4.

Exhibits at the **South Carolina State Museum,** in a large, refurbished textile mill, interpret the state's natural history, archaeology, historical development, technological and artistic accomplishments. A permanent exhibit portrays noted black astronauts (dedicated to South Carolina native Dr. Ronald McNair, who died on the *Challenger*), and another focuses on the cotton industry and slavery. An iron gate made for the museum by Phillip Simmons, the "dean of Charleston Blacksmiths," is also on display. *301 Gervais St., tel. 803/737–4921. Admission: $4 adults, $3 senior citizens, $1.50 children 6–17. Open Mon.–Sat. 10–5, Sun. 1–5.*

Time Out For a quick and tasty break, check out the **Gourmet Shop Cafe** (724 Saluda Ave., tel. 803/799–3705), in the heart of the Five Points Shopping District (*see* Shopping, *below*). You can choose from among dozens of fancy sandwiches and salads here. The Amaretto cheesecake is memorable.

Stop by the Museum Shop at Taylor and Henderson Streets in the historic district to get a map and buy tickets to tour the four Columbia houses that have been restored and opened to the public. The **Hampton-Preston Mansion** (1615 Blanding St., tel. 803/252–1770), dating from 1818, is filled with lavish furnishings collected by three generations of two influential families. The classic, columned 1823 **Robert Mills House** (1616 Blanding St., tel. 803/252–1770), was named for its architect who later designed the Washington Monument. It has opulent Regency furniture, marble mantels, silver doorknobs, and spacious grounds. **Mann–Simons Cottage–Museum of African-American Cultures** (1403 Richland St., tel. 803/252–1450) is the home of Celia Mann, one of only 200 free African-Americans in Columbia in the mid-1800s. The nearby **Woodrow Wilson Boyhood Home** (1705 Hampton St., tel. 803/252–1770) displays the gaslights, arched doorways, and ornate furnishings of the Victorian period. *Admission to each house: $3 adults, $1.50 students; combination ticket to all four houses: $10 adults, $5 students. All houses open Tues.–Sat. 10:15–3:15, Sun. 1–4.*

Riverfront Park and Historic Columbia Canal, where the Broad and Saluda Rivers meet, is made around the city's original waterworks and hydroelectric plant. Interpretive markers describe the area's plant and animal life and tell the history of the buildings. *312 Laurel St., tel. 803/733–8613. Admission free. Open daily dawn to dusk.*

Riverbanks Zoological Park and Botanical Gardens contains more than 2,000 animals and birds, some endangered, in natural habitats. Walk along pathways and through landscaped gardens to see polar bears, Siberian tigers, and American bald eagles. The South American primate collection has won international acclaim, and the park is noted for its success in breeding endangered and fragile species. There's also an aquarium-reptile complex, whose four habitats exhibit South Carolina, desert, tropical, and marine specimens. A 70-acre botanical garden will be added in spring of 1995. *I–126 and U.S. 76 at Greystone Riverbanks exit, tel. 803/779–8717 or 803/779–8730. Admission: $4.75 adults, $3.25 senior citizens, $2.25 children 3–12. Open 9–4 weekdays, 9–5 weekends.*

Camden From Columbia, drive northeast on I–20 for 32 miles to charming **Camden,** a town with a horsy history and grand Southern Colonial homes. Camden's fanciest roads remain unpaved for the sake of the hooves of the horses who regularly trot over them. A center of textile trade from the late 19th-century through the 1940s, Camden attracted Northerners escaping the cold winters; one of its early prominent families, the DuPonts, is today one of Camden's major employers. Because General Sherman spared the town during the War Between the States, most of its antebellum homes still stand. It's South Carolina's oldest inland town, dating to 1732. British General Lord Cornwallis established a garrison here during the Revolutionary War, and burned most of Camden before evacuating it. Today, the **Historic Camden Revolutionary War Site** re-creates the British occupation of 1780 on the site of the early 19th-century village. Several house restorations display period furnishings, including Cornwallis's headquarters, the **Kershaw-Cornwallis House** (ca. 1770). Nature trails, fortifications, a powder magazine, a picnic area, a farmyard with animals, and a crafts shop are also here. *U.S. 521, 1.4 mi north of I-20, tel. 803/432-9841. Admission: $4.50 adults, $1.50 children. Open for self-guided tours Tues.-Sat. 10-4, Sun. 1-4. Museum shop open daily 10-5.*

Sumter From Camden, drive southeast on U.S. 521 for 30 miles to **Sumter.** Named for the Revolutionary War hero and statesman General Thomas Sumter, the city was settled about 1740 as the center of a cultivated plantation district. Today it is home to varied industries, lumbering, agricultural marketing, and nearby Shaw Air Force Base. The **Sumter County Museum** (headquarters of the Sumter County Historical Society), in a lovely 1845 Victorian Gothic house exhibits fine period furnishings, Oriental carpeting, vintage carriages, dolls, and various memorabilia. Archival records are valuable for tracing family roots. *122 N. Washington St., tel. 803/775-0908. Admission free. Open Tues.-Fri. 10-5, weekends 2-5 (archives open Tues.-Sat. 10-5).*

Swan Lake Iris Gardens is like eden when its 6 million irises are in bloom. Royal White Mute, Black necked, Coscoroba, Whooper, Trumpeter, and Black Australian swans paddle leisurely around the 45-acre lake. The 150-acre park also includes walking trails, picnic areas, tennis courts, a playground, and concessions. *W. Liberty St., tel. 803/773-3371. Admission free. Open daily 8-sunset.*

Aiken and Beyond Head south along U.S. 301/601, then west on U.S. 78 to **Aiken,** in Thoroughbred Country, about 64 miles altogether. Aiken's fame began during the 1890s, when wealthy Northerners wintering here built stately mansions and entertained each other with lavish parties, horse shows, and hunts. Many of the mansions—some with up to 90 rooms—remain as testament to this era of opulence. Since those days, the area's horse farms have produced many national champions, which are commemorated at the **Aiken Racing Hall of Fame** with exhibitions of horse-related decorations, paintings, and sculptures, plus racing silks and trophies. The Hall of Fame is on the grounds of the 14-acre **Hopeland Gardens,** with winding paths, quiet terraces, and reflecting pools. There's a Touch and Scent Trail with Braille plaques. Open-air free concerts and plays are presented on Monday evenings mid-July-August. *Corner of Dupree Pl. and Whiskey Rd., tel. 803/642-7630. Admission free. Museum open Tues.-Sun. 2-5. Grounds open daily sunrise-sunset.*

Time Out The who's who of Aiken's horsy set can be found most mornings feasting in the **Track Kitchen** (Mead Ave., tel. 803/641-9628) on the heavy and hearty cooking of Carol and Pockets Curtis. The small dining room is quite unpretentious, with walls of mint-green cinder block and simple formica counters. The best time to people-watch is at about 4 AM.

The **Aiken County Historical Museum,** devoted to early regional culture, has Native American artifacts, firearms, an authentically furnished 1808 log cabin, and a one-room schoolhouse. *433 Newberry St. SW, tel. 803/642–2015. Donations accepted. Open Tues.–Fri. 9:30–4:30, first Sun. of each month 2–5.*

Aiken surrounds the serene and wild **Hitchcock Woods** (enter from the junction of Clark Road and Whitney Drive, Berrie Road, and Dibble Road), a 2,000-acre tract of southern forest traversed by hiking trails and bridal paths.

About 64 miles northwest of Aiken is **Hickory Knob State Resort Park,** which has everything for a complete vacation. Take SC 19 and U.S. 25 to U.S. 378, drive west to the town of McCormick, then south until you see signs for the park on the shore of Strom Thurmond Lake. There's fishing, waterskiing, sailing, motorboating, a swimming pool, boat slips and a launch, a tackle shop, nature trails, an 18-hole championship golf course, a fully equipped pro shop, tennis courts, and skeet and archery ranges. If none of these is to your liking, bring your favorite canine for a training session on the 4-mile bird-dog field-trial area. An 80-room lodge, nine duplex lakeside cottages, and campgrounds, plus a restaurant round out Hickory Knob's offerings. *Rte. 1, Box 199B, McCormick 29835, tel. 803/391–2450. Office open daily 7 AM–11 PM.*

Abbeville Return to McCormick via U.S. 378, then drive northwest 30 miles on SC 28 and SC 72 to **Abbeville.** This may well be one of inland South Carolina's most satisfying, though lesser-known, small towns. In Abbeville the "Southern cause" was born and died, for here the first organized secession meeting was held, and here on May 2, 1865, Confederate President Jefferson Davis officially disbanded the defeated armies of the South in the last meeting of his War Council. The 1830 house where the Council met—the **Burk-Stark Mansion** (306 N. Main St., tel. 803/459–4297 or 459–4000)—is now a private house. *Admission $3. Open Fri.–Sat. 1–5, or by appointment.*

In the **Abbeville Educational Garden** are the 1837 log cabin home of Marie Cromer Siegler, founder of 4–H clubs, and an old jail housing the Abbeville County Museum. *215 Poplar St., tel. 803/459–2696.*

The **Abbeville Opera House** faces the historic town square. Built in 1908, it has been renovated to reflect the grandeur of the days when lavish road shows and stellar entertainers came center stage. Current productions range from light, contemporary comedies to Broadway-style musicals. *Town Sq., Abbeville, tel. 803/459–2157. Reservations taken weekdays 10–5.*

Greenwood About 14 miles away on SC 72 is **Greenwood.** Founded by Irish settlers in 1802, the city received its name from the gently rolling landscape and dense forests. Andrew Johnson, the 17th U.S. president, operated a tailor shop at Courthouse Square before migrating to eastern Tennessee. The **George W. Park Seed Co.,** one of the nation's largest seed supply houses, maintains colorful experimental gardens and greenhouses here. The flower beds are especially vivid during mid-summer, and seeds and bulbs are for sale in the company's store. The South Carolina Festival of Flowers—with a performing-artists contest, a beauty pageant, private house and garden tours, and live entertainment—is held here annually at the end of June. *On SC 245, 7 mi north of town, tel. 803/941–4213. Admission free. Gardens open daily; store open Mon.–Sat. 9–6.*

Ninety Six Drive southeast about 10 miles to the **Ninety Six National Historic Site,** which commemorates two Revolutionary War battles. The visitor center museum has descriptive displays, and there are remnants of the old village, a reconstructed French-and-Indian-War stockade, and Revolutionary-era fortifications. The nearby town of Ninety Six, on an old Indian trade route, is so named for being 96 miles from the Cherokee village of Keowee in the Blue Ridge Mountains. *SC 248, tel. 803/543–4068. Admission free. Open daily 8–5.*

Shopping

Antiques and Flea Markets Many of Columbia's antiques outlets are in the **Congaree Vista Shopping District** around Huger and Gervais streets, between the State House and the river. A number of shops and cafés are in the **Five Points Shopping District,** which is around the intersection of Blossom and Harden streets. Other antiques shops are across the river on Meeting and State streets in West Columbia. The **Old Mill Antique Mall** (310 State St., W. Columbia, tel. 803/796–4229) and **Thieves Market Antique Flea Mall** (502 Gadsden St., Columbia, tel. 803/254–4997) show off the wares of dozens of antiques and collectibles dealers.

Art and Crafts Abbeville's Town Square is lined with attractive gift and specialty shops in restored historic buildings dating from the late 1800s. **Historic Camden** also has gifts and crafts for sale.

Farmer's Market The **State Farmer's Market** In Columbia (Bluff Rd., tel. 803/253–4041) is one of the 10 largest in the country. Seasonal fresh vegetables are sold each weekday, along with flowers, plants, seafood, herbs, and more.

Wineries Free tours and wine-tastings are offered by **Cruse Vineyards & Winery** (Woods Rd., off SC 72, 4 mi north of Chester, tel. 803/377–3944) and **Montmorenci Vineyards** (U.S. 78, 2.5 mi east of Aiken, tel. 803/649–4870. Tours by appointment).

Participant Sports

Canoeing A haunting canoe trail leads into a remote swampy depression at **Woods Bay State Park** (from Sumter, take U.S. 378E to U.S. 301N, tel. 803/659–4445), where rentals are available for $2 per hour or $10 full day. Self-guided canoe trails traverse an alluvial floodplain bordered by high bluffs at the **Congaree Swamp National Monument** (20 mi southeast of Columbia off SC 48, tel. 803/776–4396). Canoe rentals are available at **Adventure Carolina** (tel. 803/796–4505) in Columbia.

Fishing **Lakes Marion** and **Moultrie** attract serious anglers after bream, crappie, striped bass, catfish, and large- and small-mouth bass. Supplies, camps, guides, rentals, and accommodations abound. For information, contact Santee Cooper Counties Promotion Commission (Drawer 40, Santee, SC 29142, tel. 803/854–2131 or outside SC 800/227–8510).

Golf The many fine courses in the area include **Highland Park Country Club** (Aiken, tel. 803/649–6029), **Sedgewood** (Columbia, tel. 803/776–2177), and **White Pines Golf Club** (Camden, tel. 803/432–7442).

Hiking **Congaree Swamp National Monument** (*see* Canoeing, *above*) has 22 miles of trails for hikers and nature lovers and a ¾-mile boardwalk for visitors with disabilities. Guided nature walks leave Saturday at 1:30 PM. For information on trails in the **Francis Marion National Forest** and the **Sumter National Forest,** contact the National Forest Service (1835 Assembly St., Columbia 29201, tel. 803/765–5222).

White-Water Adventures Rafting, kayaking, and canoeing on the Saluda River near Columbia offer challenging Class 3 and Class 4 rapids. Guided river and swamp excursions are also offered. In the Upcountry, the Chattooga National Wild and Scenic River, on the border of South Carolina and Georgia, provides guided rafting, canoeing, and kayaking. Contact **Wildwater Ltd.** (tel. 800/451–9972) or **Nantahala Outdoor Center** (tel. 800/832–7238).

Spectator Sports

Baseball The **Columbia Mets** (tel. 803/256–4110), a Class A affiliate of the New York Mets, play from mid-April through August at Capital City Stadium.

Equestrian Events In Aiken, polo matches are played at Whitney Field (tel. 803/648–7874) on Sunday afternoons September–November and March–July. Three weekends in late March and early April are set aside for the famed **Triple Crown** (tel. 803/648–0485)—Thoroughbred trials of promising yearlings, a steeplechase, and harness races by young horses making their debut. Camden puts on two steeplechase events: the **Carolina Cup** in late March or early April and the **Colonial Cup** in November (tel. 803/432–6513).

Stock-Car Races **Darlington Raceway** (SC 34, 2 mi west of Darlington, tel. 803/393–4041) is the scene of NASCAR's TranSouth 500, Winston Cup Series, in late March, and the exciting Southern 500 on Labor Day weekend.

Dining

South Carolina Heartland fare ranges from regional specialties like barbecue and country ham with red-eye gravy to unself-conscious Continental cuisine. This is a great place to discover a Southern institution—one of the family-style "fish camps" serving lavish portions of fresh catfish and other catches from fish farms or nearby rivers and lakes. In Columbia, ethnic and specialty restaurants have appeared at a rapid clip in recent years. Costs throughout the region are usually pleasingly moderate.

The most highly recommended restaurants in each price category are indicated by a star ★.

Category	Cost*
$$$$	over $25
$$$	$15–$25
$$	$7–$15
$	under $7

**per person without 5% tax, service, or drinks*

Abbeville **Yoder's Dutch Kitchen.** In the heart of the Sun Belt, here's authentic Pennsylvania Dutch home cooking in an unassuming red-brick building with a mansard roof. There's a lunch buffet and evening smorgasbord with such choices as fried chicken, stuffed cabbage, Dutch meat loaf, sausage and kraut, breaded veal parmesan, and plenty of vegetables. Shoo-fly pie, Dutch bread, apple butter, homemade salad dressings, and other house specialties can be bought to go. *U.S. 72, tel. 803/459–5556. No reservations. Dress: casual. No credit cards. Closed Sun.–Tues. No dinner Wed. $$*

Aiken ★ **No. 10 Downing Street.** This stately Southern Colonial dates to 1837 and serves some of the best—and most diverse—food in town. The menu changes regularly: One month might focus on such Italian fare as *pollo al proscuitto* (chicken wrapped in proscuitto and fresh herbs with fettucini Alfredo) and baked beef tenderloin with tomatoes, garlic, and oregano; another month may salute Country French or regional cuisine. A delicious pâtê with french bread is always among the appetizers. A bakery on the premises is open during all meals. *241 Laurens St., tel. 803/642–9062. Reservations advised. Dress: casual. Closed Sun. and Mon. D, DC, MC, V. $$$*

Camden **1890 McLean's House.** On the first floor of the Victorian Greenleaf Inn,cane-back chairs, fox-hunting prints, elaborately tiled fireplaces, and hand-painted walls set the tone for an elegant meal. McLean's opened early in 1994 and has quickly become a success with six delicious steak specialties (from Diane to *au poivre*), plus such other options as walnut crusted chicken with a spicy apricot sauce, and good ole' shrimp and grits. *1308 Broad St., tel. 803/425–1806. Reservations advised. AE, D, MC, V. Closed Sun. No lunch Sat. $$$–$$$$*

★ **The Mill Pond Restaurant.** In a historic building overlooking a sprawling mill pond, this is one of the state's finest eateries. The creative Low Country cuisine features such starters as grits with andouille sausage, roast peppers, and garlic toast; and marinated quail on mixed greens with Boursin cheese and fried onions. Follow this with blackened mahimahi with crawfish hollandaise or perhaps the mouthwatering crab cakes on shrimp tartar sauce. About a ten-minute drive south of Camden proper, dinner here is worth the drive. *84 Boykin Mill Rd., Rembert, tel. 803/424–0261. Reservations advised. MC, V. Closed Sun. No lunch. $$$–$$$$*

Columbia **Columbia's Restaurant.** Columbia's, in the lower level of the AT&T Building, has an extensive menu. It includes fresh seafood, steaks, and egg dishes, plus daily luncheon and dinner specials and nouvelle Southern dishes like speckled hard grits cakes and seared sausage with roasted red-pepper relish. *1201 Main St., tel. 803/771–2410. Reservations advised. Dress: casual. AE, D, DC, MC, V. Closed Sun. $$–$$$*

Motor Supply Co. Bistro. Dine on cuisine from around the world at this restaurant in the heart of town. Fresh seafood and homemade desserts are among the many offerings; on Sundays there's a Thai menu. A happy hour is celebrated in the bar. *920 Gervais St., tel. 803/256–6687. Reservations advised. Dress: casual. AE, DC, MC, V. $$*

★ **California Dreaming.** A splendid example of adaptive use, here's dining in an airy, greenery-bedecked space that is the renovated old Union Train Station. Specialties include prime rib, barbecued baby back ribs, Mexican dishes, and homemade pasta. There's a lounge with a disc jockey. *401 S. Main St., tel. 803/254–6767. Reservations advised on weekends or for large parties. Dress: casual. AE, MC, V. $–$$*

★ **Maurice Gourmet Barbecue–Piggie Park.** One of the South's best-known barbecue chefs, Maurice Bessinger has a fervent national following for his mustard sauce–based, pit-cooked ham barbecue. He also serves barbecued chicken, ribs, and baked beans, plus hash over rice, onion rings, hushpuppies, cole slaw, and home-baked desserts. *1600 Charleston Hwy., tel. 803/796–0220. No reservations. Dress: casual. D, MC, V. $–$$*

Lodging

In addition to the accommodations listed here, you might seek out chains and bed-and-breakfasts in the area. For a complete list of B&Bs, write to the South Carolina Division of Tourism (Box 71, Columbia, SC 29202, tel. 803/734–0122) and ask for the pamphlet "South Carolina's Historic Inns, Country Inns & Bed & Breakfast."

The most highly recommended properties in each price category are indicated by a star. ★.

Category	Cost*
$$$$	over $100
$$$	$75–$100
$$	$40–$75
$	under $40

**double room; add 7% for taxes*

Abbeville *$$* **The Belmont Inn.** Built just after the turn of the century, this restored Spanish-style structure is a popular overnight stop with Opera House visitors. Rooms, which have seen better days, are comfortably furnished rather than opulent. White spreads cover brass beds, and antique quilts decorate some walls. Theater-and-dining package plans are offered at the inn. *Court Sq., Abbeville 29620, tel. and fax 803/459–9625. 24 rooms. Facilities: restaurant, lounge, meeting rooms. AE, MC, V.*

Aiken *$$$–$$$$* **Willcox Inn.** Winston Churchill, Franklin D. Roosevelt, and the Astors have slept at this elegant inn, built in grand style in the early 1900s. The lobby is graced with massive stone fireplaces, rosewood pine woodwork, pegged oak floors, and Oriental rugs. The room decor reflects the inn's early days, with floral-print spreads and high four-poster beds. *100 Colleton Ave., Aiken 29801, tel. 803/649–1377 or 800/368–1047, fax 803/643–0971. 30 rooms, 6 suites. Facilities: tennis, lawn croquet, dining room, bar, free use of nearby health club. AE, DC, MC, V.*

$$ **The Briar Patch.** You can learn plenty about both the Old and New South from the knowledgeable innkeepers of this terrific B&B, which was formerly tack rooms in Aiken's stable district. Choose either the frilly room with French Provincial furniture or the less dramatic one with pine antiques and a weathervane. *544 Magnolia La. SE, Aiken 29801, tel. 803/649–2010. 2 rooms. Facilities: tennis courts, Continental breakfast. No credit cards.*

Camden *$$–$$$* ★ **The Greenleaf Inn.** Alice Boykin, whose name is to Camden what Carnegie's name is to Pittsburgh, opened the Greenleaf in late 1993. The inn comprises three buildings: There are 4 rooms in the main inn, on the second floor above McLean's Restaurant; 7 rooms in a nearby carriage house; and a guest cottage—the latter is particularly good for families. All rooms are done with classic Victorian furniture and wallpaper; they're spacious and have modern baths. You won't find a nicer or more economical lodging in the region. *1308 Broad St., 29020, tel. 803/425–1806 or 800/437–5874. 8 rooms with bath, 3 suites, 1 cottage. Facilities: restaurant, access to health club. AE, D, MC, V.*

Holiday Inn. This well-maintained unit of the nationwide chain is 3 miles west of downtown Camden, in Lugoff. The restaurant is excellent. *Box 96, U.S. 1-601 S, Lugoff 29078, tel. 803/438–9441 or 800/*

465–4329, fax 803/438–9441. 120 rooms. Facilities: pool, restaurant, lounge, whirlpool baths. AE, D, DC, MC, V.

Columbia *$$$* ★ **Chestnut Cottage.** Sleep in luxurious rooms surrounded by Confederate memorabilia in this Federal-style cottage, where Mary Chestnut penned her famous Civil War diary and Jefferson Davis delivered a speech. The hosts run your bath water, turn down your bed, and treat you to afternoon beverages, brownies and milk at bedtime, and a full breakfast in bed upon request. *1718 Hampton St., 29201, tel. 803/256–1718. 4 rooms with baths. Facilities: airport transportation. MC, V.*

Claussen's Inn. This welcome retreat from the downtown bustle is a converted bakery warehouse in the attractive Five Points neighborhood. The inn has an open, airy lobby with a Mexican tile floor; the rooms, some two-story, are arranged around the lobby. There are eight loft suites, with downstairs sitting rooms and spiral staircases leading to sleeping areas furnished with period reproductions and four-poster beds. *2003 Greene St., Columbia 29205, tel. 803/765–0440 or 800/622–3382, fax 803/799–7924. 21 rooms, 8 suites. Facilities: cable TV, whirlpool, meeting facilities. AE, MC, V.*

Columbia Marriott. This upscale downtown hotel is conveniently located near state offices and the University of South Carolina. Public areas and guest rooms are contemporary in feeling, with the touches of warmth and elegance characteristic of Marriotts. The Palm Terrace Restaurant is in a spectacular atrium with stunning views of decorative details; Veronique's provides an intimate, elegant setting for gourmet dining. *1200 Hampton St., Columbia 29201, tel. 803/771–7000 or 800/228–9290, fax 803/254–2911. 298 rooms and suites. Facilities: 2 restaurants, bar, indoor pool, health club, sauna, office facilities. AE, D, DC, MC, V.*

$$–$$$ **Embassy Suites Hotel Columbia.** In the spacious seven-story atrium lobby with skylights, fountains, pools and live plants, overnight guests enjoy sumptuous breakfasts and an early evening manager's cocktail reception—both complimentary. *200 Stoneridge Dr., Columbia 29210, tel. 803/252–8700 or 800/362–2779, fax 803/256–8749. 214 housekeeping suites. Facilities: indoor pool, health club, sun decks, billiards room, disco, gift shop, cable TV. AE, D, DC, MC, V.*

$–$$ **La Quinta Motor Inn.** At this three-story inn on a quiet street near the zoo, the rooms are spacious and well lit, with large working areas and oversize beds. *1335 Garner La., Columbia 29210, tel. 803/798–9590 or 800/531–5900, fax 803/731–5574. 120 rooms. Facilities: pool, cable TV. AE, D, DC, MC, V.*

Greenwood *$$–$$$* **Inn on the Square.** This elegant inn was fashioned out of a warehouse in the heart of town. Though the rooms suffer from rather unremarkable views, they're bright and spacious with reproduction 18th-century antiques, four poster beds, writing desks, and such thoughtful touches as turndown service and complimentary morning newspapers. The staff is congenial and attuned to the needs of business travelers and vacationers alike. *104 Court Sq., 29648, tel. 803/223–4488, fax 803/223–7067. 48 rooms. Facilities: restaurant, lounge, pool. AE, D, DC, MC, V.*

Pendleton *$$* **Liberty Hall Inn.** There's great food and lodging at this country inn in the heart of Historic Pendleton near Clemson University. The inn, which was built in the 1840s and restored in the 1980s, caters to business travelers and vacationers. Rooms are furnished in antiques and family heirlooms; a Continental breakfast comes with the room. *621 S. Mechanic St., 29670, tel. and fax 803/646–7500 or 800/643–*

7944. 10 rooms with private baths. Facilities: restaurant. AE, D, DC, MC, V.

Sumter *$$* **Holiday Inn.** This well-maintained motor inn is 4 miles west of town, near Shaw Air Force Base. *2390 Broad St. ext., 29150, tel. 803/469–9001 or 800/465–4329, fax 803/469–7001. 124 rooms. Facilities: pool, tennis and golf packages, restaurant, live entertainment. AE, D, DC, MC, V.*

Magnolia House. In Sumter's Historic District, this imposing four-columned Greek Revival structure is a nice alternative to the region's generic chain motels. Antiques, many of them French, furnish the rooms; there are also stained-glass windows, inlaid oak floors, and five fireplaces. A full breakfast is included in the rate. *230 Church St., 29150, tel. 803/775–6694. 3 rooms with bath, 1 suite. AE, MC, V.*

The Arts

Concerts, Opera, and Dance In Columbia, call the **South Carolina Philharmonic and Chamber Orchestra Association** (tel. 803/771–7937) for information about scheduled conserts of the philharmonic, the chamber orchestra, and the Youth Orchestra. The **Columbia Music Festival Association** (tel. 803/771–6303) can inform callers about events of the **Choral Society,** the **Opera, Opera Guild, Dance Theatre, Brass Band, Caroliers,** and **Cabaret Company.**

Theater Columbia's **Town Theatre** (1012 Sumter St., tel. 803/799–2510), founded in 1919, stages six plays a year from September to late May, plus a special summer show, and the **Workshop Theatre of South Carolina** (1136 Bull St., tel. 803/799–4876) also puts on plays. The **Abbeville Opera House** (Town Square, tel. 803/459–2157) stages high-caliber productions in an early 20th-century setting.

Nightlife

In Columbia, **Cracker Jacks** (tel. 803/731–5692) features lively "beach" music for listening and dancing, and occasionally a lusty floor show. **Nitelites Dance Club** (tel. 803/252–8700) at the Embassy Suites Hotel boasts state-of-the-art lighting and presents a lavish free hors d'oeuvres buffet on weekdays, 5–7:30. Also try **Dance Factory** (tel. 803/731–0300) at the Sheraton Columbia Northwest, and the Columbia Marriott's **Palm Terrace Lounge** (tel. 803/771–7000).

There's live entertainment at **Jockey's Lounge** in the Holiday Inn in Aiken (tel. 803/648–4272). **Plums Restaurant & Lounge** at the Holiday Inns in Camden (tel. 803/438–7586) and Sumter (tel. 803/469–9001) provides pleasant evening unwinding with live entertainment. Another Camden option is **The Paddock Restaurant & Pub** (tel. 803/432–3222), and there's live entertainment at **Rose Anna's** lounge in the Orangeburg Holiday Inn (tel. 803/531–4600).

Elsewhere in the State

Those with more time may want to take an excursion into the **Upcountry,** the northwest corner of the state, long a favorite for family vacations. For information, contact: Discover Upcountry Carolina Association, Box 3116, Greenville 29602, tel. 803/233–2690 or 800/849–4766). The abundant lakes, waterfalls, and several state parks (including **Caesar's Head, Keowee-Toxaway, Oconee, Table Rock, and the Chattooga National Wild and Scenic River**) provide all manner of recreational activities. Beautiful anytime, the 130-mile **Cherokee**

Foothills Scenic Highway (SC 11), through the Blue Ridge Mountains, is especially delightful in spring and autumn. At **Devils Fork State Park** (161 Holcombe Circle, Salem 29676, tel. 803/944–2639) on beatiful Lake Jocassee, visitors clamor to stay in the luxurious villas.

The comfortable communities of **Greenville, Spartanburg, Clemson, Pendleton,** and **Anderson** take justifiable pride in their educational institutions, museums, historic preservation, and cultural accomplishments. Any one of them is worth a day's visit—particularly charming Pendleton, near Clemson University, which has a historic district, interesting architecture, and good restaurants.

The Greenville County Museum of Art. Housed in an innovative modern building, the museum displays American art dating from the Colonial era. Exhibited are works by Paul Jenkins, Jamie Wyeth, Jasper Johns, and noted Southern artists along with North American sculpture. *420 College St., Greenville, tel. 803/271–7570. Admission free. Open Tues.–Sat. 10–5, Sun. 1–5.*

Kings Mountain National Military Park. The "turning point" Revolutionary War battle on October 7, 1780, was fought on this site. Colonial Tories commanded by British Major Patrick Ferguson were soundly defeated by rag-tag patriot forces from the Southern Appalachians. Visitor Center exhibits, dioramas, and an orientation film describe the action. A paved self-guided trail leads through the battlefield. *20 mi NE of Gaffney off I–85 via a marked side road in North Carolina, tel. 803/936–7921. Admission free. Open daily 9–5, until 6 Memorial Day–Labor Day.*

Index

Personal Itinerary

Departure *Date*

Time

Transportation

Arrival *Date* *Time*

Departure *Date* *Time*

Transportation

Accommodations

Arrival *Date* *Time*

Departure *Date* *Time*

Transportation

Accommodations

Arrival *Date* *Time*

Departure *Date* *Time*

Transportation

Accommodations

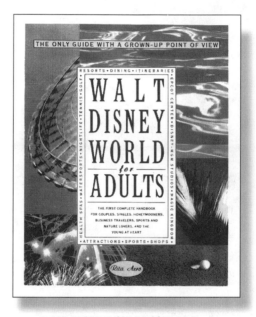

Fodor's Travel Guides

Available at bookstores everywhere, or call 1–800–533–6478, 24 hours a day.

U.S. Guides

Alaska

Arizona

Boston

California

Cape Cod, Martha's Vineyard, Nantucket

The Carolinas & the Georgia Coast

Chicago

Colorado

Florida

Hawaii

Las Vegas, Reno, Tahoe

Los Angeles

Maine, Vermont, New Hampshire

Maui

Miami & the Keys

New England

New Orleans

New York City

Pacific North Coast

Philadelphia & the Pennsylvania Dutch Country

The Rockies

San Diego

San Francisco

Santa Fe, Taos, Albuquerque

Seattle & Vancouver

The South

The U.S. & British Virgin Islands

USA

The Upper Great Lakes Region

Virginia & Maryland

Waikiki

Walt Disney World and the Orlando Area

Washington, D.C.

Foreign Guides

Acapulco, Ixtapa, Zihuatanejo

Australia & New Zealand

Austria

The Bahamas

Baja & Mexico's Pacific Coast Resorts

Barbados

Berlin

Bermuda

Brittany & Normandy

Budapest

Canada

Cancún, Cozumel, Yucatán Peninsula

Caribbean

China

Costa Rica, Belize, Guatemala

The Czech Republic & Slovakia

Eastern Europe

Egypt

Euro Disney

Europe

Florence, Tuscany & Umbria

France

Germany

Great Britain

Greece

Hong Kong

India

Ireland

Israel

Italy

Japan

Kenya & Tanzania

Korea

London

Madrid & Barcelona

Mexico

Montréal & Québec City

Morocco

Moscow & St. Petersburg

The Netherlands, Belgium & Luxembourg

New Zealand

Norway

Nova Scotia, Prince Edward Island & New Brunswick

Paris

Portugal

Provence & the Riviera

Rome

Russia & the Baltic Countries

Scandinavia

Scotland

Singapore

South America

Southeast Asia

Spain

Sweden

Switzerland

Thailand

Tokyo

Toronto

Turkey

Vienna & the Danube Valley

Special Series

Fodor's Affordables

Caribbean

Europe

Florida

France

Germany

Great Britain

Italy

London

Paris

Fodor's Bed & Breakfast and Country Inns Guides

America's Best B&Bs

California

Canada's Great Country Inns

Cottages, B&Bs and Country Inns of England and Wales

Mid-Atlantic Region

New England

The Pacific Northwest

The South

The Southwest

The Upper Great Lakes Region

The Berkeley Guides

California

Central America

Eastern Europe

Europe

France

Germany & Austria

Great Britain & Ireland

Italy

London

Mexico

Pacific Northwest & Alaska

Paris

San Francisco

Fodor's Exploring Guides

Australia

Boston & New England

Britain

California

The Caribbean

Florence & Tuscany

Florida

France

Germany

Ireland

Italy

London

Mexico

New York City

Paris

Prague

Rome

Scotland

Singapore & Malaysia

Spain

Thailand

Turkey

Fodor's Flashmaps

Boston

New York

Washington, D.C.

Fodor's Pocket Guides

Acapulco

Bahamas

Barbados

Jamaica

London

New York City

Paris

Puerto Rico

San Francisco

Washington, D.C.

Fodor's Sports

Cycling

Golf Digest's Best Places to Play

Hiking

The Insider's Guide to the Best Canadian Skiing

Running

Sailing

Skiing in the USA & Canada

USA Today's Complete Four Sports Stadium Guide

Fodor's Three-In-Ones (guidebook, language cassette, and phrase book)

France

Germany

Italy

Mexico

Spain

Fodor's Special-Interest Guides

Complete Guide to America's National Parks

Condé Nast Traveler Caribbean Resort and Cruise Ship Finder

Cruises and Ports of Call

Euro Disney

France by Train

Halliday's New England Food Explorer

Healthy Escapes

Italy by Train

London Companion

Shadow Traffic's New York Shortcuts and Traffic Tips

Sunday in New York

Sunday in San Francisco

Touring Europe

Touring USA: Eastern Edition

Walt Disney World and the Orlando Area

Walt Disney World for Adults

Fodor's Vacation Planners

Great American Learning Vacations

Great American Sports & Adventure Vacations

Great American Vacations

Great American Vacations for Travelers with Disabilities

National Parks and Seashores of the East

National Parks of the West

The Wall Street Journal Guides to Business Travel

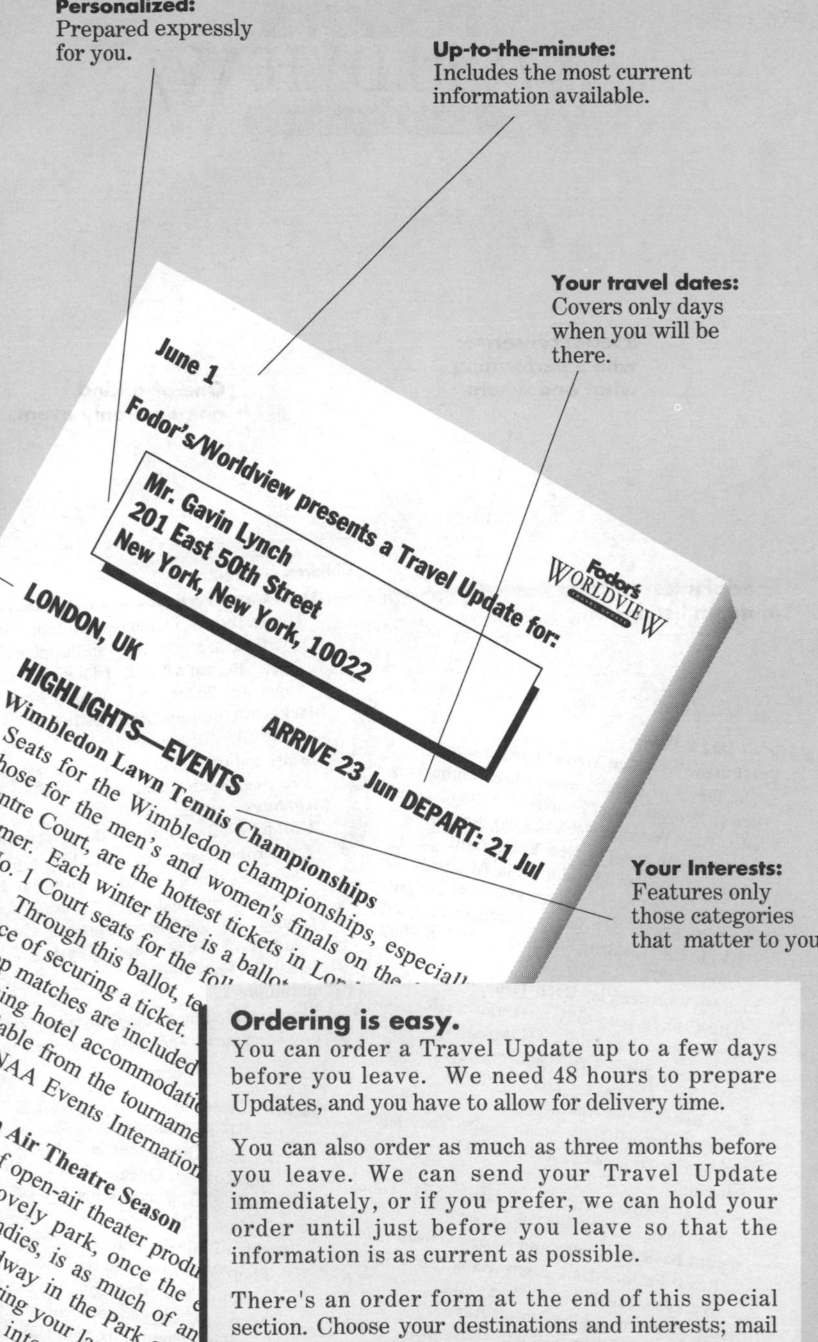

Ordering is easy.

You can order a Travel Update up to a few days before you leave. We need 48 hours to prepare Updates, and you have to allow for delivery time.

You can also order as much as three months before you leave. We can send your Travel Update immediately, or if you prefer, we can hold your order until just before you leave so that the information is as current as possible.

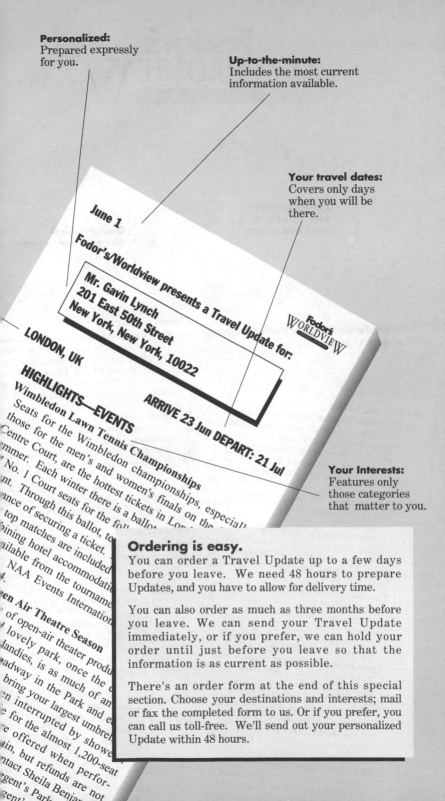

There's an order form at the end of this special section. Choose your destinations and interests; mail or fax the completed form to us. Or if you prefer, you can call us toll-free. We'll send out your personalized Update within 48 hours.

Special concerts— who's performing what and where

One-of-a-kind, one-time-only events

Special interest, in-depth listings

Music — Jazz & Blues

Tito Puente's Golden Men of Latin Jazz
The father of mambo and Cuban rumba king comes to town. Royal Festival Hall. South Bank. SE1. Tube: Waterloo. Tel: 928 8800. 8pm. 7/15.

Georgie Fame and The New York Band
Riding a popular tide with his latest album, the smoky-voiced Fame and his keyboard are on a tour yet again. The Grand. Clapham Junction. SW11. BR: Clapham Junction. Tel: 738 9000. 7:30pm. 7/07.

Jacques Loussier Play Bach Trio
The French jazz classicist and colleagues. Kenwood Lakeside. Hampstead Lane. Kenwood. NW3. Tube: Golders Green, then bus 210. Tel: 413 1443. 7pm. 7/10.

Tony Bennett and Ronnie Scott
Royal Festival Hall. South Bank. SE1. Tube: Waterloo. Tel: 928 8800. 8pm. 7/11.

Santana
Royal Festival Hall. South Bank. SE1. Tube: Waterloo. Tel: 928 8800. 8pm. 7/12.

Count Basie Orchestra and Nancy Wilson Trio
Royal Festival Hall. South Bank. SE1. Tube Waterloo. Tel: 928 8800. 8pm. 7/14.

King Pleasure and the Biscuit Boys
Royal Festival Hall. South Bank. SE1. Tube Waterloo. Tel: 928 8800. 6:30 and 9pm. 7/16.

Al Green and the London Community Gospel Choi
Royal Festival Hall. South Bank. SE1. Tube Waterloo. Tel: 928 8800. 8pm. 7/13.

BB King and Linda Hopkins
Mother of the blues and successor to Bessi Smith, Hopkins meets up with "Blues Boy Royal Festival Hall. South Bank. SE

Children — Events

Angel Canal Festival
The festivities include a children's fun entertainers, a boat rally and displays on water. Regent's Canal. Islington. N1. T Angel. Tel: 267 9100. 11:30am-5:30pm. 7/

Blackheath Summer Kite Festival
Stunt kite displays with parachuting te bears and trade stands. Free admission. S BR: Blackheath. 10am. 6/27.

Megabugs
Children will delight in this infestation giant robotic insects, including a prayi mantis 60 times life size. Mon-Sat 10a 6pm; Sun 11am-6pm. Admission 4. pounds. Natural History Museum, Cromw Road. SW7. Tube: South Kensington. T 938 9123. Ends 10/01.

Childminders
This establishment employs only wome providing nurses and qualified nannies to

Music — Classical

Marylebone Sinfonia
Kenneth Gowen conducts music by and Rossini. Queen Elizabeth Hall Bank. SE1. Tube: Waterloo. Tel: 92 7:45pm. 7/16.

London Philharmonic
Franz Welser-Moest and George B conduct selections by Alexander Messiaen, and some of Benjamin's o positions. Queen Elizabeth Hall. Sou SE1. Tube: Waterloo. Tel: 928 8800.

London Pro Arte Orchestra and Fore
Murray Stewart conducts selec Rossini, Haydn and Jonathan Willco Queen Elizabeth Hall. South Ba Tube: Waterloo. Tel: 928 8800. 7:45

Kensington Symphony Orchestra
Russell Keable conducts Dvorak

Here's what you get . . .

Detailed information about what's going on — precisely when you'll be there.

Show openings during your visit

Handy pocket-size booklet

Reviews by local critics

Exhibitions & Shows—Antique & Flower

Westminster Antiques Fair

Over 50 stands with pre-1830 furniture and other Victorian and earlier items. Thu-Fri 11am-8pm; Sat-Sun 11am-6pm. Admission 4 pounds, children free. Old Royal Horticultural Hall. Vincent Square. SW1. Tel: 0444/48 25 14. 6-24 thru 6/27.

Royal Horticultural Society Flower Show

The show includes displays of carnations, summer fruit and vegetables. Tue 11am-7pm; Wed 10am-5pm. Admission Tue 4 pounds, Wed 2 pounds. Royal Horticultural Halls. Greycoat Street and Vincent Square. SW1. Tube: Victoria. 7/20 thru 7/21.

mpton Court Palace International Flower Show

Major international garden and flower show taking place in conjunction with

Theater — Musical

Sunset Boulevard

In June, the four Andrew Lloyd Webber musicals which dominated London's stages in the 1980s (Cats, Starlight Express, Phantom of the Opera and Aspects of Love) are joined by the composer's latest work, a show rumored to have his best music to date. The 1950 Billy Wilder film about a helpless young writer who is drawn into the world of a possessive, aging silent screen star offers rich opportunities for Webber's evolving style. Soaring, aching melodies, lush technical effects and psychological thrills are all expected. Patti Lupone stars. Mon-Sat at 8pm; matinee Thu-Sat at 3pm. In-person sales only at the box office; credit card bookings, Tel: 344 0055. Admission 15-32.50 pounds. Adelphi Theatre. The Strand. WC2. Tube: Charing Cross. Tel: 836 7611. Starts: 6/21.

Leonardo A Portrait of Love

A new musical about the great Renaissance artist and inventor comes in for a London pre- ... tested by a brief run at Oxford's Old ... The work explores

Spectator Sports — Other Sports

Greyhound Racing: Wembley Stadium

This dog track offers good views of greyhound racing held on Mon, Wed and Fri. No credit cards. Stadium Way. Wembley. HA9. Tube: Wembley Park. Tel: 902 8833.

Benson & Hedges Cricket Cup Final

Lord's Cricket Ground. St. John's Wood Road. NW8. Tube: St. John's Wood. Tel: 289 1611. 11am. 7/10.

Business-Fax & Overnight Mail

Post Office, Trafalgar Square Branch

Offers a network of fax services, the Intelpost system, throughout the country and abroad. Mon-Sat 8am-8pm, Sun 9am-5pm. William IV Street. WC2. Tube: Charing Cross. Tel: 930 9580

Fodor's
WORLDVIEW
TRAVEL UPDATE

London, England
Arriving: June 23
Departing: July 21

Interest Categories

For your personalized Travel Update, choose the categories you're most interested in from this list. Every Travel Update automatically provides you with *Event Highlights* - the best of what's happening during the dates of your trip.

	Category	Includes
1.	**Business Services**	Fax & Overnight Mail, Computer Rentals, Photocopying, Protocol, Secretarial, Messenger, Translation Services
	Dining	
2.	**All Day Dining**	Breakfast & Brunch, Cafes & Tea Rooms, Late-Night Dining
3.	**Local Cuisine**	In Every Price Range—from Budget Restaurants to the Special Splurge
4.	**European Cuisine**	Continental, French, Italian
5.	**Asian Cuisine**	Chinese, Far Eastern, Japanese, Other
6.	**Americas Cuisine**	American, Mexican & Latin
7.	**Nightlife**	Bars, Dance Clubs, Casinos, Comedy Clubs, Ethnic, Pubs & Beer Halls
8.	**Entertainment**	Theater—Comedy, Drama, English Language, Musicals, Dance, Ticket Agencies
9.	**Music**	Country/Western/Folk, Classical, Traditional & Ethnic, Opera, Jazz & Blues, Pop, Rock
10.	**Children's Activities**	Events, Attractions
11.	**Tours**	Local Tours, Day Trips, Overnight Excursions, Cruises
12.	**Exhibitions, Festivals & Shows**	Antiques & Flower, History & Cultural, Art Exhibitions, Fairs & Craft Shows, Music & Art Festivals
13.	**Shopping**	Districts & Malls, Markets, Regional Specialities
14.	**Fitness**	Bicycling, Health Clubs, Hiking, Jogging
15.	**Recreational Sports**	Boating/Sailing, Fishing, Golf, Ice Skating, Skiing, Snorkeling/Scuba, Swimming, Tennis & Racquet
16.	**Spectator Sports**	Auto Racing, Baseball, Basketball, Boating & Sailing, Football, Golf, Horse Racing, Ice Hockey, Rugby, Soccer, Tennis, Track & Field, Other Sports

Please note that interest category content will vary by season, destination, and length of stay.

Destinations

The Fodor's/Worldview Travel Update covers more than 160 destinations worldwide. Choose the destinations that match your itinerary from this list. (Choose bulleted destinations only.)

Europe
- • Amsterdam
- • Athens
- • Barcelona
- • Berlin
- • Brussels
- • Budapest
- • Copenhagen
- • Dublin
- • Edinburgh
- • Florence
- • Frankfurt
- • French Riviera
- • Geneva
- • Glasgow
- • Istanbul
- • Lausanne
- • Lisbon
- • London
- • Madrid
- • Milan
- • Moscow
- • Munich
- • Oslo
- • Paris
- • Prague
- • Provence
- • Rome
- • Salzburg
- * Seville
- • St. Petersburg
- • Stockholm
- • Venice
- • Vienna
- • Zurich

United States (Mainland)
- • Albuquerque
- • Atlanta
- • Atlantic City
- • Baltimore
- • Boston
- * Branson, MO
- * Charleston, SC
- • Chicago
- • Cincinnati
- • Cleveland
- • Dallas/Ft. Worth
- • Denver
- • Detroit
- • Houston
- * Indianapolis
- • Kansas City
- • Las Vegas
- • Los Angeles
- • Memphis
- • Miami
- • Milwaukee
- • Minneapolis/St. Paul
- * Nashville
- • New Orleans
- • New York City
- • Orlando
- • Palm Springs
- • Philadelphia
- • Phoenix
- • Pittsburgh
- • Portland
- * Reno/Lake Tahoe
- • St. Louis
- • Salt Lake City
- • San Antonio
- • San Diego
- • San Francisco
- * Santa Fe
- • Seattle
- • Tampa
- • Washington, DC

Alaska
- • Alaskan Destinations

Hawaii
- • Honolulu
- • Island of Hawaii
- • Kauai
- • Maui

Canada
- • Quebec City
- • Montreal
- • Ottawa
- • Toronto
- • Vancouver

Bahamas
- • Abaco
- • Eleuthera/Harbour Island
- • Exuma
- • Freeport
- • Nassau & Paradise Island

Bermuda
- • Bermuda Countryside
- • Hamilton

British Leeward Islands
- • Anguilla
- • Antigua & Barbuda
- • St. Kitts & Nevis

British Virgin Islands
- • Tortola & Virgin Gorda

British Windward Islands
- • Barbados
- • Dominica
- • Grenada
- • St. Lucia
- • St. Vincent
- • Trinidad & Tobago

Cayman Islands
- • The Caymans

Dominican Republic
- • Santo Domingo

Dutch Leeward Islands
- • Aruba
- • Bonaire
- • Curacao

Dutch Windward Island
- • St. Maarten/St. Martin

French West Indies
- • Guadeloupe
- • Martinique
- • St. Barthelemy

Jamaica
- • Kingston
- • Montego Bay
- • Negril
- • Ocho Rios

Puerto Rico
- • Ponce
- • San Juan

Turks & Caicos
- • Grand Turk/Providenciales

U.S. Virgin Islands
- • St. Croix
- • St. John
- • St. Thomas

Mexico
- • Acapulco
- • Cancun & Isla Mujeres
- • Cozumel
- • Guadalajara
- • Ixtapa & Zihuatanejo
- • Los Cabos
- • Mazatlan
- • Mexico City
- • Monterrey
- • Oaxaca
- • Puerto Vallarta

South/Central America
- * Buenos Aires
- * Caracas
- * Rio de Janeiro
- * San Jose, Costa Rica
- * Sao Paulo

Middle East
- * Jerusalem

Australia & New Zealand
- • Auckland
- • Melbourne
- * South Island
- • Sydney

China
- • Beijing
- • Guangzhou
- • Shanghai

Japan
- • Kyoto
- • Nagoya
- • Osaka
- • Tokyo
- • Yokohama

Pacific Rim/Other
- * Bali
- • Bangkok
- • Hong Kong & Macau
- • Manila
- • Seoul
- • Singapore
- • Taipei

* Destinations available by 1/1/95

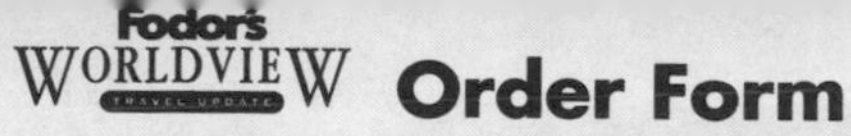

Order Form

THIS TRAVEL UPDATE IS FOR (Please print):

Name

Address

City **State** **Country** **ZIP**

Tel # ( ) - **Fax #** ( ) -

Title of this Fodor's guide:

Store and location where guide was purchased:

INDICATE YOUR DESTINATIONS/DATES: You can order up to three (3) destinations from the previous page. Fill in your arrival and departure dates for each destination. **Your Travel Update itinerary (all destinations selected) cannot exceed 30 days from beginning to end.**

		Month / Day		Month / Day
(Sample) LONDON	*From:*	6 / 21	*To:*	6 / 30
1	From:	/	To:	/
2	From:	/	To:	/
3	From:	/	To:	/

CHOOSE YOUR INTERESTS: Select up to eight (8) categories from the list of interest categories shown on the previous page and circle the numbers below:

1 2 3 4 5 6 7 8 9 10 11 12 13 14 15 16

CHOOSE WHEN YOU WANT YOUR TRAVEL UPDATE DELIVERED (Check one):

❑ Please send my Travel Update immediately.

❑ Please hold my order until a few weeks before my trip to include the most up-to-date information.

Completed orders will be sent within 48 hours. Allow 7-10 days for U.S. mail delivery.

ADD UP YOUR ORDER HERE. ***SPECIAL OFFER FOR FODOR'S PURCHASERS ONLY!***

	Suggested Retail Price	Your Price	This Order
First destination ordered	~~$ 9.95~~	$ 7.95	$ 7.95
Second destination (if applicable)	~~$ 6.95~~	$ 4.95	+
Third destination (if applicable)	~~$ 6.95~~	$ 4.95	+

DELIVERY CHARGE (Check one and enter amount below)

	Within U.S. & Canada	Outside U.S. & Canada
First Class Mail	❑ $2.50	❑ $5.00
FAX	❑ $5.00	❑ $10.00
Priority Delivery	❑ $15.00	❑ $27.00

ENTER DELIVERY CHARGE FROM ABOVE: +

TOTAL: $

METHOD OF PAYMENT IN U.S. FUNDS ONLY (Check one):

❑ AmEx ❑ MC ❑ Visa ❑ Discover ❑ Personal Check (U. S. & Canada only)

❑ Money Order/ International Money Order

Make check or money order payable to: Fodor's Worldview Travel Update

Credit Card **Expiration Date:**

Authorized Signature

SEND THIS COMPLETED FORM WITH PAYMENT TO:

Fodor's Worldview Travel Update, 114 Sansome Street, Suite 700, San Francisco, CA 94104

OR CALL OR FAX US 24-HOURS A DAY

Telephone **1-800-799-9609** • Fax **1-800-799-9619** (From within the U.S. & Canada)

(Outside the U.S. & Canada: Telephone 415-616-9988 • Fax 415-616-9989)

(Please have this guide in front of you when you call so we can verify purchase.)

Code: FTG

Offer valid until 12/31/95